An Introduction to Data Visualisation of the Writing Process

Studies in Writing

VOLUME 41

The series was founded by Gert Rijlaarsdam and Eric Espéret in 1994. It was pursued by Gert Rijlaarsdam until 2014. Since its inception in 1994 it has become one of the most influential book series in the field of writing research.

The titles published in this series are listed at *brill.com/siw*

An Introduction to Data Visualisation of the Writing Process

Edited by

Christophe Leblay
Hakim Usoof
Gilles Caporossi

BRILL

ISSN 1572-6304
ISBN 978-90-04-75819-3
ISBN 978-90-04-76026-4 (PDF)
DOI https://doi.org/10.1163/9789004760264

Library of Congress Control Number: 2026932372

Brill and Koninklijke Brill BV are part of De Gruyter Brill.
www.degruyterbrill.com

Questions about General Product Safety Regulation: productsafety@degruyterbrill.com

Contents

List of Figures, Maps, and Tables VII
Notes on Contributors XIV

1 Dimensions of Visualisation Applied to the Writing Process 1
Christophe Leblay, Hakim Usoof and Gilles Caporossi

2 Visualisation Toolkit for the Humanities 19
Juuso Koponen

3 Keystroke Data Logging and Visualisation: Design Process and Possibilities and Limitations 48
Pavithra Basnayake and Hakim Usoof

4 Graph Models: What Do the Coloured Forms Tell Us about the Writing Process? From Numbers to Visual and Coloured Forms 73
Christophe Leblay, Hakim Usoof and Gilles Caporossi

5 Visualising the Stages of a Writing Process 106
Florence Tanoï Namio, Gilles Caporossi and Alain Hertz

6 Towards a 3-Sided Behavioural/Linguistic/Machine Learning Analysis and Visualisation of Key-Log Data 124
Georgeta Cislaru, Nistor Grozavu and Maxime Olivié

7 Visualising the Genesis of a Text: a Workflow for Analysing Keystroke Logging Data with a Text Genetic Approach 148
Lamyk Bekius and Floor Buschenhenke

8 Visualising Real-World Writing Processes with Progression Analysis 176
Daniel Perrin

9 Visualising the Process of Answering Clinical and Diagnostic Linguistic Tests 191
Andreas Sellstone, Linda Sandström and Kirk P.H. Sullivan

10 Visualising Multilingual Writers' Bursts and Profiles in the Initial Writing Phase 214
Maarit Mutta, Mari Mäkilä, Päivi Laine and Anne-Maj Åberg

11 The Visualisation of Writing 236
Thierry Olive

Glossary 249

Figures, Maps, and Tables

Figures

1.1 Graph of the relations between chapters according to the similarities of their vocable 13
2.1 The information graphics continuum 20
2.2 A comparison of a table and a vertical bar chart depicting the same data set. The jump in Swiss population from 2000 to 2010 is hard to discern from the table on the left but stands out in the chart on the right 22
2.3 A stacked vertical bar chart showing the population of Switzerland, 1910–2021, broken down by main language 28
2.4 A grouped horizontal bar chart showing the sizes of the German-speaking and non-German-speaking population in each Swiss region 29
2.5 A line chart showing the sizes of linguistic groups of Switzerland, 1910–2021 30
2.6 An area chart showing the population of Switzerland, 1910–2021, broken down by main language 30
2.7 A donut chart showing the distribution of languages spoken in Switzerland The donut chart is a purely aesthetic variant of the pie chart: Kosara & Skau (2016) have shown that there is no functional difference in pie and donut charts except in a few edge cases. 31
2.8 A scatter plot of Swiss districts (Bezirk), showing the number of German-speakers by district on the x-axis and non-German-speakers on the y-axis 32
2.9 A univariate scatter plot of Swiss districts (Bezirk), showing the number of German-speakers by district in the first row and the number of French-speakers in the second 33
2.10 A box plot showing the distribution of the share of speakers of each of Switzerland's national languages by municipality (Gemeide) 34
2.11 A histogram showing the distribution of the share of German-speakers in Switzerland's municipalities (Gemeide), network diagrams 35
2.12 A tree diagram showing the relationships of the Romance languages, focusing especially on the three Romance languages traditionally spoken in Switzerland: French, Italian, and Romansch 36
2.13 A network diagram depicting the relationships between the Romance and Germanic languages (based on Steinbach 2015), focusing on the Swiss national languages 36
2.14 A flow diagram depicting the Swiss population over 15 by language, region, and age group 37

2.15 A simplified timeline of the history of the Italian language 38
2.16 A word cloud of the 200 most common Swiss surnames with their linguistic origins, created using the online tool Wordclouds.com (n.d.) and slightly edited 39
2.17 The recommended alternative for word clouds is word bubbles, where each of the words is placed inside a bubble whose area is scaled according to the frequency of each word, instead of scaling the words directly 40
2.18 Jakobson's Cube—a highly specific qualitative infographic originally created by linguist Roman Jakobson to show the interrelated meanings of the eight cases of the Russian language 43
3.1 Event count and cursor position over time 58
3.2 Cognitive pause (> = 2000 ms) vs. time 59
3.3 Pause location analysis created using Microsoft PowerBI 60
3.4 Bigram distribution as a count (where the count is > = 10) 63
3.5 Bigram distribution as a percentage of all occurrences of bigrams (where the count is > = 10) 64
3.6 Burst and efficiency distribution over time 65
3.7 Deletion vs. node distance plot 66
3.8 Editing distance distribution 67
3.9 Heat map of fixation in Eye and Pen. Adapted from Alamargot & Chesnet (2018) 67
3.10 Gaze map of fixation in Eye and Pen. Adapted from Alamargot & Chesnet (2018) 67
4.1 LS Graph associated to the toy example/problem/model 76
4.2 S-notation representation of the sequence 77
4.3 Graph associated with the S-notation model (based on Figure 4.1) 77
4.4 The atomic DNA graph after phase 1 78
4.5 The atomic DNA graph after phase 2 78
4.6 The atomic DNA graph after phase 3 79
4.7 The atomic DNA graph after phase 4 79
4.8 The atomic DNA graph after phase 5 80
4.9 The atomic DNA graph after phase 6 81
4.10 The atomic DNA graph after phase 7 81
4.11 The aggregated DNA graph after phase 1 83
4.12 The aggregated DNA graph after phase 2 83
4.13 The aggregated DNA graph after phase 3 83
4.14 The aggregated DNA graph after phase 4 83
4.15 The aggregated DNA graph after phase 5 84
4.16 The aggregated DNA graph after phase 6 84
4.17 The aggregated DNA graph after phase 7 84

4.18 The final enhanced aggregated DNA graph 85
4.19 The atomic lossless graph 87
4.20 The aggregated lossless graph 88
4.21 Decomposition of the process in revision campaigns 90
4.22 Graph of a linear writing process, with few inserts and frequent deletes 94
4.23 Graph of a complex writing process, with many inserts and the writer moving back and forth within the text and frequent deletes 94
4.24 Graph depicting an edit, the revision of a text with a delete and a reconstitution of the presentation 95
4.25 Graph depicting the same edit as Figure 4.24, but with the inclusion of pause nodes that are greater than a certain threshold (e.g., > 2000ms) 96
4.26 Graph illustration of an insertion event 96
4.27 Graph representation of the use of the Backspace key for deletion 97
4.28 Graph representation of the use of either a highlight and deletion or a deletion using the Delete key 98
4.29 Edit distribution of Amelia (novice writer) 99
4.30 Edit distribution of Clair (proficient writer) 100
5.1 Visualisation of an episode of modifications 111
5.2 Visualisation of the four episodes of our simple example 111
5.3 Visualisation of the single episode of the second example 112
5.4 An example of a writing process with 18 episodes 114
5.5 Visualisation of the 18 episodes of the example of Figure 5.4 115
5.6 Distribution of the insertions and deletions for the example of Figure 5.4 116
5.7 Contribution of each episode to the final text 117
5.8 Merge of episodes for the example of Figure 5.4 with the proximity criteria and threshold of 20 (at the left) and 60 (at the right) 119
5.9 Merge of episodes for the example of Figure 5.4 with the size criteria and threshold of 20 (at the left) and 70 (at the right) 119
6.1 Number of rewriting operations for a 14-session writing process. The tool's interface is in French only 128
6.2 Inputlog representation of a writer's productivity during a social report writing session 131
6.3 Reconstruction of deletions from Inputlog .idfx files and visualisation based on handwriting strategies 131
6.4 A flat multi-level representation: different text representations displayed in several windows 132
6.5 Tabular view of the bursts (excerpt from the Pro-TEXT platform, see section 7). Some burst columns can be visualised via a horizontal scroll 133
6.6 Text display with pause (or burst border) marking and POS (part-of-speech) marking option 133

6.7 Cascading representation compiling bursts and pauses (in seconds) 134
6.8A Dependency trees including part-of-speech annotations and lemmatization (bottom line) 135
6.8B Dependency trees including pause visualisation. Pause length was measured in seconds 135
6.9 Bursts clustering visualisation based on the Bert-Sentence Transformer model 138
6.10 Dynamic behaviour of clusters based on the Bert-Sentence Transformer model 138
6.11 Clustering visualisation based on the Doc2Vec Method 139
6.12 Dynamic behaviour of clusters based on the Doc2Vec method 139
6.13 Burst content visualisation with color-coded information on cluster affiliation 139
6.14 File import panel of the visualisation platform 140
6.15 Analysis creation panel (i.e., choice of clustering algorithm) of the visualisation platform 141
6.16 1D bar chart created with the visualisation platform 142
6.17 2D scatter plot created with the visualisation platform 142
6.18 3D scatter plot created with the visualisation platform 143
7.1 Page from Mary W. Shelley's draft of *Frankenstein*, MS. Abinger c. 56, r4, 1816 (Shelley) 150
7.2 Visualisation of the collation output by MEDITE, comparing the end product of session 5 with the end product of the preceding session 156
7.3 Visualisation of the text comparison by Diff Annotator, comparing the end product of session 5 with the end product of the preceding session 157
7.4 Visualisation that visualises all the writing actions in Roos van Rijswijk's sixth writing session 164
7.5 Visualisation that hides all the additions, from Van Rijswijk's 6th session 166
7.6 Visualisation that obscures all the deletions, Van Rijswijk's sixth session 166
7.7 Visualisation with the numbers indicating the order of the writing actions, representing a fragment of Van Rijswijk's sixth writing session 168
7.8 Visualisation of the writing path, sample taken from Van Rijswijk's 5th writing session. Blue lines represent movement towards the top of the document, orange lines movements towards the bottom. 170
8.1 S-notation basics shown in a simplified example 178
8.2 S-notation of screen activity in the text production window (extract) 178
8.3 Transcription of collaborative text production (extract) 180
8.4 Key stills of video-recorded collaborative text production 180

8.5 Dynamic progression graph. On screen, moving the yellow slider plots the graph dot by dot, revision by revision, in the order of their appearance in the writing process. 182
8.6 Progression score based on writer's cue-based retrospective verbal protocol 183
8.7 Daily newsroom workflow and predominant activity fields 184
8.8 Synopsis of research activities in the Idée suisse project 186
8.9 Interplay of activity fields in professional real-life writing 187
8.10 Visualisation of empirically based good practices 188
9.1 Overview of the total score for each participant over each subtest—(a) displaying unstandardised test scores and (b) displaying standardised test scores. The test scores are visualised in the y-axis, while each subtest is categorically divided and visualised in the x-axis. 201
9.2 Overview of the number of pauses (a) and deletions (b) for each subtest 202
9.3 Each participant's number of pauses in the x-axis and score in the y-axis for the morphological spelling subtest 203
9.4 Each participant's number of pauses in the x-axes and score in the y-axes (a) displaying standard deviations and mean for score and (b) displaying standard deviations and mean for number of pauses 204
9.5 Individual and standardised overview of one participant's number of scores (a), pauses (b), and deletions (c) for each subtest. Each subtest is categorically represented in the y-axis, while the participants' standard deviations of each measurement (score, pauses, or deletions) are represented in the x-axis. 205
9.6 Individual overview of the number of pauses (a), mean pause length (b), and number of deletions (c) for each item in the morphological spelling subtest. Correct answers are represented by blue bars and incorrect answers by red bars. Each target word is categorically represented in the y-axis, while the measures (pauses, mean pause length, or deletions) are represented in the x-axis 206
9.7 Answer revisions for one participant in the multiple-choice task Word Detectives and the duration between answers, with the question-number in the y-axis, time in the x-axis. Correct answers are represented by blue data points and incorrect answers by red data points. 207
9.8 Pause graph analysis with the start of each item by the participant visualised by a dotted line (Q1–Q10). The left y-axis represents the pause duration in milliseconds, the right y-axis represents the cursor position in characters, and the x-axis represents the time in minutes of the whole subtest session. Each dotted line (Q1–Q10) represents the time at which the participant started writing a word. Each dot is a type of pause, and its colour indicates what type of pause it was (as seen in the right-hand graph legend). The grey line represents cursor position. 208

10.1 Criteria for V-bursts in GGXLog 221
11.1 A figure depicting the transitional probabilities between the writing processes pf Planning (P), Translating (T), evaluating (E), and revising (R) of two writers in different phases of a writing session 243

Maps

2.1 A dot map depicting all municipalities of at least 5,000 inhabitants in Switzerland, and their majority language 24
2.2 A symbol map depicting the population of the districts (Bezirk) of Switzerland, and their majority language 25
2.3 A categorical (qualitative) choropleth map of the majority language in each Swiss district (Bezirk) 26
2.4 A quantitative choropleth map of the share of German speakers in each Swiss district (Bezirk) 26
2.5 A Dorling cartogram depicting the population of the districts (Bezirk) of Switzerland, and their majority language 27

Tables

3.1 Illustrations of a selection of the collected data with examples and variable types 55
3.2 Example of variables created by aggregating raw keystroke log data 61
4.1 Graph parameters generated by GenoGraphiX-LOG 2.0 for four L2 writers 102
4.2 Node and character distribution generated by GenoGraphiX-LOG 2.0 for four writers in L2 102
7.1 Overview of the different writing actions that can be encoded in the TEI-XML 162
9.1 Morphological skill and subtest with an example (Sellstone, 2023) 198
10.1 Example of GGXLog's different presentation tools (ID 2019, L2 Swedish, C1 level) 217
10.2 Example of P-bursts alternating with pauses (ID 2013, L2 English, B2 level, time 01:32) 218
10.3 Example of R-bursts in text production (ID 2017, L2 English, B1 level, time 00:40) 219
10.4 Example of pauses and revisions in text production (ID 2011, B2 level, time 01:11) 220

10.5 Number of writers at each CEFR level in English, French, and Swedish 223
10.6 Explicit planner 226
10.7 Implicit planner 226
10.8 Slow production starter 227
10.9 Tentative starter 228
10.10 Quick starter 229
10.11 Quick and productive starter 230
10.12 Number of starter writer profiles in L1 and L2 230

Notes on Contributors

Pavithra Basnayake
is Lecturer in the Department of Statistics and Computer Science, University of Peradeniya, Sri Lanka. She is reading for a PhD in Statistics at the Department of Statistics & Computer Science, University of Kelaniya, Sri Lanka. Her research interests include data science, time series forecasting and statistical modelling. Pavithra is passionate about applying modern statistical methods to solve real-world problems and enhance data-driven decision-making. She has published several articles in reputed journals, presented her work at numerous international conferences, contributed to organizing academic events, and received awards in recognition of her research contributions. Contact: pavithrab@sci.pdn.ac.lk.

Lamyk Bekius
holds a PhD in Literary Studies and is currently a postdoctoral researcher at the University of Antwerp, Belgium. Her research focusses on digital literary writing, especially applying genetic criticism to born-digital literary archives and keystroke logging data. She is also the University of Antwerp's coordinator of CLARIAH-VL+. Contact: lamyk.bekius@uantwerpen.be.

Floor Buschenhenke
has her PhD from Amsterdam, The Netherlands. Her doctoral thesis, "Entering stories: Decoding born-digital fiction writing through keystroke logging" (2025) [https://hdl.handle.net/11245.1/16460778-7a64-4134-8df5-321e8ece96ef], investigated the creative writing processes of eleven professional Dutch and Flemish authors. She used both quantitative and hermeneutical approaches to assess the temporal dynamics and individual characteristics of these processes. Contact: floor@buschenhenke.nl.

Gilles Caporossi
is a professor at HEC Montréal in the department of decision sciences. His research interests include graph theory, algorithmic and artificial intelligence. He is a member of the GERAD, group for research in decision analysis since 2004, of the international academy for mathematical chemistry since 2010. In collaboration with Christophe Leblay and Hakim Usoof, he co-developed the Genographix (ggxlog.net) keylogger software, which was based on a combination of text genetics and graph theory. Contact: gilles.caporossi@hec.ca.

Georgeta Cislaru
is Full Professor in Linguistics at University Sorbonne Nouvelle, Paris, France. Her research areas are Text Linguistics, Writing, Semantics, Discourse Analysis. Her recent research aims at modelling textualization processes in writing and elaborating a unified linguistic model to explain expectations, projections and predictions expressed through language. She is the head of the Pro-TEXT ANR Project, co-authored *Le processus de textualisation* (2018, with T. Olive), edited several books and special issues: "Written performance operating units: Linguistic and behavioural markers" (SI of *Journal of Writing Research*, 2025, with C. Doquet & T. Olive), *Writing(s) at the Crossroads. The Process–product Interface* (2015), *Linguistic Approaches to Emotions in Context* (2014, with F. Baider). Contact: georgeta.cislaru@sorbonne-nouvelle.fr.

Nistor Grozavu
is Full Professor and Director of the ETIS Laboratory at CY Cergy Paris University. He holds a PhD in Computer Science from University of Paris 13 (2009) and an Habilitation to Supervise Research (2021). His research focuses on unsupervised learning, multi-modal data analysis, and collaborative learning, with applications in scalable AI systems. He has supervised 9 PhD theses and authored 12 journal articles and over 60 conference papers. Nistor actively contributes to the scientific community by organizing international workshops and tutorials, including on topological clustering. He also teaches Artificial Intelligence and Data Analysis at CY Cergy Paris University. Contact: nistor.grozavu@cyu.fr.

Alain Hertz
graduated in mathematical engineering and obtained a PhD in operations research at the École Polytechnqiue Fédérale de Lausanne. Since 2001, he is professor at the department of mathematics and industrial engineering at Polytechnique Montréal, Canada. He is also a member of the multidisciplinary GERAD research group that includes nearly sixty researchers and experts in operations research and discrete mathematics. He is the author of around 200 scientific publications and 4 detective novels. His main research domains are combinatorial optimization, graph theory, algorithmics, and the development of decision aid systems for scheduling and distribution problems. Contact: alain.hertz@gerad.ca.

Juuso Koponen

is an information designer and data journalist. He teaches data journalism and data visualisation at Haaga-Helia University of Applied Sciences and other Finnish universities, and is a co-founder of the Helsinki, Finland-based information design studio Koponen+Hildén. Contact: juuso.koponen@haaga-helia.fi.

Päivi Laine

is Associate Professor and University Lecturer of Finnish Language in the School of Languages and Translation Studies at the University of Turku, Finland. Her research primarily focuses on Finnish as a first language, but she is also interested in multilingual writing. In her studies on writing, she has concentrated on writing processes and fluency, such as bursts, pauses and multi-word sequences. Through this research, she aims to enhance the teaching of language and writing. Contact: paipel@utu.fi.

Christophe Leblay

is Adjunct Professor at the School of Languages and Translation Studies at Turku University, Finland. His research interests include text genetics with a particular focus on revision during writing and professional writing. He is also an associate researcher at Institut des textes et manuscrits modernes (ITEM). In collaboration with Gilles Caporossi and Hakim Usoof, he co-developed the Genographix (ggxlog.net) keylogger software, which was based on a combination of text genetics and graph theory. Contact: Christophe.leblay@utu.fi.

Maarit Mutta

is Senior University Lecturer (PhD) and the Deputy Head of the School of Languages and Translation Studies (Education and Development; 2025–2029). She also holds the title of Associate Professor of Applied Linguistics at the University of Jyväskylä. She is an expert in online processing perspectives on written fluency and the impact of meta-language on language learning and production. Currently, she is leading the KISUVI project on the visualisation of fluency patterns (Kone Foundation, 2022–2026) and has expertise in digital learning and sustainability in language teaching and learning. She has led two ERASMUS+ projects in Finland for adult education (LALI 2017–2020; CORDIALIS 2022–2024). Contact: maarit.mutta@utu.fi.

Mari Mäkilä
is a postdoctoral researcher in the Department of Scandinavian Languages at the University of Turku, Finland. She specialises in syntactic complexity, but her research interests cover all the aspects in the CAF triad—that is, accuracy and fluency in addition to complexity. In her research, she has focused on, for instance, individual variation and the differences between written and spoken learner language. Her most recent work focuses on fluency in multilingual language learners' written production. Contact: mari.makila@utu.fi.

Thierry Olive
is Senior Research Scientist in psychology at the Centre National de la Recherche Scientifique, France (CNRS). His research investigates writing and learning to write in adult writers, in typically developing children as well as in writers with language difficulties. He has published numerous articles and books on writing and note-taking, in which he studies cognitive processes, orthographic skills, the involvement of working memory, and the role of digital writing tools. He is a co-editor of the *Studies in Writing* series published by Brill and of the *Journal of Writing Research*. Contact: thierry.olive@cnrs.fr.

Maxime Olivié
is a fullstack developer with an academic background in Artificial Intelligence and Pattern Recognition, collaborating with the ANR Pro-TEXT project in Paris, France. He is responsible for the development of a web platform aimed at presenting, organizing, and disseminating the project's research outputs. His professional interests include data visualisation, machine learning, and software architecture. Contact: contact@maximeolivie.fr.

Daniel Perrin
is Professor of Applied Linguistics, Dean of the School of Applied Linguistics at the Zurich University of Applied Sciences, Past President of the International Association of Applied Linguistics AILA, Board Member of the Swiss Academy of Social Sciences and Humanities, as well as Editor of the de Gruyter *Handbook of Applied Linguistics* series. His areas of research include media linguistics, methodology of applied linguistics, text production research, and analysis of language use in professional communication. Perrin worked as a journalist and writing coach before his academic career. For more information see: www.danielperrin.net. Contact: daniel.perrin@bluewin.ch.

Linda Sandström
is an assistant professor of linguistics with a focus on language development and processing at Umeå University, Sweden. She holds a PhD in Speech-Language Pathology (SLP) and teaches on the SLP and special education programmes. She also conducts school-based dyslexia research with universities in Norway and Sweden. Linda's other research interests include morphological development and processing in relation to reading and writing. Contact: linda.sandstrom@umu.se.

Andreas Sellstone
holds a master's degree in Cognitive Science from Umeå University, Sweden. His research focuses on the cognitive processes involved in writing during computer interactions and how they vary depending on the type of writing activity. Specifically, his work has explored the role of Artificial Intelligence in writing, the use of computer keystroke logging for diagnostic and educational purposes, and the visualisation of keystroke data for practical applications in schools and clinics. Contact: andreas@sellstone.se.

Kirk P.H. Sullivan
is Professor of Linguistics at the Department of Language Studies, Umeå University, Sweden, and an honorary professor at Prifysgol Bangor University, Wales. His research interests lie at the nexus of linguistics, cognition, and education, and include special education, writing processes, the teaching of writing, multilingualism, doctoral studies, and forensic linguistics. Together with Coppélie Cocq and Eva Lindgren, Kirk has edited several books in Brill's *Studies in Writing* series. Contact: kirk.sullivan@umu.se.

Florence Tanoï Namio
obtained her PhD from Polytechnique Montréal (Canada) in 2025. She has a master's in statistics from the National Advanced School of Engineering of the University of Yaoundé 1 (Cameroon) and a bachelor degree in mathematics from the University of Yaoundé 1 (Cameroun). She is an expert in mathematics and focuses her work on the mathematical modeling of the writing activity. Contact: florence.tanoi-namio@polymtl.ca.

Hakim Usoof
is Senior Lecturer in Computer Science at the University of Peradeniya's Department of Statistics & Computer Science, which he rejoined in 2019 after a 15-year tenure at the University of Colombo School of Computing. He began

his academic career at Peradeniya in 2003 and earned his PhD in Technology and Education from Sweden's Umeå University (2012) through a SIDA/SPIDER scholarship. During a 2020 sabbatical, he researched at Finland's University of Turku on the GenoGaphiX-LOG project for visualising writing data. His expertise spans human–computer interaction, educational technology, human–data interaction, data visualisation, explainable AI, and digital humanities, with extensive postgraduate supervision at the University of Colombo, Queensland University of Technology, and Peradeniya. His work bridges technological innovation and education, emphasizing interdisciplinary collaboration and applied research methodologies. In collaboration with Gilles Caporossi and Christophe Leblay, he co-developed the GenoGraphiX (ggxlog.net) keylogger software, which was based on a combination of text genetics and graph theory. Contact: hau@sci.pdn.ac.lk.

Anne-Maj Åberg
is a university teacher in Scandinavian languages at the School of Languages and Translation Studies at the University of Turku in Finland. She received her PhD degree in Scandinavian languages in 2020 at the University of Turku. In her dissertation, she examines the effects of explicit form-focused instruction (FFI) on formal second language (L2) learners' explicit and implicit knowledge of Swedish. The focus is on syntax in Swedish. In her research, she studies writing processes in Swedish as second language in addition to second language acquisition in Swedish. Contact: anne-maj.aberg@utu.fi.

CHAPTER 1

Dimensions of Visualisation Applied to the Writing Process

Christophe Leblay, Hakim Usoof and Gilles Caporossi

The field of writing studies has undergone significant transformations over the past two decades, driven largely by advancements in hardware and software that enable the collection and analysis of data captured during the computer-based writing process. In the *Studies in Writing* series, preceded by two volumes, the first, published in 2006, *Computer Keystroke Logging and Writing* (edited by Kirk P.H. Sullivan and Eva Lindgren) and the second, published in 2019, *Observing Writing: Insights from Keystroke Logging and Handwriting* (edited by Eva Lindgren and Kirk K.P. Sullivan), this volume *An introduction to Data Visualisation of the Writing Process*, aims to address the growing need for sophisticated methods to interpret and analyse the complex and comprehensive data available through various data acquisition techniques.

This volume covers a range of academic and professional writing settings and a range of disciplines, including linguistics, text genetics, psychology, mathematical modelling, computer science, information science, engineering neuroscience, modern languages, education and other professional degree programmes. The chapters in this new volume provide readers with basic knowledge on data visualisation from a methodological and practical perspective.

1.1 The Timely Need for This Volume

The necessity of this volume arises from several key developments in the study of writing processes. First, writing research now benefits from a variety of data capture techniques, including keystroke logging, mouse tracking, eye-tracking, screen capture, video and audio recording, stylus tracing and touch inputs. These data sources provide unprecedented insights into the writing process but also present challenges in terms of volume and complexity.

Second, the sheer scale of the data collected through these techniques demands more advanced analytical approaches to decipher the complex information hidden within. Writing process data is often longitudinal, multimodal and multi-layered, requiring tools capable of handling and synthesising large

 | HTTPS://DOI.ORG/10.1163/9789004760264-002

datasets. Traditional quantitative and qualitative methods alone are inadequate for detecting and comprehending complex patterns and trends in such complex datasets.

Third, the limitations of conventional methods for analysing writing data underscore the need for data visualisation. Traditional numerical and text-based approaches often fail to reveal complex relationships, progression patterns and behavioural shifts in the writing process. Data visualisation provides a means to translate raw data into meaningful, interpretable forms that can highlight significant patterns, anomalies and structural elements in writing behaviour.

Finally, the importance of data visualisation extends beyond writing studies and into various disciplines, including the humanities, social sciences, business, finance, education and the sciences. In these fields, visualisation has proven to be an invaluable tool for making sense of large and complex datasets, enabling researchers and practitioners to extract meaningful insights that inform theory and practice.

Much has happened since then, and the present volume focuses on presenting an introduction to the visualisation of the data of the writing process, with an emphasis on theoretical and methodological groundings and case studies. This volume also includes a glossary of chapter terms. Data visualisation is seen as a tool that tells stories from data for a specific purpose. As data visualisation is both an art and a science, the authors in this volume highlight existing writing capture tools and the unique uses of their built-in visualisation features and/or share their own visualisations, created using generic software or especially developed for the study of the writing process.

1.2 Thematic Analysis of Chapters

This thematic analysis synthesises insights from a comprehensive corpus of literature spanning nine chapters and their associated references, each contributing to the interdisciplinary study of data visualisation and writing processes. The analysis was conducted through a meticulous examination of recurring concepts, methodologies and theoretical frameworks across the chapters and the works cited by their authors. By integrating primary discussions from the chapters—ranging from foundational visualisation principles to applications in clinical and educational settings—with the broader scholarly landscape reflected in their bibliographies, this work identifies nine interconnected themes that encapsulate the field's breadth and depth.

The process involved tracing theoretical lineages, such as Bertin's semiology of graphics (1983) and Hayes' cognitive models of writing (2009), while also highlighting contemporary innovations in machine learning and genetic criticism. Special attention was given to how authors engaged with historical milestones (e.g., Minard's flow maps) and modern tools (e.g., keystroke logging software) to bridge theory and practice. The resulting themes, which span foundational theories, methodological advancements and ethical considerations, reflect the dynamic interplay between cognitive science, digital humanities and applied linguistics.

By mapping these themes, the analysis not only clarifies the current state of research but also underscores emerging challenges and opportunities in understanding writing as a multidimensional, iterative process. The following sections elaborate on these nine themes, offering a cohesive framework to navigate the complexities of visualising and analysing textual creation.

1.2.1 *Foundations of Data Visualisation: Bridging Theory and Practice*

The evolution of data visualisation as a scientific tool and as an interpretive art is rooted in foundational works that blend quantitative rigour with humanistic enquiry. Jacques Bertin's Semiology of Graphics (1967, 2011) revolutionised the field by establishing principles for encoding data, such as position, colour and size, which align with human perceptual systems. Bertin's insistence on 'graphic efficiency' emphasised stripping away superfluous elements to foreground meaningful patterns, a philosophy later echoed in Edward Tufte's The Visual Display of Quantitative Information (1983). Tufte's concept of the 'data–ink ratio' became a mantra for designers, advocating minimalism to avoid distorting data through decorative clutter. These principles found practical application in tools such as GenoGraphiX-Log (Usoof et al., 2020), which visualises keystroke data using colour gradients to represent revision intensity, allowing researchers to track the ebb and flow of writing processes.

However, the humanities pose unique challenges to these quantitative paradigms. Johanna Drucker (2011) critiqued the dominance of (science-technology-engineering-mathematics) STEM-centric visualisation methods, arguing that humanistic data—often ambiguous and context-dependent—demand interfaces that embrace multiplicity and subjectivity. Her concept of a *humanistic interface design* rejects static charts in favour of interactive, layered visualisations that invite interpretation. For example, Drucker's temporal mapping eschews linear timelines to represent drafting processes as overlapping strata, reflecting the nonlinear nature of creative work. This tension between precision and ambiguity is epitomised in Matejka and Fitzmaurice's (2017) 'same stats, different graphs,' which demonstrates how identical statistical summaries can mask radically divergent narratives, reinforcing the necessity of visualisation for exploratory analysis.

Historical milestones further contextualise this evolution. Michael Friendly (2009) chronicled breakthroughs, including Edmond Halley's thematic maps (Thrower, 1981), which visualised trade winds to aid navigation, and Charles-Joseph Minard's flow diagrams, which mapped Napoleon's disastrous Russian campaign through variables such as troop numbers and temperature. These works underscore visualisation's power to synthesise complex narratives—a theme later mirrored in Chapter 7's genetic criticism of textual evolution.

Visualisation serves as the unifying thematic thread that binds the diverse explorations in this volume. Although it permeates every chapter, its foundational role is most explicitly articulated in Chapter 2, which establishes the core principles of visualisation within the broader context of the humanities and social sciences. Here, the discussion bridges theoretical frameworks—from Bertin's semiology to Drucker's humanistic critiques—with practical applications, grounding visualisation as an analytical tool and an interpretive act. Building on this foundation, subsequent chapters narrow their focus. Chapter 3 delves into the specialised domain of writing studies and examines how keystroke logging data is transformed into visual narratives that decode cognitive and behavioural patterns. This chapter demonstrates how techniques of keystroke logging, data visualisation and writing process analytics provide concrete means of uncovering hidden aspects of writing behaviour. By addressing the difficulty of capturing and interpreting the dynamic, non-linear nature of text production, the chapter shows how these methods transform raw writing traces into interpretable insights. The specific contribution lies in offering a framework that integrates visualisation with empirical analysis, enabling researchers and educators to answer critical questions about writing development and decision-making with greater clarity and precision. Chapters 4 and 5 further sharpen this lens, introducing graph-theoretical visualisations and visualisation writing stages, respectively, both rooted in text-genetic scholarship to map the nonlinear, iterative nature of drafting processes. Together, these chapters illustrate how visualisation evolves from abstract theory to domain-specific practice, maintaining its centrality as a bridge between data and meaning.

1.2.2 *Keystroke Logging: Capturing the Dynamics of Writing*

Keystroke logging emerged as a transformative methodology for dissecting the cognitive and behavioural intricacies of writing. Its development built upon earlier efforts to capture the writing process, such as video recordings of composing (Matsuhashi, 1981). A significant leap occurred with Claudine Fabre's

(1991) integration of text genetics, which highlighted the challenge of observing the act of writing itself. This was soon followed by pioneering software like Genèse du texte (Foucambert, 1995), which recorded all keyboard operations, functioning like a video recorder for text creation and enabling researchers to replay and analyse a dynamic digital (pre-)text.

The 1990s saw the development of several key keystroke logging (KSL) tools, including TraceIt (Kollberg et al., 1996), ScriptLog (Strömqvist & Malmsten, 1998), and Translog (Jakobsen & Schou, 1999). These programs established the core KSL function of faithfully recording keyboard and mouse events with millisecond precision. In a manner consistent with all subsequent KSL software (Johansson et al., 2018; Leijten & Van Waes, 2013; Usoof et al., 2020), these early tools formed a foundation upon which various analysis modules were later built, necessitating that researchers select tools based on their specific research goals.

A prominent example of such a tool is Inputlog (Leijten & Van Waes, 2005, 2013), which records keystrokes, mouse movements, and pauses. The integration of eye-tracking with KSL, a milestone pioneered by Andersson et al. (2006) using ScriptLog, provides a multimodal lens into writing phases—planning, drafting and revising—that align with Hayes and Flower's (1980) cognitive model.

Recent advances in machine learning have further expanded analytical possibilities. Conijn et al. (2024) developed algorithms to categorise revisions as formative (e.g., spelling corrections) or conceptual (e.g., rephrasing arguments), enabling large-scale analysis of writing strategies. Many software further advanced the field of keystroke logging, drawing on the works such as Burns et al. (2020), who proposed a multi-level evaluation framework for visualisations, distinguishing perceptual effectiveness (e.g., colour contrast) from cognitive effectiveness (e.g., inference accuracy) in the field of human–computer interaction. These innovations underscore keystroke logging's evolution from a niche research tool to a cornerstone of interdisciplinary writing analysis.

Chapter 2 provides general information on visualisation in humanities, while the remaining chapters in this volume provide a detailed overview of studies on the writing process using KSL.

1.2.3 *Graph Theory: Mapping Nonlinear Writing Processes*

Graphs and networks are built from nodes (points) and arcs (lines) eventually joining pairs of nodes. By their nature, they are both useful for visualisation and to represent relations between objects. They are applied in a wide variety of fields through different means. Beside the metro map or the road network for which the data is originally a graph, other complex data may also be represented as graphs after applying transformations which may not be obvious.

For instance, business relations or task scheduling may be studied by the mean of graphs.

In all cases, graphs either help understanding the data, or they help in building meaningful models that could later be analysed through the graph theory point of view. In the same way as data may be standardized for the purpose of statistical analysis, it may be converted to graph for a graph theory-based analysis, a different tool that provides a different way to study a process.

In the context of writing, graphs have provided access to new elements enabling researchers to show that the process is non-linear and iterative. Caporossi and Leblay (2011) modelled 'rumination writing'—an expression coined by Irène Fenoglio (2009a, 2009b) to describe texts revised recursively—as dynamic graphs. The nodes in these graphs represent events contributing to the evolution of the text, such as insertions, deletions or displacements, while edges denote the relations among these events. For example, a novice writer's graph may show dense clusters of nodes around introductory paragraphs, reflecting repeated attempts to refine a thesis statement. GenoGraphiX-Log (Usoof et al., 2020) enhanced this model by colour-coding nodes (red for deletions, green for insertions) and weighting edges using temporal intervals, revealing patterns such as 'hesitation clusters' in which writers vacillate between alternatives.

Alternative approaches, such as Kollberg's (1998) S-notation, use hierarchical trees to trace sentence evolution. Each branch represents a draft version, enabling researchers to reconstruct how a sentence is morphed from passive to active voice or how metaphors are replaced. These methods intersect with Almuth Grésillon's (1994) genetic criticism, which treats manuscripts as palimpsests of layered creative decisions. For example, Bekius (2023) applied TEI-XML encoding to digitise Mary Shelley's Frankenstein drafts, visualising marginalia and interlinear additions that reveal her evolving ethical framing of the Creature.

Despite its utility, static visualisation faces criticism. Leblay and Caporossi (2014) argued that it obscures temporal flow, advocating instead for dynamic visualisations that simulate real-time drafting. This critique spurred tools such as GenoGraphiX-Log's playback feature, which animates the writing process, allowing researchers to observe how a text unfolds moment by moment.

In this volume, Chapters 4, 5 and 10 are strongly related to the concept of graphs. Chapter 10 describes an application with analysis based on the graph model. It introduces a new type of burst based on the GGXLog analysis, namely visualisation bursts (V-bursts), in order to define and illustrate different writer profiles in the initial writing phase. Chapters 4 and 5 are more methodological. Both provide tools to visualise the successive stages in the development of a text, from the blank page to the final version, a process that may seem linear at first glance but is, in reality, iterative and complex. In Chapter 5, process is broken down into episodes of modifications, each consisting of successive character insertions and deletions made without moving the cursor. The option to merge episodes of modifications offers a more holistic view of the writing process, while additional diagrams synthesize information to evaluate the quantitative contribution of each episode to the final text.

1.2.4 *Revision Analysis: from Cognitive Models to Pedagogical Tools*

Revision—the recursive process of evaluating and altering text—has been dissected through cognitive, pedagogical and computational lenses. Hayes and Flower's (1980) seminal model distinguishes monitoring (assessing text against goals) from revising (executing changes), a framework expanded upon earlier work by Donald Murray (1978) into internal (pre-textual ideation) and external (post-textual edits) revisions. For example, a writer may internally restructure an argument before drafting (internal) or delete redundant paragraphs post-drafting (external).

Keystroke logging quantifies these stages. Lindgren and Sullivan (2002) introduced LS Graphs to map revision trajectories, in which the 'distance' between drafts reflects the extent of changes. A case study of student essays revealed dense clusters of revisions around thesis statements, illustrating iterative refinement. Modern tools, such as Mahlow et al.'s (2024) (natural language processing) NLP pipeline, automate this analysis, extracting 'sentence histories' to track syntactic and semantic shifts. For example, a sentence may evolve from a declarative structure ('The experiment succeeded') to a speculative one ('The results suggest partial success'), reflecting the writer's growing nuance.

Pedagogical applications abound. Daniel Perrin's (2019) progression analysis combines macro-level workflow charts (e.g., collaborative writing stages) with micro-level S-notation diagrams to train journalists in reflective practice. In one intervention, reporters learned to identify 'scaffolded drafting', in which they iteratively integrate sources rather than drafting linearly. Similarly, Olmanson et al. (2016) developed mapping tools that visualise revision patterns, helping students recognise over-reliance on surface edits (e.g., grammar fixes) at the expense of conceptual restructuring.

Expert–novice differences further illuminate revision's cognitive demands. Sommers (1980) found that experienced adult writers revise at all levels and make changes to "form, balance, rhythm, and communication," whereas student writers primarily correct spelling, punctuation, and diction—fixating on local errors rather than global restructuring. This dichotomy underscores the role of metacognition in writing development—a theme explored in Lindgren and Sullivan's (2003) use of keystroke logs to prompt L2 learners to verbalise their strategies during pauses.

Revision analysis, as a methodological framework and a pedagogical imperative, finds its most granular exploration in the chapters that anchor this section. Chapter 7 centres on the text-genetic approach, using keystroke data to reconstruct the layered evolution of drafts, thereby illuminating how writers navigate recursive cycles of creation and revision. Building on this, Chapter 8 adopts progression analysis—a hybrid framework blending macro-level workflow mapping with micro-level temporal tracking—to visualise writing processes in real-world contexts and uncover patterns, such as iterative drafting in collaborative journalism or metacognitive pauses in L2 learners. Expanding the scope, Chapter 9 transitions into clinical applications, demonstrating how visualisation of writing processes during diagnostic tests can reveal biomarkers for language impairments or neuropsychiatric disorders, such as aphasia or early-stage Alzheimer's. Together, these chapters underscore revision not only as an editorial act but also as a window into cognitive, pedagogical and clinical dimensions of writing, bridging theoretical models with transformative educational and diagnostic practices.

1.2.5 *Genetic Criticism: Digitizing Textual Evolution*

Genetic criticism, rooted in the study of drafts and marginalia, has embraced digital tools to analyse text genesis. Grésillon (1994) framed writing as a 'slow-motion' process in which each draft captures a picture of creative decision-making. This approach gained new traction with born-digital texts, with Deppman et al. (2004) arguing that genetic criticism demands fresh analytical frameworks.

Digital tools have had a profound impact on the field of genetics research by opening up a wide range of possibilities. Fenoglio and Ganascia's (2007) and Ganascia's (2011) MEDITE software compare draft versions to highlight variants, such as lexical substitutions that alter the narrative tone. For example, in Flaubert's Madame Bovary, MEDITE revealed how the replacement of 'passion' with 'ennui' in later drafts shifted the protagonist's portrayal from fiery to listless.

Studies by Bekius (2023), Buschenhenke (2025) and Butzek (2023) have highlighted the renewal of genetic criticism when combined with KSL tools in the analysis of born-digital literary works. It is within this precise context that the term 'nanogenetics' was first coined.

Critics, such as Mathijsen (2009), question genetic editing's viability, arguing that its emphasis on documenting processes over establishing texts limits its usefulness for traditional textual scholarship. However, Fiormonte and Pusceddu (2006) argue that many digital approaches expand access to previously restricted archival materials.

Chapters 4 and 7 of this volume reflect this orientation towards text genetics. Both use KSL tools to show how genesis can be visualised. Chapter 4 constitutes an exploratory investigation into the potential of coloured graph-based modelling to deliver pertinent information concerning the writing process using toy examples. Conversely, Chapter 7 proposes a workflow for adapting the text genetic methodology to work with keystroke logging data upon extensive experience in long-term literary writing. It presents visualisations of keystroke logging data showing the production process, the text produced so far along with all the textual changes made along the way in their temporal and spatial context.

1.2.6 *Machine Learning and High-Dimensional Analytics*

Machine learning has unlocked new frontiers in analysing writing's linguistic, temporal and behavioural dimensions. Reimers and Gurevych (2019) leveraged BERT embeddings to detect semantic coherence in drafts, flagging sections in which rapid drafting led to disjointed arguments.

Topological data analysis (TDA), which was applied by Hensel et al. (2021), maps nonlinear writing trajectories. Persistent homology—a TDA technique—identified 'holes' in data representing drafting bottlenecks, such as prolonged pauses before introducing new characters in fiction. In case studies such as Lardilleux et al.'s (2013), Allongos software align draft versions longitudinally and visualise how writers progressively refine rhetorical structures.

Ethical concerns loom large. Berber Sardinha (2024) demonstrated that artificial intelligence (AI)-generated text detectors have some bias that could lead to the penalisation of some classes of writers. Similarly, de Villiers et al. (2024) cautioned against opaque AI models in sustainability reporting and advocated algorithmic transparency to prevent greenwashing.

The integration of machine learning and high-dimensional analytics into writing research has emerged as a pivotal yet underexplored frontier, especially with the escalation of data complexity. While keystroke logging traditionally captures 10–15 features per data point, recording metrics such as pause duration and revision frequency, advances in sensor technology, as noted in Chapter 3, now enable the collection of hundreds of multimodal features, from gaze-tracking patterns and video data capturing body language to physiological signals, such as heart rate variability and brain wave patterns, measured via EEG. This proliferation of data dimensions necessitates sophisticated analytical frameworks, a challenge briefly acknowledged in Chapters 6, 7 and 8. Although these chapters only indicate AI's potential, they collectively underscore its capacity to unearth latent patterns, such as predictive biomarkers for cognitive load (via brain wave oscillations) or stylistic evolution in multilingual writing (linked to gestural pauses in video recordings), which defy conventional analysis. As the field advances, the fusion of high-dimensional data with machine learning promises not only to refine existing methodologies but also to redefine the very boundaries of how writing is studied, providing that ethical and interpretive challenges are navigated with rigour.

As described in Chapter 6, the visualisation tools developed by the Pro-TEXT project make it possible to link temporal and spatial information with linguistic information, thus offering a more complete representation of the writing process as a linguistic practice.

The visual techniques, in Chapter 8, make the often-invisible processes of writing visible and easier to understand, from small edits to large-scale workflows. They help researchers and practitioners to see where difficulties arise—for example in translation, collaboration, or decision-making—and to trace how these challenges are resolved step by step.

1.2.7 *Multilingual Writing: Fluency, Code-Switching and Pedagogy*

Multilingual writing research explores how L1/L2 differences manifest in fluency, bursts and code-switching. The Common European Framework of Reference (CEFR, 2001) provides standardised proficiency levels, while Tavakoli and Uchihara (2020) linked L2 fluency to the automated retrieval of multiword sequences (e.g., 'on the other hand'). Mutta et al. (2025) profiled writers using burst–pause ratios and found that L2 writers' shorter bursts seemed to reflect cognitive load during lexical retrieval.

Visual tools, such as GenoGraphiX-Log (Usoof et al., 2020), map code-switching patterns. In a study of Finnish–Swedish bilinguals (Ivaska et al., 2025), heatmaps revealed L1 syntactic structures influencing L2 clause formation, such as the placement of adverbs post-verbally in Swedish drafts due to Finnish interference. Storto et al. (2023) extended this to the classroom context using node-link diagrams to visualise translanguaging practices in which students blend L1 and L2 resources to scaffold argumentation.

Pedagogical strategies have evolved in response. Skein et al. (2020) discuss translanguaging practices that support multilingual writers' flexible language use rather than prescribing fixed L1-to-L2 drafting sequences. Lindgren, Stevenson and Sullivan (2008) examine keystroke logging as a tool to support learner reflection on writing processes, including pauses and revisions.

The exploration of multilingual writing in this volume is enriched by interdisciplinary approaches that bridge behavioural, linguistic and computational perspectives. Chapter 6 establishes a methodological foundation through its three-pronged framework, visualising features such as fluency, bursts and pauses by integrating behavioural patterns, linguistic structures and machine learning analytics, a model readily adaptable to multilingual contexts. Chapter 10 builds on this foundation by exemplifying how visualisations of initial drafting phases, including code-switching dynamics and fluency variations, illuminate the unique cognitive rhythms of multilingual writers. Chapter 9 primarily addresses clinical diagnostics. Its insights into pedagogical interventions, such as tailoring feedback based on keystroke patterns or pause analysis, have indirect yet transformative potential for multilingual education, offering strategies to address the diverse needs of linguistically heterogeneous classrooms. Collectively, these chapters underscore the volume's central aim: to decode writing processes through visualisation not only as an academic exercise but also as a catalyst for developing pedagogies that empower multilingual learners. By mapping the interplay of language systems and cognitive behaviours, this work equips educators to design nuanced, data-informed interventions that honour the complexity of writing across linguistic boundaries.

1.2.8 *Clinical and Educational Applications: from Theory to Practice*

In clinical settings, keystroke logging has proven transformative. Johansson-Malmeling et al. (2020) correlated pause duration with aphasia severity and informed personalised therapy plans that target lexical retrieval. Van Waes et al. (2017) identified irregular inter-key intervals as markers of Alzheimer's, thus enabling pre-symptomatic intervention.

Wengelin (2007) linked dysfluent bursts—characterised by mid-word pauses and frequent deletions—to conditions such as dyslexia and aphasia. For example, individuals with aphasia often exhibit prolonged pauses before high-frequency words, signalling lexical retrieval deficits. Van Waes et al. (2017) extended this to neurodegenerative contexts by identifying irregular typing rhythms as early markers of Alzheimer's disease. These findings validated keystroke logging's diagnostic potential, although Baaijen et al. (2012) cautioned that keystroke logging measures—pauses, bursts, and revisions—do not provide an unambiguous interpretation of cognitive processes. They identified this as a "problem of alignment" between keystroke units and writing models, noting that pauses may reflect planning, re-reading, or revision activities. To address this, they developed refined analytical procedures including burst classification by initiation/termination type and mixture models for pause data.

Education has similarly benefited. Olmanson et al. (2016) explored how students used a semantic concept mapping tool to create visualisations of the content and organization of their first drafts. Their qualitative analysis suggested that this process scaffolded self-evaluation and helped students develop meta-awareness of gaps or misalignments in their writing, with implications for supporting the revision process. Perrin (2019) employed progression analysis, a multi-method approach combining keystroke logging, ethnographic observation, and retrospective verbalisation to investigate how journalistic writing practices have evolved with digitalization.

In this volume, Chapter 9 alone opens up this clinical perspective. Nevertheless, this chapter is crucial in demonstrating how the visualisation of keystroke recording data is particularly well suited to clinical and educational settings. The authors highlight the slow adoption of such a protocol, pointing out that research-focused visualisations can make keystroke recording programmes unattractive to clinicians and teachers.

1.2.9 *Ethical and Interdisciplinary Futures*

The future of writing research hinges on ethical innovation and interdisciplinary synergy. Berber Sardinha (2024) shows that some bias could arise from AI tools, which suggest the need for fairness audit to prevent against this bias. Drucker (2011) called for training programmes that merge humanities with computational literacies, fostering scholars adept at both qualitative nuance and algorithmic rigour.

Emerging technologies promise real-time interventions, such as KSL approaches. Bekius (2023) advocated open-access genetic archives to democratise textual scholarship.

The final theme is cross-cutting in nature, with implications for all chapters. The integration of a keystroke logging system with a data visualisation function exemplifies the value of interdisciplinary collaboration and underscores the need for such approaches in contemporary writing research.

In addition to this fundamental choice, which is shared by all chapters, certain chapters cross-reference specific disciplines.

We conducted an exploratory analysis based on the vocables used in the different chapters to visualise the relationship between them. That is, nouns and verbs were associated with their roots (lemma), and we used the Jaccard coefficient to evaluate the strength of this relationship. In the next step, each chapter was linked to two more similar others, thus building the graph in Figure 1.1, in which each node represents a chapter and arcs indicate vocabulary proximity.

The first remark is that nodes 4 and 6 are more central, which may be explained by the nature of the corresponding chapters. Chapter 4 creates the relation between three topics, namely linguistics, graphs and analysis, while Chapter 6 creates the relation between behaviour, linguistics and machine learning from analysis and visualisation perspectives.

Chapters 2, 3 and 7 are related to both Chapters 4 and 6, with Chapter 2 being dedicated to visualisation in humanities, Chapter 3 being dedicated to

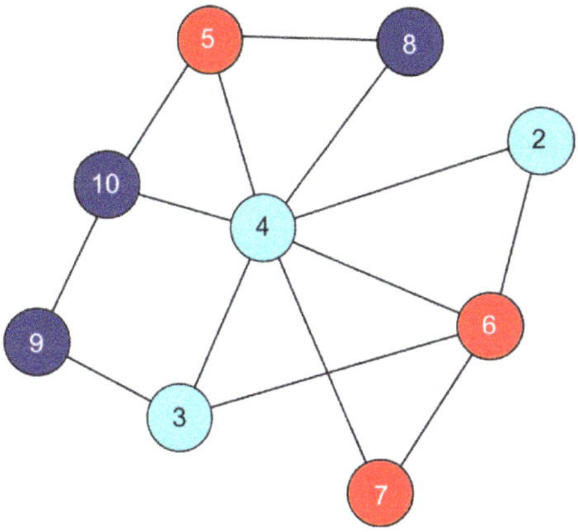

FIGURE 1.1
Graph of the relations between chapters according to the similarities of their vocable

visualisation based on KSL and Chapter 6 providing a framework for analysing KSL data.

In this network, we also notice that Chapters 4, 5 and 10 form a triangle. They are all based on the use of graph models, with Chapter 10 being on the application side and Chapters 4 and 5 being more methodological.

Surprisingly, Chapter 8 is related to nodes 4 and 5 but not to node 10. It is not a numerical artefact, but Perrin (this volume, p. 176) envisioned AI-driven dashboards that adapt to writers' needs, offering prompts during pauses or suggesting structural reorganisations, which could be related to the analysis tools proposed in Chapters 4 and 5 that are not graphs.

Finally, Chapter 9 describes an application of visualisation based on KSL, the methodology described in Chapter 3. It is also related to other applications used in Chapter 10.

From a global perspective, this volume is organised as follows: Chapters 2, 3 and 4 are related to methodology, mainly dealing with visualisation, while Chapters 5, 6 and 7 involve analysis. Chapters 8, 9 and 10 describe applications that eventually use tools or methods described in the previous chapters. These three groups are represented by colours in Figure 1.1. Combining colours and the graph structure, Figure 1.1 shows that various concepts are interrelated in a way that is far from linear.

This thematic analysis of the chapters collectively redefines writing as a dynamic, multidimensional and interdisciplinary practice. Visualisation transcends its role as a tool, becoming a theoretical lens that bridges cognitive processes with tangible outputs. From Proust's recursive drafts to AI-driven pedagogy, these advances underscore the need for interdisciplinary collaboration, ethical vigilance and innovative thinking to unravel writing's complexities. As technology evolves, so too must our approaches to ensure that visualisation remains a mirror that reflects human creativity and a window into its boundless possibilities.

This volume proceeds in two directions that may appear paradoxical. First, it provides visualisations of the writing process, as expected. Second, and surprisingly, it provides a list of terms and their definitions. This is intended to demonstrate the crucial role of conceptual tools in a volume devoted to shapes and colours. Please refer to the glossary at the end of this volume for definitions used in each chapter.

References

Andersson, B., Dahl, J., Holmqvist, K., Holsanova, J., Johansson, V., Karlsson, H., & Wengelin, A. (2006). Combining keystroke logging with eye-tracking. In L. Van Waes, M. Leijten, & C. Neuwirth (Eds.), *Writing and digital media* (vol. 17, pp. 166–172). Elsevier.

Baaijen, V. M., Galbraith, D., & de Glopper, K. (2012). Keystroke analysis: Reflections on procedures and measures. *Written Communication*, 29(3), 246–277. https://doi.org/10.1177/0741088312451108.

Baaijen, V.M., Galbraith, D., & De Glopper, K. (2012). Keystroke analysis: Reflections on procedures and measures. *Written Communication*, *29*(3), 246–277.

Bekius, L.L. (2023). *Behind the computer screens: The use of keystroke logging for genetic criticism applied to born-digital works of literature* [Doctoral dissertation, Antwerp University & University of Amsterdam]. https://repository.uantwerpen.be/docstore/d:irua:19149.

Berber Sardinha, T. (2024). AI-generated vs human-authored texts: A multidimensional comparison. *Applied Corpus Linguistics*, *4*(1), 100083. https://doi.org/10.1016/j.acorp.2023.100083.

Bertin, J. (1967). *Sémiologie graphique: Les diagrammes, les réseaux, les cartes.* Gauthier-Villars.

Bertin, J. (2011). *Semiology of graphics: Diagrams, networks, maps* (W.J. Berg, Trans.). Esri Press. (Original work published 1967).

Burns, A., Xiong, C., Franconeri, S., Cairo, A., & Mahyar, N. (2020, October). How to evaluate data visualizations across different levels of understanding. In *2020 IEEE Workshop on Evaluation and Beyond-Methodological Approaches to Visualization (BELIV)* (pp. 19–28). IEEE.

Buschenhenke, F. (2025). *Entering stories: Decoding born-digital fiction writing through keystroke logging* [Doctoral dissertation, University of Antwerp & University of Amsterdam]. University of Amsterdam Digital Academic Repository. https://hdl.handle.net/11245.1/16460778-7a64-4134-8df5-321e8ece96ef.

Butzek, A.M. (2023). *Les processus de l'écriture littéraire du point de vue génétique et psycholinguistique: étude de cas* [*Literary writing processes from a genetic and psycholinguistic perspective: a case study*] [Doctoral dissertation, Aix-Marseille Université]. https://theses.fr/2023AIXM0588.

Caporossi, G., & Leblay, C. (2011, October). Online writing data representation: A graph theory approach. In International Symposium on Intelligent Data Analysis (pp. 80–89). Berlin, Heidelberg: Springer Berlin Heidelberg. https://link.springer.com/chapter/10.1007/978-3-642-24800-9_10.

Conijn, R., Dux Speltz, E., & Chukharev-Hudilainen, E. (2024). Automated extraction of revision events from keystroke data. *Reading and Writing*, *37*, 483–508. https://doi.org/10.1007/s11145-021-10222-w.

Council of Europe. (2001). *Common European framework of reference for languages: Learning, teaching, assessment*. Cambridge University Press.

Deppman, J., Ferrer, D., & Groden, M. (Eds.). (2004). *Genetic criticism: Texts and avant-textes*. University of Pennsylvania Press.

de Villiers, C., Dimes, R., & Molinari, M. (2024). How will AI text generation and processing impact sustainability reporting? *Sustainability Accounting, Management and Policy Journal*, *15*(1), 96–118. https://doi.org/10.1108/SAMPJ-02-2023-0097.

Drucker, J. (2011). Humanities approaches to graphical display. *Digital Humanities Quarterly*, *5*(1). http://www.digitalhumanities.org/dhq/vol/5/1/000091/000091.html.

Fabre, C. (1991). La linguistique génétique: une autre entrée dans la production d'écrits [*Genetic linguistics: another approach to writing*]. *Repères. Recherches en didactique du français langue maternelle*, *4*(1), 49–58.

Fenoglio, I. (2009a). Les notes de travail d'Émile Benveniste: où la pensée théorique naît via son énonciation [*Émile Benveniste's working notes: where theoretical thought is born through its enunciation*]. *Langage et société*, *127*(1), 23–49.

Fenoglio, I. (2009b). Conceptualisation et textualisation dans le manuscrit de l'article « Le langage et l'expérience humaine » d'Emile Benveniste. Une contribution à la génétique de l'écriture en sciences humaines [*Conceptualisation and writing in the manuscript of the article 'Le langage et l'expérience humaine' by Emile Benveniste. A contribution to the genesis of writing in the Humanities*]. *Modèles linguistiques*, *30*(59), 71–99.

Fenoglio, I., & Ganascia, J.-G. (2007). MEDITE: un logiciel pour l'approche comparative de documents de genèse [*MEDITE is a software for comparative genetic analysis*]. *Genesis*, *29*, 166–168.

Fiormonte, D., & Pusceddu, C. (2006). The text as product and process. History, genesis, experiments. In D. Van Hulle & M.D.S. Corrêa (Eds.), *Manuscript, variant, genese—Genesis* (pp. 109–128). Koninklijke Academie voor Nederlandse Taal.

Foucambert, J. (1995). La recherche Genèse du texte [*Research with the software* Genèse du texte]. *Repères, recherches en didactique du français langue maternelle, 11*, 47–57. https://doi.org/10.3406/reper.1995.2142.

Friendly, M. (2009). *Milestones in the history of thematic cartography, statistical graphics, and data visualization.* http://euclid.psych.yorku.ca/SCS/Gallery /milestone/milestone.pdf.

Ganascia, J.-G. (2011, November 15–17). *MEDITE—A unilingual text aligner for humanities. Application to textual genetics and to the edition of text variants* [Conference presentation]. Supporting Digital Humanities (SDH 2011), Copenhagen, Denmark.

Grésillon, A. (1994). *Éléments de critique génétique: Lire les manuscrits modernes* [*Elements of genetic criticism: Reading modern manuscripts*]. Presses Universitaires de France.

Hayes, J.R., & Flower, L.S. (1980). Identifying the organization of writing processes. In L.W. Gregg & E.R. Steinberg (Eds.), *Cognitive processes in writing* (pp. 3–30). Erlbaum.

Hayes, J.R. (2009). From idea to text. In R. Beard, D. Myhill, M. Nystrand, & J. Riley (Eds.), *The SAGE handbook of writing development* (pp. 65–79). SAGE. https://doi .org/10.4135/9780857021069.

Hensel, F., Moor, M., & Rieck, B. (2021). A survey of topological machine learning methods. *Frontiers in Artificial Intelligence, 4*, 681108. https://doi.org/10.3389 /frai.2021.681108.

Ivaska, I., Toropainen, O., & Lahtinen, S. (2025). Pauses during a writing process in two typologically different languages. *Journal of Writing Research, 16*(3). 407–433. https://doi.org/10.17239/jowr-2025.16.03.03.

Jakobsen, A.L., & Schou, L. (1999). Translog Documentation—Appendix. I.G. Hansen (Ed.), *Probing the process in translation: methods and results* (ss. 151–186). Samfundslitteratur.

Johansson, V., Frid, J., & Wengelin, Å. (2018). *ScriptLog—an experimental keystroke logging tool* [Conference abstract]. ELN 1st Literacy Summit, Porto, Portugal.

Johansson-Malmeling, C., Wengelin, Å., & Henriksson, I. (2020). Aphasia and spelling to dictation: Analysis of spelling errors and editing. *International Journal of Language & Communication Disorders, 56*(1), 145–160. https://doi.org/10.1111/1460-6984.12591.

Kollberg, P. (1998). *S-notation—A computer-based method for studying and representing text composition* [Licentiate thesis, Royal Institute of Technology].

Kollberg, P., Kim, H.-C., & Eklundh, K.S. (1996). Trace-It: An Interactive Tool for Revision Analysis. In *European Writing Conferences Barcelona*, Spain (23–25. or.). Barcelona.

Lardilleux, A., Fleury, S., & Cislaru, G. (2013). Allongos: Longitudinal alignment for the genetic study of writers' drafts. In *International Conference on Intelligent Text Processing and Computational Linguistics* (pp. 537–548). Springer. https://doi.org /10.1007/978-3-642-37256-8_44.

Leblay, C. & Caporossi, G. (Eds.) 2014. *Temps de l'écriture. Enregistrements et représentations.* [*Time of writing. Recordings and representations.*] Coll. "Sciences du langage : Carrefours et points de vue", Louvain-La-Neuve, Academia-L'Harmattan. 257 p. https://digital.casalini.it/9782336337401.

Leijten, M., & Van Waes, L. (2005). Inputlog: A logging tool for the research of writing processes. *Proceedings of the European Writing Conferences.*

Leijten, M., & Van Waes, L. (2013). Keystroke logging in writing research: Using Inputlog to analyze and visualize writing processes. *Written Communication, 30*(3), 358–392. https://doi.org/10.1177/0741088313491692.

Lindgren, E., Stevenson, M., & Sullivan, K.P.H. (2008). Supporting the reflective language learner with computer keystroke logging. In F. Zhang & B. Barber (Eds.), *Handbook of research on computer-enhanced language acquisition and learning* (pp. 189–204). IGI Global.

Lindgren, E., & Sullivan, K.P.H. (2002). The LS graph: A methodology for visualizing writing revision. *Language Learning, 52*(3), 565–595.

Lindgren, E., & Sullivan, K.P.H. (2003). Stimulated recall as a trigger for increasing noticing and language awareness in the L2 writing classroom: A case study of two young female writers. *Language Awareness, 12*(3–4), 172–186.

Mahlow, C., Ulasik, M.A., & Tuggener, D. (2024). Extraction of transforming sequences and sentence histories from writing process data: A first step towards linguistic modeling of writing. *Reading and Writing, 37*(2), 443–482. https://doi.org/10.1007/s11145-021-10234-6.

Matejka, J., & Fitzmaurice, G. (2017). Same stats, different graphs: Generating datasets with varied appearance and identical statistics through simulated annealing. In *Proceedings of the 2017 CHI Conference on Human Factors in Computing Systems* (pp. 1290–1294). ACM. https://doi.org/10.1145/3025453.3025912.

Mathijsen, M. (2009). Genetic textual editing: The end of an era. In G. Mitterauer, U. Müller, M. Springeth, & V. Vitzthum (Eds.), *Was ist Textkritik?* (pp. 233–240). Max Niemeyer Verlag. https://doi.org/10.1515/9783484970786.4.233.

Matsuhashi, A. (1981). Pausing and planning: The tempo of written discourse production. *Research in the Teaching of English, 15*(2), 113–134.

Murray, D. (1978). "Internal Revision: A Process of Discovery." *Research on Composing: Points of Departure, edited by* Charles R. Cooper and Lee Odell, National Council of Teachers of English, 1978, pp. 85–104.

Mutta, M., Peltonen, P., Laine, P., & Lintunen, P. (2025). Fluency across modes: An exploratory study of L1 and L2 spoken and written fluency. *International Review of Applied Linguistics in Language Teaching*, 1–30. https://doi.org/10.1515/iral-2024-0187.

Olmanson, J., Kennett, K., Magnifico, A., McCarthey, S., Searsmith, D., Cope, B., & Kalantzis, M. (2016). Visualizing revision: Leveraging student-generated between-draft diagramming data in support of academic writing development.

Technology, Knowledge and Learning, *21*, 99–123. https://doi.org/10.1007/s10758-015-9265-5.

Perrin, D. (2019). Progression Analysis: Working with Large Data Corpora in Field Research on Writing. In E. Lindgren & K.P.H. Sullivan (Eds.), *Observing writing: Insights from keystroke logging and handwriting* (pp. 143–162). Brill. https://doi.org/10.1163/9789004392526_008.

Reimers, N., & Gurevych, I. (2019). Sentence-BERT: Sentence embeddings using Siamese BERT-networks. *arXiv*. https://arxiv.org/abs/1908.10084.

Skein, E., Yvonne Knospe, Y., & Sullivan K. P. H. (2020). Supporting Advanced Multlingual Speakers as Individuals: Translanguaging in Writing. In *Research Anthology on Bilingual and Multilingual Education* (pp.1638–1656). https://doi.org/10.4018/978-1-6684-3690-5.ch082.

Sommers, N. (1980). Revision strategies of student writers and experienced adult writers. College Composition and Communication, 31(4), 378–388. https://doi.org/10.2307/356588.

Storto, A., Haukås, Å., & Tiurikova, I. (2023). Visualising the language practices of lower secondary students: Outlines for practice-based models of multilingualism. *Applied Linguistics Review*, *15*(5), 2035–2059. https://doi.org/10.1515/applirev-2022-0010.

Strömqvist, S., & Malmsten, L. (1998). Scriptlog Pro 1.04—*User's manual.* Technical report, Sweden, Gothenburg: Göteborg University, Department of Linguistics.

Tavakoli, P., & Uchihara, T. (2020). To what extent are multiword sequences associated with oral fluency? *Language Learning*, *70*(2), 506–547. https://doi.org/10.1111/lang.12384.

Thrower, N. J. W., ed. (1981). T*he Three Voyages of Edmond Halley in the Paramore 1698–1701.* London: Hakluyt Society. 2nd series, vols. 156–157.

Tufte, E.R. (1983). *The visual display of quantitative information.* Graphics Press.

Usoof, H., Leblay, C., & Caporossi, G. (2020). *GenoGraphiX-Log version 2.0 user guide*. Les Cahiers du GERAD G-2020-68.

Van Waes, L., Leijten, M., Marin, P., & Engelborghs, S. (2017). Typing competencies in Alzheimer's disease: An exploration of copy tasks. *Computers in Human Behavior*, *73*, 311–319. https://doi.org/10.1016/j.chb.2017.03.050.

Wengelin, Å. (2007). The word-level focus in text production by adults with reading and writing difficulties. In M. Torrance, L. Van Waes, & D. Galbraith (Eds.), *Writing and cognition: Research and applications* (pp. 67–82). Brill. https://doi.org/10.1163/9781849508223_006.

CHAPTER 2

Visualisation Toolkit for the Humanities

Juuso Koponen

Data visualisation is the practice of turning abstract information into visual form in order to better understand and gain insights from it. Though there are numerous historical and modern examples of visualisation methods being applied in the humanities, the practice of supporting arguments in research papers with insightful visualisation is less well-established in contemporary humanities than it is in statistics, science, and social sciences.

2.1 A Definition Visualisation

What exactly is a **visualisation**? One succinct definition is: "graphical representation of data to make patterns perceptually visible." (Brath, 2021, p. 28)

The term refers both to the process of turning information into pictorial form, and to the result thereof. For the *process* of visualisation, Kosara (2007) has proposed the following as the minimal set of requirements: it is based on (non-visual) data, it produces an image, and the result is readable and recognizable.

I would add to Kosara's definition that visualisation involves *consistently following a set of clearly defined rules*; in other words, it is based on "an agreed-upon set of rules for converting the information into visual form" (Koponen & Hildén, 2019, p. 26). In bar charts, for example, such rules include that all bars are of equal width, but their lengths vary in proportion to the values being shown. Though the rules are not made explicit in most contexts, it should be easy for the reader to infer what they are merely by looking at the visualisation and reading any accompanying explanatory texts.

For visualisation as an *end result*, I have proposed (in Koponen & Hildén, 2019, p. 27) that visualisation can be thought of as a continuum in two dimensions:

 | HTTPS://DOI.ORG/10.1163/9789004760264-003

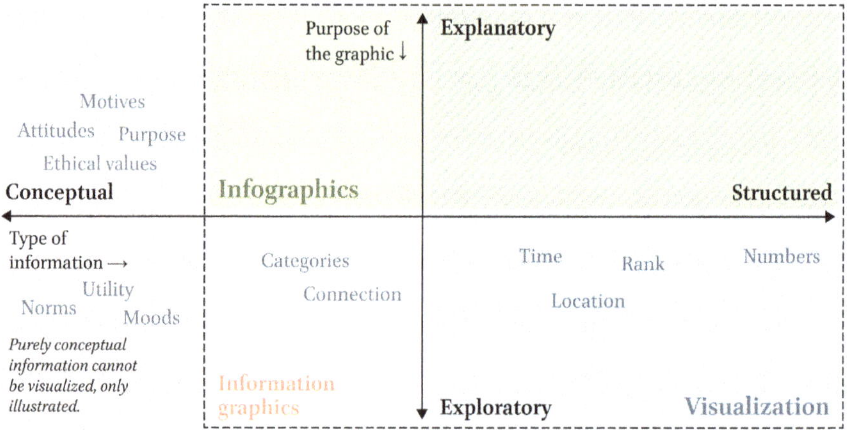

FIGURE 2.1 The information graphics continuum

Strictly speaking, this continuum (Figure 2.1), which builds on the work of Berinato (2016), encompasses all of information graphics—a hypernym that covers both infographics and visualisations proper (Koponen & Hildén, 2019, p. 27). The vertical dimension refers to the purpose of the graphic, from *exploratory* to *explanatory*—from thinking aid to communication aid, and the horizontal dimension refers to the type of information being depicted, from *conceptual* to *structured*.

As pointed out by Ware (2013, p. 2), "thinking is not something that goes on entirely, or even mostly, inside people's heads." Instead, cognitive processes usually take place in constant interaction with external devices, such as pen and paper, calculators, and computer software. At the bottom of the information graphics continuum, exploratory visualisations—also called infographics—work as such a thinking aid: they are meant to help the person creating the graphic to understand the data better themselves more than to be used as tools of communication (Koponen & Hildén, 2019, p. 27). The opposite is true of explanatory visualisation, at the top, which aims to disseminate some information that the person creating the graphic already has (*ibid.*). Most graphics lie somewhere between the two extremes on the continuum: a well-made visualisation usually supports both inquiry and interchange, even if the emphasis is on one of the two tasks.

On the right of the continuum, we have graphics that show structured, quantitative information such as numbers and ranks, and on the left conceptual, extremely qualitative information such as ethical values and attitudes. (It should be noted that such of categorization of information into "objective" data and less objective non-data is not universally accepted within the humanities. See Drucker 2011 for a thoughtful critique of the supposed neutrality and observer-independence of data, specifically in the context of visualisation.) In the center lie types of information that have both conceptual and structured characteristics. They are still qualitative in nature, but have some structure to them, such as categorizations of and connections between data points. The types of information on the very left of the continuum are too conceptual to be visualised *per se*, though they often can be transformed into more structured data using methods such as *natural language processing* (e.g., Brath, 2021, pp. 82–86), categorization, or by constructing a composite indicator that gives numerical scores to the entities found in the data.

Within this universe of information graphics "visualisation" (the end result) refers to images that depict at least some structured information, such as numbers, and "infographics" to graphics that have primarily an explanatory purpose, "graphics that tell a story." (Koponen & Hildén, pp. 26) As can be seen, the terms overlap considerably, meaning that they are partial synonyms, but that there also exist visualisations for which "infographic" would not be an appropriate description—and vice versa (*ibid.*).

2.2 Why Visualise?

Humans have documented their surroundings in visual form for tens of thousands of years, preceding the invention of writing by countless millennia. Adjacent to purely pictorial representations of the natural world, abstract and conceptual images such as maps also started developing early on (Friendly & Denis, 2008). After the Industrial Revolution the rapid development of science, technology, and society lead to a Cambrian explosion of new presentation methods, such as statistical charts, that greatly expanded the visual horizon. The late 1800s and the first half of 1900s saw the first attempts to standardize these methods, to coalesce them into clearly delineated categories and types based on their form and function, and to document them in an accessible format (e.g., Levasseur 1885, Brinton, 1919). In the present century, easy-to-use automated tools have placed the power to create compelling visualisations in the hands of nearly anyone with an access to a personal computer.

Many experts (e.g., Brath, 2021, p. 3) argue that one of the main benefits of visualisation is that visual patterns can be processed pre-attentively by the viewer—that is, extremely fast and before consciously focusing their attention on its details. The notion of pre-attentive processing of visualisations has been challenged by modern perception research (e.g., Haroz & Whitney, 2012), but what seems to me to beyond doubt is that visualisation is at least *pre-lexical*: lexemic information does not require to be processed for a visualisation to make at least some sense—though language does play an important supporting role

Population of Switzerland by native language

	German	French	Italian	Other*
1970	2,987,747	855,603	507,871	219,620
1980	3,252,689	920,853	460,426	311,902
1990	3,549,782	1,060,538	439,601	450,591
2000	3,767,623	1,173,714	399,063	527,088
2010	4,289,684	1,491,682	548,164	1,256,182
2015	4,424,920	1,567,197	581,381	1,511,259
2021	4,492,394	1,641,398	591,122	1,678,125

*) incl. Romansh

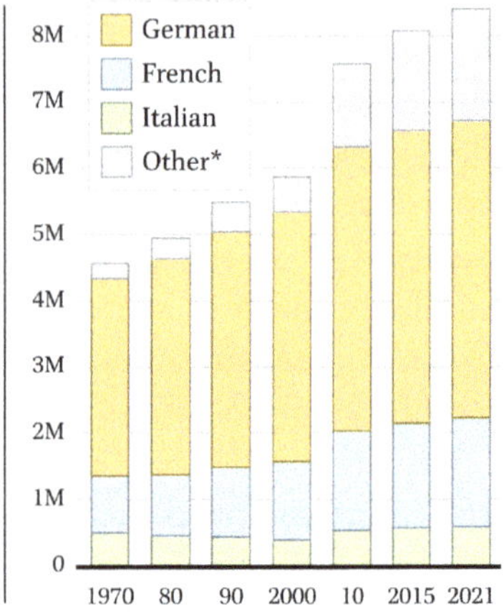

FIGURE 2.2 A comparison of a table and a vertical bar chart depicting the same data set. The jump in Swiss population from 2000 to 2010 is hard to discern from the table on the left but stands out in the chart on the right.

both within visualisations themselves, and in communication using visualisations more broadly, as shown in the Figure 2.2 above.

Bertin (2011, pp. 2–3) divides visual signs into two broad categories: *monosemic* (having a single meaning) and *polysemic* (having multiple meanings). The meaning of monosemic signs such as mathematical symbols is given, and their interpretation is therefore unambiguous. The meaning of polysemic signs, however, like the individual details that make up a drawing, depends on the context of other symbols present: for instance, a circle can represent different things in different drawings. Polysemic signs are read "between the sign and its meaning," making their interpretation, to some extent, ambiguous and debatable. According to Bertin, information graphics are read "among the given meanings" of monosemic signs. While the meaning of each individual element in isolation is known in advance from convention and through legends, colour keys, etc., the majority of the information in a visualisation is embedded in the *relationships* between the signs, letting the reader infer much more than the individual pieces of information explicitly included in the graphic by its designer.

Unlike text or tables, visualisation gives the reader an intuitive "feel" for abstract data, revealing with a quick glance patterns and outliers that might otherwise remain hidden and facilitating discovery of insights that would otherwise easily be missed (Anscombe, 1973). Consequently, reading visualisations of complex data sets is orders of magnitude faster than trying to extract the same information from a table of numbers. Bertin (2011, p. 3) notes that "[i]t would take at least 20,000 successive instants of perception compare two data tables of 100 rows by 100 columns. If the data are transcribed graphically, comparison becomes easy; it can even be instantaneous." The upshot is that whereas a text or a summary table can only present a selection of the research data for the reader, a well-made visualisation can include *all* the data in a still-digestible format.

2.3 Common Visualisation Types

Different visualisation types have different representational characteristics, which makes them suited for different tasks. For example, if the most interesting patterns in the data aren't geographic, a map is probably not the optimal method for presenting it (Ericson, 2011). Below, I will discuss some of the most commonly used visualisation types and demonstrate some visualisation best practices.

2.3.1 *Maps*

Maps, often defined as "measurement-based miniature image[s] of a geographical area" (Koponen & Hildén, p. 137), are the oldest form of abstract, non-naturalistic visual representations of information. According to Tiitta (1999), despite the different vantage point, early maps were conceptually similar to landscape painting: both were attempts to distill the essential features of the terrain into a representative visual form. As cartographic expression developed, however, maps became more and more detached from purely pictorial representations such as painting, and developed a unique idiom, detached from direct visual observation. Modern maps are not representational images of landscape, but data visualisations, constructed from measurement-based and other data.

In contrast with *general purpose maps*, which focus on showing the locations of *spatial phenomena* such as lakes or cities, thematic maps, also known as data maps, depict *spatial patterns* in predominantly *non-geographic phenomena*—for instance, population distribution. Though there are individual examples of data maps from as early as the 3rd century BCE (Hsu, 1993), and Early Modern maps often also included non-geographic information (e.g., Rossby, 2003), the beginning of modern thematic mapping can be dated to the late 17th century, to the work of the British astronomer Edmond Halley (e.g., Thrower, 1969).

Creating maps used to be a laborious task requiring highly specialized technical skills. However, in the recent years easy-to-use software and openly available geographic data has made it feasible for researchers to create basic maps to complement their work. The most common types of data maps seen in academic publications include *dot*, *symbol*, and *choropleth maps*. *Cartograms*, which, according to some definitions, are not maps because they do not strive for geographical accuracy, are also often discussed in connection with data maps.

Dot maps (see Map 2.1), sometimes called *dot distribution maps*, show individual recordings or observations of some phenomenon as dimensionless locations marked by dots of equal size (Koponen & Hildén, 2019, p. 145). Each observation can correspond to things such as a person, a location of an event, or a building, depending on the topic of the map. Sometimes categories of recordings can be differentiated by use of differently colored or shaped markers.

Symbol maps (see Map 2.2), sometimes called *graduated symbol maps*, are similar to dot maps, but with the size of each symbol, usually a circle, varying

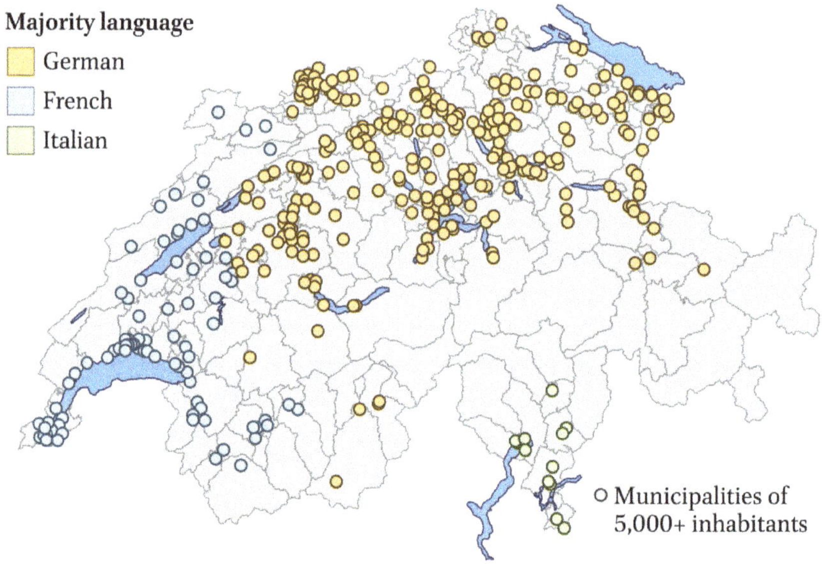

MAP 2.1 A dot map depicting all municipalities of at least 5,000 inhabitants in Switzerland, and their majority language

Though lacking detail, because all dots are of equal size and, consequently, smaller settlements are missing, the map gives a fairly accurate picture of the varying population distribution within the country. Notice the sparse geographic context: only the boundaries of the districts (Bezirk) of Switzerland and major lakes are shown.

Best practices followed: the map uses a muted colour scheme, where the main colours are light and bordered by a thin line of a darker shade. The chosen colours are colourblind-safe. The base map on which the dots are placed is sparse, so as not to interfere with the depiction of the actual data.

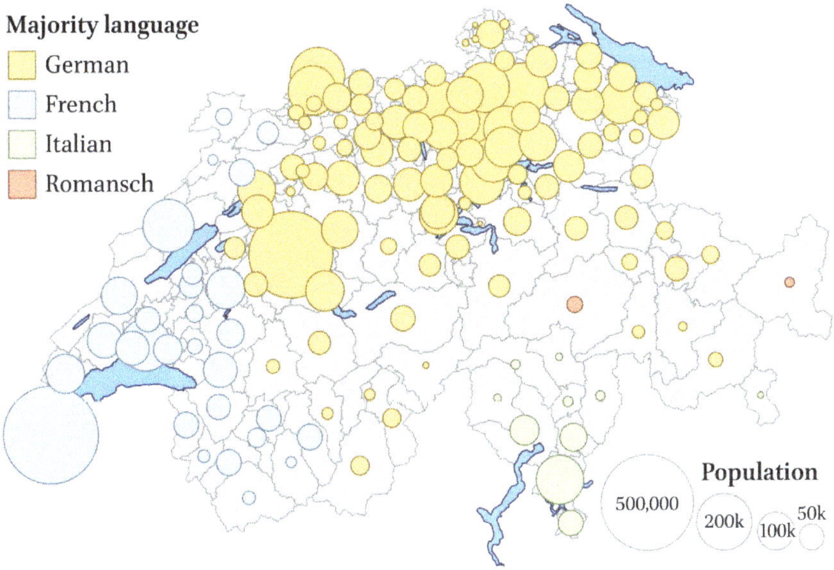

MAP 2.2 A symbol map depicting the population of the districts (Bezirk) of Switzerland, and their majority language

Notice the considerable overlap of bubbles in the Zürich region in the Northern part of the country, which makes the map hard to read at places.

Best practices followed: the circles are scaled using the Flannery method (Flannery 1971). The drawing order of the bubbles is controlled so that the smallest are on top, which minimizes the risk of a bubble being completely obscured by others.

based on a value of a variable of interest (*ibid.*, p. 146). The symbols are most commonly circles, often called *bubbles* in this context, but occasionally other symbols, such as squares, are used.

Symbol maps should only be used to show absolute values such as counts or totals, not relative number such as percentages, for which choropleth maps are the better option.

Choropleth maps—sometimes incorrectly called "heat maps"—are probably the most commonly used data maps. In these maps, the region being depicted is divided into smaller areas which correspond to previously defined geographic regions and are assigned a colour based on the value of a specific variable (Koponen & Hildén, 2019, pp. 147–148). This variable is typically quantitative (see Map 2.4) but can also be qualitative in nature (see Map 2.3). The areas, such as municipalities or postcodes, are collectively called *enumeration units*.

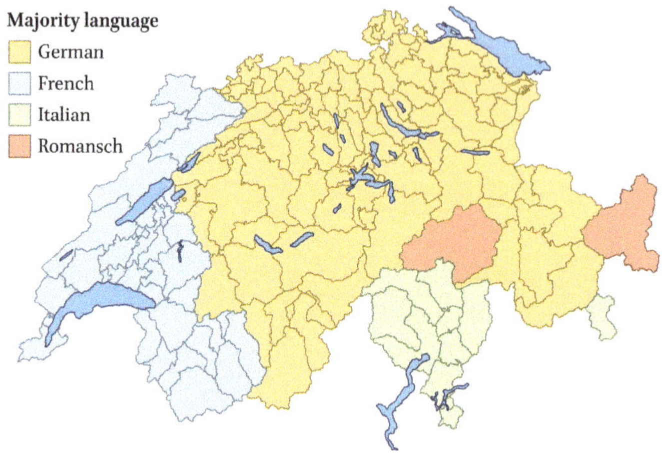

MAP 2.3 A categorical (qualitative) choropleth map of the majority language in each Swiss district (Bezirk)

The map gives a clear picture of the linguistic landscape but overemphasizes the Romansch-speaking areas which are in reality mountainous and sparsely populated.

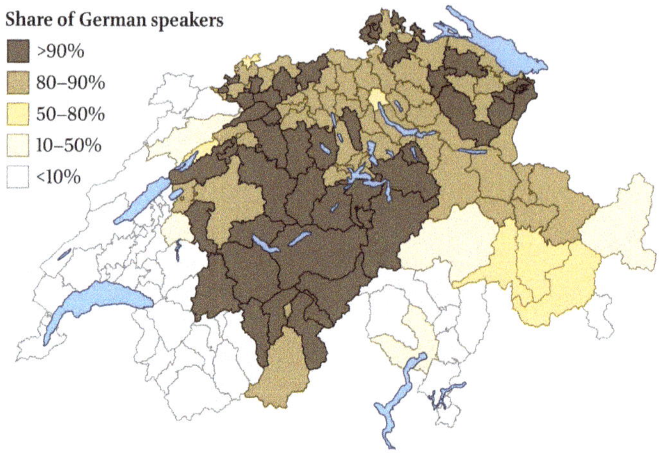

MAP 2.4 A quantitative choropleth map of the share of German speakers in each Swiss district (Bezirk)

Best practices followed: instead of a continuous colour gradient, the map uses a colour scale with five discrete steps each depicting a class of values. While somewhat less precise in theory, the discrete scale is easier to read in practice, and less prone to the distorting effects of simultaneous contrast—a phenomenon of colour vision which causes adjoining areas of colour to influence the perception of each other (Arnkil 2013, pp. 102–110). The class boundaries are chosen so as to correspond to meaningful categorical breakpoints in the value continuum and to result in an insightful map.

Choropleth maps suffer from a number of issues (see e.g., Schiewe, 2019), the most important being that in most cases the pre-defined areal units usually exhibit wide variation in some of their primary characteristics such as area and population. Such dissimilarities mean the overall impression given by a choropleth map can be seriously misleading because they tend to overemphasize large, but sparsely populated areas over dense, more populous ones where political and economic power in most societies lies.

Choropleth maps should not be used to show absolute values. They work best when used to show relative values—percentages, "per 100,000 of population," and so on—aggregate values, such as averages, or categorical data, as seen in Map 2.3.

Cartograms are graphics that combine statistical and geographical information, where areas of geographical regions are scaled in proportion to some statistic (Nusrat & Kobourov, 2016). In other words, they are map-like visualisations where the surface area, or less commonly, some other visual property

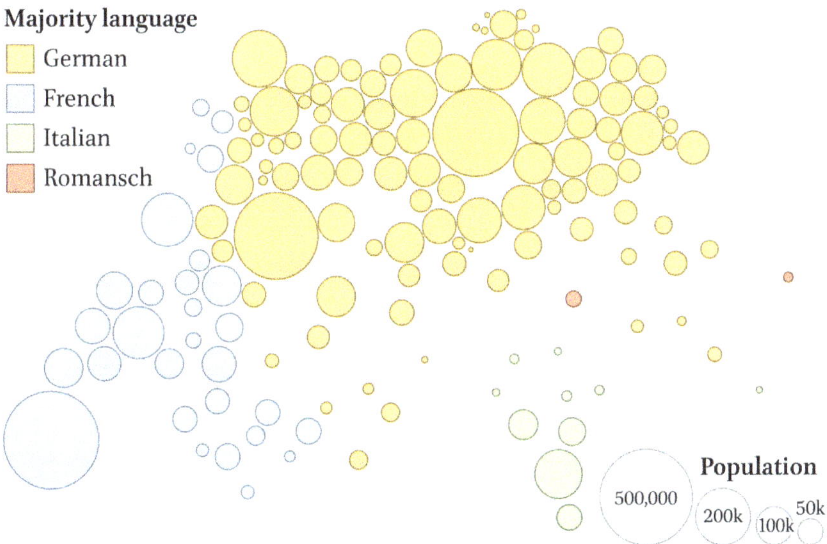

MAP 2.5 A Dorling cartogram depicting the population of the districts (Bezirk) of Switzerland, and their majority language

Compare this with Map 2.2, which shows the same data set. With no base map, the geographical context is less clear in the cartogram, but with the overlap removed the districts in the Zürich area stand out much better than in Map 2.2.

Best practices followed: the bubbles are located as close to the centroids of the districts on the (unseen) base map as possible, so that the circles are only pushed from their initial location when it is necessary to fit all of them without overlap. Likewise, preservation of topology is attempted, so that neighbouring districts should appear next to each other whenever possible.

of the shapes corresponding to the enumeration units is used to encode non-geographic data. This means they do not retain most of the units' geographic characteristics such as area, shape and/or topology. Despite this, cartograms get around many of the limitations of symbol and choropleth maps, and can be a good alternative to either in many use cases.

There are several subtypes of cartograms (see Nusrat & Kobourov, 2016), but I will limit the discussion to Dorling cartograms (see Map 2.5), where each region is drawn as a circle with its area in proportion to its population or other another statistic and is then treated as an object in a gravity model which is repelled by other circles with which it overlaps, but is attracted to circles which were neighbouring regions on the original map (Dorling, 1996). These cartograms resemble symbol maps, with the most visible difference being that the circles' positions are not always geographically correct but adjusted instead to make sure they never overlap. In other words, Dorling cartograms prioritize reducing clutter over retaining correct positioning or topology.

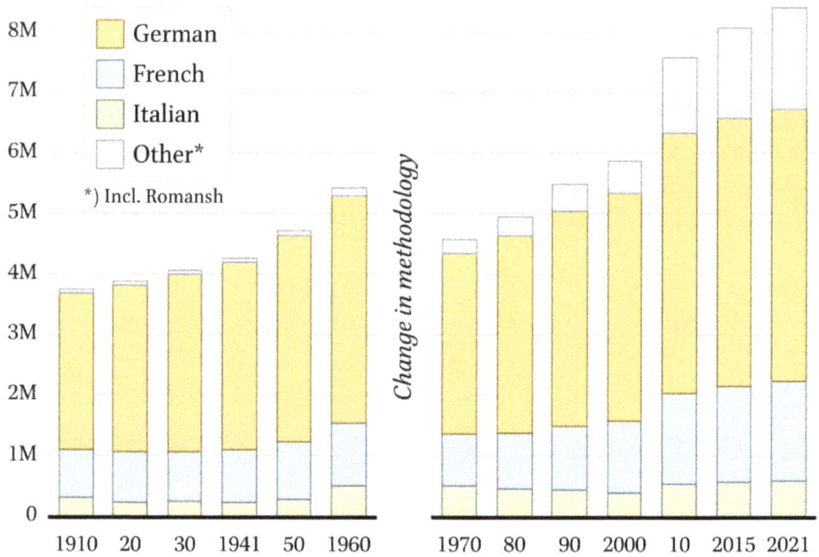

FIGURE 2.3 A stacked vertical bar chart showing the population of Switzerland, 1910–2021, broken down by main language

Vertical bar charts are suitable for depicting time-series and other continuous data, but not recommended for categorical data. (For further information, see Koponen & Hildén 2019, pp. 180–181.)

Best practices followed: the grid connected to the vertical axis is presented in a light colour, so that it is clearly visible, but only barely so, so as to not compete for attention with the actual data. A change in the methodology of data collection is clearly visually indicated as a break in the series.

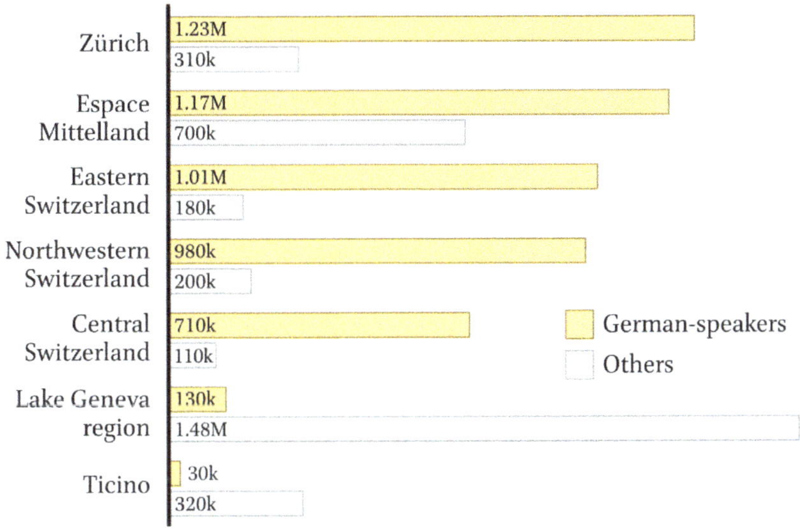

FIGURE 2.4 A grouped horizontal bar chart showing the sizes of the German-speaking and non-German-speaking population in each Swiss region

Horizontal bar charts are recommended when the data is categorical instead of a time-series, as here. Note: in grouped bar charts, two series (bars) per group works well, but a larger number quickly becomes unwieldy. (See Koponen & Hildén, 2019, pp. 180–183.)

Best practices followed: the bars are organized by the size of the German-speaking population, instead of alphabetically. Alphabetical ordering is recommended in tables to facilitate quick look-up of values, but in visualisations it is preferable that the order of elements is based on the data itself, and not merely on a convention such as the alphabetical order. (See Koponen & Hildén, 2019, pp. 37–42.) Values are labelled directly so that the grid can be left out.

2.3.2 *Charts*

The most common type of visualisation seen today are statistical charts, or charts for short—visual representations of quantitative data that employ graphic symbols with varying dimensions and positions within a Cartesian or polar coordinate system to express numerical relationships. Though a handful of proto-bar charts had already been included in the work of 14th century philosopher Nicole d'Oresme (Weaver, 2014, Friendly & Denis, 2008), the history of charts properly begins with *The commercial and political atlas* of 1786, the magnum opus of the Scottish economist William Playfair (Costigan-Eaves & Macdonald-Ross, 1990). The book included the first modern bar charts (see Figures 2.3 and 2.4)—stylized graphs where data in the form of a bar or a line is plotted against x and y axes (Weaver, 2014)—and line charts (see Figures 2.5 and 2.6)—charts consisting of data points that are connected to each other

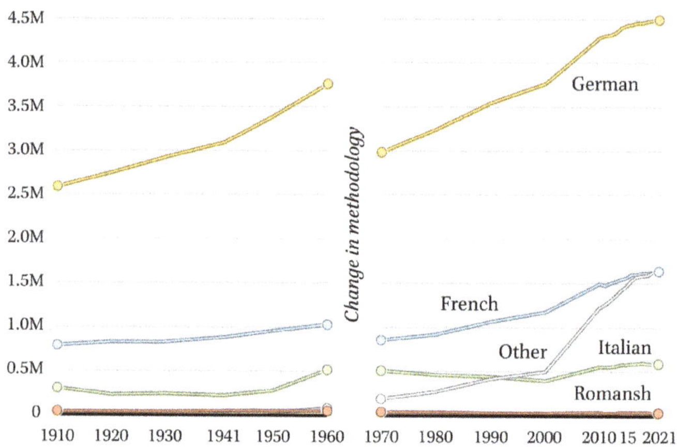

FIGURE 2.5 A line chart showing the sizes of linguistic groups of Switzerland, 1910–2021

Best practices followed: the series are directly labelled, precluding the need for a separate legend. The horizontal axis is scaled to take account of the non-equally spaced data provided by the Swiss Federal Statistical Office: for example, the period from 2010 to 2011 is shown as 10% of the width of the preceding period, 2000 to 2010. Between 2010 and 2021 there is data available for each year, but only 2010, 2015 and 2021 are labelled to prevent cluttering of the x-axis.

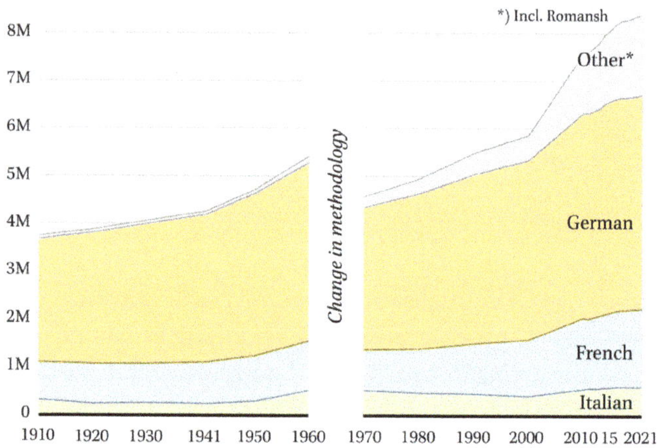

FIGURE 2.6 An area chart showing the population of Switzerland, 1910–2021, broken down by main language

Area chart is a subtype of the line chart that focuses the reader's attention first on the combined total of the series, with the breakdown by series provided as secondary information.

Best practices followed: to increase legibility, the underlying darker outline is interrupted under the label "Other," which is partially overlaid on the edge of the topmost series.

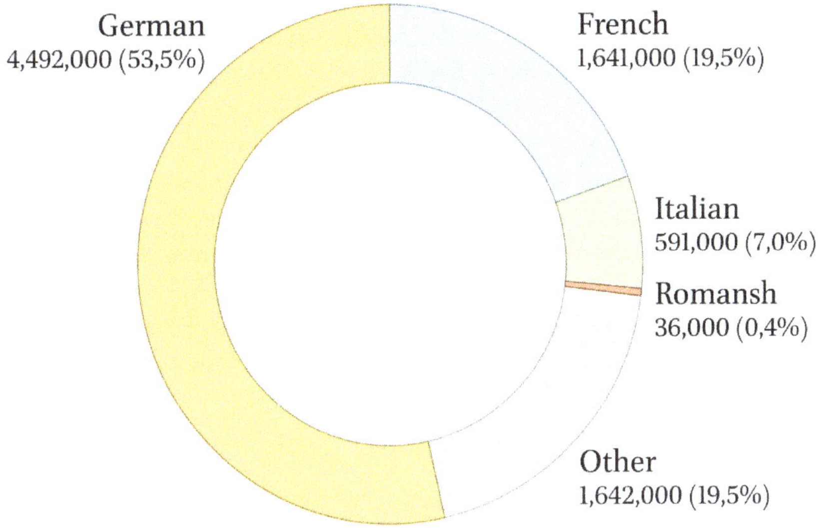

FIGURE 2.7 A donut chart showing the distribution of languages spoken in Switzerland

The donut chart is a purely aesthetic variant of the pie chart: Kosara & Skau (2016) have shown that there is no functional difference in pie and donut charts except in a few edge cases.

Best practices followed: the slices are ordered so that the two largest slices meet at the top of the chart, the visually most prominent part. (See Wong, 2010, p. 74–75.)

with a line representing an approximation of the values between the recorded observations (Koponen & Hildén, 2019, p. 184). A few years later, Playfair also invented the pie chart (see Figure 2.7)—a circular chart that encodes data using central angle, wedge area, and arc length (Kosara & Skau, 2016), completing the trio of what I call the basic chart types (Costigan-Eaves & Macdonald-Ross, 1990, Friendly & Denis, 2008).

Dozens of different types of statistical charts have been developed since, but bar and line charts still dominate academic literature (Weissgerber et al., 2015). Although it has been shown that pie charts work well for part-to-whole comparisons (Simkin & Hastie, 1987, Kosara & Skau, 2016), this chart type has not achieved popularity in academia, and its use is sometimes seen—unfairly, in my opinion—as an indicator of lack of visual sophistication.

In addition to the basic chart types, three other charts have been particularly popular in academic literature: the scatter plot, the box plot, and the histogram.

The scatter plot (see Figures 2.8 and 2.9) is a chart consisting of data points whose two characteristics are recorded as values on the horizontal and vertical axes, revealing the relationship between the variables and their distributions (Koponen & Hildén, 2019, p. 190) first seen in the work of Sir John Herschel in 1832 (Friendly & Denis, 2008; see also Friendly & Denis, 2005).

Regular scatter plots are used for exploring the interrelationship between two variables. Though correlation and other interesting pattern in the data can be revealed with purely mathematical analysis, many relationships are beyond the reach of purely statistical methods but would pop out from the page if visualised using a scatter plot (Anscombe, 1973, Matejka & Fitzmaurice, 2017). Univariate scatter plots, where quantitative data is plotted only along one

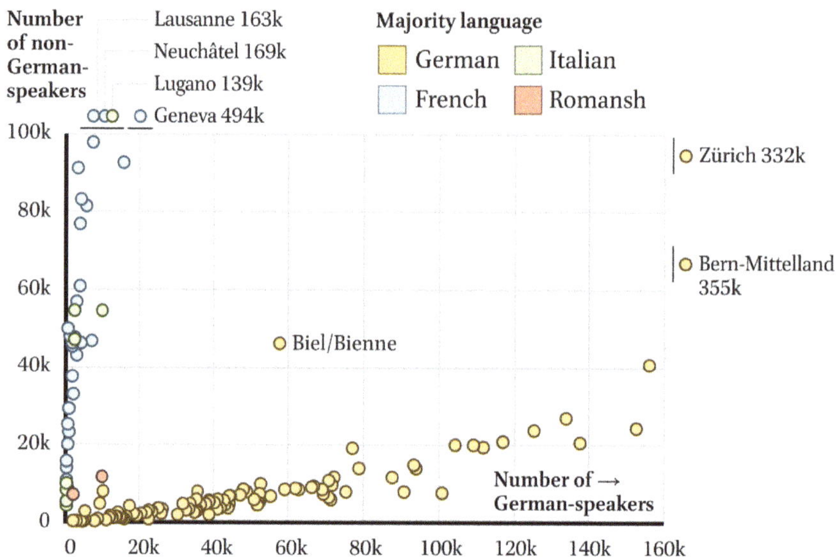

FIGURE 2.8 A scatter plot of Swiss districts (Bezirk), showing the number of German-speakers by district on the x-axis and non-German-speakers on the y-axis

In districts where the majority language is German, the ratio of non-German to German-speakers stays roughly stable regardless of overall population size. For other districts the trend is less clear, or at least the average share of German-speakers is smaller. Biel/Bienne stands out as a large, truly bilingual district.

Best practices followed: because both axes show the number of speakers, they use matching scales, meaning that the same distance always implies a similar increase or decrease, regardless of which axis it is measured on. The axes have been truncated so that the few outlier values do not squeeze everything else into a small area in the corner. These outliers are labelled, and their locations indicated. The exceptional district of Biel/Bienne is also directly labelled.

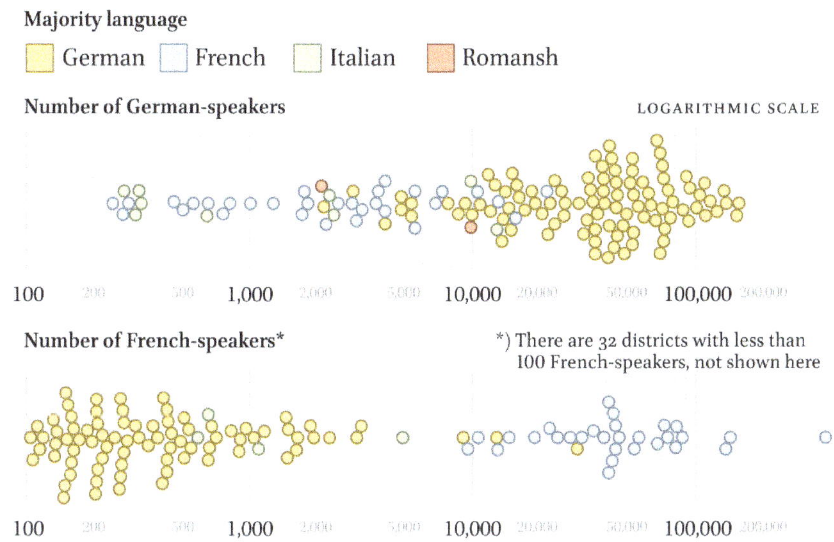

FIGURE 2.9 A univariate scatter plot of Swiss districts (Bezirk), showing the number of German-speakers by district in the first row and the number of French-speakers in the second

A logarithmic scale is used to help visual comparison across several orders of magnitude.

The variant shown here is the so-called beeswarm plot, where some of the dots are moved to the side to prevent overlap. The varying breadth of the "swarm" gives a good indication of the shape of the distribution. Another variants of the univariate scatter plot include the so-called strip plot or density plot, where the dots are semi-translucent and allowed to overlap, and the jitter plot, where total overlap is prevented by randomly moving the points around a bit.

Best practices followed: the use of logarithmic scale is indicated using unevenly spaced grid lines, as well as explicitly with the label "logarithmic scale."

dimension (x or y), are instead used to visualise distributions, similar to box plots and histograms.

The box plot (see Figure 2.10) is a chart made up of five components—a median line, two hinges, and two fences—chosen to give a summary of the distribution of a dataset (Wickham & Stryjewski, 201; Tukey, 1977, pp. 39–44). It was first documented and possibly invented by Mary Eleanor Spear in 1952 (Wickham & Stryjewski, 2011; Jones, 2019). Most box plots seen today are so-called *Tukey's box plots*, a subtype popularized by John Tukey (Tukey, 1977, pp. 39–44).

Despite their popularity, it has been persuasively argued that box plots are sub-optimal in cases where the underlying data is not normally distributed—in

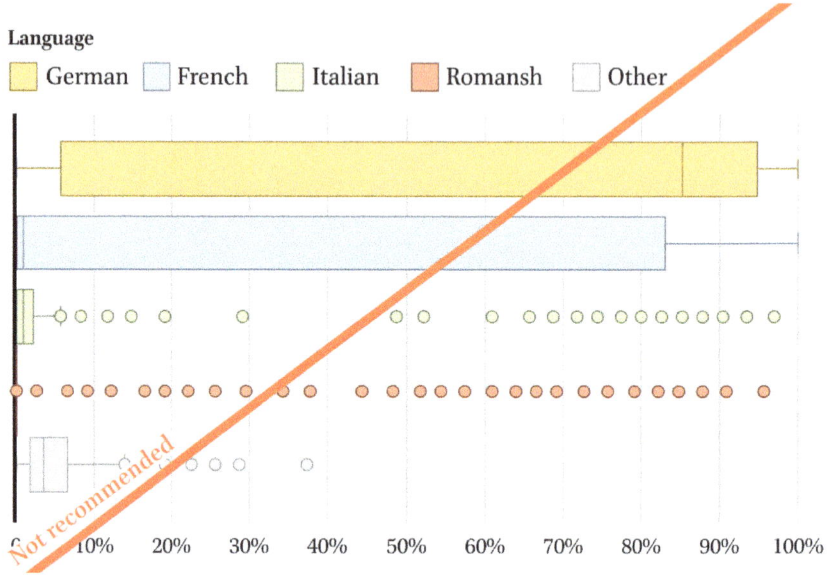

FIGURE 2.10 A box plot showing the distribution of the share of speakers of each of Switzerland's national languages by municipality (Gemeide)

The visualisation is nearly useless due to the extremely skewed distribution. The chart is confusing and hard to read, and does not give a clear picture of the underlying distribution in the data. Compare this with the histogram in Figure 2.11, showing a part of the same dataset. Though box plots perform considerably better than this when the distributions shown are more akin to a normal distribution, they still tend to hide most of the variation in the data.

other words, precisely when it would be useful to visualise the distribution in the first place. This is because this chart type hides most of the underlying variation in the data (Desbarats, 2021, Scherer, 2021). Box plots are nearly useless when the distribution shown is extremely skewed, as seen in Figure 2.10. Scherer (2021) offers an extensive selection of alternatives to the box plot, but for many use cases, simple univariate scatter plots and histograms work well and have the added benefit of being reasonably easy to interpret for most readers. I recommend favouring these two chart types over the box plot for visualising distributions.

The histogram (see Figure 2.11) is a bar, line, or area chart that shows the distribution of a variable, where individual data points are classified into bins of equal intervals, and the chart shows the number of observations that fall into each. The histogram was first described by Karl Pearson (Pearson, 1895) but probably invented earlier.

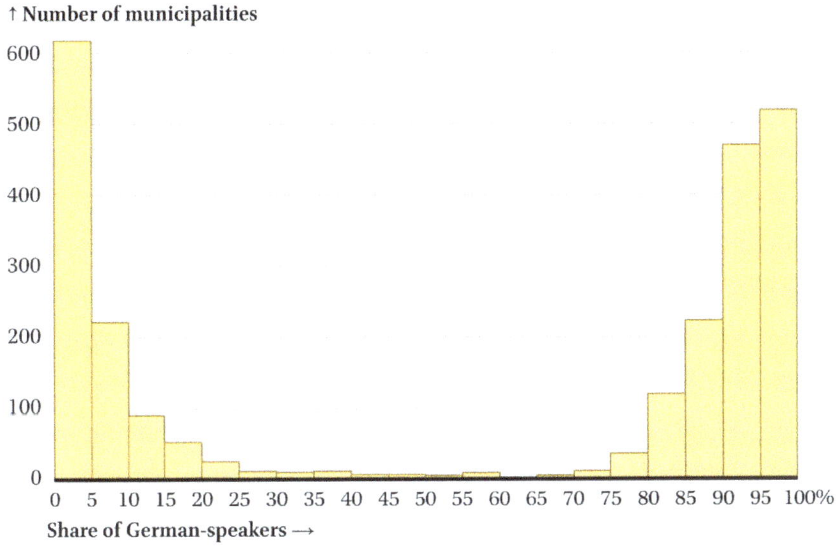

FIGURE 2.11 A histogram showing the distribution of the share of German-speakers in Switzerland's municipalities (Gemeide)

Network diagram which reveals a U-shaped distribution where most municipalities have either a very small or very large share of German-speakers, with very few falling into the 25–75% range. Compared to the box plot in Figure 2.10, showing the same data, the interpretation of this visualisation is much easier and more intuitive. In terms of clarity and insightfulness, histograms outperform box plots in almost all use cases, but especially when the distribution of the underlying data does not resemble a normal distribution at all, as here.

Best practices followed: the histogram bins are labelled at their boundaries, 0–5–10–20, etc., instead of labelling each bracket with 0–5, 5–10, 10–15, 15–20, etc. This reduces clutter and makes the chart easier to read.

Network diagrams (see Figure 2.13) are visualisations that display the relationships between objects or concepts using connecting lines, typically in such a way that connected elements are fairly close to each other (Koponen & Hildén, 2019, p. 227). The network consists of data points called nodes that are connected to each other by lines, often called edges, which depict the relationships between the nodes. In the case of a *directed graph*, in which the edges have an associated direction, the nodes are connected by arrows (also called directed edges).

Tree diagrams (see Figure 2.12) are network diagrams which have a hierarchical structure (Koponen & Hildén, 2019, p. 230). They are much older than

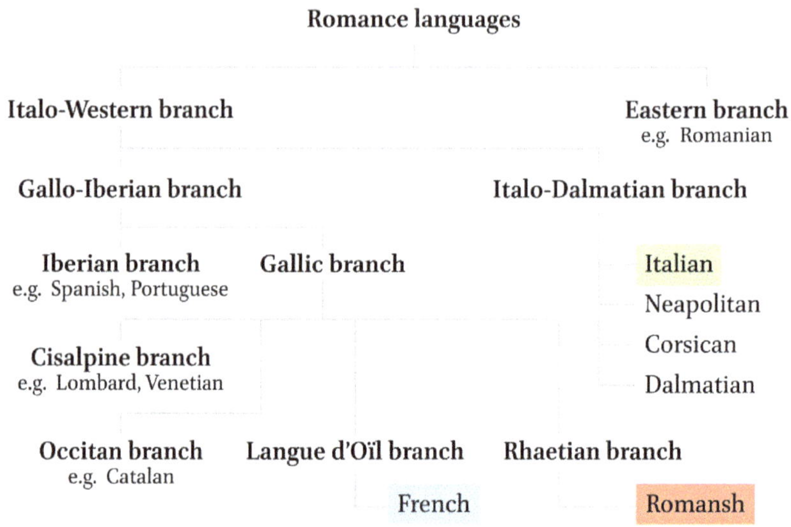

FIGURE 2.12 A tree diagram showing the relationships of the Romance languages, focusing especially on the three Romance languages traditionally spoken in Switzerland: French, Italian, and Romansch.

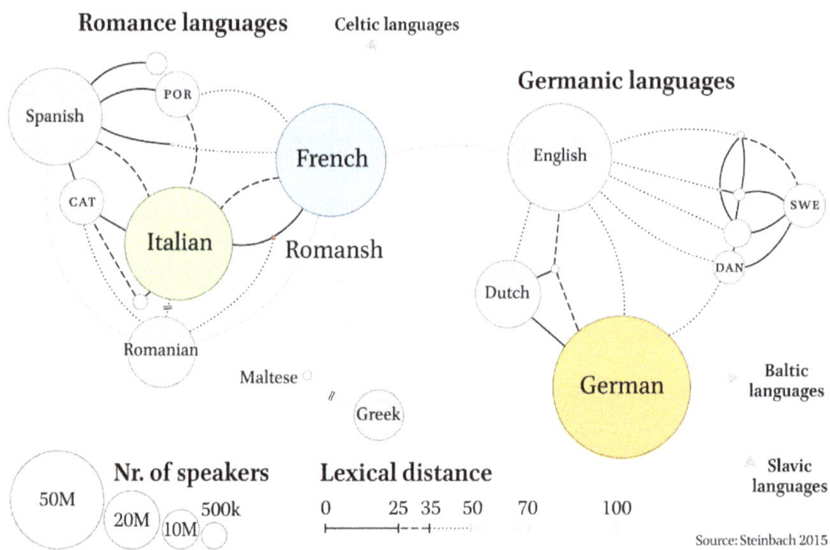

FIGURE 2.13 A network diagram depicting the relationships between the Romance and Germanic languages (based on Steinbach, 2015), focusing on the Swiss national languages

The lexical distance is shown as the length of the connecting line as well as its colour and dash pattern, and the bubbles are scaled according to the number of speakers (in Europe, not globally). Due to constraints of the two-dimensional picture plane, a few of the lines are too short—these have been indicated with a truncation mark.

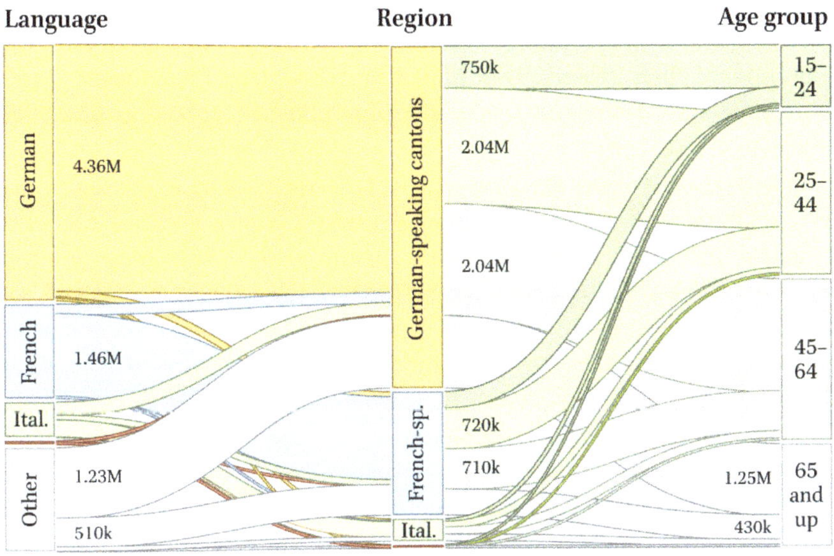

FIGURE 2.14 A flow diagram depicting the Swiss population over 15 by language, region, and age group

This is a subtype of the flow diagram called an alluvial diagram, where the nodes are organized in neat vertical columns. The other subtype is the Sankey diagram, where the layout is more freeform.

"free" network diagrams which have no such hierarchy, tracing their lineage to the Neoplatonic *Porphyrian tree* (Dardağan, 2017) or possibly even further back.

Flow diagrams (see Figure 2.14) are tree structure diagrams where the connections have numeric values or weights attached to them, and which are visualised using line thickness. They are a highly versatile group of visualisations with many use cases—in addition to visualising flows (of people, goods, etc.) they can be used to depict, for example, complex hierarchical distributions. Flow diagrams can also be presented on a map, in which case they are called flow maps. (See, e.g., Rendgen, 2018.)

2.3.3 *Qualitative Infographics*

After maps, charts, and network diagrams, I want to mention a fourth group of visualisations I call qualitative infographics. They are diagrams that are neither charts or maps, and depict information that is typically more conceptual than structured in nature. This category is much less clearly defined than the three previous ones and includes graphics that are often highly specific to a particular use case—or even one-off creations. They are typically used to depict information that is more conceptual than structured in nature, and thus find a lot of use within the humanities.

Within qualitative infographics there are much fewer established visualisation types than in the previous categories, as these more conceptual presentations are often created ad hoc to fit a particular need. Nevertheless, I want to mention three commonly used and well-established types of graphics that belong to this category.

Timelines (see Figure 2.15) are a chart type with a long and glorious history, explored in detail by Rosenberg & Grafton (2010). They are historical diagrams that depict chronology using straight, curved, branching, or crossing line(s) (*ibid.*). Though there are many different conventions for creating timelines—and a lot of room for improvisation—the essential characteristics are clear: they should show the sequence of events, the rhythm of events, and the concurrence of events (if any). A timeline that manages to depict only the sequence without the two other factors is not much more insightful than a bullet-point list.

Word clouds (see Figure 2.16), sometimes termed *Wordles* in the literature (after a popular tool for creating them)—diagrams that visualise frequencies of words in text by varying font size, so that the most common words are shown in a larger size than less common ones (Koponen & Hildén, 2019, p. 224)—are an extremely common way of visualising word frequencies in

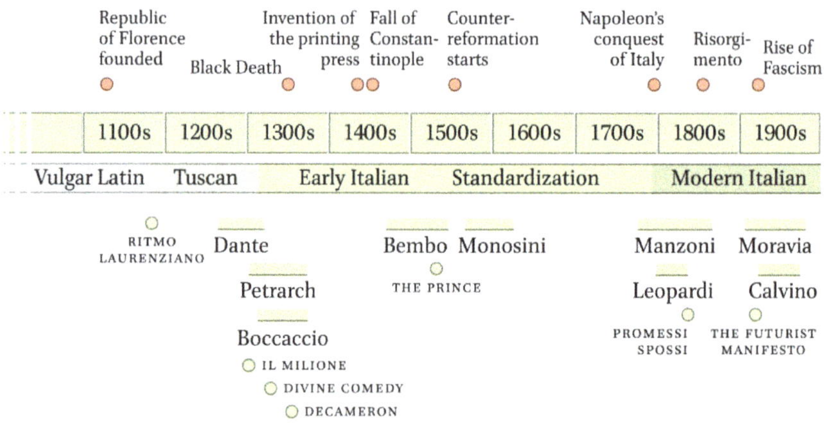

FIGURE 2.15 A simplified timeline of the history of the Italian language

In the middle, we see the actual timeline—the years—and the phases of development of the language. Above are depicted key political events, and below, the lives of prominent authors and other figures, whose work has shaped the language, as well as some landmark texts from them and others.

Best practices followed: sequence, rhythm, and timeline of the events are shown.

FIGURE 2.16 A word cloud of the 200 most common Swiss surnames with their linguistic origins, created using the online tool Wordclouds.com (n.d.) and slightly edited

Though word clouds are extremely commonly used for visualising word frequencies, this chart type is not recommended for scientific use, as it is extremely imprecise and gives a distorted picture of the relative abundance of each word in the data.

Even the best word cloud algorithms overemphasize long words at the expense of short ones, but many, such as the tool used here, do not seem to care much about relative frequencies at all. Compare this figure with the adjoining Figure 2.17 to see how distorted the picture is. For example, Schmid and Müller look about the same size, though Müller is 75% more abundant in the data than Schmid. On the other hand, Schmid looks at least three times larger than Keller, though the former name is only about 30% common than the latter.

text corpuses. Different word cloud tools produce slightly different results with different problems but all share a central weakness: they tend to misrepresent the relative frequencies of short vs. long words—as can be seen in figure 2.16. A better approach is to use word bubbles (see Figure 2.17), visualisations of word frequencies where words are located inside circles whose size is proportional to their frequency (Koponen & Hildén, 2019, p. 225), and the circles are clustered using a *circle packing* algorithm. Because this facilitates visual comparison of areas of similar shapes—the circles—instead of sizes of words of varying length and shape, the chart gives a much better idea of the

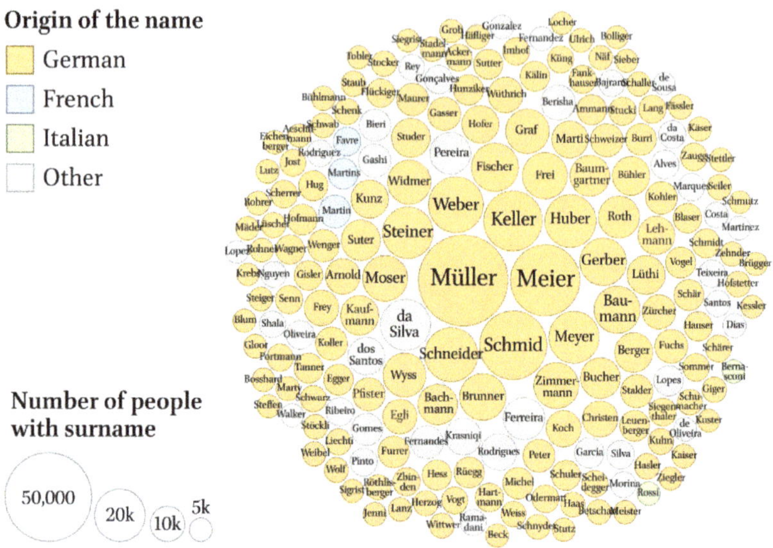

FIGURE 2.17 The recommended alternative for word clouds is word bubbles, where each of the words is placed inside a bubble whose area is scaled according to the frequency of each word, instead of scaling the words directly.

This gives a much better picture of how common each word is compared to others. The graphic above shows the exact same data set as Figure 2.16—the 200 most common Swiss surnames—but is much easier to read.

Best practices followed: instead of dark, intense colours, pale fill colours are used with a darker outline, making the chart easier and more pleasant to read. Font size is varied with bubble size, but only in a few steps. Long names are hyphenated to better fit inside the circles.

relative word frequencies than does the word cloud. The circle is also a more flexible shape design-wise: for instance, pale fill colours with dark edges can be used. This would not work with the word cloud, where each word needs to be single-coloured, as outlines make text harder to read.

A more straightforward way of visualising word frequencies is to use a simple horizontal bar chart.

Successful use of visualisation hinges not only on selecting a presentation type that is suitable for the data, intended audience, and context, but also on more intricate factors, such as the use of colour and the typography and positioning of labels. The space available does not permit a detailed discussion of these factors, but the examples above attempt to exemplify visualisation best practices. Further practical advice on both the choice of visualisation type and design details can be found in, e.g., Koponen & Hildén 2019, Mason 2019, Franconeri et al. 2021, and Rougier et al. 2014.

2.4 Towards Better Visualisations in the Humanities

In the past decade or so, the humanities have seen a substantial shift towards incorporating visualisation as an integral part of the research toolkit. To a significant extent, this has been thanks to the Digital Humanities movement, which is no longer a niche pursuit as it was in the past century, but instead a very mainstream part of current research.

Visualisation in the humanities is, however, not a new concept and predates the emergence of digital methods by centuries. Some of the earliest non-map visualisations were, in fact, created in areas of inquiry that would today be considered a part of the humanities. Among the earliest known network diagrams is the *Tree of Jesse*, a visual representation of Jesus' ancestry, depicted in the *Vyšehrad codex* of 1086 (Hayes-Williams, 2000). Timelines were used to visualise histories hundreds of years before statistical charts became commonplace in economics and science, and reached a mature form with Thomas Jefferys' Chart of *Universal History* in 1753—decades before Playfair's *Atlas* (Rosenberg & Grafton, 2010, pp. 114–115). Linguistics has, in some measure, made good use of visualisations since at least Schleicher's tree diagrams of genetic relatedness of Indo-European languages (Lauersdorf, 2018), and archaeology papers have traditionally been among some of the most visual in academia.

Despite the illustrious history and recent progress, I argue that visualisation is still underused in humanities, despite its potential as a tool for exploring and communicating the complex and at times abstract concepts that humanities operate with. By visualising their data, scholars can see patterns and connections that might be difficult to discern through traditional textual analysis alone. This can lead to new insights and can also help to validate or challenge existing theories. Qualitative infographics can be used to explain and demonstrate interrelatedness of research concepts, to make complex arguments more accessible to the audience, to illustrate historical timelines and map the evolution of ideas, and to reveal connections between languages, cultural practices, and historical artifacts, to name but a few examples of use cases that might be relevant in the humanities.

Visualisation is, of course, not a replacement for humanities' traditional methods of research and communication, but a complement to them. The process of quantizing and simplifying information for visualisation inevitably imposes some limitations on its ability to fully represent the complex and multi-faceted phenomena that are the objects of inquiry in humanities. A visualisation will never be able to fully answer the fundamental questions humanities scholars typically are interested in—about meanings, intents, identities, and so on—but the things visualisations *can* show they show in precision and breadth that is hard to match with any other means of communication. Box & Norman (1987, p. 74) note of statistical models, "all models are wrong, but some are useful; the practical question is how wrong do they have to be to not be useful." I think this is, to some extent, true of visualisations as well: though a visualisation can never tell the full story on its own, it can be extremely useful in telling a part of it. Fruitful approaches could include *narrative visualisation*, a technique borrowed from visual journalism where the visualisation is interspersed with text to contrast the data with more qualitative information (Segel & Heer, 2010), or *interactive visualisations* that let the reader explore the full data set to make their own interpretations (see e.g., Tenney et al., 2020).

The use of visualisation in the humanities presents challenges which are unique to the field. Even more so than in other areas of inquiry, humanities data is often messy, ambiguous, and open to interpretation. This may require a domain-specific approach that can better accommodate the complexity and nuance inherent in the subject matter. Indeed, Drucker (2011) cautions against unquestioningly accepting visualisation techniques originally developed for the empirical sciences which "[conceal] their epistemological biases under a guise of familiarity." Even if one does not hold a position as critical as this, there are certainly many practical reasons to question whether the set of visualisation types discussed above is sufficient for all use cases in the humanities.

Consequently, many areas of research within the humanities have developed their own, specialized visualisation types, which are rarely, if ever, utilized elsewhere. In linguistics, for example, though the common visualisation types discussed above find much use in subfields such as sociolinguistics or corpus linguistics—according to data compiled by Sönning & Schützler (2023), 85% of graphics in corpus-based articles published between 2015 and 2020 were of one of chart types mentioned above—they may not fully cover the needs of some other branches. As a result, a large number of specialized visualisation types or subtypes have been specifically invented for use in linguistics. Lauersdorf (2018) has compiled an interesting collection of some of these, including the Jakobson's Cube, a unique qualitative infographic (see Figure 2.18), various network diagrams such as *syntax trees* and linguistic *cladograms*—a chart type borrowed from biological cladistics—several examples of *geospatial visualisation* (maps) from dialect atlases, and a *kernel density plot* of vowel measurements. Though Lauersdorf's list is not comprehensive, it already gives an idea of the breadth of specialized visualisation types employed in linguistics.

Impressive as this wide variety of visualisation types already is, I believe there is still room for improvement and increased usage of visualisations in the humanities. They are a powerful tool for finding patterns and connections that might otherwise be overlooked by scholars, and for communicating

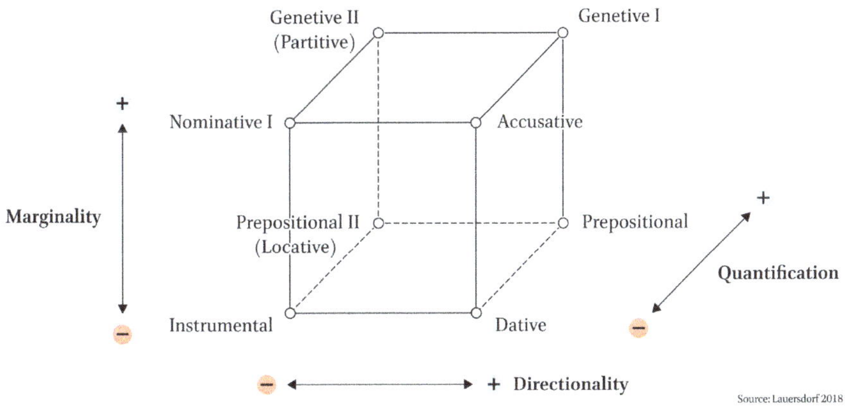

FIGURE 2.18 Jakobson's Cube—a highly specific qualitative infographic originally created by linguist Roman Jakobson to show the interrelated meanings of the eight cases of the Russian language

The graphic is not a variation of any established chart type but created ad hoc for this singular purpose. Though Lauersdorf (2018) sees this particular presentation type as flawed and a "cautionary tale," it is nevertheless an interesting example of a visualisation created for an extremely specific use case in the humanities. Adapted from Lauersdorf (2018)

their research results in a clear and compelling way. Following design best practices, humanities researchers can make use of visualisation types developed in science, statistics, and cartography or domain-specific alternatives invented within their own field—or even create custom presentation types, suitable for the particular subject matter of their own research. Though visualisation will not replace more traditional methods of analysis and communication, it can be an effective complement to them and help scholars better answer fundamental questions about human beings and their cultures.

Acknowledgments

The data used in the examples comes from the Swiss Federal Statistical Office or Wikipedia, unless otherwise stated. Please note that the examples are meant only to showcase the visualisation types being discussed, and limited effort has been put to ensuring the accuracy and timeliness of the data being visualised. Consequently, some of the data used in the graphics may be incomplete, inaccurate, or out of date.

References

Anscombe, F.J. (1973). Graphs in statistical analysis. *American Statistician* 27:1, pp. 17–21.

Arnkil, H. (2013). *Colours in the visual world.* Helsinki, Finland: Aalto ARTS Books. 294 p. ISBN 978-952-60-5246-5.

Berinato, S. (2016). Good charts: the HBR guide to making smarter, more persuasive business graphics. Boston (MA), USA: Harvard Business School Publishing Corporation. 255 p. ISBN 978-1-63369-070-7.

Bertin, J. (2011). *Semiology of graphics: diagrams, networks, maps.* Translated by William J. Berg. Redlands (CA), USA: Esri Press. 438 p. ISBN 978-1-58948-261-6.

Box, G.E.P. & Draper, N.R. (1987). *Empirical model-building and response surfaces.* New York (NY), USA: Wiley. 688 p. ISBN 978-0-471-81033-9.

Brath, R. (2021). Visualizing with text. Boca Raton (FL), USA: CRC Press. 268 p. ISBN 978-0-367-25926-6.

Brinton, W.C. (1919). Graphic methods for presenting facts. New York (NY), USA: The Engineering Magazine Company. 386 p.

Costigan-Eaves, P. & Macdonald-Ross, M. (1990). William Playfair (1759–1823). Statistical Science, 5:3, pp. 318–326.

Dardağan, A. (2017). Neoplatonic "Tree of Life": Arbor Porphyriana—a diagram of logic and mystical theology. Unpublished.

Desbarats, N. (2021). 'I've stopped using box plots: should you?', *Nightingale*, 4 November. Available at: https://nightingaledvs.com/ive-stopped-using-box-plots-should-you/. (Accessed 7 January 2024).

Dorling, D. (1996). *Concepts and Techniques in Modern Geography 59. Area cartograms: their use and creation.* Norwich, UK: University of East Anglia. 70 p. ISBN 1-872464-09-2.

Drucker, J. (2011). Humanities approaches to graphical display. *Digital Humanities Quarterly* 5:1.

Ericson, M. (2011). 'When maps shouldn't be maps.' *Matthew Ericson.* Available at: https://www.ericson.net/content/2011/10/when-maps-shouldnt-be-maps/. (Accessed 23 February 2024.).

Flannery, J.J. (1971). The Relative effectiveness of some common graduated point symbols in the presentation of Quantitive data. *Cartographica: The International Journal for Geographic Information and Geovisualization*, 8:2, pp. 96–109.

Franconeri, S.L., Padilla, L.M., Shah, P., Zacks, J.M. & Hullman, J. (2021). The science of data communication: what works. *Psychological Science in Public Interest* 22:3, pp. 110–161.

Friendly, M. & Denis, D. (2005). The early origins and development of the scatterplot. *Journal of the History of the Behavioral Sciences*, 41:2, pp. 103–130.

Friendly, M. & Denis, D.J. (2008). *Milestones in the history of thematic cartography, statistical graphics, and data visualization: an illustrated chronology of innovations.* Available at: http://euclid.psych.yorku.ca/SCS/Gallery/milestone/index.html. (Accessed 6 January 2024).

Haroz, S. & Whitney, D. (2012). How capacity limits of attention influence information visualization effectiveness. IEEE Transactions on Visualization and Computer Graphics, 18:12, pp. 2402–2410.

Hayes-Williams, J.A. (2000). The earliest dated Tree of Jesse image: thematically reconsidered. Athanor, 18, pp. 17–23.

Hsu, M.-L. (1993). The Qin maps: a clue to later Chinese cartographic development. *Imago Mundi* 45, pp. 90–100.

Jones, B. (2019). 'Credit where credit is due: Mary Eleanor Spear', *Nightingale*, 6 August. Available at: https://nightingaledvs.com/credit-where-credit-is-due-mary-eleanor-spear/. (Accessed 7 January 2024).

Koponen, J. & Hildén, J. (2019). *Data visualization handbook*. Helsinki, Finland: Aalto ARTS Books. 352 p. ISBN 978-952-60-7449-8.

Kosara, R. (2007). Visualization criticism: the missing link between information visualization and art. In 2007 11th International Conference Information Visualization (IV '07), pp. 631–636. Los Calamitos (CA), USA: IEEE Computer Society. ISBN 0-7695-2900-3.

Kosara, R. & Skau, D. (2016). Arcs, angles, or areas: individual data encodings in pie and donut charts. *Computer Graphics Forum*, 35:3, pp. 121–130.

Lauersdorf, M.R. (2018). 'Linguistic visualizations as objets d'art?' In Bubenhofer, Noah & Kupietz, Marc (eds.) *Visualisierung der sprachlicher Daten: visual linguistics—praxis—tools*. Heidelberg, Germany: Heidelberg University Publishing. ISBN 978-3-946054-75-7.

Levasseur, É. (1885). La statistique graphique [Graphical statistics]. Journal of the Statistical Society of London, pp. 218–250.

Mason, B. (2019). Why scientists need to be better at data visualization. *Knowable Magazine*, 11 December. Available at: https://knowablemagazine.org/content/article/mind/2019/science-data-visualization. (Accessed 27 February 2024).

Matejka, J. & Fitzmaurice, G. (2017). Same stats, different graphs: generating datasets with varied appearance and identical statistics through simulated annealing. *Proceedings of the 2017 CHI conference on human factors in computing systems*, pp. 1290–1294.

Nusrat, S. & Kobourov, S. (2016). The state of the art in cartograms. *Computer Graphics Forum* 35:3, pp. 619–642.

Pearson, K. (1895). Contributions to the mathematical theory of evolution. II: skew variation in homogeneous material. *Phil. Trans. R. Soc. Lond. A* 186, pp. 343–414.

Rendgen, S. (2018). The Minard system: the complete statistical graphics of Charles-Joseph Minard from the collection of the École nationale des ponts et chaussées. Hudson (NY), USA: Princeton Architectural Press. 173 p. ISBN 978-1-6168933-1.

Rosenberg, D. & Grafton, A. (2010). *Cartographies of time: a history of the timeline.* Princeton (NJ), USA: Princeton Architectural Press. 272 p. ISBN 978-1-568-98763-7.

Rossby, T.H. (2003). Ocean Eddies in the 1539 Carta Marina by Olaus Magnus. *Oceanography* 16:4, pp. 77–88.

Rougier, N.P., Droettboom, M. & Bourne, P.E. (2014). Ten simple rules for better figures. *PLOS Computational Biology* 10:9, p. e1003833.

Scherer, C. (2021). *Beyond bar and box plots.* 4 November. Available at: https://z3tt.github.io/beyond-bar-and-box-plots/. (Accessed 7 January 2024.).

Schiewe, J. (2019). Empirical studies on the visual perception of spatial patterns in choropleth maps. *KN—Journal of Cartography and Geographic Information* 69, pp. 217–228.

Segel, E. & Heer, J. (2010). Narrative visualization: telling stories with data. *IEEE Transactions on Visualization and Computer Graphics* 16:6, pp. 1139–1148.

Simkin, D. & Hastie, R. (1987). An information processing analysis of graph perception. *Journal of the American Statistical Association*, 82:398, pp. 454–465.

Steinbach, S.F. (2015). 'Lexical distance among languages of Europe 2015', *Alternative Transport.* Available at: https://alternativetransport.wordpress.com/2015/05/05/34/. (Accessed 3 February 2024.).

Sönnig, L. & Schützler, O. (2023). 'Data visualization in corpus linguistics: critical reflections and future directions'. In Sönnig, Lukas & Schützler, Ole (eds.) *Studies in Variation, Contacts and Change in English* 22. Helsinki, Finland: VARIENG. Available at: https://varieng.helsinki.fi/series/volumes/22/introduction.html. (Accessed 26 February 2024.).

Tenney, I., Wexler, J., Bastings, J., Bolukbasi, T., Coenen, A., Gehrmann, S., Jiang, E., Pushkarna, M., Radebaugh, C., Reif, E. & Yuan, A. (2020). The language interpretability tool: extensible, interactive visualizations and analysis for NLP models. *arXiv* preprint, arXiv:2008.05122.

Thrower, N.J.W. (1969). Edmond Halley as a thematic geo-cartographer. *Annals of the Association of American Geographers*, 59:4, pp. 652–676.

Tiitta, A. (1999). Suomen karttakuvan kehitys. *Tieteessä tapahtuu* 17:4, pp. 16–23.

Tukey, J. (1977). *Exploratory data analysis.* Reading (MA), USA: Addison-Wesley Publishing Company. 506 p. ISBN 0-201-07616-0.

Ware, C. (2013). *Information visualization: perception for design.* Third edition. San Fransisco (CA), USA: Morgan Kaufmann. 536 p. ISBN 978-012-381464-7.

Weaver, P. (2014). The origins of bar charting. *PM World Journal*, 3:4.

Weissgerber, T.L., Milic, N.M., Winham, S.J. & Garovic, V.J. (2015). Beyond bar and line graphs: time for a new data presentation paradigm. *PLOS Biology* 13:4, p. e1002128.

Wickham, H. & Stryjewski, L. (2011). *40 years of boxplots*. Unpublished.

Wong, D.M. (2010). The Wall Street Journal guide to information graphics: the dos and don'ts of presenting data, facts and figures. New York (NY), USA: W.W. Norton & Company. 157 p. ISBN 978-039-307295-2.

Wordclouds.com n.d. *Wordclouds.com*. Available at: https://wordclouds.com. (Accessed 3 February 2024.).

CHAPTER 3

Keystroke Data Logging and Visualisation: Design Process and Possibilities and Limitations

Pavithra Basnayake and Hakim Usoof

3.1 Introduction

Owing to the use of digital media, such as computers and smartphones, the generation of textual content and data visualisation techniques across diverse contexts and by individuals from varied backgrounds has increased. The field of data visualisation includes the creation, design, and utilisation of graphical depictions to convey information effectively such that it supports enhancing comprehension and interpretation of data, facilitating informed decision-making processes (Amar & Stasko, 2013; Gandhi & Pruthi, 2020; Munzner, 2014). The fundamental concept of keystroke logging involves recording every event within the process of writing, allowing researchers to observe writing procedure and enhance their comprehension of the underlying dynamics during text production (Caporossi et al., 2020; Edwards et al., 2020; Leijten & Van Waes, 2005; Leijten & Van Waes, 2013; Wengelin & Johansson, 2023). The work carried out by Bridwell and Duin (1985) was an initial investigation that highlighted the transformation of the writing context with the use of computers related to research writing. Nevertheless, keystroke logging was subsequently utilised in other diverse fields such as human–computer interaction and computer security, in assessing children's writing skills and in the analysis of challenges in writing and spelling (Bridwell & Duin, 1985; Hinbarji et al., 2016; Leijten & Van Waes, 2005; Leijten & Van Waes, 2013).

Keystroke logging and data visualisation are two distinct concepts, but they can be related in many scenarios (Andersson et al., 2006; Leijten & Van Waes, 2013). For instance, data visualisation can be used to analyse the data collected by keystroke loggers for security purposes. By visualising patterns in keystroke data, such as unusual typing behaviour or frequent entry of sensitive information, security analysts can detect potential security breaches or unauthorised access attempts. Further, keystroke logging can be used for monitoring and analysing user behaviour within software applications or websites. Data visualisation techniques can then be applied to the logged keystroke data to gain insights into user interactions, navigation patterns, and preferences. This

HTTPS://DOI.ORG/10.1163/9789004760264-004

analysis can inform user experience improvements, such as optimising interface design or identifying usability issues.

3.1.1 *Keystroke Logging*

The term keystroke logging refers to the recording of key presses and releases on a computer keyboard (Sullivan & Lindgren, 2008). This technique is used for various purposes, one of which is to study the processes involved in computer-based text development (Leijten & Van Waes, 2013). While initial keystroke logging software only captured keystrokes, modern versions can also capture data such as mouse movements, clicks, system tasks (cut-copy-paste), use of external applications, screenshots, audio recordings, and even eye-tracking (Andersson et al., 2006; Stromqvist et al., 2006). In the context of computer-based text development, the purpose of keystroke logging is to gain insights into the writing process with the cognitive processes involved, and the development of the text itself (Miller & Sullivan, 2013). It's important to acknowledge that this data, while valuable, is not a direct representation of the writing processes themselves, but rather a reflection of various processes at play (Wengelin, 2009).

3.1.2 *Data Visualisation*

Data visualisation is the act of representing data through graphical elements like charts, plots, infographics, and even animations (Amar & Stasko, 2013; Gandhi & Pruthi, 2020; Munzner, 2014; Koponen, 2025). The goal of designing visualisations is to effectively communicate and present data in a way that fosters comprehension (Few, 2009; Gandhi & Pruthi, 2020). Well-designed visualisations don't force understanding, but they can significantly improve a viewer's ability to perceive, interpret, and grasp the data (Amar & Stasko, 2013). Prior to selecting a particular visualisation technique, careful consideration is essential. The data to be presented should be carefully selected to ensure relevance and focus on the objective. Once these foundational steps are completed, additional considerations such as colours, fonts, and other visual elements may be addressed.

Keystroke logging data can be numerical (number of keystrokes, time between keystrokes), categorical (key pressed), time series (sequence of keystrokes over time), spatial (location of clicks), and even multivariate (combining various data types) (Graesser & McNamara, 2017). This raw data may require transformations or can be used directly to create informative visualisations relevant to learners, teachers, and researchers (Liu et al., 2020). Visual elements like position, length, angle, direction, area, volume, saturation, and hue can be positioned on Cartesian, polar, or geographic coordinates with scales that are linear, categorical, logarithmic, ordinal, percentage, or time-based (Cleveland, 1993). The effectiveness of data visualisation for keystroke logging data is ultimately influenced by factors like computational limitations, statistical accuracy, the appropriateness of the specific data being represented, and the constraints of the available display space (Gandhi & Pruthi, 2020; Munzner, 2014).

3.1.3 *Aim of the Chapter*

This chapter explores the conceptual foundations and potential applications of data visualisation within the context of keystroke logging and writing research. Our primary objective is to exemplify the key concepts and possibilities inherent in this approach. By equipping readers with a comprehensive understanding of the principles, we aim to empower them with the knowledge to create their own conceptualizations and design novel visualisations tailored to their specific research questions and interests.

3.2 Tools for Keystroke Logging

At present, several software exist that enable monitoring and recording of computer activities. The fundamental idea underlying various keystroke logging tools is to record every keystroke and mouse movement. Many tools have been developed over the years for the logging of keystroke data with the aim of using them for writing research. However, their scope and objectives have been driven by various research interests. For examples, the Scriptlog software was primarily developed for experimental research, with optional integration with eye-tracking (Andersson et al., 2006; Leijten & Van Waes, 2005; Leijten & Van Waes, 2013; Wengelin & Johansson, 2023), the software Translog is designed for experimental research on translation using source texts, whereas the software Inputlog's focus is on multimodal professional writing environments. The more recent, GenoGraphiX-LOG is focused on experimental research with high-accuracy data capture and data visualisation with a primary focus on the application of graph theory (Caprossi et al., 2020). Nevertheless, keystroke logging offers more than just process-level analysis. By capturing data on pausing and revision behaviours, it allows researchers to make inferences about a writer's resource allocation, including aspects like working memory, long-term memory, and reading (Beattie & Magnusson, 2007; Ericsson & Delaney, 2011). This is because these cognitive resources are known to be involved in the very acts of pausing, reflecting, and revising during writing (Jarvis et al., 2009).

3.2.1 *LoggerMan*

LoggerMan is an extensive logging tool designed to capture various facets of human–computer interaction (HCI) experiments mainly focusing on finding significant insights about user behaviour by facilitating the execution of advanced analysis and developing personalised services. (Hinbarji et al., 2016). LoggerMan operates on Mac OSX 10.7 or newer and this software uses all data stored locally on the computer aiming to protect user privacy and a local reporting tool is available for the purpose of visualising and providing insights to the users regarding their computer usage. There are numerous logging modules that are individually operable; each module records several data types where each entry is timestamped. The modules related to the keyboard are tasked with recording keystroke events and saving them into local files offering details on two levels where one is based on words and the other on individual keys. The mouse Module monitors all mouse actions, and the screenshots module is designed to take a screenshot of the currently active window. Users can choose from various shooting intervals or for a smart-shooting feature where in this it captures a screenshot after each window transition. The apps module is specifically used to monitor transitions between applications and the clipboard Module is responsible for tracking copy-paste operations. Each module is crafted to ensure Unicode compatibility, enabling the tool to accurately work with various programming languages.

3.2.2 *ScriptLog*

ScriptLog was initially created as a Mac application, and the present version is compatible across multiple platforms, including Mac, Windows, and Linux. The program provides multiple experimental configurations, including diverse elicitation formats using images, texts and sound. Additionally, it offers opportunities for the post-editing of previously developed text within a new writing session. The Software provides a basic integrated text editor with rich-text functionality, which accurately records keystroke and mouse interaction data. Additionally, the software integrates complete synchronisation with SensoMotoric Instruments (SMI) and Tobii eye trackers (Andersson et al., 2006; Wengelin & Johansson, 2023) as well as allows working with recorded audio instructions. This software application generates fundamental summary statistics, temporal data, and a linear file, however, lacking revision analysis functionality. It provides users with real-time playback, step-by-step playback, and fast-forward playback features. The developers suggest exporting keystroke data to InputLog and facilitating this process by offering an export function.

3.2.3 *Inputlog*

Many writing logging tools were either built to be used in the word processing environment or inadequately suited to Windows environments where researchers were unable to conduct their investigations using commercial word processors accustomed to copying and pasting from the Internet or logging programs designed for HCI studies lack in writing-focused analyses (Leijten & Van Waes, 2005; Leijten & Van Waes, 2013). These factors have been considered in building the Inputlog. Inputlog is a keystroke logging tool that runs on the Windows operating system, and it is based on JEdit, Trace-It and ScripTlog programs programmed in Visual C++ and the user interface built using Visual Basic. The Inputlog tool facilitates researchers in documenting writing sessions within MS Word which is a foremost distinctive feature, and it can create data files for statistical, textual, pause and model analysis (Leijten & Van Waes, 2005; Leijten & Van Waes, 2013). Further, it can adjust playback speeds for recorded sessions and capture dictation input through speech recognition software. In contrast to Trace-it and ScriptLog, this tool records each keystroke and mouse movement irrespective of the specific word processor in use. Inputlog extends its functionality by monitoring keyboard and mouse actions within other Windows-based programs. Overall, Inputlog facilitates the observation not only of writing procedures but also of fundamental processes such as programming related to Windows-based language and web consultant procedures.

The Inputlog system consists of five modules. The Record module is designed to log data using keyboard, mouse, and speech inputs within Microsoft Word and other Windows-based applications, accompanied by a distinctive timestamp in milliseconds. In the pre-processing module, it facilitates the processing of data in multiple ways such as including event-based, time-based, and window-changes. The analyse module consists of three representations of processes of general and linear logging files and s-notation of text and four levels of aggregated analysis including pause, summary, revision, and source analyses. The post-process module involves the integration of either single or multiple log files generated from Inputlog software or other tools such as morae, eye-tracking data and dragon naturally speaking. Additionally, the capability exists to combine multiple output files to facilitate advanced analysis using SPSS or MLWin. The Play module provides researchers the capability to review recorded sessions. The playback operates on data rather than video, with adjustable playback speeds. Moreover, a logged session can be rebuilt considering the required revisions. The combination of log data from Inputlog with eye-tracking devices such as Eyelink and Tobii facilitates researchers to evaluate reading activities throughout the writing process.

3.2.4 *GenoGraphiX*

GenoGraphiX (www.ggxlog.net) is a keystroke logging software developed using Java programming language with text genetics and graph theory methodologies for writing studies (Caporossi et al., 2020). It operates on Windows, Mac OS X and the Linux operating systems, and its primary functionalities include recording writing sessions, storing session data and analysing and visualising the data. The software interface is structured into five main areas: main-menu, interface language selection, work-window, task-in-progress, and task-clock. In GenoGraphiX, the real-time graph indicates the in-progress writing session related to short texts in the text editor. Further, this logging tool is capable of recording activities from third-party applications used during the writing session such as Word documents and web browsers.

For data analysis and data visualisation purposes, this software provides different views: (i) Replay—This feature permits the replay of the writing session. (ii) Graph representation—Here, the session graph method employs graph theory to visualise the writing session (Caporossi et al., 2020), graph statistics provide both numerical statistics and visual summaries of the session graph, and progressive graphs progressively make the session graph, based on significant events throughout the writing session (Caporossi et al., 2020). (iii) Notation—The linear text format illustrates the writing session employing two notational structures, summarising the progression of events throughout the session utilising textual descriptions and symbolic representations, S-Notation serves as a method for analysing revisions and text generation throughout the session (Caporossi et al., 2020). (iv) Analysis—statistics feature provides the fundamental statistics of the session, burst and efficiency analyses bursts and efficiency metrics associated with interruptions during the session, micro analysis feature provides a micro-level analysis of events and text within the writing session, edit distance tool calculates the distance between two edits made during the session. (v) Session Log—This view exhibits a filtered subset of fields extracted from the session log file.

3.2.5 *TransLog*

Translog-II is a computer program designed to capture and investigate human reading and writing processes within a digital environment (Jakobsen, 1999; CRITT, 2024; Wengelin & Johansson, 2023). However, it was originally developed for the exploration of translation in research. It functions as a research instrument facilitating the acquisition of objective, digital data on human translation activities. Like previous versions of Translog, Translog-II comprises two primary components:

- **Translog-II Supervisor**: This component allows researchers to create project files and replay recorded user sessions.
- **Translog-II User**: This component enables the execution of text production experiments, where participants can read, write, or translate a text.

Translog-II generates log files containing user activity data associated with the reading, writing, and translation processes. The software is compatible with SR Research EyeLink, SensoMotoric Instruments (SMI) eye trackers and TobiiPro eye trackers. The log files generated by the software can be further analysed using external tools for a deeper understanding of human text processing behaviour (CRITT, 2024).

3.3 Data, Definitions and Visualisation

Raw data or unprocessed data in computer-based writing research can take various forms, including logged keystrokes, stylus tracking, mouse movements, eye tracking, and application tracking (Andersson et al., 2006; Caporossi et al., 2020; Graesser & McNamara, 2017; Liu et al., 2020; Stromqvist et al., 2006).

3.3.1 *Data Acquisition*

3.3.1.1 Keystroke Logs

Keystroke logs typically consist of key characters, modifier keys (e.g., Shift, Ctrl), and navigation keys (e.g., arrows, Home, End) logged with timestamps for both keypress and key release events (Andersson et al., 2006; Angelino et al., 2013; Caporossi et al., 2020; Hinbarji et al., 2016; Leijten & Van Waes, 2013). Additionally, cursor position data, including caret and anchor positions, is often captured (Granville et al., 2009). Keystroke logging may also encompass key depression duration, key hold duration, pauses between key releases and subsequent keypresses, and time elapsed since the writing session began (Christopulos et al., 2004).

In addition keystroke logs allow for the curser may be tracked or edits may be tracked to illustrate paths of the writer's navigation of the document (Bekius and Buschenhenke, this volume, p. 148).

3.3.1.2 Stylus Tracking

Stylus tracking data typically includes x and y coordinates at the beginning and end of an event, the pressure exerted by the stylus, timestamps for both the beginning and end of the event, and event categorization (e.g., pen up, pen down, move) (Gong et al., 2004). Additional data points may include the time between the event's start and end and the distance travelled between the starting and ending points.

3.3.1.3 Mouse Movement Tracking

Mouse movement tracking data typically includes the x and y coordinates of the cursor, along with event categorization such as left click, right click, double click, and move events (Hinbarji et al., 2016; Vertega et al., 2001).

3.3.1.4 Eye Tracking Logs

Eye tracking logs typically capture screen coordinates (x and y) and the corresponding timestamp of each fixation (Andersson et al., 2006; Liu et al., 2020; Holmqvist et al., 2011).

3.3.1.5 Application Logging

Application logging data typically includes the application name, timestamps for when the application gains and loses focus, and the name of the opened file or URL (Garnefski et al., 2010). In some cases, application logging may also capture screenshots of the application window.

3.3.1.6 Video and Audio Recording

Video and audio recordings (Perrin, this volume, p. 176) of writers engaged in writing sessions could also be used as means to capture data that may not necessarily be captured in the keystroke log or other data captured on the writing device. These data may be coded to provide a quantitative or qualitative analysis providing an option for data triangulation to gain insights into the writing session.

In any research procedure, understanding the data, its types and statistical classification of variables is crucial for effective analysis and interpretation.

TABLE 3.1 Illustrations of a selection of the collected data with examples and variable types

Data	**Type**	**Variable type**	**Examples**
Device	String/ numerical	Categorical	Computer, laptop, Tobii eye tracker
Key character	Character	Categorical	'A', 'b', 'Enter', 'Space'
Timestamp	Numerical	Date/time	2024-03-19 14:30:15
Duration of event	Numerical	Continuous	Seconds, minutes, hours
Cursor position	Numerical	Numerical	x = 300, y = 200
X and Y coordinates	Numerical	Numerical	x = 500, y = 350
Pause duration	Numerical	Continuous	30 seconds, 2 minutes
Pause location	String/ numerical	Categorical	Main menu, submenu, screen X

Data types define how information is stored, guiding researchers on appropriate analytical methods. Statistical classification of variables categorises data into types such as numeric, categorical and date type helping researchers choose suitable statistical tests. For instance, a project that involves analysing keystroke logging data to understand typing behaviour among users with different levels of expertise can create various plots or charts to explore and communicate findings effectively based on the collected data with their correct data types: a scatter plot showing the relationship between pause duration and typing speed could reveal patterns in typing behaviour, a time-series plot could illustrate changes in typing speed over time, heat maps could visualise common typing errors or frequently used keys. These visualisations help researchers gain insights into user behaviour and identify areas for further investigation or improvement in user interface design.

3.3.2 *Limitations of Traditional Data Analysis and Data Visualisation*

In research, the management of data mainly involves three sequential procedural stages: data formalisation, data analysis, and data visualisation (Burns et al., 2020, Cavalier, 2021). Formalization of data arises through preprocessing procedures, while data analysis yields valuable insights, and data visualisation facilitates comprehension and interpretation, ultimately leading to the generation of knowledge. The meaningful data visualisation lies in establishing a connection between data and its representation. Designers strategically make decisions regarding design elements under data visualisation techniques, aiming to effectively communicate the accurate interpretation of the data to the readers. Mainly, the data visualisation evaluation approaches often focus on perceptual understanding, such as comparing mean values, calculating descriptive statistics, tabular analysis or retrieving values, which is inadequate for assessing the knowledge or insights gained. Traditional data analysis and data visualisation techniques often struggle to handle large volumes of data efficiently and can produce static charts that may not effectively convey the dynamic nature of data where they are difficult to interpret, especially for non-technical users (Gandhi & Pruthi, 2020). Further, they struggle to integrate with other systems and platforms limiting their ability to access and analyse data from diverse sources and not adequately address security and privacy concerns, particularly in handling sensitive or confidential information. Hence, there are several interactive visualisation tools and taxonomies introduced to implement structured methodologies for data visualisation based on the levels of information abstraction, the capabilities of the graphical representation tools, the visualisation setup specifics, the strategic approaches to visualisation and the efficiency of communication across various graphical tools (Burns et al., 2020; Cavalier, 2021; Gandhi & Pruthi, 2020).

3.3.3 *Representations and Visualisation of Keystroke Data*

Traditionally representing and visualising keystroke data from a computing perspective can provide insights into typing behaviour, user interaction patterns, and potentially identify anomalies or security breaches. From a writing research perspective these patterns can represent fluency, processes, psychomotor activities, and cognition during writing.

Here are some examples:

- Heat maps can represent the frequency or intensity of keystrokes across the keyboard. Each key is coloured based on the number of times it's pressed, with dark colours indicating higher activity.
- Time-series plots show the frequency or timing of keystrokes over time. They can reveal typing speed, rhythm, and pauses between keystrokes. Time-series analysis can detect changes in typing behaviour or anomalies such as sudden spikes in activity.
- Histograms and bar charts can display the distribution of various typing metrics such as key hold times or digraph frequencies.
- Scatter plots can visualise relationships between different typing metrics. For example, plotting key hold times against key digraph frequencies can reveal correlations between typing speed and accuracy.

Furthermore, interactive visualisations allow users to explore keystroke data dynamically, zooming in on specific time periods, filtering by typing metrics or comparing multiple users' typing behaviour. Interactive dashboards or tools enable deeper analysis and insights into keystroke data.

3.3.4 *Levels of Data Visualisation*

Unprocessed data, referred to as raw data, can be transformed into valuable information where this conversion necessitates data extraction, systematic organisation, and proper analysis to facilitate effective data visualisation. For instance, Hinbarji et al., 2016 implemented a reporting tool to illustrate the pattern of raw data (utilised applications, typed words and titles of windows) in Loggerman using normalised frequencies of incident occurrences within the user-selected date range by apps cloud, time-series graphs, and windows title clouds. Leijten & Van Waes in 2013 investigated the potential for aggregating data from the letter-to-word level considering the logging data with lexica and natural language processing (NLP) tools focusing on linguistics aspects in writing where the language-based and process-based analyses enabled in finding of innovative research inquiries such as: are pauses prior to verb lengthier compared to those preceding nouns? compared to new writers, to professional writers frequently replace high-frequency terms with low-frequency terms, etc. Within the inputlog software, users could define and adjust the pause threshold to their preferred level (Leijten & Van Waes, 2013). Here, pauses are quantified at both a general level with pause counts along with mean and standard deviation of pause durations, and at a more specific level through the division of writing sessions into ten distinct time slots. Furthermore, pauses are categorised within various text components, including within and between words, sentences, and paragraphs. The analysis also includes the identification and reporting of pause bursts detailing both their quantity and duration.

3.3.4.1 Raw Data

There are certain visualisations that are possible based on the raw data. As the timestamp is continuous, we can visualise certain data by having one of the axes as the time dimension. Typically line graphs, histograms with time intervals, Gantt charts and scatter plots may be used to visualise such data. A few examples are given in Figure 3.1 to Figure 3.3.

Figure 3.1 illustrates the movements of the cursor position (represented by the orange line) and event count (indicated by the blue line) over time. Initially, both exhibit a similar upward trend, yet as time progresses, the event count diverges from the cursor position. Noticeable downward fluctuations occur in the cursor position, which are not visible in event counts. This chart was generated using the chart feature in MS Excel.

Figure 3.2 depicts the duration of cognitive pauses (≥ 2000 milliseconds) over time. Most observations fall within the range of 1000 ms to 10,000 ms, with a notable increase in one observation between 5 and 8 minutes. Overall, the trend line fitted to the data suggests a downward trend. This was performed by filtering pause values over 2000ms using MS Excel and then using the chart feature to plot the graph.

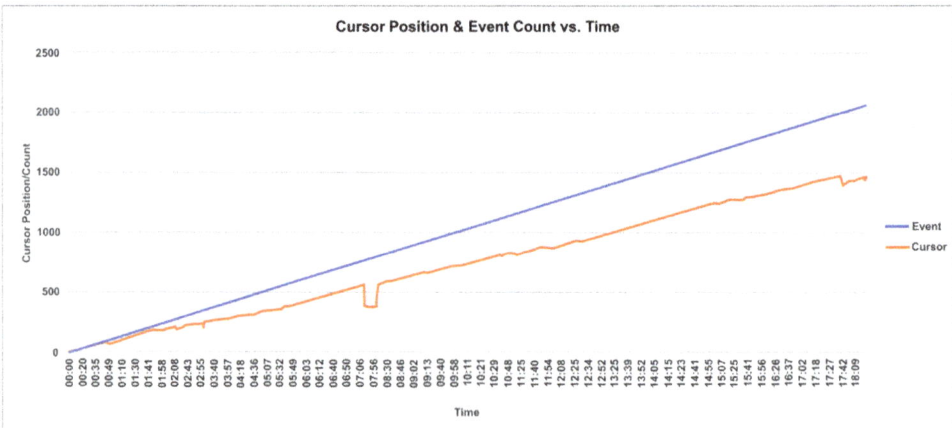

FIGURE 3.1 Event count and cursor position over time

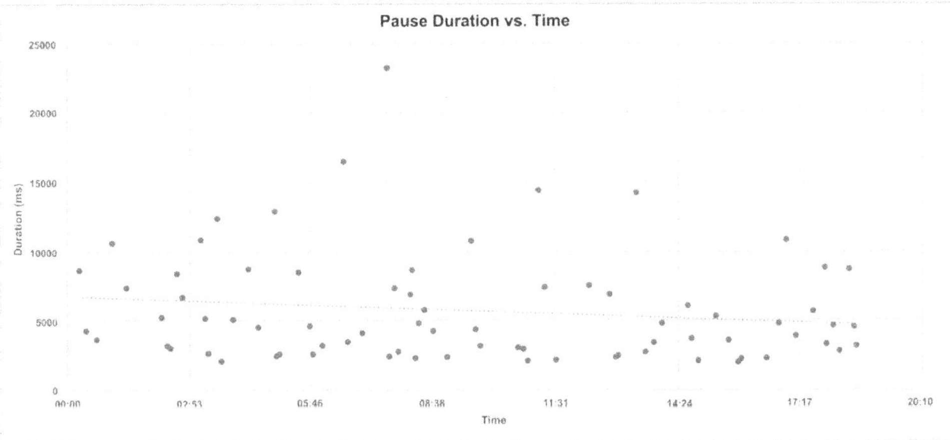

FIGURE 3.2 Cognitive pause (> = 2000 ms) vs. time

The analysis of pause locations generated through Microsoft PowerBI, as illustrated in Figure 3.3, the top left corner bar chart indicates summations of counts corresponding to various pause locations: between words, navigation, unknown, delete, paragraph end, within word and sentences end where they are displayed descending order sum of count values. The same pattern is observed for the total duration in milliseconds for the identified pause locations as per the bar chart in the right-hand side corner in Figure 3.3, except the least sum of total duration is observed for the within-word pause location and the next highest value is observed at the sentence end. In contrast to the bar charts, the pattern of mean pause duration in milliseconds across different pause locations has shifted, as illustrated in the orange colour bar chart in Figure 3.3. The highest sum of the mean pause is observed for sentence end and the lowest value for within word. The right-side bottom bar chart includes the behaviour sum of counts against total duration in milliseconds

3.3.4.2 Aggregated Data

The raw data in the logs can be processed to create new data points which we refer to as aggregated data. Table 3.2 provides us with some examples of how different data can be aggregated in various data collection methods.

The aggregation of data can be done from two perspectives. The first around language-based concepts such as words, sentences, and paragraphs and the second process-based concepts such as inserts, deletions, and pauses. These aggregated variables can be visualised to provide researchers with insight into various aspects of the writing session. The aggregation of this data can

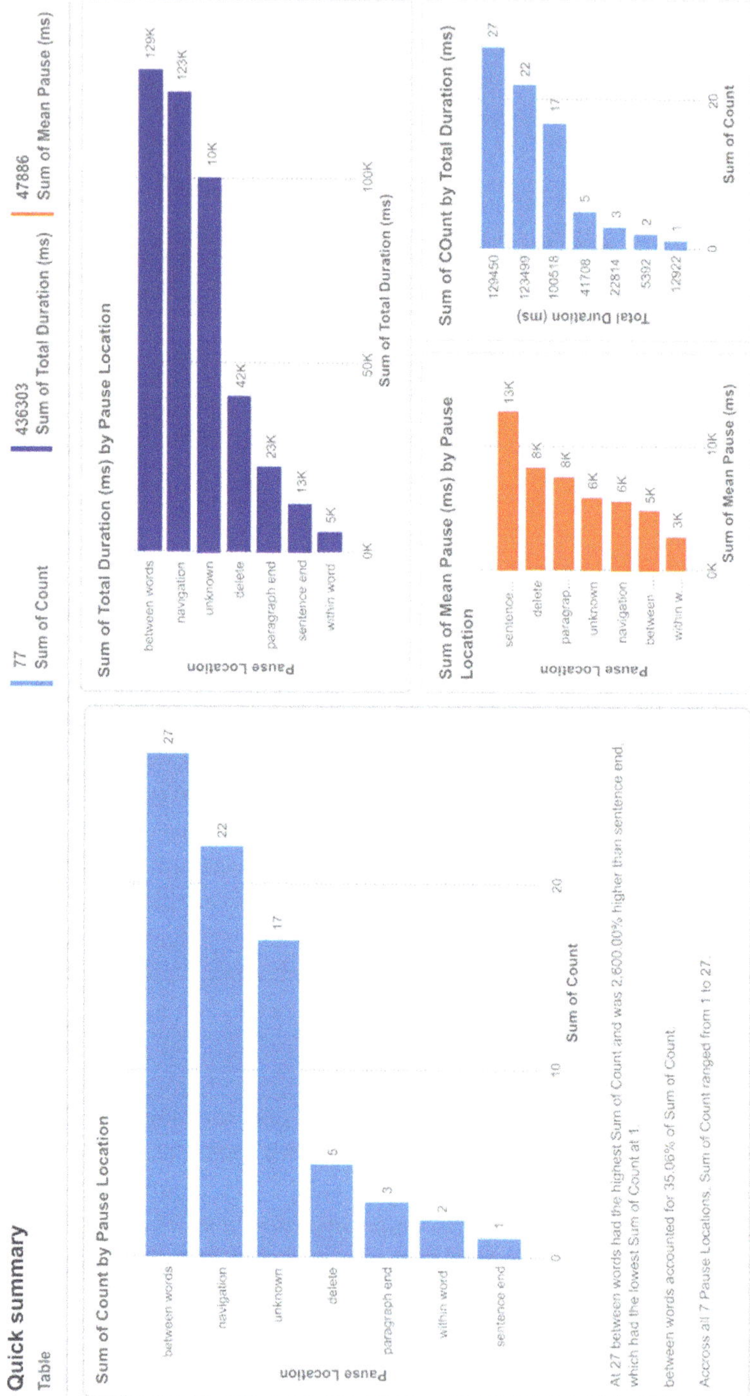

FIGURE 3.3 Pause location analysis created using Microsoft PowerBI

TABLE 3.2 Example of variables created by aggregating raw keystroke log data

Variable	Aggregation	Description
Bigrams, trigrams, words, sentences, paragraphs	Combining key characters, separated by spaces, punctuations, and return keys	Provides basic structures of language and writing
Pauses	The time between the end of one event and the beginning of another	The pauses can be classified into such notions as motor pauses and cognitive pauses. If the pause duration exceeds a specified threshold, they are considered cognitive.
Bursts	By aggregating events between cognitive pauses, insertions and/or deletions	Represents a contiguous series of events
Fluency	A burst divided by the duration of the burst	Provides an idea of how fluent a writer might be during a particular sub-session of writing.
Counts	Various counts based on numerous classifications of events	These may include event counts, character counts, word counts, pause counts, bigram and/or trigram counts.
Frequencies	The counts described above are divided by the duration of the session.	Provides an idea about various proficiencies, writers' limitations, etc. Example events per minute, words per minute.
Means	Means of parameters above	Provides an idea about various characteristics of the writer, task and language. May include values such as mean word length and mean cognitive pauses.
Pause type	A categorization of pauses	Cognitive pauses may be classified according to where they occur. For example, between sentences, between words, deletion or edits, etc.

be achieved through simple manipulations using software such as spreadsheets or might require statistical packages or even more complex unique computer programs specifically written for this purpose. The visualisations of these aggregated data can be done using tools such as spreadsheets but might require specialised data visualisation tools such as R, PowerBI, Tableau, and Datawrapper and in unique and specific visualisations are required, one might be required to develop code using JavaScript visualisation frameworks such as D3.js and Chart.js. Figure 3.4 depicts the distribution of bigrams as a count while Figure 3.5 visualises bigram distribution as a percentage of all bigrams. These have had the data aggregation and visualisation performed using MS Excel. Figure 3.6 illustrates the Bursts and fluency in a writing session and the data aggregation has been performed using the Java programming language and the visualisation using the D3.js JavaScript framework.

Tools such as Microsoft Excel, PowerBI and many statistical packages are not capable of complex visualisation such as multi-dimensional cartesian charts, focussing on the specific interest of researchers in writing studies, which limits their use. For example, in the burst and efficiency analysis chart in Figure 3.6, the two-dimensional chart not only represents two dimensions of the x–y axes but using shapes, colours and a secondary y-axis on the right-hand side, represents four factors as time, fluency, no of characters in a burst, type of burst. These types of multidimensional visualisations require specific computer code to illustrate such information.

A similar multi-dimensional chart is the Delete Node distribution given in Figure 3.7. Even though the chart has only two primary axes, which are Node No. as the x-axis and Average Node distance as the y-axis, the radius of the spheres used indicates the number of characters deleted, and the darkness or lightness of the sphere is used to indicate Relative node distance with respect to the current number of nodes. Therefore, this chart has four dimensions represented in a 2-dimensional space.

Figure 3.8 illustrates the distribution of editing distances. The data for this chart is derived firstly, by counting events between editing actions (insertions, deletion, mouse clicks, etc.), and next by deriving the distribution of these edits in different ranges. The initial aggregation was provided by GGXLog software, and that dataset was clustered into ranges using spreadsheet software. Thus, it is important to investigate aggregations provided by the software, which can be visualised on their own, but also these aggregations can be further transformed by third-party software for more specific purposes and unique visualisations.

Other such customised visualisations are gaze maps and heat maps for eye-tracking data. This data can be captured using special wearable devices such as those used in the Eye and Pen software and MetaQuest as well as passive devices such as the Tobii eye tracker. These complex visualisations require specific software for unique visualisations. Examples of Heat maps and Gaze maps are given in Figure 3.9 and Figure 3.10 respectively.

A substantial body of visualisations exists, driven by a robust research interest and ultimately constrained only by the researcher's creativity. While the accessibility of generic software and its inherent functionalities impose

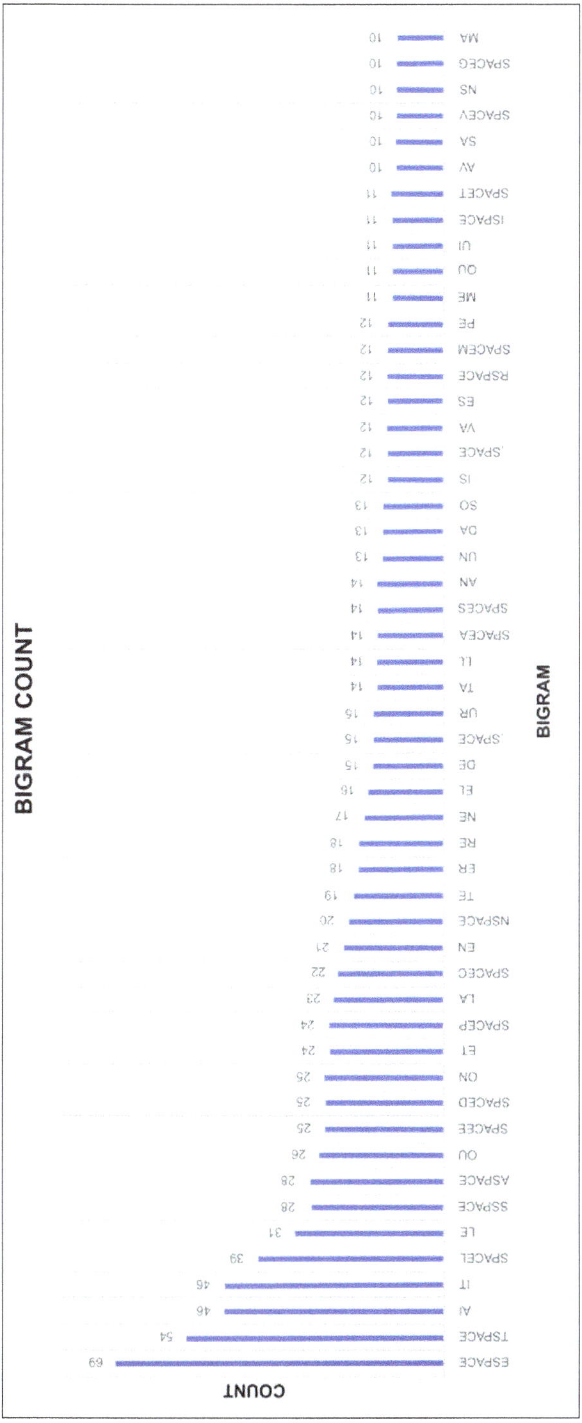

FIGURE 3.4 Bigram distribution as a count (where the count is > = 10)

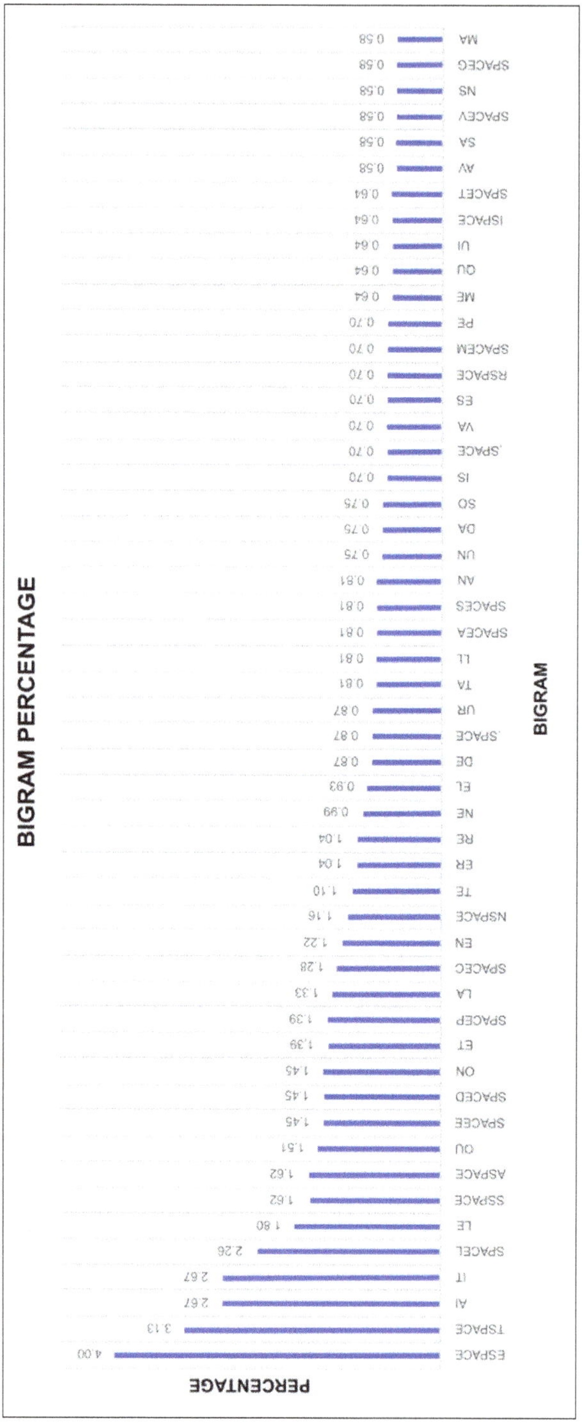

FIGURE 3.5 Bigram distribution as a percentage of all occurrences of bigrams (where the count is > = 10)

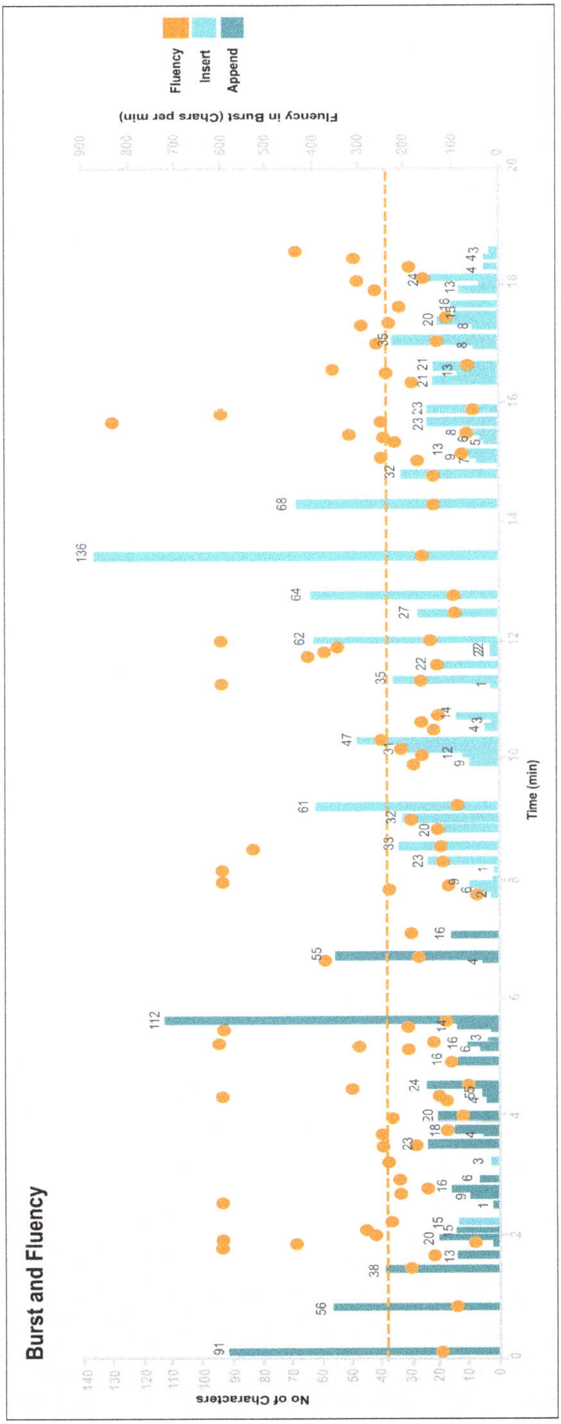

FIGURE 3.6 Burst and efficiency distribution over time

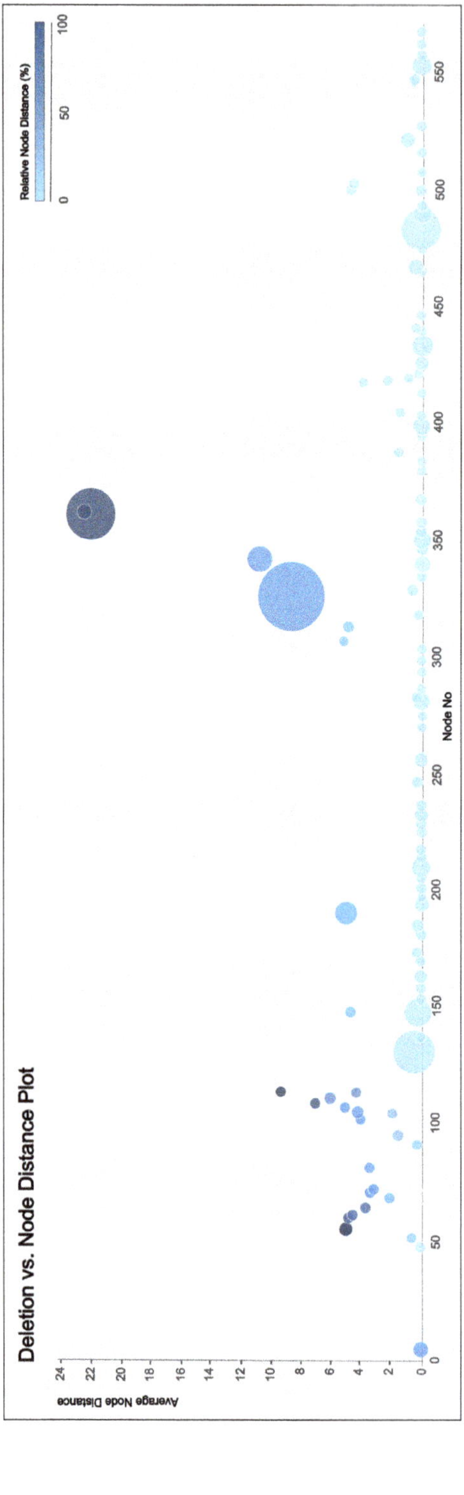

FIGURE 3.7 Deletion vs. node distance plot

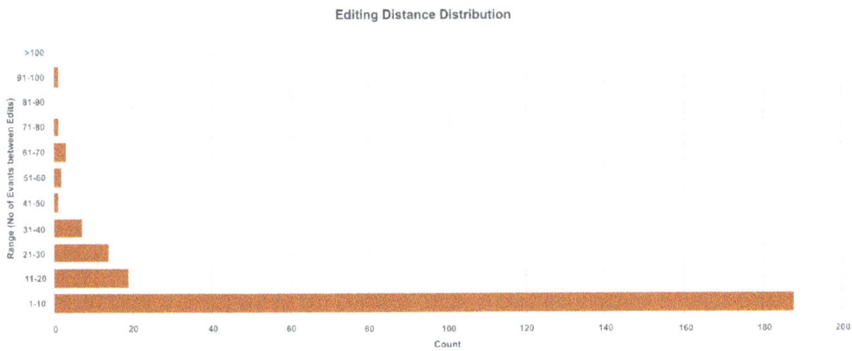

FIGURE 3.8 Editing distance distribution

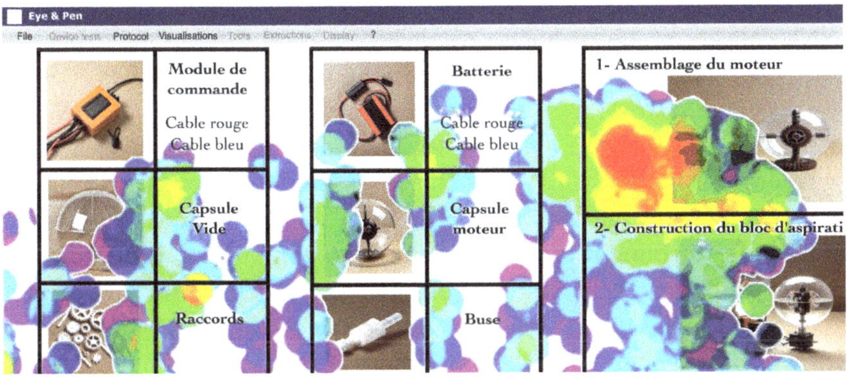

FIGURE 3.9 Heat map of fixation in Eye and Pen. Adapted from Alamargot & Chesnet (2018)

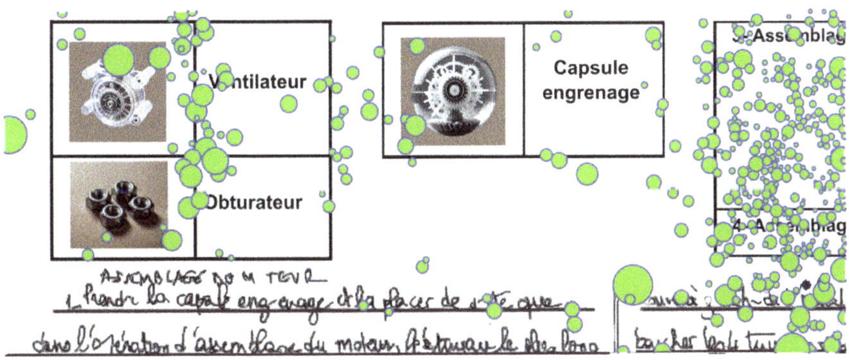

FIGURE 3.10 Gaze map of fixation in Eye and Pen. Adapted from Alamargot & Chesnet (2018)

limitations, the potential for creating even more intricate visualisations is unbounded if researchers leverage the capabilities of more advanced software and programming languages.

3.3.4.3 Limitations

Data aggregation plays a critical role in the visualisation process, particularly when dealing with large, complex datasets like those generated from keystroke logging. Aggregating data allows for summarization and pattern recognition, but it comes with both advantages and limitations (Elmqvist & Fekete, 2010). The decision to aggregate or not, significantly influences the type of visualisation and the insights that can be drawn.

3.3.4.3.1 *Limitations of Visualisation with Data Aggregation*

While data aggregation simplifies complex datasets and makes them easier to interpret, it can also have certain limitations. Some key limitations include:
- **Loss of granularity**: Aggregation reduces the level of detail in the data. For instance, summarizing keystroke logs into bursts or pauses may hide variations in keystroke timing or individual typing behaviour that could be important for certain analyses.
- **Risk of oversimplification**: Aggregating data into higher-order structures (e.g., words, sentences) may oversimplify underlying patterns. For example, aggregating pause durations into mean values may obscure outlier pauses that signify cognitive difficulties or complex editing processes.
- **Bias in data interpretation**: Aggregated data can introduce bias, especially if inappropriate aggregation methods are used. For example, calculating average pause durations might misrepresent the distribution of pauses, leading to misinterpretations about writing fluency.
- **Limited ability to detect anomalies:** Aggregated visualisations may fail to reveal outliers or anomalies in the dataset, such as sudden spikes in keystroke speed or editing frequency, which could provide critical insights into user behaviour.

3.3.4.3.2 *Limitations of Visualisation without Data Aggregation*

Visualising unaggregated or raw data provides a more detailed representation but also comes with its own challenges. For example:
- **Overload of information**: Visualising raw data can overwhelm the viewer, especially in large datasets. For example, representing every keystroke individually in a time-series plot can make it difficult to identify meaningful patterns or trends.

- **Complexity in interpretation**: Raw data visualisations often require more sophisticated analysis skills to interpret effectively. Without aggregation, patterns may be difficult to discern, especially for non-technical users.
- **Inefficiency in communicating insights**: Raw data can produce overly complex visualisations that are not easily communicable. For instance, plotting every individual pause and keystroke may be insightful for an expert, but less useful for communicating broader patterns to a general audience.

3.4 Discussion and Conclusions

This chapter emphasises the importance of integrating keystroke logging data and data visualisation techniques for a comprehensive understanding of the writing process. Keystroke logging offers a precise and detailed record of user activities, encompassing keypresses, mouse movements, application usage, and even eye-tracking data. Data visualisation is an effective analytical tool that facilitates the extraction of insights and interpretation of this rich data. The convergence of these two techniques fosters a holistic perspective on the writing process, and reveals the underlying cognitive process involved.

Furthermore, the chapter underscores the significance of statistical literacy in data analysis and visualisation design. A fundamental understanding of statistical principles is crucial for the appropriate analysis of keystroke logging data and the development of meaningful visualisations. This chapter explores the potential of utilising both raw (unaggregated) and aggregated data for this purpose. While raw data offers granular detail, aggregated data provides a broader view of trends and patterns. The decision to aggregate data necessitates careful consideration of statistical validity and the intended value of the analysis. Aggregation can be performed using basic tools like spreadsheets, while more sophisticated techniques may require specialised software or programming languages. Notably, the information inferred from data analysis is intrinsically linked to the specific research questions, the writing aspect under investigation, and the overall research domain.

The chapter also highlights the critical role of research objectives in guiding data visualisation practices. Both raw and aggregated data visualisations require alignment with the research question, domain of interest, and the specific aspect of writing being explored. Data visualisation software options range from widely accessible tools like Microsoft Excel or Power BI to more specialised software capable of generating multifaceted, multidimensional visualisations that enhance data comprehension, pattern identification, and knowledge extraction.

In conclusion, this chapter emphasises that the tasks of utilising raw data, performing data aggregation, and designing effective visualisations are all dependent upon the specific focus of the writing research. While some of these tasks can be accomplished using readily available software, others necessitate more specialised tools. Lastly, the chapter underscores the power of data visualisation. Humans possess a remarkable ability to perceive visual information and identify patterns significantly faster than reading text or analysing numerical data. This inherent strength renders data visualisation a powerful tool for investigating the writing process captured through keystroke logging.

References

Alamargot, D. & Chesnet, D. (2018). Eye and Pen User Manual. Available from https://eyeandpen.net/wp-content/uploads/sites/495/2020/02/EP3Manual_en.pdf.

Amar, R., & Stasko, J. (2013). Interactive visualization: Communication with data. John Wiley & Sons.

Anderson, B., Dahl, J., Holmqvist, K., Holšánová, J., Strömqvist, S., Tufvesson, S., & Wengelin Asa. (2006). Combining keystroke-logging with eye-tracking. In *Writing and digital media* (pp. 166–172). Elsevier. https://www.researchgate.net/publication/303496626.

Angelino, F., Baur, M., & Moreno, A.M. (2013). Keyboard dynamics for text entry biometrics. *Expert Systems with Applications*, *40*(4), 1391–1405.

Beattie, K., & Magnusson, M. (2007). Using keystroke logging to investigate aspects of writing fluency in L1 and L2 writers. *Applied Linguistics*, *28*(4), 633–657.

Bridwell, L.S., & Duin, A.H. (1985). Looking in-depth at writers: Computers as writing medium and research tool. In J.L. Collins & E.A. Sommers (Eds.), *Writing on-line* (pp. 115–121). Upper Montclair, NJ: Boynton/Cook.

Burns, A., Xiong, C., Franconeri, S., Cairo, A., & Mahyar, N. (2020). How to evaluate data visualizations across different levels of understanding. *IEEE Workshop on Evaluation and Beyond: Methodological Approaches to Visualization* (*BELIV*), 19–28. https://doi.org/10.1109/BELIV51497.2020.00010.

Caporossi, G., Leblay, C., & Usoof, H. (2020). *GenoGraphiX-Log version 2.0 User Guide*. Available from https://www.ggxlog.net/download/User%20Guide_20230130.pdf.

Cavaller, V. (2021). Dimensional Taxonomy of Data Visualization: A Proposal From Communication Sciences Tackling Complexity. *Frontiers in Research Metrics and Analytics*, *6*, 1–22. https://doi.org/10.3389/frma.2021.643533.

Christopulos, C., Dimitrakopoulos, A., & Magoulas, G. (2004). Keystroke dynamics in typing fluency discrimination. *Lecture Notes in Computer Science*, 3072, 1007–1016.

Cleveland, W.S. (1993). *Visualizing data.* Hobart Press.

CRITT (2024) Centre for Research and Innovation in Translation and Translation Technology, https://sites.google.com/site/centretranslationinnovation/home.

Elmqvist, N. & Fekete, J. (2010). 'Hierarchical Aggregation for Information Visualization: Overview, Techniques, and Design Guidelines', *IEEE Transactions on Visualization and Computer Graphics*, 16(3), 439–454.

Ericsson, K.A., & Delaney, P.F. (2011). How theories of expertise inform the design of optimal learning environments. *Educational Psychologist, 46*(1), 6–10.

Few, S. (2009). Now you see it: And endless improvement cycle for visualizing information. Information Design Press.

Garnefski, N., Koopman, P., & Komdeur, J. (2010). Measuring computer use with application logging. *Computers in Human Behavior, 26*(2), 339–348.

Gong, J., Xiang, X., Liao, J., Yang, J., & Xu, Y. (2004). Stylus interaction and its applications. In CHI '04 *Extended Abstracts on Human Factors in Computing Systems* (pp. 801–802). ACM.

Graesser, A.C., & McNamara, D.S. (2017). From Discourse Comprehension to Problem Solving: A Cognitive Psychology Approach. Psychology Press.

Granville, L.A., Murray, W.S., & Bates, D.M. (2009). Typing interface for people with dyslexia: Can improved feedback help?. In *Proceedings of the 12th International Conference on Computers Helping People with Special Needs* (pp. 542–549). Springer-Verlag.

Hinbarji, Z., Albatal, R., O'connor, N., & Gurrin, C. (2016). LoggerMan, A Comprehensive Logging and Visualization Tool to Capture Computer Usage. *International Conference on Multimedia Modeling*, 342–347. https://www.insight-centre.org.

Holmqvist, K., Lundström, M., Mathiassen, L., & Duchowski, A. (2011). Eye tracking in user experience research: A systematic review and meta-analysis of fixations, saccades, and scanpaths. *PLoS ONE*, *6*(12), e26855.

Jakobsen, A.L. (1999). Logging target text production with Translog. *Copenhagen studies in language*, (24), 9–20.

Jarvis, R., Ainley, J., & Murray, J. (2009). Metacognitive regulation in writing: A case-study approach. *Metacognition and Learning*, *4*(2), 127–150.

Kollberg, P., & Eklundh, K.S. (2002). Studying writers' revising patterns with S-notation analysis. *Contemporary tools and techniques for studying writing*, 89–104.

Leijten, M., & Van Waes, V.L. (2005). *Inputlog: A logging tool for the research of writing processes.* University of Antwerp, Department of Management, Faculty of Applied Economics.

Leijten, M., & Van Waes, L. (2013). Keystroke Logging in Writing Research: Using Inputlog to Analyze and Visualize Writing Processes. *Written Communication, 30*(3), 358–392. https://doi.org/10.1177/0741088313491692.

Liffick, B.W., & Yohe, L.K. (2001). Using Surveillance Software as an HCI Tool. *Information Systems Education Conference*. https://www.researchgate.net/publication/241351931.

Liu, Z., Luo, L., Liu, H., & Xu, Y. (2020). A review of eye-tracking research in L2 writing. *Reading in a Second Language, 53*(2), 242–273.

Miller, K.S., & Sullivan, K.P. (2013). *Computer Key-Stroke Logging and Writing*. John Benjamins Publishing Company.

Munzner, T. (2014). Visualization analysis and design. CRC Press.

Stromqvist, S., Karlsson, F., & Wengelin, A. (2006). Keystroke logging in writing research; Observing writing processes with Inputlog. *Research in Writing Processes, 19*(1), 1–37.

Sullivan, P., & Lindgren, E. (2008). Keystroke Logging: An Introduction. In K.S. Miller & K.P. Sullivan (Eds.), *Computer Key-Stroke Logging and Writing* (pp. 1–17). John Benjamins Publishing Company.

Vertega, P., Maguire, M., & Sundaresan, R. (2001). Modeling user focus with gaze location and velocity distributions. In *Proceedings of the SIGCHI Conference on Human Factors in Computing Systems* (pp. 205–212). ACM.

Wengelin, Å., & Johansson, V. (2023). Investigating Writing Processes with Keystroke Logging Theory, Research, and Practice. In *Digital Writing Technologies in Higher Education* (pp. 405–420). Springer International Publishing. https://doi.org/10.1007/978-3-031-36033-6.

Wengelin, A. (2009). Examining Pauses in Writing: Theory, Methods and Empirical Data. John Benjamins Publishing Company.

CHAPTER 4

Graph Models: What Do the Coloured Forms Tell Us about the Writing Process? From Numbers to Visual and Coloured Forms

Christophe Leblay, Hakim Usoof and Gilles Caporossi

What kind of writing is this chapter interested in? Mainly, as Fenoglio (2009) puts it, in *rumination writing*, as opposed to writing produced in a *single stride*. That is, the former is "recomposed several times before arriving at a stabilised product for a variety of reasons".

4.1 Variable-Focus Genesis

Taking the time of writing as the object of observation, we are entitled to wonder about the reality of temporal data in writing. This chapter attempts to provide some answers by taking as a prerequisite the distinction proposed by Lebrave (2008; 1998) between *visible* data and *legible* data; the former concerns data that can, in Lebrave's words, "only be the object of a descriptive commentary, an analysis or an interpretation", while the latter makes it possible to "make traces speak [...] by transforming them into a discourse in which [we] are the enunciator" (1998) [our translations]. In other words, legibility is concerned with description, classification or inventory, while visibility is concerned with interpretation, which in this work is called transcription and representation. Visibility concerns the manuscript, the readability of the draft.

4.2 On the Threshold of Visualisation

Grésillon's work (1994) on transcription methods, which has become a reference for anyone interested in genetics, dedicates over ten pages to the subject due to its predominant place in the genetic method. The first observation highlights the paradoxical search for the dimension of time, also known as the third dimension, in an eminently spatial universe—the page. The second observation relates to the futile search for transcription harmonisation. These remarks remain valid today.

 HTTPS://DOI.ORG/10.1163/9789004760264-005

Despite this, the principle set out by Grésillon in the same book (1994, 129), according to which "the aim of transcription is not perfection, but perfectibility" [our translation], remains more than relevant. Since the early 1970s, the work of the Flaubert, Proust and Joyce teams at ITEM (Institut des textes et manuscrits modernes) has made it possible to disseminate the transcriptions of working manuscripts.

Genetic criticism has clearly distanced itself from philological criticism over the last 30 years. It has refused to make value judgements and, therefore, to seek out the best texts among the various versions available.

Philology recognises the passage of time, but from the perspective of deterioration: manuscripts suffer losses as time goes by. This is unlike text genetics, where the passage of time does not result in a loss of quality, since textual quality often comes from the succession of versions of the same text.

ITEM's definition of text genetics is clear: (1) collect the material traces of the creative processes, (2) relate these traces to each other and to the works to which these processes have generally led, (3) arrange these traces in a chronological sequence that reflects the stages of the work's development, and (4) analyse these traces and interpret them as clues to the temporal and spatial course of the genesis to identify recurring elements and regularities or, on the contrary, singularities, ruptures.

In order to build on this early work, we propose a model that has already been well researched (Caporossi & Leblay, 2011, 2015; Leblay & Caporossi, 2014; Bécotte et al., 2019; Foucambert et al., 2022; Leblay et al., 2022), which does not break with the achievements of these pioneering works in process linguistics. On the contrary, the mathematical theory of graphs, used to model pairwise relations between objects, intersects ideally with the linguistic theory of process.

The focus of this chapter will be on the development of graph-based models and the ways in which they can be used.

4.3 Graph-Based Models

The goal of visualisation is to exhibit some properties that would be difficult to assess in a clear way (see Koponen, this volume, p. 19). In the case of the writing process, the main aspect is linearity. First, when writing with a word processor, the output, i.e. the text, is linear in essence. This means that it is a sequence of characters (jumping from one line to the next is managed by the software or handled through a special character that indicates the end of the line).

On the other hand, the process by the writer is linear from the chronological point of view. Indeed, the text is built by a sequence of keystrokes or mouse moves/clicks. That sequence is linear, as shows the nature of a classical logfile in which each action is associated with a line describing its nature and content. The complexity of the process comes from the fact that these linearities do not match. For instance, the writer may come back to the written text and insert some characters. It may also happen that some portions are deleted, which also breaks the coherence of the two linearities.

To visualise the process, various techniques may be considered, but the main two are the LS Graph model (Lindgren & Sullivan, 2002) and the S-notation (Kollberg, 1998).

To better illustrate the models, let us consider an example of a sentence that was constructed by a 7 phases sequence involving 40 keystrokes. The boldface characters correspond to edition between two phases, and the crossed-out characters are suppressed.

1. The mak
2. The ma~~k~~
3. The ma**n draws**
4. The **young** man draws
5. The ~~young man~~ draws
6. The **boy** draws
7. The boy draws **a line**

Before exposing graph models, let us illustrate this example with the well-known LS Graph and the S-notation.

4.3.1 *LS Graph*

In the case of the LS Graph model, statistics are computed all along the process and drawn as curves on a 2d-plot where the x-axis is associated with the sequence (either chronological or temporal) while the y-axis is associated with the statistics. These statistics are typically the total number of keystrokes, the number of characters in the text, the position of the cursor or other measures that may be of interest.

The main weakness of this model is that each position is not associated with a specific portion of the writing. Thus, at a time t, when an action is performed in the written text, as soon as some insertions or deletions have occurred, it may be difficult to identify what is being changed. The model allows for some high-level analysis, such as to see roughly where the text was changed or to see whether the writer applied some revision of the text, but detailed analysis is not possible.

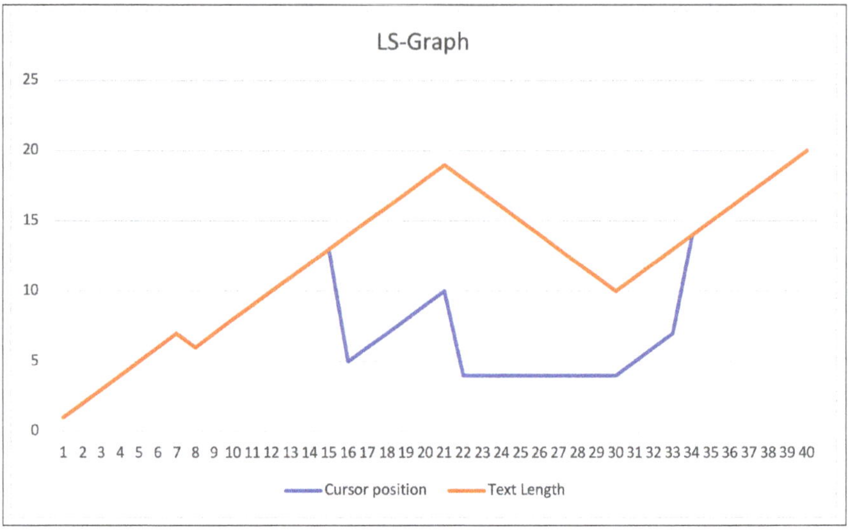

FIGURE 4.1 LS Graph associated to the toy example/problem/model

The LS Graph corresponding to this sequence is represented in Figure 4.1, where the x-axis represents the total number of keystrokes and the y-axis lines represent the cursor position and the text length.

4.3.2 *Progressive Visualisation*

To combine both the chronological and topographical dimensions, the so-called progressive visualisation was proposed as a tentative model (Becotte-boutin et al., 2019), wherein the x-axis is associated with topography and the chronology is represented by the y-axis (in that way, each keystroke is alone on one line). Unlike the LS Graph, in the progressive graph, the x-position of a keystroke is adjusted. For instance, an insertion before a given character leads to the last one being shifted, so that the x-position of an action allows the researcher to determine which part of the text was modified. Unfortunately, this model is not usable in practice since it requires huge space, except for with *toy examples*.

4.3.2.1 S-notation

Beside the LS Graph and its variants like the progressive graph, which are based upon chronology or temporality (x-axis), the S-notation provides a completely different approach to the edition presented by Kollberg (1998) and by Nilsson & Kollberg (1994). In this case, the edition of the text is the main focus while temporality or chronology is difficult to follow. S-notation provides a visualisation that looks like a text where no character is removed (deletions are represented by crossed characters); it implicitly associates the x-axis to topography while chronology is represented by ***hyperlinks***. Therefore, in essence, the S-notation is linear.

Using the S-notation transcription, the sequence would be represented as:

The $^{3}[^{2}\{\text{young }\}^{2}|_{3}\text{ma}^{1}[\text{k}]^{1}|_{1}\text{n}]\ ^{3}|_{4}{}^{4}\{\text{boy}\}^{4}$ draws$|_{2}$ a line

FIGURE 4.2 S-notation representation of the sequence

Indeed, we consider S-notation to be a graph that is unaware of itself. In the mathematical sense, a graph is a set of points called nodes that are eventually linked by arcs. These hyperlinks, or arcs, may be used to exhibit relations between portions of writing that remove constraints on the x-axis or the y-axis.

In Figure 4.2, portions of text or letters may be represented by nodes while references indicate movements, i.e., a rupture in the sequence that may be viewed as arcs with an implicit chronology indicated either by the position of the letter in the case of the raw text or by the numbering of the link between the subscript label to its corresponding superscript encapsuled in [] for deletions or {} for insertions. This hypertext model corresponds to a graph model where the position of the nodes is linear.

In Figure 4.3, we note that the linearity of the S-notation—which means that the letters or symbols are placed one after the other on a line—does not hold for the graph representation. Therefore, some implicit relations need to be explicitly stated. In this graph, red arrows represent topological relations, i.e., sequences that are next to the other on the S-notation representation, while arrows with numbers correspond to the hyperlinks indicated by the numbered labels. Arcs in blue show the portion of text that are removed during a deletion (corresponding to the content that is within [] in the S-notation).

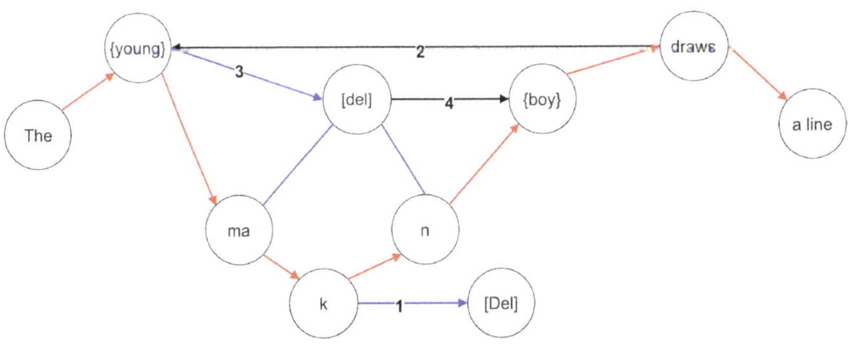

FIGURE 4.3 Graph associated with the S-notation model (based on Figure 4.1)

Apart from the S-notation graph, there are multiple ways to build graphs from keystroke logging data. In this chapter, we will present four of them based upon two principles: the so-called DNA models and lossless models. From each principle, variants may be designed: The atomic models have one node per keystroke while some nodes are merged in aggregated versions. In the case of the DNA model, an enhanced version is also presented where it is possible to identify all the successive versions of the text, which is not possible from the DNA models. Such a variant is not needed for the lossless aggregated model as it already has this property.

4.3.3 *Atomic DNA Graph Model*

The most straightforward way to build a graph to represent the process is to assign each keystroke to a node.

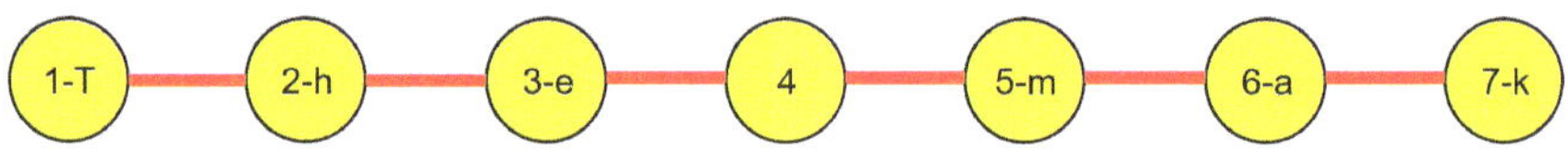

FIGURE 4.4 The atomic DNA graph after phase 1

When no editing is done, the graph simply represents the sequence of letters that appear in the text. The solid line indicates the chronological order of the keystrokes and, in this case, it is the same as the topographical order of the characters in the text.

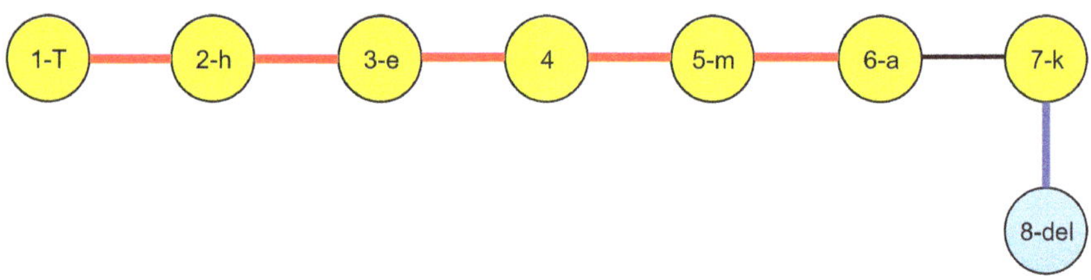

FIGURE 4.5 The atomic DNA graph after phase 2

The 8th keystroke is the deletion of the letter "k", which seems to be a typo. After that, the letter "k" is no longer visible and the topological sequence ends at the letter "a". The chronological and spatial representations will then be different. Node 8 corresponds to a deletion. Since addition or insertion and deletion are different in nature, it was decided that the visualisation should particularity stress this and the colour associated with deletion has to be different. Blue was chosen as the colour for deletion nodes.

Note also that the relation between nodes 8 (deletion) and 7 (the deleted character) is neither chronological nor topological. It was decided that the colour blue would be used to show this specificity. The arc between 6 and 7 does not represent a topological relation since 7 is now invisible. It was thus changed to the colour black.

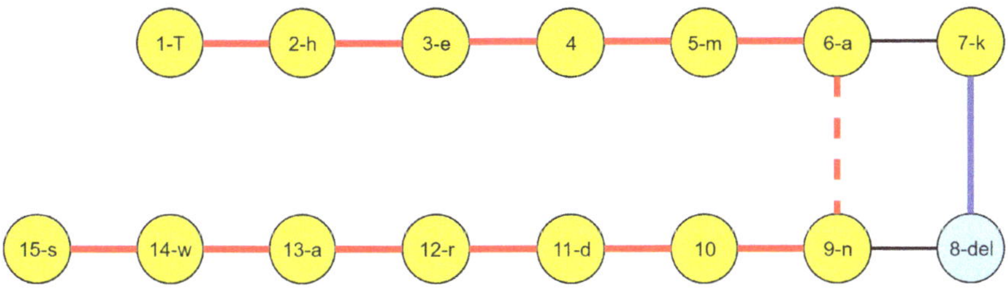

FIGURE 4.6 The atomic DNA graph after phase 3

Compared to phase 1 and 2, in phase 3, the text is again augmented by the addition of "n draws". There is a topological link between node 6 (letter "a") and node 9 (letter "n"), but these two nodes are not chronologically related. The corresponding arc is thus shown in red but dashed.

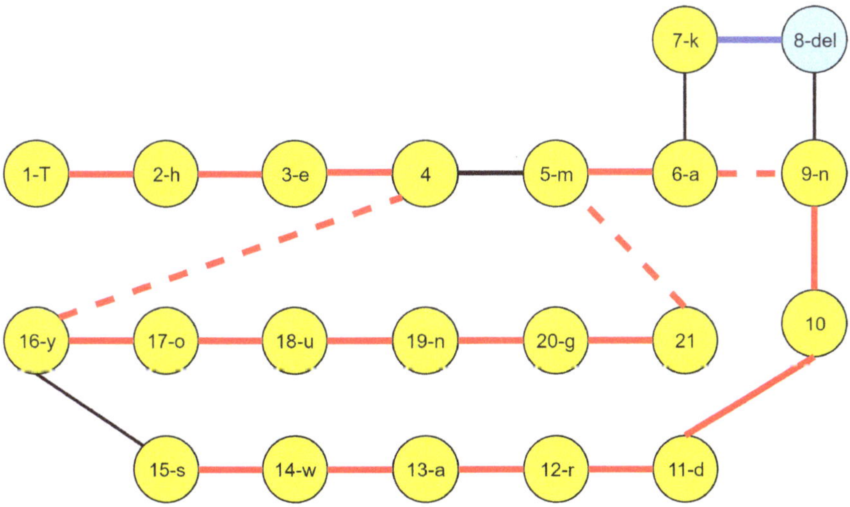

FIGURE 4.7 The atomic DNA graph after phase 4

In phase 4, the word “young” is inserted in the text between nodes 4 (space) and 5 (letter “m”). Chronologically, this insertion appears after the addition of the word “draws”. Like in the graph from phase 3, dashed red lines show the topological continuity, while the chronological order is still represented by solid lines.

Since the graph model does not provide any specific position for nodes, the drawing of the process may be done in various ways. We decided here to change the positions of some nodes so that the drawing is easier to read.

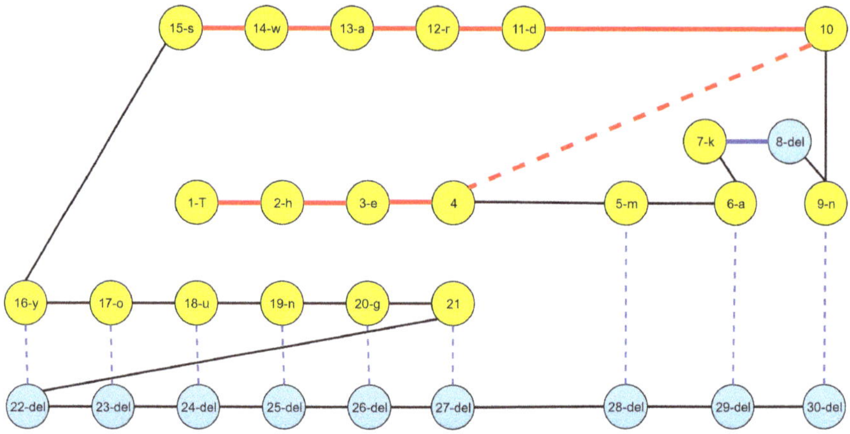

FIGURE 4.8 The atomic DNA graph after phase 5

Phase 5 consists of deleting portions of text; namely, the sequence “young man” was erased. As a consequence, the red arcs joining the corresponding letters are either switched to black (in the case they also correspond to chronological relations) or removed if they had no other function than displaying a topological relation. The arc between nodes 21 and 5 on the graph from phase 4 thus disappear in that of phase 5.

After phase 6, the erased sequence “young man” is replaced with “boy”. The new word is inserted on the topological sequence between nodes 4 and 10.

At the very end of the process, the graph has 40 nodes; the chronological order from 1 to 40 corresponds to the path drawn in solid lines (1-2, 2-3, …, 32-40).

The final text could be read by following the red line 1-2-3-4-31-32-33-10-11-12-13-14-15, which reads “The boy draws a line”.

Although this visualisation is easier to read than the original log, it remains a little difficult for the researcher because of the huge number of nodes. This

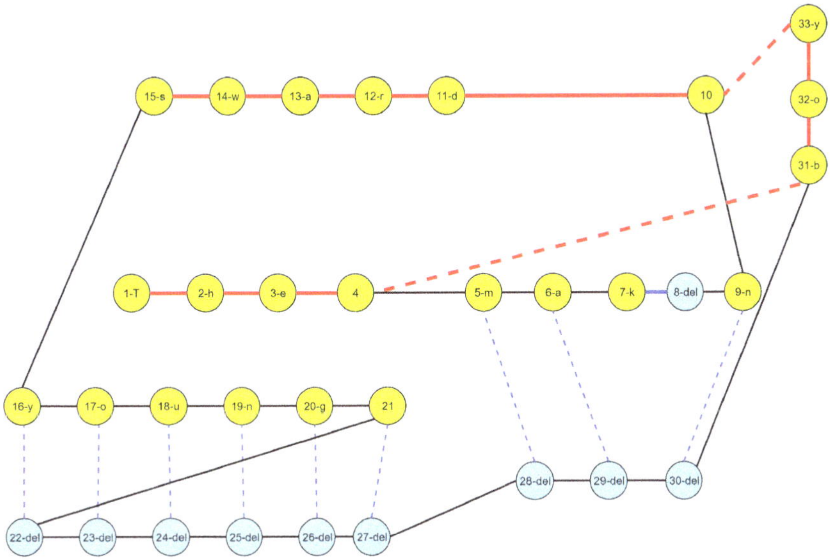

FIGURE 4.9 The atomic DNA graph after phase 6

sequence is typically smaller than any real recording. For comparison, 15 minutes of writing usually provides about 2000 to 3000 keystrokes, which would correspond to a large graph. If the graph is too large, the advantage of using a visualisation model vanishes.

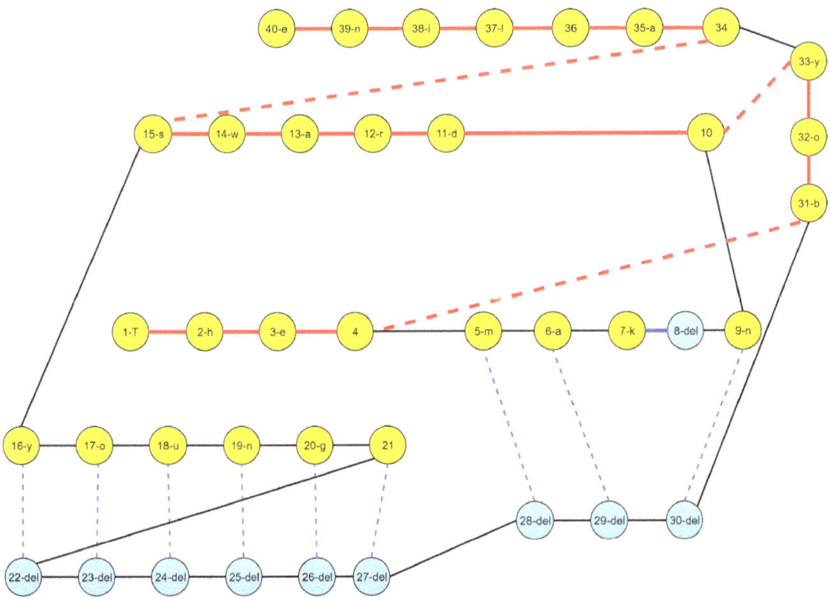

FIGURE 4.10 The atomic DNA graph after phase 7

4.3.4 *Aggregated DNA Graph Model*

To improve the readability of the graph, it is possible to merge nodes under certain circumstances.

A sequence of nodes may be merged if the following conditions are met:

- They are of the same nature, either addition/insertion or deletion.
- They occur chronologically in consecutive order.
- They are consecutive in space.
- They are additions/insertions that happen to be deleted and their deletion is consecutive.

In the case of the graph from the last phase of the atomic DNA model, the following nodes could be merged:

- (1-2-3-4), addition
- (5-6), deletion
- (7), addition
- (8), deletion of 7
- (9), addition to be deleted by 30
- (10-11-12-13-14-15), addition
- (16-17-18-19-20-21), addition to be deleted by 22-29
- (22-23-24-25-26-27-28-29-30), deletion
- (31-32-33), insertion
- (34,35,36,37,38,39,40), addition

The number of nodes then drops to 10 from 40. The rules for arcs are the same as for the previous model. Namely, by the nature of the merging conditions, two merged nodes A and B will be adjacent if and only if at least one node from A is adjacent to one node of B and the nature of the arc between A and B is the same as that of the arcs from nodes in A and nodes in B.

In Figure 4.15, it can be seen that node 8 consists of the deletion of nodes 2, 5 and 7. There is no special reason to split the deletion, but some graph models used previously were built using the rule that one deletion node is associated with exactly one corresponding addition/insertion node. The deletion would then be represented by 3 distinct nodes.

The aggregated DNA model is naturally much easier to follow and understand. Indeed, the number of nodes is quite restricted. Each addition of a sequence of characters will add at most one node, each insertion will add at most two nodes and each deletion will add at most three nodes, which is quite small given that the sequences of characters corresponding to each phase are generally much larger.

FIGURE 4.11 The aggregated DNA graph after phase 1

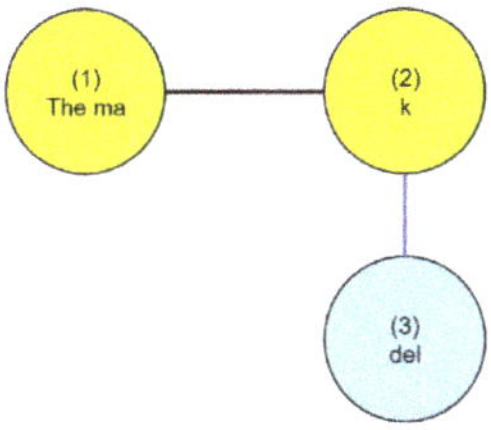

FIGURE 4.12 The aggregated DNA graph after phase 2

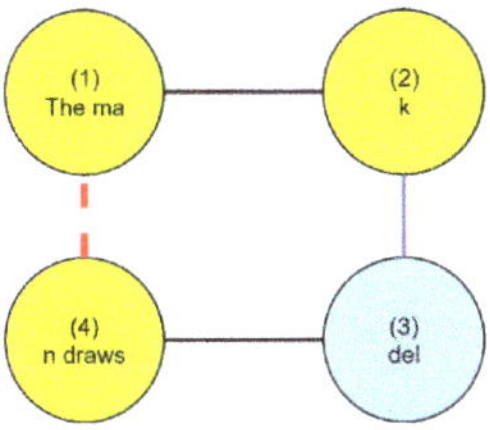

FIGURE 4.13 The aggregated DNA graph after phase 3

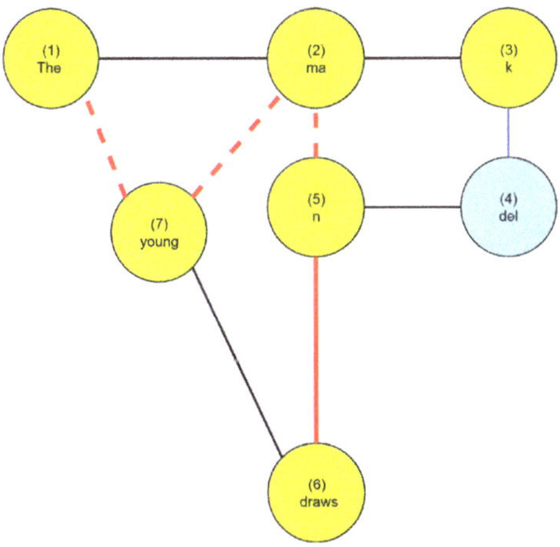

FIGURE 4.14 The aggregated DNA graph after phase 4

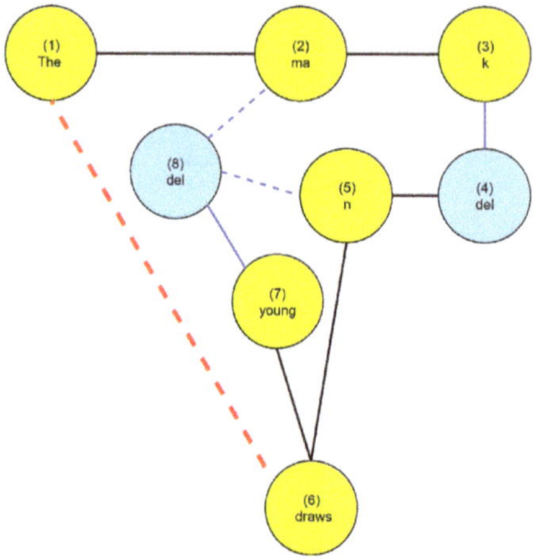

FIGURE 4.15
The aggregated DNA graph after phase 5

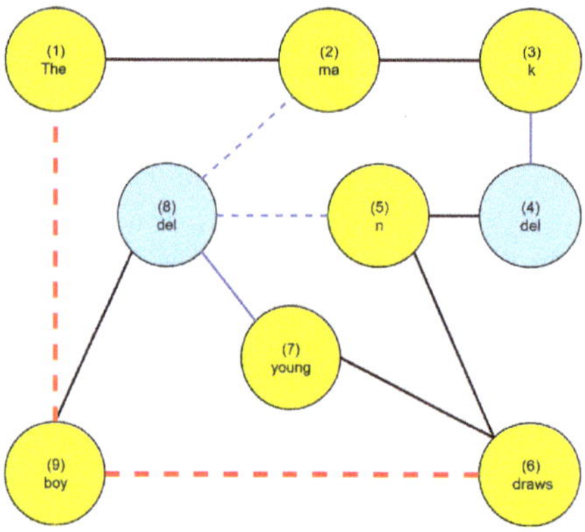

FIGURE 4.16
The aggregated DNA graph after phase 6

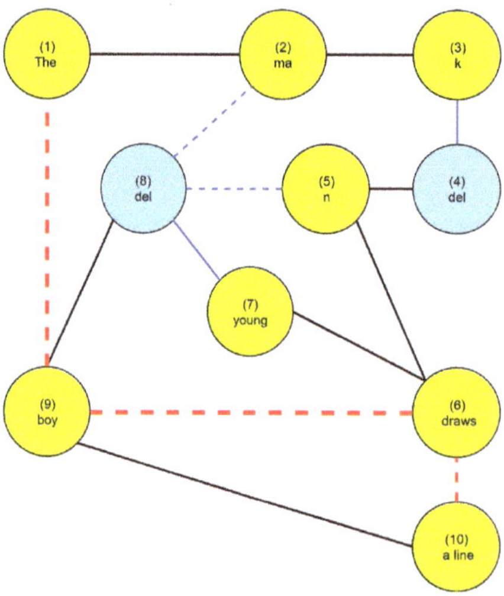

FIGURE 4.17
The aggregated DNA graph after phase 7

4.3.5 *Enhanced DNA Graph Model*

Even if the DNA model is helpful to identify portions of text that involved a deeper work, as soon as a character is deleted, its previous role will vanish. For instance, after phase 6, it is impossible to know where the word "young" was placed. Only the characters that appear in the final text may properly be analysed, and thus some information is lost with this model. It may, however, be enhanced by keeping a record of topographical arcs that used to exist. The enhanced aggregated DNA graph model is built in this manner.

4.3.6 *Atomic-Lossless Graph Model*

Should one want to be able to reconstruct all versions of the text during the process by only studying one single graph, another model is required to store the information lost by the DNA models, the so-called lossless models. The best way to build such a model is to use only additions of nodes and arcs and no removals. When the nodes are added by following their order, i.e., the number associated with each node corresponds to the number of the keystroke in the writing sequence. Also, if no node and no arc is deleted from the model, it will always be possible to reconstruct any previous version of the graph by just removing or not considering later nodes.

The rules to build such a graph are as follows:

- For any addition of character, identify the node corresponding to the last visible character before the insertion, say c. Then, find the following node on the lower boundary of the graph, say s. Add then connect the new character, say k, to c and to s by adding arcs (arrows) from c to k and from k to s.

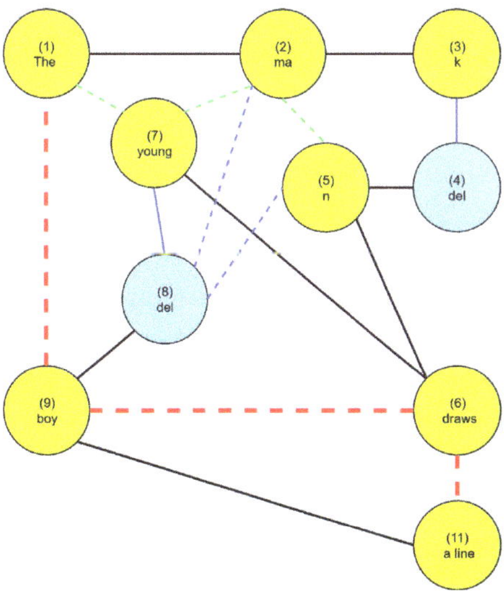

FIGURE 4.18 The final enhanced aggregated DNA graph

- Suppose a character c is now deleted. Consider the node corresponding to the character before c, say b, and the node after, say s. The new deletion node k will be added as well as arcs from b to k and from k to s.

To start the graph, one needs to initialize the empty document using two nodes: *start* (with number –1) and *end* (with number 0). Each keystroke is then added to the graph as a new node with its number. To read the text at any given time, for instance before keystroke *k*, one can simply start from node –1, then recursively move to the next node with the higher label smaller than *k*. The end of the text will therefore be at node 0. Should a character *c* be inserted between two nodes *a* and *b* (which may be –1 or 0), an arc between *a* and *c* as well as an arc between *c* and *b* are added, so that the node following *a* is *c* and the one after *c* is *b*. Another possibility is that the character from node *c* is deleted by keystroke *k*. In this case, the arcs from *a* to *k* and from *k* to *b* should be added so that the text after keystroke *k* will not have character *c* as it will be bypassed by *k*.

Lossless graph models are oriented in nature. We decided to explicitly draw the orientation, even if it is not strictly needed when drawn properly, i.e., by adding nodes outside the boundary of the graph representation. At each step, the boundary may be used to read the text. For instance, the last version of the text may be read by the sequence of nodes –1, 1, 2, 3, 4, 31, 32, 33, 22, 23, 24, 25, 26, 27, 28, 29, 30, 10, 11, 12, 13, 14, 15, 34, 35, 36, 37, 38, 39, 40, 8, 0. In this sequence, the nodes from 22 to 30 as well as node 8 are deletions that do not correspond to any added or inserted character in the text, but they indicate that some nodes should be skipped as they have been deleted. The final text thus reads "The boy draws a line".

Since the graph is built by outer additions on its shape, and because the process only consists of additions, it is possible to read the text at any stage. Suppose, for instance, that one wishes to read the version of the text just after the keystroke *k*. We just need to remove (or not consider) nodes numbered *k + 1* or more. Identifying the text, for instance, just after hitting keystroke 22 will be achieved by the following simple rule: From node –1, always go to the node with highest number not larger than *k* (here that is 22).

This leads to the sequence (1,2,3,4,22,17,18,19,20,21,5,6,9,10,11,12,13,14,15,8) that reads "The young man draws". This model is lossless because, unlike the DNA model, it is possible to characterize each step of the whole process by using one single graph. Note, however, that the numbering of the nodes is then important and the start node (–1) as well as the end node (0) are also important to be able to use one single rule to build any version of the text.

4.3.7 *Aggregated Lossless Graph Model*

Like the original model, it may be condensed by using the following rules:

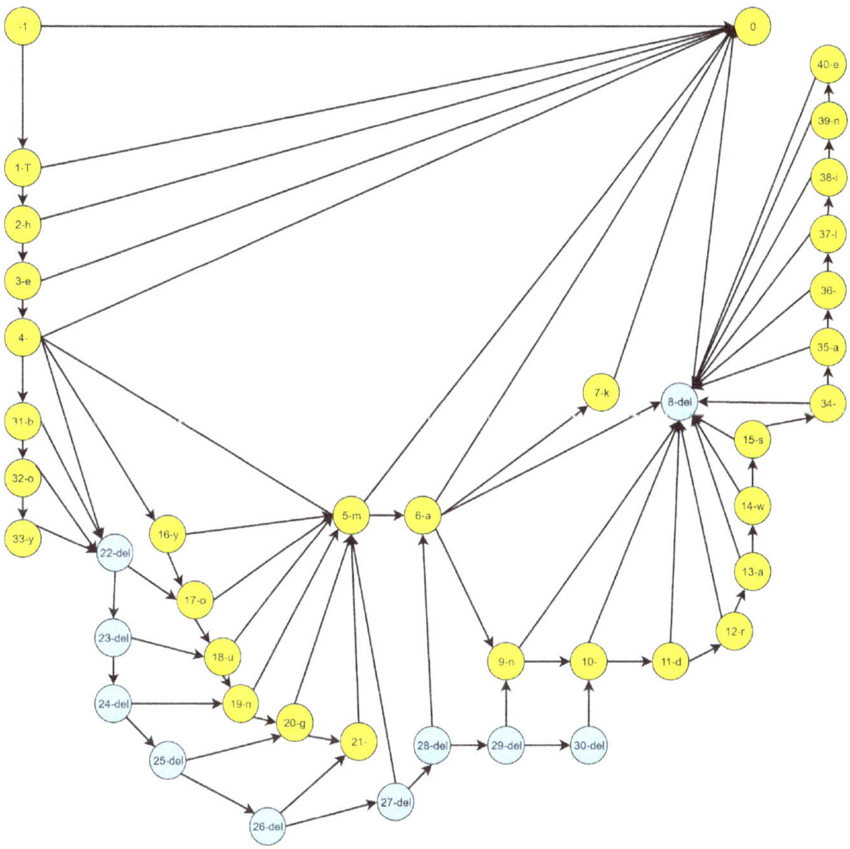

FIGURE 4.19 The atomic lossless graph

- Two addition/insertion nodes may be merged if they are consecutive (by their numbers), adjacent, have the same neighbour, and either none of them was later deleted or they were deleted consecutively (by consecutive deletion keystrokes).
- Two deletion nodes may be merged if they are adjacent and their corresponding deleted nodes are adjacent and consecutive.

Because of the lossless property, some merges may not be the same in this model as the DNA model. Namely, as there are some constraints to ensure reconstruction, it may happen that some nodes are merged in the DNA model but cannot be in the lossless model. It is therefore to be expected that the residual number of nodes will be larger in the aggregated lossless model in the aggregated DNA model.

> (1, 2, 3, 4)-(5, 6)-(7)-(8)-(9)-(10, 11, 12, 13, 14, 15)-(16, 17, 18, 19, 20, 21)-(22, 23, 24, 25, 26, 27)-(28, 29)-(30)-(31, 32, 33)-(34, 35, 36, 37, 38, 39)

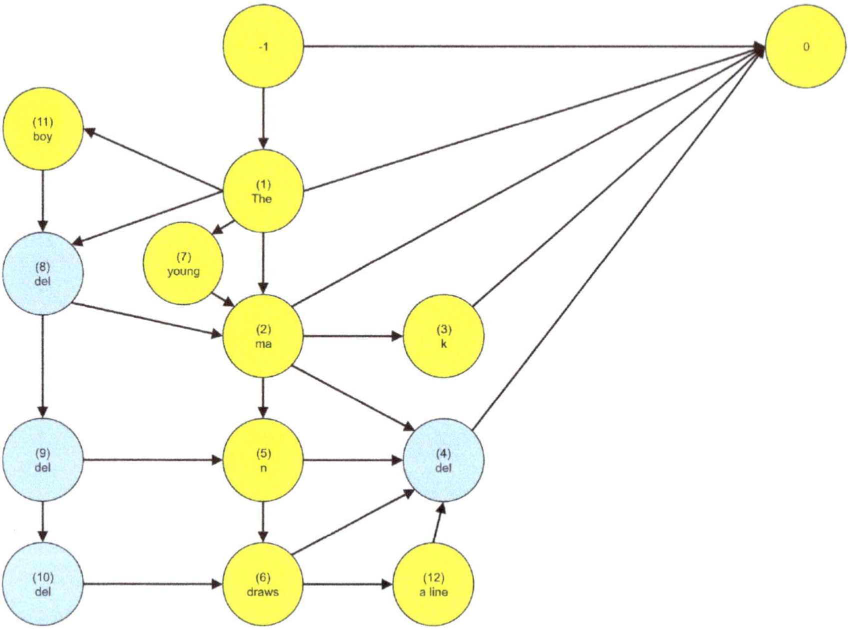

FIGURE 4.20 The aggregated lossless graph

Although this model is certainly much easier to read, it is no more additive, which means that it may only be built after the whole process is complete. That is, it should be constructed after the complete lossless graph is constructed.

4.4 Analysing the Evolution of the Text and Identifying Revision Campaigns

Recall that the final text is drawn from the oriented graph by always following the path using the largest number accessible at any time, which corresponds to the exterior path. For the lossless atomic model in Figure 4.19, that sequence is 1,2,3,4,31,32,33,22,23,24,25,26,27,28,29,30,10,11,12,13,14,15,34,35,36,37,38,39,40,8. If we remove deletion nodes from that sequence, it becomes 1,2,3,4,31,32,33, 10,11,12,13,14,15,34,35,36,37,38,39,40.

Let us now consider an intermediate version. For instance, what was the text just before keystroke 23 occurred, when the character "o" from "young" was deleted? The text would then read "The yung man draws", and it is represented by the sequence 1,2,3,4,22,17,18,19,20,21,5, 6,9,10,11,12,13,14,15,8.

It is possible, by looking at the final graph to find some *revision campaigns*, which is when the author goes through the existing text to correct or adjust it. In the case of the DNA model, since the deleted nodes are no longer attached to any sequence, they cannot be considered. The technique therefore relies only on the remaining text whose creation is described by the sequence of nodes it contains. The proposed technique consists of finding a series of nodes in increasing order that appear in the final text and cover the whole text by these series.

In our example, the final text consists of the keystrokes 1,2,3,4,31,32,33,10,11, 12,13,14,15.

The sequence may be covered by two series of increasing numbers, shown below:

> **1,2,3,4,31,32,33,10,11,12,13,14,15**
> C1 = {**1,2,3,4,10,11,12,13,14,15**}, and an insertion that occurred later:
> C2 = {31,32,33}

In the same way as in the compact DNA model, it is possible to analyse the successive modifications and identify *revision campaigns* with the lossless model in a more precise way, as deleted sequences are also considered. Every alteration of the text is considered whether it is kept or not.

The campaign analysis algorithm may be described as follows:

- Set the number of campaigns c = 1.
- Set the current node k = 1 and the first keystroke of the campaign as 1.

As long as *k* is less than the number of keystrokes, do the following:

- If there exists an oriented path from k to k + 1 only using nodes with labels less than or equal to k, change k to k + 1, and repeat.
- If such a path does not exist, it is because another campaign was used with moves to the previous position in the text.

We will then start the next campaign, and note the first keystroke of that new campaign, *k*.

Applying this algorithm to the graph from Figure 4.19, one gets:

- C1 = {1,2,3,4,5,6,7}
- C2 = {8}
- C3 = {9,10,11,12,13,14,15}
- C4 = {16,17,18,19,20,21}
- C5 = {22,23,24,25,26,27,28,29,30}
- C6 = {31,32,33,34,35,36,37,38,39,40}, which is illustrated in the following figure (arcs that are not related to campaigns are omitted to improve readability)

A simple way to represent the succession of campaigns is that, during a campaign, the position of the cursor always goes to an increasing position. A new campaign starts as soon as the cursor moves backward.

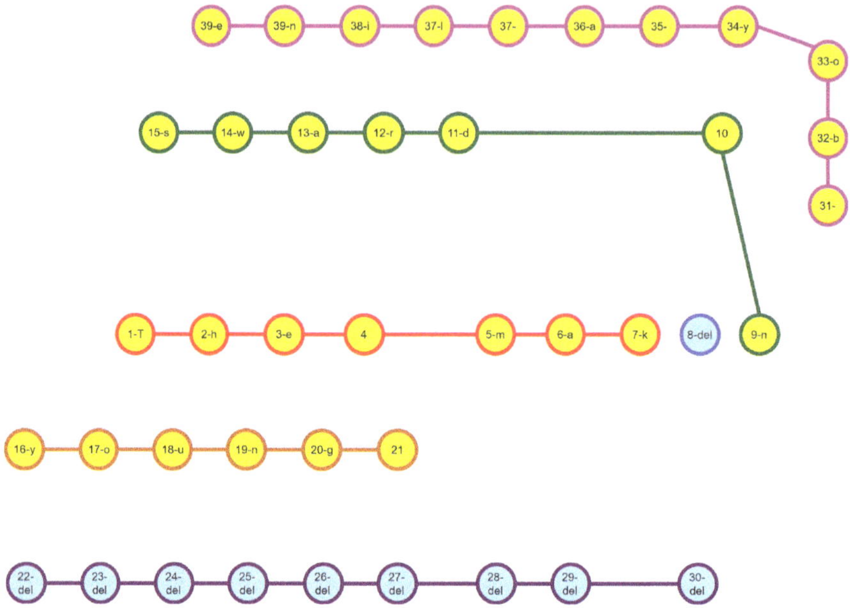

FIGURE 4.21 Decomposition of the process in revision campaigns

It can be noted that, using the lossless model, six campaigns are found while only two were detected when analysing the DNA model. First, we realize that keystroke 1,2,3,4,5,6 and 11,12,13,14,15 are considered as a single campaign in the DNA model because some portion of work is simply not considered.

From these models, the aggregated DNA model is the best compromise as it is easy to read yet informative enough. It was therefore more commonly used in practice and often adapted or improved. For instance, extra nodes may be used to represent pauses and the original basic operations may be improved to handle more complex transformations of the text, such as moving a portion of the text or replacement. This last version is used in the GenoGraphiX-Log 2.0 system described in the following section.

4.5 Use of Graph Models

In this section, several writing session graph examples are explored, which closely examine tangible instances of writing logs using graphs. The graph model we use in this section is based on the current model given in GenoGraphi-X 2.0 (Usoof, Leblay & Caporossi, 2020). This provides an opportunity for a more profound comprehension of the methodologies that form the foundation of the application of the graph model for studying writing. Moreover, it serves as a platform to showcase the information that can be easily identified from a graphical model. The primary focus will be highlighting useful information, patterns and key writing processes that can be achieved through the application of graph models.

4.5.1 *Definitions Used in the Graph Model Example*

Prior to delving into the graph representation of writing sessions, we define a set of operations in addition to the operations defined in the previous two sections. First, we define pauses. In writing research and keystroke logging, we identified four distinct categories of pauses—psychomotor, cognitive, strategic and technical. *Psychomotor* pauses are defined as brief interruptions in the physical activity of writing caused by the need for motor adjustments, such as finger movements, key transitions or hand repositioning. These pauses reflect the mechanical execution of writing tasks rather than cognitive activities like planning or problem-solving. They are typically shorter in duration than cognitive pauses and occur naturally due to the physical requirements of typing or handwriting. *Cognitive* pauses are defined as pauses that occur when the writer stops to think, plan or solve a problem during the writing process. They are often longer than psychomotor pauses and can indicate decision-making, language retrieval or composing strategies. Pausing to choose the next word, structure a sentence or plan a paragraph are examples of the same. *Strategic* pauses are defined as pauses taken by the writer to revise, re-read or reflect on the written text. Strategic pauses are more deliberate and often related to editing or re-evaluating the work. Pausing to review a paragraph and revise wording or punctuation are examples of strategic pauses. *Technical* pauses are defined as pauses that occur due to technical or external interruptions, such as dealing with software issues, system delays or non-writing-related distractions. For example, pausing due to a computer lag or checking a reference in another document are considered technical pauses (Alves & Limpo, 2015; Van Waes et al., 2010). Second, we define the process of displacing a text, which is the process of moving a portion of text from one location of the document to another; in colloquial terms, a cut-and-paste operation. Third, we define the process of copying text. This refers to the process of copying a portion of the text from one location of the document to another, commonly referred to and copy-and-paste (Christianson et. al, 2005; Van Waes et. al, 2010; Lijten & Van Waes, 2013). Furthermore, we also clearly distinguish between the processes of adding text at the extreme end of the existing writing as append and in the middle or beginning of the text as insert (Van Waes et al., 2010; Chenoweth & Hayes, 2001).

The specific implementation of the graph model utilized for the study of writing involves distinct components that require preliminary definitions that also includes colour coding. It is essential to outline the key elements of the graph, which consist of nodes and arcs, as explained earlier. A breakdown of the nodes and arcs are given below to help the reader comprehend the visual examples and the corresponding terminology. First, nodes are categorized into the following groups:

- **Append (red)**: a node that contains text added at the end of the existing content
- **Insert (pink)**: a node that contains text added somewhere in the middle of the existing content
- **Removed (yellow)**: a node that contains text that was typed but was deleted and not included in the final text (such a node is required to keep track of the chronological order of typed text)
- **Delete (blue)**: a node that contains text that was deleted (such a node is needed to keep track of when the deletion occurred as well as the order of the removal of characters)
- **Pause (green)**: a node that contains the duration of a cognitive pause; if a pause duration exceeds a specified threshold, it is considered a cognitive pause
- **Copy (brown)**: a node that contains text that was copied and pasted in the text
- **Displaced (orange)**: a node that contains text that was cut and pasted in the text

Second, arcs or edges—which serve to point to connections between nodes and their colour coding and pattern—focus on the relationships between nodes. These arcs can be organised into three distinct categories:

- **Chronology arc (black continuous)**: indicates the chronological order of events (nodes) during the text development
- **Final text arc (red dashed arrow)**: indicates the flow of the construction of the final text
- **Deletion arc (blue dashed)**: indicates the connection between the removed text and the delete node

In addition to the above definitions of colours and patterns for nodes and arcs, we also define the visual parameter "radius of a node". The radius of a node is directly proportionate to the number of characters inside it. For example, if 25 characters were inserted during a writing event and 5 characters were deleted in another event, the insert node would be proportionately larger than the delete node.

The graphical depiction under consideration serves as a visual representation encompassing both the written content and the complex dynamics of the writing process. This affords a macroscopic interpretation, enabling a comprehensive assessment of the entirety of the written work, alongside a microscopic scrutiny that facilitates the clear comprehension of specific events from perspectives such as writing process, revisions or cognition (Lindgren et al., 2019). Beyond the primary graphical representation, a comprehensive analysis of diverse matrices derived from graph-related parameters holds the potential to yield additional insights by selectively isolating patterns inherent in the writing.

4.5.2 *Macroscopic View of Graphs*

An initial macroscopic examination of the graph—devoid of specific node analysis and devoid of examination of node types distinguished by colour and content—serves to differentiate whether the writing process is predominantly linear or exhibits a more dynamic and iterative processes. These observations provide insights into potential scenarios, including the writer's predisposition for pre-planned compositional tasks, engagement in copying text, execution of a simplistic or rudimentary writing task, involvement in a complex cognitive process during writing, continuous revision, development of a sophisticated textual structure or simply the manifestation of frequent errors.

A comprehensive analysis of the graph of a writing session involves considering node types, arcs and their spatial arrangement. For instance, when examining Figures 4.22 and 4.23, one can observe a notable prevalence of yellow nodes (indicating removed text) and blue nodes (representing delete actions) distributed evenly across the writing process. This pattern may suggest that the writer is consistently engaged in revision or may be prone to typing errors. Furthermore, the size of the nodes' radius could potentially signify that the writer produces substantial portions of text in a continuous manner, suggesting an inclination for developing extended text without encountering errors or engaging in any revision operations.

4.5.3 *Microscopic View of Graphs*

A closer examination at the microscopic level allows for a thorough understanding of specific events through the utilization of graphs. To illustrate, consider Figure 4.23, where indications suggest that the writer, in the act of composing, maybe concurrently be contemplating the most effective way to convey their idea. This inference might be supported by the alteration from "be an appended" to "contains appended, inserted, …"—signifying a shift in the writer's objective and presentation. In terms of writing methodology, this may imply that the writer tends to think spontaneously while writing, rather than meticulously planning each section beforehand. To gain deeper insights into this potential writing process, the incorporation of pause nodes within

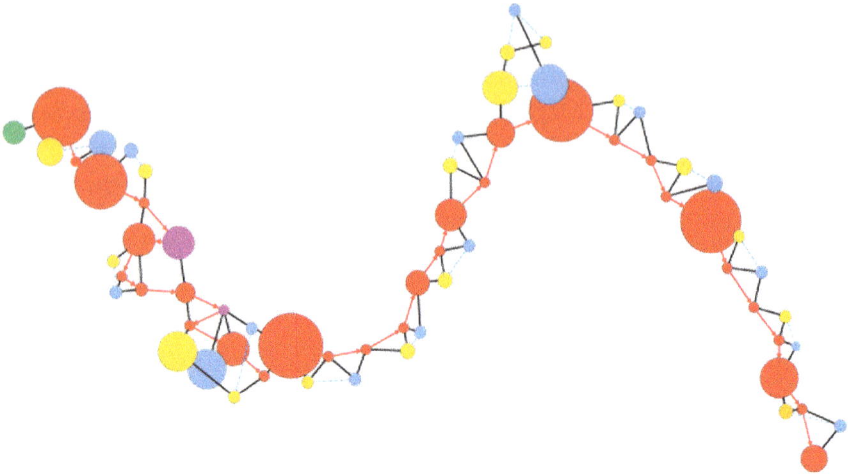

FIGURE 4.22 Graph of a linear writing process, with few inserts and frequent deletes

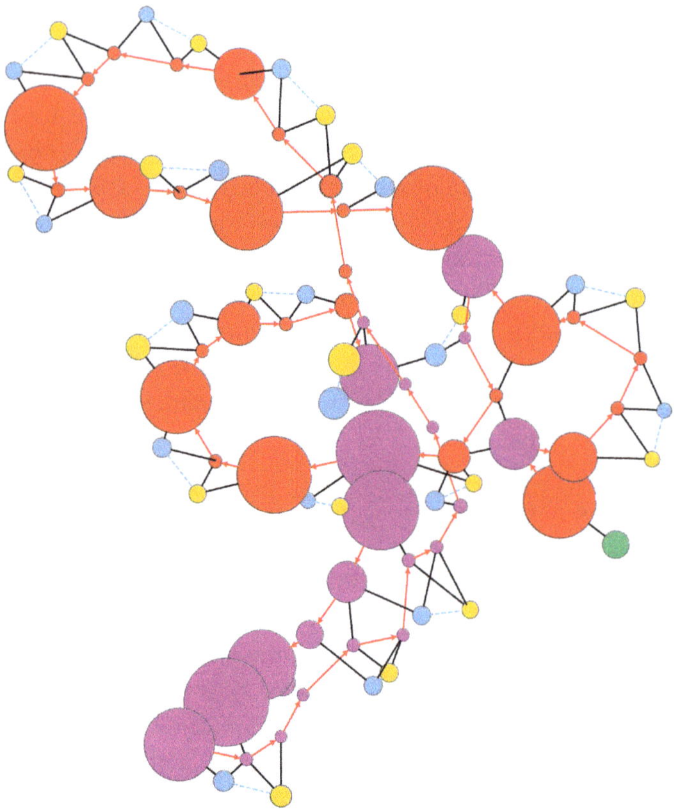

FIGURE 4.23 Graph of a complex writing process, with many inserts and the writer moving back and forth within the text and frequent deletes

the same graph, as depicted in Figure 4.24, holds promise for providing additional clarifications and understanding.

The next microscopic example is presented in Figure 4.26. This visualisation clearly illustrates the process where the writer types "The graph consists on" and then revises it as "A mathematical graph consists of". The deletions and insertions are easily comprehendible with very limited effort required.

An additional illustration of specific operations the writer might have undertaken can be understood from the following examples. In Figure 4.27, there is a deletion where the writer removes the phrase "in the writing". The blue delete node contains the text "gnitirw eht ni", indicating that the writer

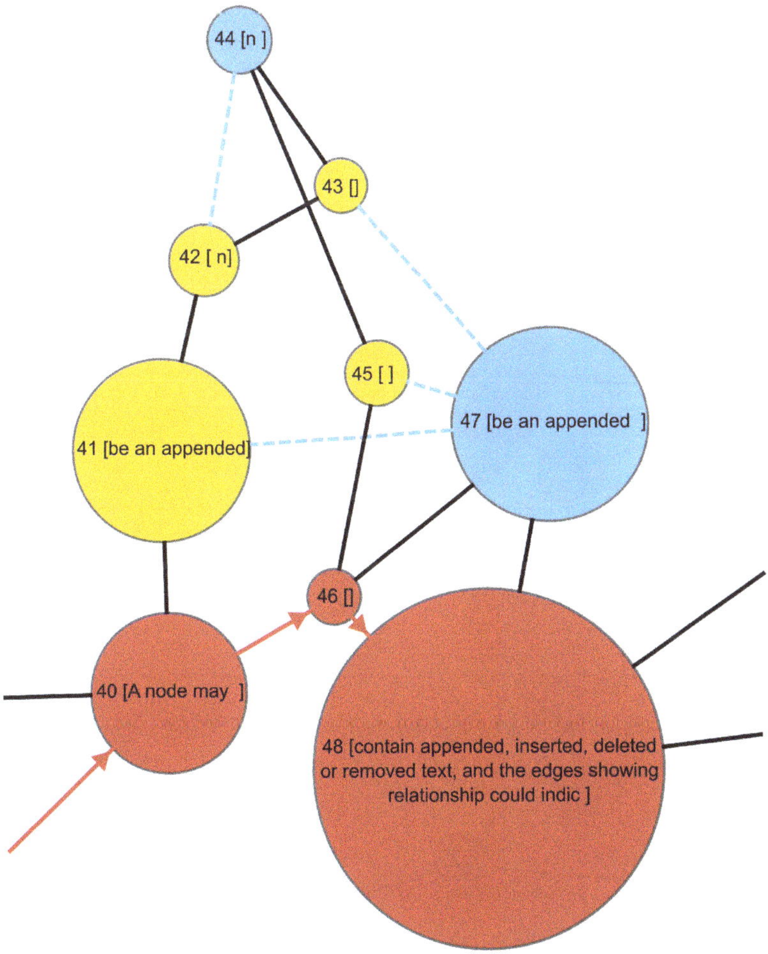

FIGURE 4.24 Graph depicting an edit, the revision of a text with a delete and a reconstitution of the presentation

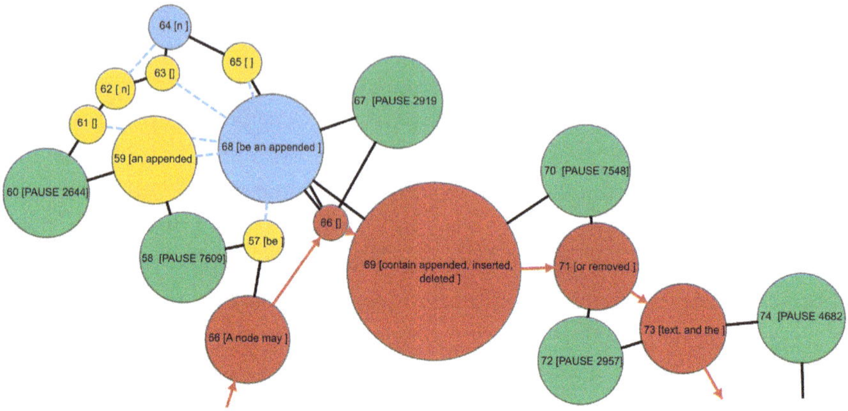

FIGURE 4.25 Graph depicting the same edit as Figure 4.24, but with the inclusion of pause nodes that are greater than a certain threshold (e.g., > 2000ms)

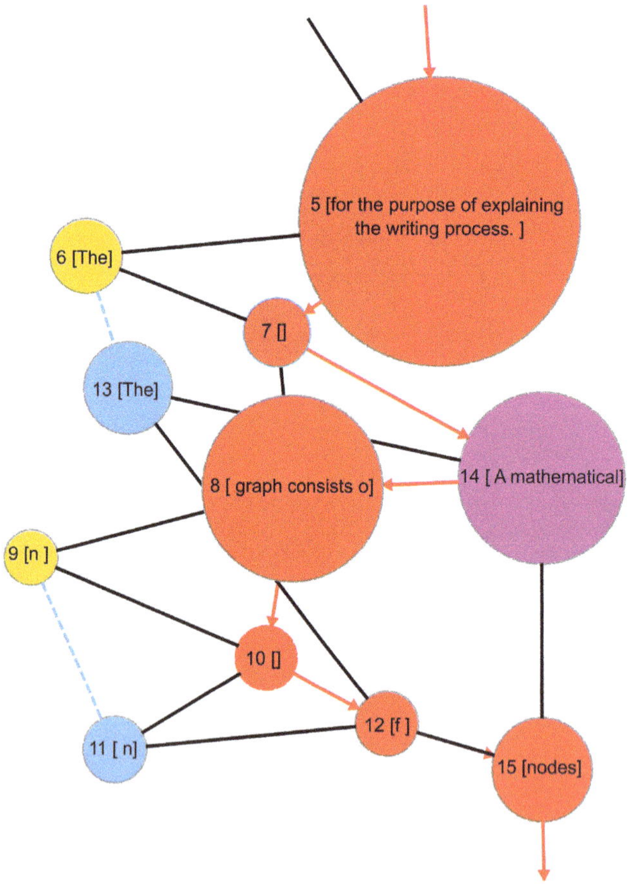

FIGURE 4.26 Graph illustration of an insertion event

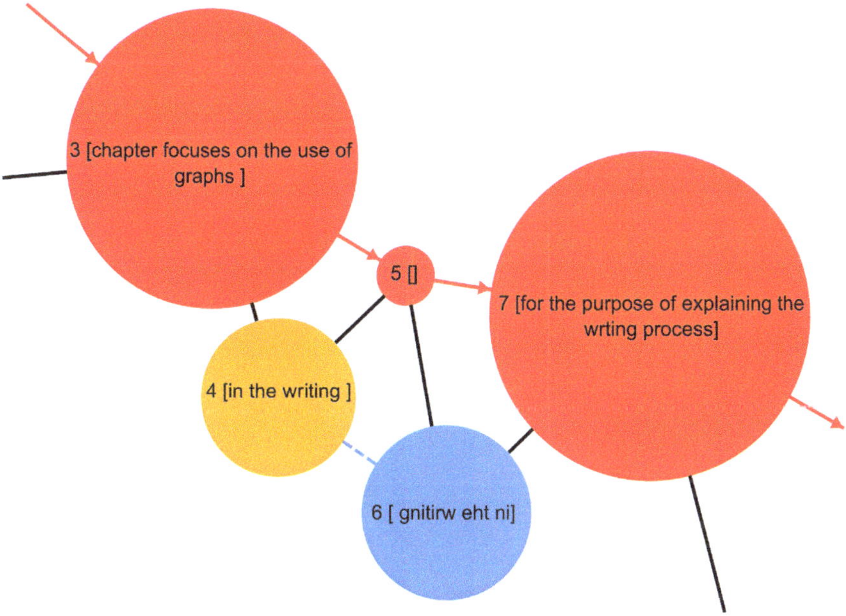

FIGURE 4.27 Graph representation of the use of the Backspace key for deletion

likely employed the Backspace key for this deletion. Moving on to Figure 4.28, another deletion occurs where the writer eliminates the phrase ", typically with text". The corresponding delete node mirrors this text precisely. This similarity suggests that the writer may have either highlighted the text with the mouse or Shift + Arrow keys, followed by overwriting with text or deleting it using the Delete or Backspace key. Alternatively, this may imply a continuous use of the Delete key for the entirety of the text removal. These instances shed light on the writer's specific actions during the editing process. A reference to this event in the raw keystroke log data would help identify exactly which sequence of operations was performed.

4.5.4 *Analysis and Secondary Visualisations of Graphs*

A macroscopic or microscopic analysis is possible even if the graph becomes highly complex, with many nodes and complex relationships indicated by arcs. The immediate identifications of unique events and overall patterns, however, may be challenging and time consuming. In such scenarios, it is possible to conduct an analysis of the graph. This analysis may include counts, averages, ratios, percentages and further specific visualisations to help identify key patterns in the larger graph. To illustrate some of these analyses, we refer to graph visualisations of four second language (L2) writers, two of whom are novice (Amelia and Brian) and the other two are proficient (Clair and Dave).

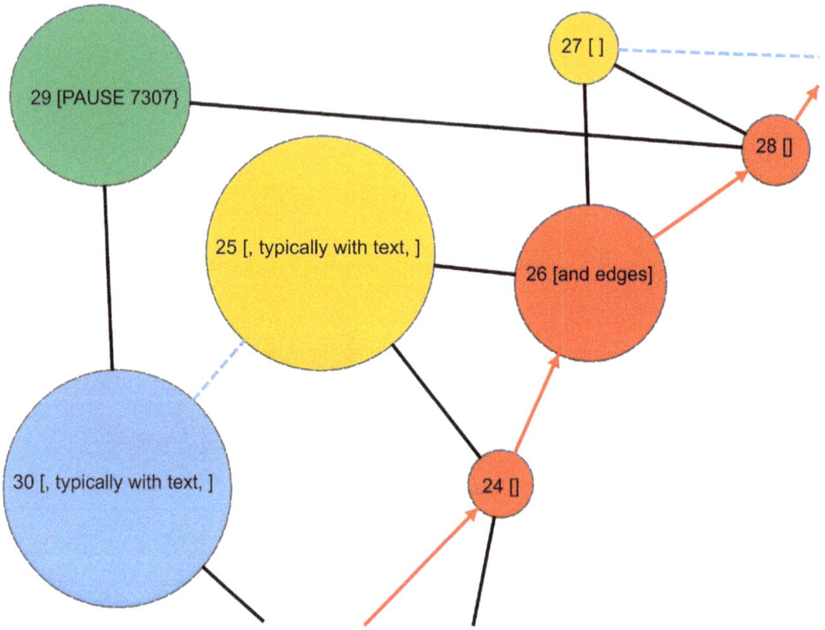

FIGURE 4.28 Graph representation of the use of either a highlight and deletion or a deletion using the Delete key

Secondary visual representations can be generated by using the time or node number as one of the axes and examining the corresponding distribution of node types. The distribution of nodes can be presented as a percentage or cumulatively. The depiction of time and nodes may either be continuous or organized in blocks, such as per minute, every 5 minutes, every 5 nodes or every 20 nodes. The choice of granularity depends on the specific requirements, duration of the writing session or complexity of the primary graph. However, doing this provides a chronological dimension to the visualisation. Furthermore, in the examination of writing processes, a pivotal consideration is the scrutiny of edits, primarily encompassing insertions and deletions. A comprehensive analysis involves plotting the distribution of insertion and deletion nodes over time, complemented by additional data, such as the character count (captured through for example the radius of the circles) and the spatial distance between the last writing action within the text and the location of the edit (captured through the lightness or darkness of the respective colour indicating whether the edit is closer to the last position of writing or further away, respectively). This multifaceted distribution has the potential to unveil valuable insights into the writer's behaviour. Figures 4.29 and 4.30 serve as examples to illustrate these secondary visualisations, where the distribution of insert nodes and deletion nodes are highlighted.

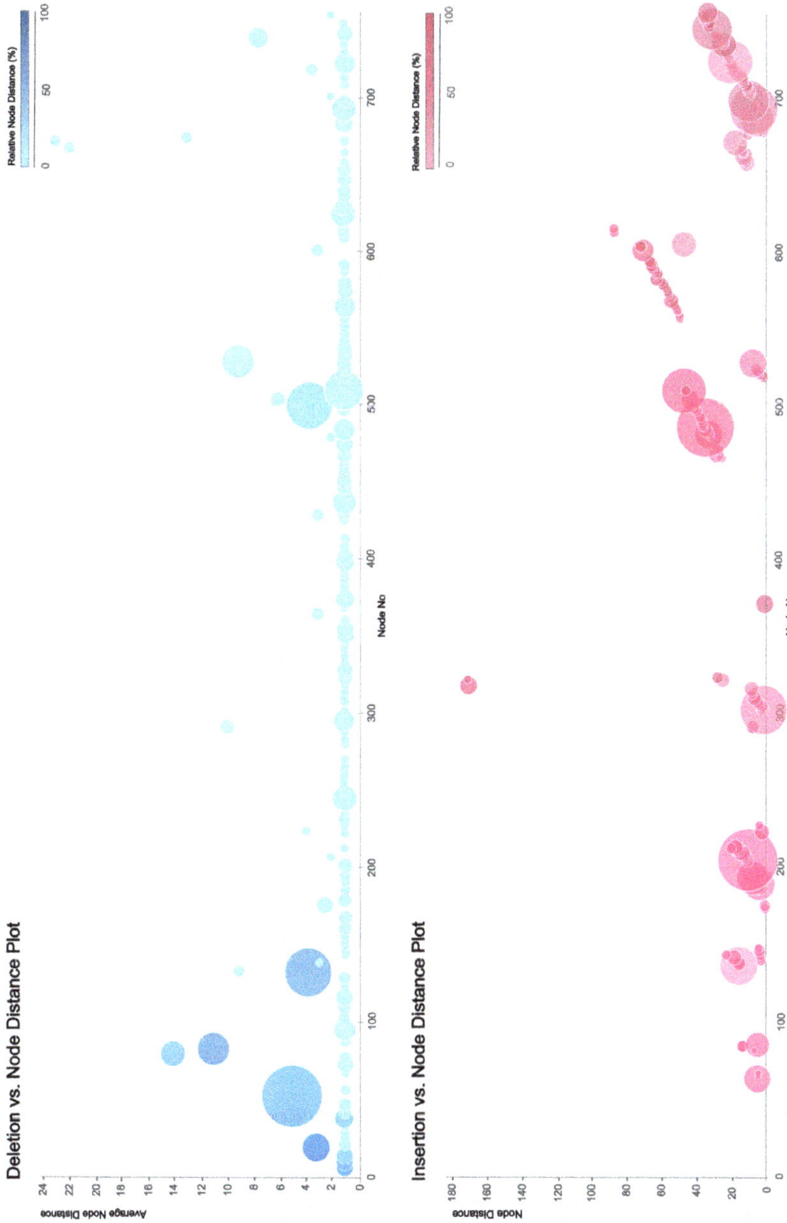

FIGURE 4.29 Edit distribution of Amelia (novice writer)

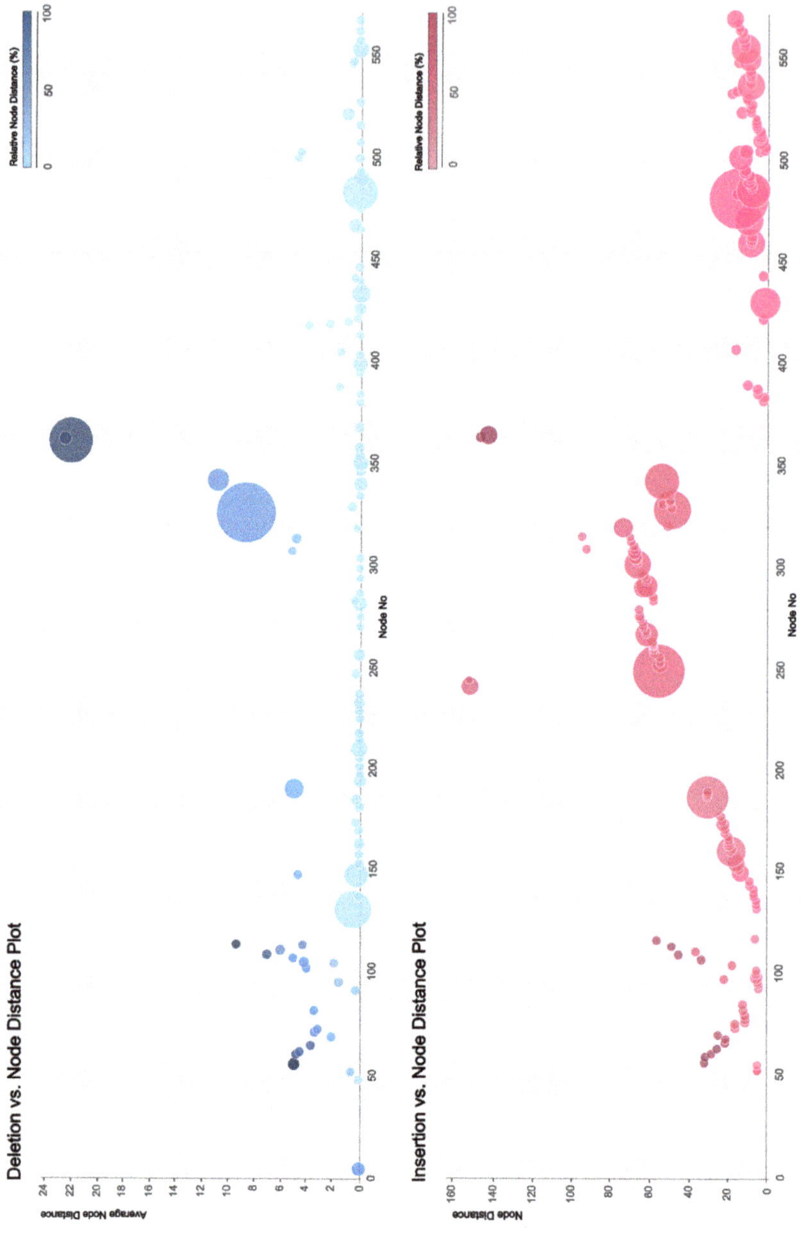

FIGURE 4.30 Edit distribution of Clair (proficient writer)

The examination of such a distribution can provide important information about the writer's habits, including the frequency of text revisions or typos, whether the writer engages in frequent editing tasks, navigates through the text repeatedly or opts to edit once the core of the text is complete. Furthermore, this analysis can shed light on the scale of the edits, distinguishing between substantial modifications and minor adjustments. By exploring these facets of the editing process, a richer understanding of the writer's approach and patterns emerges, contributing significantly to the study of writing dynamics.

Further information in Figures 4.29 and 4.30 illustrates the distribution of edits for Amelia, a novice L2 writer, and Clair, a proficient L2 writer, respectively. These visualisations reveal distinct differences in the deletion distribution in terms of both frequency and relative node distance between the two groups. Similarly, a notable contrast is observed in the frequency and relative node distance of insertions between Amelia and Clair. Additionally, the insertions tend to be longer in character length and occur at a greater distance from the preceding writing event for Clair. These findings may imply that there exist distinct editing patterns between novice and proficient writers in their second language composition.

As mentioned before, the secondary analysis of the graphs may include numerical values as well. For example, Table 3.1 and Table 3.2 provide a comparison of selected graph parameters, the distribution of different types of graph nodes and characters among four instances of writing. A noticeable disparity emerges in the nodes per minute, indicating a lower frequency for expert writers compared to novices. This discrepancy may stem from novice writers engaging in more frequent editing activities, including deletions and insertions, typing errors and misspellings as well as pausing frequently. This phenomenon is particularly evident in the average node length for append nodes, suggesting that novice writers tend to input fewer characters between editing and pausing. Conversely, proficient writers undertake more extensive writing tasks, resulting in fewer nodes with a higher character count per node. Moreover, it may be inferred that edits performed by proficient writers are relatively more substantial in size (character count).

In the above writing examples, graphs, secondary analysis and visualisations help identify findings that provide insights into the distinctive writing behaviours and patterns exhibited by novice and proficient writers. This, in turn, provides valuable insights into their respective cognitive processes and skill levels in second language composition.

In the broader context, diverse categories of writers, their distinct approaches to writing, cognitive methodologies and the exploration of various writing tasks—including but not limited to descriptive, narrative, expository and argumentative (Richard and Schmidt, 2010), copy tasks (Olive, 2024), translation and creative writing (Lindgren et. al, 2019)—can be discerned through the identification of patterns within the primary graph or through secondary analyses and visualisations derived from the graph. This comprehensive examination enables a deep understanding of the diverse aspects encompassing writers, their writing strategies and the intricate cognitive processes involved across different literary genres and writing tasks.

TABLE 4.1 Graph parameters generated by GenoGraphiX-LOG 2.0 for four L2 writers

	Amelia—novice L2	Brian—novice L2	Clair—proficient L2	Dave—proficient L2
Nodes per minute	26.46	32.72	19.7	16.58
Final text arcs to chronology arcs ratio	0.49	0.54	0.54	0.51
Final text arcs to total arcs ratio	0.3	0.31	0.31	0.31

TABLE 4.2 Node and character distribution generated by GenoGraphiX-LOG 2.0 for four writers in L2

Node type	Node percentage (%)				Mean node length (chars.)			
	Amelia—novice L2	Brian—novice L2	Clair—proficient L2	Dave—proficient L2	Amelia—novice L2	Brian—novice L2	Clair—proficient L2	Dave—proficient L2
Non-empty append nodes	11.47	8.2	9.38	13.08	4.31	10.64	26.77	23.52
Empty append nodes	17.07	7.21	10.42	8.47	–	–	–	–
Insert nodes	20.51	38.2	33.68	29.78	1.25	4.26	7.74	11.35
Displaced nodes	0.27	0	.23	0	3.33	–	60	–
Copy nodes	0	0	0	0	–	–	–	–
Removed nodes	16.98	18.36	17.36	15.74	–	–	–	–
Delete nodes	14.81	15.41	12.5	13.8	2.01	2.66	7.05	5.6
Pause nodes	18.88	12.62	16.44	19.13	–	–	–	–

4.6 Discussion

The above example demonstrates that graph-based visualisation of the writing process offers clear advantages over alternative notations and statistical analyses. Graph visualisations facilitate the identification of trends and patterns in writing data, enhanced by the natural ability of humans to comprehend visual data much more efficiently as opposed to textual or numerical data. Additionally, they provide both macroscopic and microscopic perspectives, enabling researchers to explore the writing process from various angles and based on differing levels of detail. However, when graph representations become overly complex, analysing them at a macroscopic level can become overwhelming. To address this limitation, we propose the use of supplementary visualisations based on the graphs and other characteristics of the graph to enhance the understanding of writing sessions.

The most significant drawback of graph visualisations is the need for specialised software and coding skills to generate graphs from keystroke logs. Moreover, these logs must be highly precise and accurate, as errors can result in inaccurate graphs construction. This requirement limits researchers to writing environments capable of achieving such precision, which may restrict the use of more natural or commonly used writing platforms.

4.7 Conclusion

In conclusion, we propose the following systematic approach for utilizing the graph model in the study of writing:

1. Begin by obtaining an initial overview of the graph, aiming to grasp its complexity and gain insights into the writing process in its entirety.
2. Conduct an in-depth analysis of the primary graph, generating secondary visualisations and extracting various statistical measures from the graph data.
3. Identify distinctive patterns and trends observed in the secondary visualisations.
4. Refer back to the primary graph and proceed with either a macroscopic or microscopic analysis of the identified subsections of the graph, depending on the specific research objectives.
5. Investigate the analysis further by examining specific events or sequences of events within the original keystroke log, thereby further enhancing the understanding of the underlying writing dynamics.

By following this structured approach, researchers can effectively utilize the graph model to explore and gain valuable insights into the intricacies of the writing process.

References

Alves, R.A., & Limpo, T. 2015. Progress in written production studies through the use of Inputlog: Challenges and opportunities. *Writing and Pedagogy*, vol. 7, no. 1, pp. 133–150.

Becotte, H.S., Caporossi, G., Leblay, C., & Hertz, A. 2019. Writing and rewriting: Keystroke logging's colored numerical visualization. In K.P.H. Sullivan & E. Lindgren (Eds.) *Observing writing: Logging handwriting and computer keystrokes*. Leyde: Brill Academic Publishers.

Brun, B. (Ed.). 2008. *Marcel Proust*. Paris: [The blue rider], coll. « Les idées reçues ».

Caporossi, G., & Leblay, C. 2015. A graph theory approach to online writing data visualization. *In* G. Cislaru (Ed.) *Writing(s) at the crossroads: The process-product interface*. Amsterdam: John Benjamins, pp. 171–181.

Caporossi, G., & Leblay, C. 2011. Online writing data representation: A graph theory approach. *In* J. Gama, E. Bradley, & J. Hollmén (Ed.) *Lecture notes in computer sciences* 7014 (Advances in Intelligent Data Analysis X). Dordrecht, London, New York: Springer Heidelberg, pp. 80–89.

Chenoweth, N.A., & Hayes, J.R. 2001. Fluency in writing: Generating text in L1 and L2. *Written Communication*, vol. 18, no. 1, pp. 80–98.

Christianson, K., et al. 2005. The copy-and-paste generation: Net literacy in the composition classroom. *Computers and Composition*, vol. 22, no. 1, pp. 4–13.

Fenoglio, I. 2009. [Emile Benveniste's working notes: Where theoretical thought is born through its enunciation.] *Langage & Société*, vol. 127, pp. 23–49.

Foucambert, D., Heranic, T., Leblay, C., Mutta, M., & Zhong, M. 2022. [Integration of visualisation in the analysis of complex processes: writing and rewriting in a multilingual academic corpus.] *In 8ème Congrès Mondial de Linguistique française* 2022; SHS Web of Conferences 138, 06010. DOI: https://doi.org/10.1051/shsconf/202213806010.

Grésillon, A. 1994. [Elements of genetic criticism: Reading modern manuscripts.] Paris: Presses Universitaires de France.

Kollberg, P. 1998. *S-notation—A computer-based method for studying and representing text composition*. Licentiate thesis, Stockholm, Sweden. Department of Numerical Analysis and Computing Science, Royal Institute of Technology.

Kollberg, P., & Eklundh, K.S. 2002. Studying writers' revising patterns with S-notation analysis. *In* T. Olive & C.M. Levy (Eds.) *Contemporary tools and techniques for studying writing. Studies in writing*, vol 10. Dordrecht: Springer. https://doi.org/10.1007/978-94-010-0468-8_5.

Leblay, C. 2011. [The time of writing. Genesis, duration, representations.] Doctorate thesis. Online publication in PDF format. (ISBN: 978-951-39-4519-0).

Leblay, C., & Caporossi, G. (Ed.). 2014. [Time of writing. Recordings and representations.] Coll. "Sciences du langage: Carrefours et points de vue", Louvain-La-Neuve, Academia-L'Harmattan, p. 257.

Leblay, C., Usoof, H., & Caporossi, G. 2022. [Dynamic visualization of the writing process.] *Kieli, Koulutus ja Yhteiskunta*, vol. 13, no. 3.

Lebrave, J.-L. 1998. [From visible to readable: electronic genetic editing.] In C. Luc (éd.) Actes du Colloque *Genèses*. [http://aleph.ens.fr/item_ancien/contenus/publications/articles_cher/Lebrave/JLL_Coll_Gen.pdf].

Lebrave, J.-L. 2008. [From computerized publishing to electronic publishing.] *In* A. Crasson (Ed.) [Manuscript editing. From the creative archive to the electronic scriptorium.] Louvain la Nevue: Academia Bruylant, pp. 169–187.

Leijten, M., & Van Waes, L. 2013. Keystroke logging in writing research: Using Inputlog to analyse and visualise writing processes. *Written Communication*, vol. 30, no. 3, pp. 358–392.

Lindgren, E., Knospe, Y., & Sullivan, K.P.H. 2019. Researching writing with observational logging tools from 2006 to the present. *BRILL EBooks*, pp. 1–29. https://doi.org/10.1163/9789004392526_002.

Lindgren, E., & Sullivan, P.H. (2002). The LS graph: A methodology for visualizing written revision. *Language Learning*, vol. 52, no. 3, pp. 565–595.

Nilsson, M., Kollberg, P. 1994. *Trace-it 2.0 user's manual*. IPLab, Department of Numerical Analysis and Computing Science, KTH.

Olive, T. 2004. Working memory in writing: Empirical evidence from the dual-task technique. *European Psychologist*, vol. 9, no. 1, pp. 32–42.

Richards, J.C., & Schmidt, R. 2010. *Longman dictionary of language teaching and applied linguistics* (4th ed.). Harlow, England: Longman.

Strömqvist, S. 2006. [An experimental approach to the writing process: recording keyboard typing.] *Genesis*, vol. 27, pp. 45–58.

Usoof, H., Leblay, C., & Caporossi, G. 2020. *GenoGraphiX-Log version 2.0 user guide*. Technical report Les Cahiers du GERAD G-2020-68, GERAD, HEC. Montreal, Canada.

Van Waes, L., Leijten, M., & Quinlan, T. 2010. Translating writing processes into research data: Using Inputlog to analyse and visualise writing processes. *Journal of Writing Research*, vol. 2, no. 2, pp. 139–170.

CHAPTER 5

Visualising the Stages of a Writing Process

Florence Tanoï Namio, Gilles Caporossi and Alain Hertz

5.1 Introduction

Writing is part of almost everyone's daily life. Every day, we write messages, notes and much more, but in most case, what is written initially does not appear in the final text. We constantly change what we write, because of a mistake or a new idea. Since these changes do not appear in the final text, no one knows how they helped improve the quality of the text. For example, if it is a text to be evaluated, the teacher will not know the steps and the efforts that the students made to produce their text, nor how to help the students to improve their process of writing. Knowing how changes are made and how they contribute to the final text would be an important asset.

The writing process is complex to analyse. Early studies described this process as a linear activity in which writers produce a draft that they then revise. The writing process is then likened to the growth of a plant (Rohman and Wlecke, 1964), because of the different stages of the growth of a writing idea from thoughts and sensations into words on paper (Sharp, 2016). The writing process is then divided into three stages: prewriting, which refers to everything that takes place before the text appears on paper; writing the text; and then rewriting, which consists of revising the written text (Rohman and Wlecke, 1964). These stages are also called by Murray (1978) the prevision, the vision, and the revision. However, research shows that the writing process is more complex than a linear presentation. The work of Emig (1967, 1971) questioned the linearity of the writing process; for her, writing can include the three stages defined previously, but these stages can occur recursively. She then defines ten steps in the composition of a text and highlights the influence of speech in the writing process. Furthermore, with the work of Flower and Hayes (1980), the writing process is seen as a hierarchically structured cognitive process in which writing is carried out recursively. According to them, during written production, an expert writer uses three cognitive processes: planning, translation, and revision. Planning is considered the first step, followed by translation and revision. During planning, the writers use their knowledge and the writing topic to develop a writing goal and plan. When they finish with planning, they

 | HTTPS://DOI.ORG/10.1163/9789004760264-006

move on to translation, which consists of producing a text following the established plan. Then, during revision, they read, identify, and correct errors and imperfections. Over time this model was modified, with the addition of motivation among the elements that influence the writers in writing (Hayes, 1996) and the removal of planning and revision (Hayes, 2012). In fact, planning and revision are considered a particular application of the writing process. In other words, when writers plan and revise, they write a text but of a different nature. Revision is therefore a fundamental component of the writing process, so fundamental that for some scholars, writing is largely a matter of revision (Allal et al., 2004).

Over the years, the definition of revision has evolved. Researchers no longer see revisions as simple error correction, but as a process involving a cognitive process. For Fitzgerald (1987), revision means making any change at any point in the writing process. Just as the writing process is subdivided, Witte (1985) also subdivides revision into three parts: pretextual revision, for revision which affect intention, plan or mental formulation of text; online revision for revision which refers to changes while reviewing a word or group of words that has just been written; and deferred revision which takes place when the draft is complete. For other researchers, revision can be grouped into two types: internal revision takes place in the mind of the author before the text is transcribed or produced; external revision concerns any changes made during the writing of the text (Conijin et al., 2004). Hence, a revision can include a spontaneous correction as well as a more elaborate change. Revision can also include a number of subprocesses that have been defined in various ways (see for example Alamargot and Chanquoy, 2001). In summary, the concept of revision has evolved a lot over time (for a survey, see for example Horning and Becker, 2006; Alla et al., 2004; Alamargot and Chanquoy, 2001). More recently, revision was studied using keystroke logging mainly from the burst/pauses perspective (Baaijen et al., 2012). For example, for Conijn et al., (2024) a revision event starts with a deletion located at the lower/outer boundary of the text or away. In this chapter, we will only consider external revisions, because these are the only ones for which we have concrete traces. More specifically, we do not consider what the writers say but focus only on the modifications they make to the texts without considering the meaning.

The evolution of computer tools has made it possible to record the writer's keystrokes, which are then analysed to determine how the writers wrote and revised their text. This analysis is, however, very complex. Some use statistical data analysis techniques such as data mining (Baaijen et al., 2012; Abdel Latif, 2008; Leijten and Van Waes, 2013). Graph theory is also used to structure the information contained in the file containing the keystroke record (Caporossi and Leblay, 2013; Bécotte-Boutin, 2019; Leblay et al., p. 73).

In this chapter, we will analyse keystroke logging from the perspective of data analysis and mathematical modelling. The model described in the current chapter is obtained from a keystroke logging software that generates a file in which each line is associated with a keystroke. Keystrokes are described by attributes as the key that was pressed (a letter most of the time, but also the "deletion" or "backspace" keys, as well as arrows). Each keystroke is also assigned a timestamp as well as the position of the cursor when it was hit. A typical writing session of 15 minutes yields 2000 to 3000 keystrokes, which indicates that a short writing session provides a large data file. Log files are very precise in the sense that the whole process is recorded and it is possible to "play" the writing session in great detail. However, these large data files are difficult to analyse manually. In order to understand the information they contain, a translation phase is needed. In the same way as a compiler translates a human readable document (usually called computer program) to a machine understandable one, we somehow propose the reverse here and translate data that is hard to read for humans into a more insightful representation.

The concept of insightful representation varies depending on the task the researcher wishes to accomplish. The level of detail required when studying typos is certainly not the same as when studying the importance of writing planning. For this reason, different levels of aggregation may be needed. Our objective is to offer a tool which allows to visualise and interpret the successive stages which led to the production of a final text. Several other tools exist in the literature to analyse the writing process (for an overview see Lindgren et al., 2019), the most recent being that of Malhow et al. (2024) which presents an approach for the analysis of writing processes with a focus on linguistic structures based on transforming sequences, text history, and sentence history. Here we do not consider linguistic structures, we simply consider sequences of character insertions or deletions performed without moving the cursor from one place to another in the text.

The model we propose is a generic framework that could be used to better understand the writing activity from keystroke logging. In the next section, we show how to break the writing process into so-called episodes of modifications, and to visualise them. Additional diagrams are described in Section 3 to synthesize the information contained in the episodes. Also, merging procedures are proposed in Section 4 to produce a more concise view of the writing process.

5.2 Breaking the Writing Process into Episodes of Modifications

Although the writing process is very complex, we simplify it by considering it as a series of actions carried out by the writer, these being of three different types:

- Type 1: The writer can move the cursor to another place in the text, using the mouse or keyboard arrows.
- Type 2: The writer can insert a character where the cursor is located.
- Type 3: The writer can delete a character adjacent to the cursor, either on its left (type 3.1) or on its right (type 3.2).

For illustration, consider the following simple example. The final text produced by the writer is "An Example." We assume it is not produced all at once. Initially, the writer writes "A sam".

Text at the end of the first step: A sam

Then the writer moves the cursor before the "s", inserts "ex" and deletes "s". Insertions are shown with bold letters, and removed letters are presented as strikeout text.

Text at the end of the second step: A **ex**~~s~~am

The cursor is then moved before the "m" and the writer inserts "mple", deletes the last "m" and replaces it with a dot.

Text at the end of the third step: A exa**mple**~~m~~**.**

Finally, the writer moves the cursor after the initial "A", writes an "m", deletes it (because of a typing error) and replaces it with an "n".

Text at the end of the fourth step: A**~~m~~n** example.

We can observe in this example the three types of action. For example, at the end of the first step, the writer *moves* (type 1) the cursor from the end of the text to the left of "s". He then performs some *insertions* (type 2). After having written "ex'" he *deletes* the "s" *at the right of the cursor* (type 3.1). Also, at the fourth step, after having written "m", he *deletes* this character which is located *at the left of the cursor* (type 3.2).

The term *episode* generally refers to an event or a group of events occurring as part of a larger sequence. We use this term here as a synonym of a *writing phase* which we define as a maximal set of consecutive actions made without using the mouse or keyboard arrows to move the cursor. This set of actions is called an episode of modifications. In other words, it is a maximal set of consecutive actions of type 2 or 3. In the above simple example, each step constitutes an episode of modifications since the cursor is moved to a new location at the end of each step. We visualise each episode as shown in Figure 5.1.

- (1a) and (1b). We use two horizontal bars: the first one is the illustration of the text at the beginning of the modification, the second one is the text at the end of the modification.
- (2a) and (2b). A pointer on the first bar indicates the cursor position at the start of the modification made in this episode, and another pointer at the bottom of the second bar indicates the cursor position at the end of the modification.
- (3) An arrow below the second pointer represents the movement made to go to the start of the modification made in the next episode, therefore towards the next pointer.
- (4a), (4b), (4c) and (4d). The white areas in the horizontal bars are the parts of the text that have not been modified during the writing phase.
- (5) The red portion in the first horizontal bar indicates the part of the text that is deleted. A deletion can take place to the left or right of the cursor, which explains why the pointer that indicates the start of the modification can be in the middle of the red zone.
- (6) The blue area in the second horizontal bar indicates the new text visible at the end of the modification. Other character insertions may have taken place during the modification, but these were subsequently deleted, which explains why they do not appear at the end of the modification.
- (7) The green rectangle between the two horizontal bars indicates the number of characters that were inserted and then deleted during this modification phase.

In summary, the number of characters the writer inserted within an episode of modifications is equal to the sum of the lengths of the blue and green rectangles, while the number of characters he removed is equal to the sum of the lengths of the red and green rectangles.

For illustration, we show in Figure 5.2 the four episodes of our simple example. In addition to the episodes, we indicate on the left the evolution of the text and which stages are part of each episode. Also, at the bottom of all the episodes, we add a rectangle whose length is that of the final text. The space occupied by a character is colored with a shade of grey. We use k different hues,

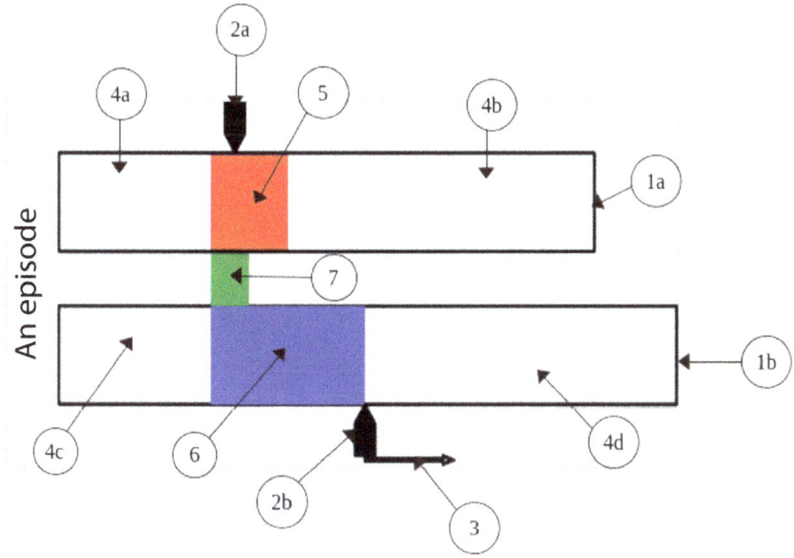

FIGURE 5.1 Visualisation of an episode of modifications

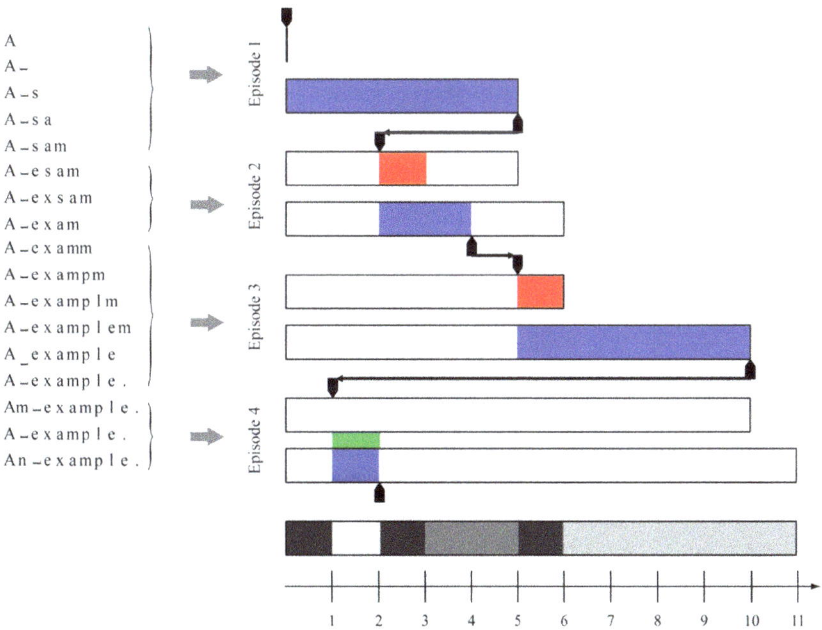

FIGURE 5.2 Visualisation of the four episodes of our simple example

where k is the total number of episodes. The first episode has colour black, and the last one is white (unless there is only one episode). Each location in the final text has the colour of the episode in which the character that occupies that location was inserted. If colours of very different hues are adjacent to each other in this rectangle, it means that the part of the text where this can be observed was changed long after a first version was written. As an illustration, in our example, we see at the beginning of the text a white space surrounded by two black spaces. This is because the "n" in the second position was inserted at the very end, while the "A" to its left and the white space to its right had been written at the very beginning.

For comparison, as second example, another writer possibly produced the same text by first writing "A sam", then deleting " sam", and finally adding "n example.". This gives only one, episode and the associated visualisation is given in Figure 5.3. The green rectangle represents the insertion and the deletion of the four characters in " sam", while the blue rectangle is for the insertion of "An example."

The representation of the episodes that we have chosen has various advantages. It allows to visualise the extent of changes at each writing phase, their position in the text as well as their composition, in addition to indicating the direction of the cursor movement during the writing process. The number of episodes corresponds to the number of writing phases, while the size of the

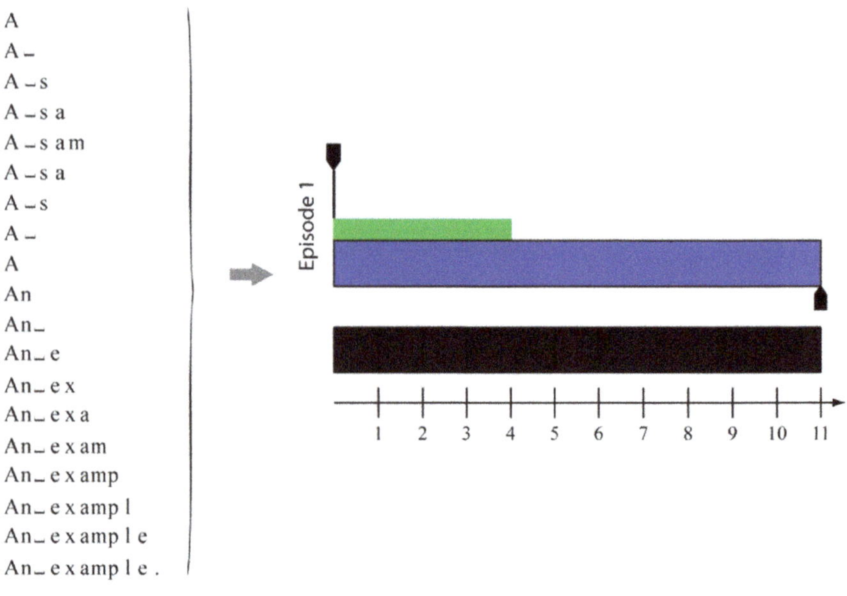

FIGURE 5.3 Visualisation of the single episode of the second example

red and blue zones of the episodes tells us about the extent and composition of the modifications. The larger the blue and red parts of an episode, the greater the change. If there is only a red part in an episode, it means that the writer simply deleted some of the existing text without adding new text. If there is only a blue area, the author has simply added new text. The presence of green rectangles indicates that newly inserted text was immediately deleted. In summary, by observing the diagrams representing the episodes, we can have a fairly precise idea of the text modifications made by the writer, their extent and their position in the final text.

5.3 Additional Diagrams

We now describe diagrams which allow to synthesize the information contained in the episodes. To clearly illustrate our points, we consider an example a little more complex than that of the previous section. It is described in Figure 5.4 and is made of 18 episodes. As in the previous example, the newly inserted characters in an episode are shown with bold letters, and deleted characters are presented as strikeout bold text.

A visualisation of these 18 episodes appears in Figure 5.5. We observe that the modifications mainly occur at the final part of the current text. The part of the text written at the beginning is hardly modified at all, except for modifications that occur in episodes C_2, C_4 and C_{15}. This is confirmed by the final bar: the darkest portions of the text are at the beginning, while the light ones are mostly at the end. This illustrates the fact that a piece of text is written and then modified until a satisfactory version is obtained before continuing. We also observe that there are very few red portions in the episodes, which indicates that little of the written text is subsequently deleted. Also, the only green rectangle appears in episode C_5, which indicates that almost no text has been written and deleted immediately. We now describe new diagrams that allow a more in-depth analysis of the process.

As already mentioned, an episode of modifications is made up of insertions and deletions. When writers insert new characters into their text, they may decide to delete them, either immediately after writing them (for example if they realize that they have made typos), or later (e.g., after proofreading). If they never delete the new text written in an episode, it will become part of the final text. We can therefore classify the insertions into three groups: insertions deleted immediately (I_1); insertions deleted in a subsequent episode (I_2); insertions never deleted, and which appear in the final text (I_3). Deletions made in an episode are divided into two groups: deletions of a text which has just been

Text produced by a writer.

A community of modifications is a series of successive insertions and/or deletions at a specific point in the text. For example, if you write "am" between "x" and "p" in the word "Exple", you get "Example". So "am" represents the community of modifications of the word "Exple". In graph terms, the community of modifications is the set of nodes with successive numbers (chronological links) and arcs (spatial links). However, due to the high number of nodes in very large graphs, it is sometimes not easy to observe communities.

Decomposition into episodes **C_i of modifications.**

C_1 ***A modifications are series of successive insertions.***

C_2 *A community of modifications are series of successive insertions.*

C_3 *A community of modifications are series of successive insertions* ***and/or deletions***.

C_4 *A community of modifications ~~are~~**is a** series of successive insertions and/or deletions.*

C_5 *A community of modifications is a series of successive insertions and/or deletions.* ***For example, if you write "xyz" between "b" and "c", "xyz" represents the community of modifications of "abcd".***

C_6 *A community of modifications is a series of successive insertions and/or deletions. For example, if you write "**~~xyz~~am**" between "b" and "c", "xyz" represents the community of modifications of "abcd".*

C_7 *A community of modifications is a series of successive insertions and/or deletions. For example, if you write "am" between "**~~b~~x**" and "c", "xyz" represents the community of modifications of "abcd".*

C_8 *A community of modifications is a series of successive insertions and/or deletions. For example, if you write "am" between "x" and "**~~c~~p**", "xyz" represents the community of modifications of "abcd".*

C_9 *A community of modifications is a series of successive insertions and/or deletions. For example, if you write "am" between "x" and "p",* ***in the word*** *"xyz" represents the community of modifications of "abcd".*

C_{10} *A community of modifications is a series of successive insertions and/or deletions. For example, if you write "am" between "x" and "p", in the word "**~~xyz~~Exple**" represents the community of modifications of "abcd".*

C_{11} *A community of modifications is a series of successive insertions and/or deletions. For example, if you write "am" between "x" and "p", in the word "Exple",* ***you get "Example". So "am"*** *represents the community of modifications of "abcd".*

C_{12} *A community of modifications is a series of successive insertions and/or deletions. For example, if you write "am" between "x" and "p", in the word "Exple", you get "Example". So "am" represents the community of modifications of* ***the word*** *"abcd".*

C_{13} *A community of modifications is a series of successive insertions and/or deletions. For example, if you write "am" between "x" and "p", in the word "Exple", you get "Example". So "am" represents the community of modifications of the word "**~~abcd~~Exple**".*

C_{14} *A community of modifications is a series of successive insertions and/or deletions. For example, if you write "am" between "x" and "p", in the word "Exple", you get "Example". So "am" represents the community of modifications of the word "Exple".* ***In graph terms, the community is the set of nodes. However, due to the high number of nodes it is sometimes difficult to observe communities.***

C_{15} *A community of modifications is a series of successive insertions and/or deletions* ***at a specific point in the text****. For example, if you write "am" between "x" and "p", in the word "Exple", you get "Example". So "am" represents the community of modifications of the word "Exple". In graph terms, the community is the set of nodes. However, due to the high number of nodes it is sometimes difficult to observe communities.*

C_{16} *A community of modifications is a series of successive insertions and/or deletions at a specific point in the text. For example, if you write "am" between "x" and "p", in the word "Exple", you get "Example". So "am" represents the community of modifications of the word "Exple". In graph terms, the community is the set of nodes* ***with successive numbers (chronological links) and arcs (spatial links)****. However, due to the high number of nodes it is sometimes difficult to observe communities.*

C_{17} *A community of modifications is a series of successive insertions and/or deletions at a specific point in the text. For example, if you write "am" between "x" and "p", in the word "Exple", you get "Example". So "am" represents the community of modifications of the word "Exple". In graph terms, the community is the set of nodes with successive numbers (chronological links) and arcs (spatial links). However, due to the high number of nodes* ***in very large graphs,*** *it is sometimes difficult to observe communities.*

C_{18} *A community of modifications is a series of successive insertions and/or deletions at a specific point in the text. For example, if you write "am" between "x" and "p", in the word "Exple", you get "Example". So "am" represents the community of modifications of the word "Exple". In graph terms, the community is the set of nodes with successive numbers (chronological links) and arcs (spatial links). However, due to the high number of nodes in very large graphs, it is sometimes* ***~~difficult~~not easy*** *to observe communities.*

FIGURE 5.4 An example of a writing process with 18 episodes

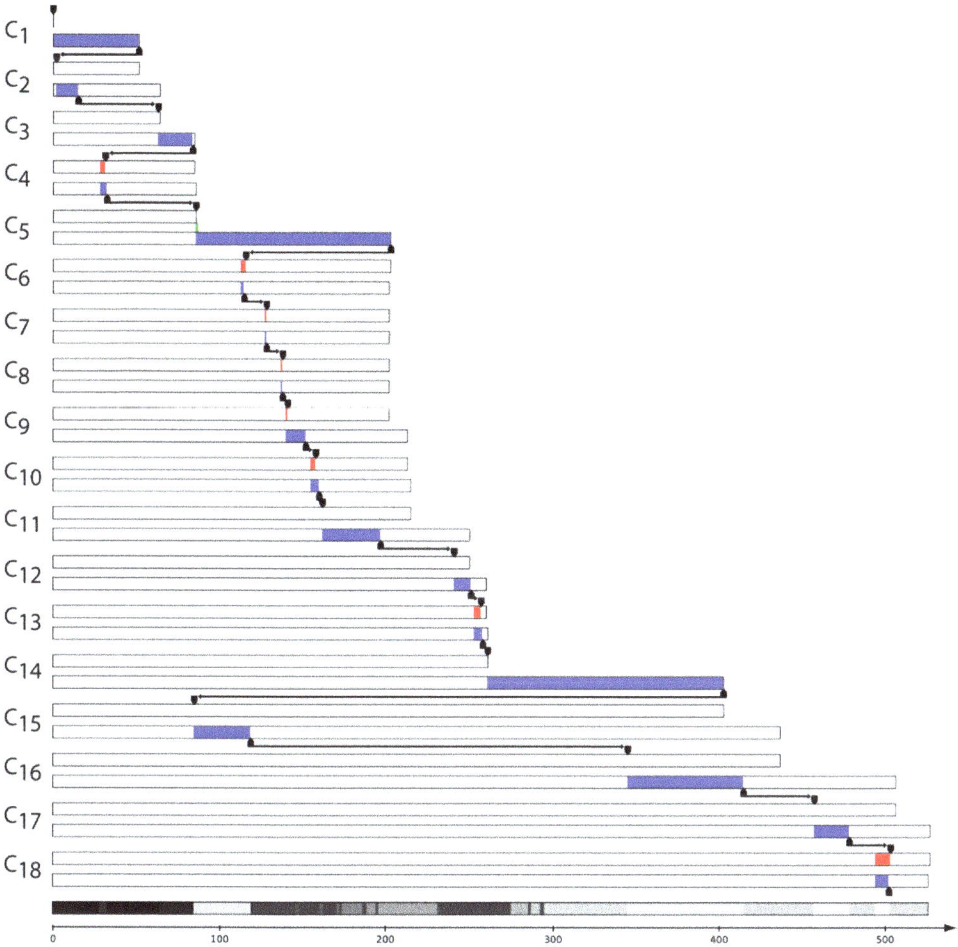

FIGURE 5.5 Visualisation of the 18 episodes of the example of Figure 5.4

written in the same episode (D_1); deletions of pieces of text that existed at the beginning of the episode (D_2).

The diagram in Figure 5.6 shows the distribution of insertions and deletions for the example of Figure 5.4. The blue part, which represents insertions, covers $100\frac{|I_1|+|I_2|+|I_3|}{|I_1|+|I_2|+|I_3|+|D_1|+|D_2|}$% of the circle, while the rest of the circle corresponds to deletions. For each type I_i of insertion, we indicate its proportion $100\frac{|I_i|}{|I_1|+|I_2|+|I_3|}$, and we do the same with the two types of deletions.

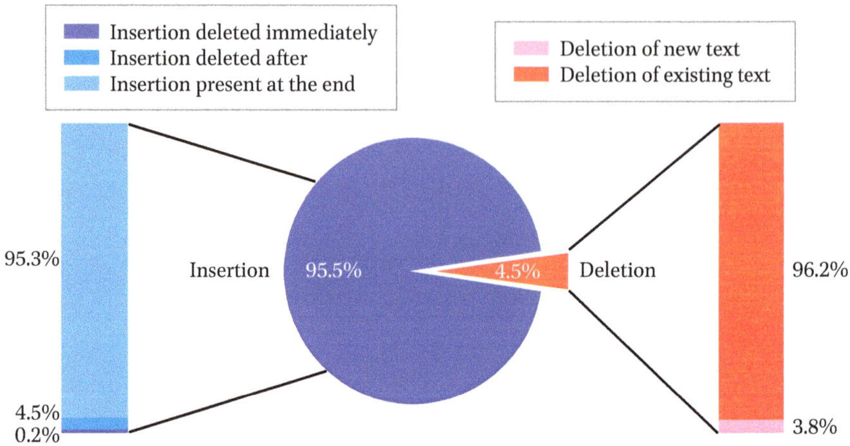

FIGURE 5.6 Distribution of the insertions and deletions for the example of Figure 5.4

The figure shows that 95.5% of the actions performed by the writer are insertions, and 4.5% are deletions. Moreover, 96.2% of the deletions concern text written in previous episodes. We can also see that 95.3% of the insertions remain until the final version of the text and that less than 1% are deleted immediately. This means that when the writer writes something, it's more likely to stay until the end. This can help to know how authors revise their text. For example, for an author who is a very intensive reviser, we will observe a high percentage of deletions, a high percentage of insertions deleted (immediately or later in subsequent episodes). Authors who revise their text immediately after writing will have a high percentage of insertions deleted immediately while authors who do not revise their text immediately will have a higher percentage of insertions deleted in subsequent episodes.

A question that can be asked is: what is the contribution of each episode to the final text? If we denote N the number of characters of the final text, and N_i the length of the portion of the blue rectangle of the ith episode which is present in the final text, we have that the ith episode contributes to $\frac{N_i}{N}100\%$ of the final text. This contribution is given in terms of the percentage of the number of characters present in the final text resulting from a given modification. This can be represented using a diagram, such as the one given in Figure 5.7.

For our example, we observe that nearly 25% of the final text comes from the 14th episode, 20% from the 5th and 15% from the 16th. So, the insertions performed in these three episodes cover more than 60% of the final text, while the combined contributions to the final text performed in the 4th, 6th, 7th and

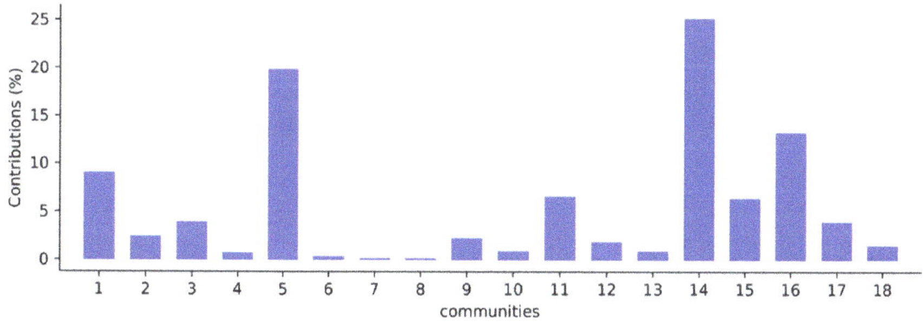

FIGURE 5.7 Contribution of each episode to the final text

8th episodes represent less than 5%. In other words, 60% of the characters in the final text come from three episodes and only 5% of the characters come from four other episodes.

5.4 Episode Merging

When revising a text, it sometimes happens that small changes are made in parts of text that are close to each other. The movement of the cursor, to move a little to the right or to the left, makes these modifications appear in different episodes while it could be interesting to group these changes so that they constitute only one episode.

Also, it may be that short modifications here and there temporarily interrupt a writing phase. For example, the writer may have observed a few typos in various parts of the text far from each other. The cursor is thus possibly moved to various places for short modifications, and it could be interesting to group these successive episodes into one.

In other words, it may be useful to merge episodes according to various criteria. We are interested here in two types of fusion based on two different criteria.

- Proximity of the episodes. The first type of fusion concerns successive episodes which only require a small movement of the cursor to move from one episode to the next. The principle is therefore to merge two successive episodes if the movement of the cursor between the two episodes is less than a given threshold. This reflects the fact that the author makes changes to various parts of the text that are close to each other.
- Size of the episodes. The second type of fusion concerns the extent of the changes made in an episode. When two successive episodes have only few

modifications, we can decide to group them. The number of modifications made in an episode is defined as the sum of the lengths of the red and blue parts and therefore corresponds to the number of newly inserted characters which are visible at the end of the episode at which we add the number of characters that were present at the start of the episode and that have been removed.

For the example of Figure 5.5, the move of the cursor between two episodes varies from 2 to 309 characters, and a large portion of these moves are smaller than 20 characters while only three moves are more than 80 characters long. As shown in Figure 5.8, if we merge two consecutive episodes when the move is at most 20 characters long, we decrease the number of episodes to 11: the 6 episodes from the 6th to the 11th merged into one, and the 12th, 13th and 14th also merged. With a threshold of 60 instead of 20, we get only four episodes. For example, the 16th, 17th, and 18th episodes of Figure 5.5 merged into one episode and represent the following set of modifications which are performed in parts of the text that are close to each other, at the end of the text.

> A community of modifications is a series of successive insertions and/or deletions at a specific point in the text. For example, if you write "am" between "x" and "p" in the word "Exple", you get "Example". So "am" represents the community of modifications of the word "Exple". In graph terms, the community is the set of nodes **with successive numbers (chronological links) and arcs (spatial links)**. However, due to the high number of nodes **in very large graphs**, it is sometimes **not easy** to observe communities.

As the threshold increases, the number of episodes decreases, giving us a more concise view of the drafting process and the revisions made. We observe that fewer revisions are made to the second half of the text. This confirms previous observations.

To summarize, by applying proximity-based episode merging, we obtain episodes that provide information on all the changes made successively at a specific location with a chosen gap for the move of the cursor. This makes it possible to detect revision episodes based on the proximity of modifications.

Let's now consider fusion of episodes based on their size. In the example of Figure 5.4, most of the episodes have a size smaller than 20 characters, while only two episodes have a size larger than 100. Let's consider 20 and 70 as a threshold for the fusion. The result of the merging procedure appears in Figure 5.9. For a threshold equal to 20 we get 13 episodes, while by increasing the threshold to 70, we get 5 episodes.

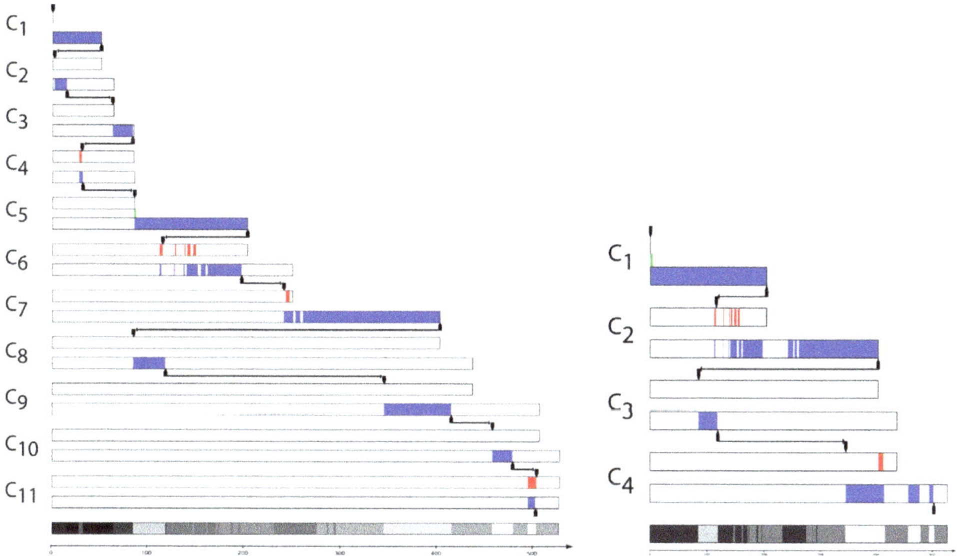

FIGURE 5.8 Merge of episodes for the example of Figure 5.4 with the proximity criteria and threshold of 20 (at the left) and 60 (at the right)

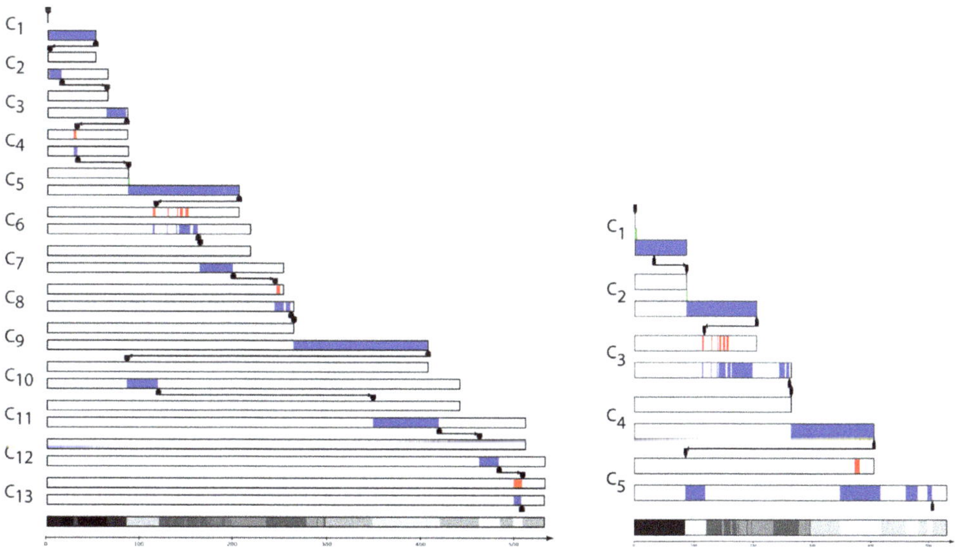

FIGURE 5.9 Merge of episodes for the example of Figure 5.4 with the size criteria and threshold of 20 (at the left) and 70 (at the right)

Using size-based episode merging, we obtain episodes that provide information about successive changes made with a size smaller than the chosen threshold. This allows us to observe revision episodes based on the extent of changes made without moving the cursor. We can thus link two various episodes of modification which are distant from each other in the final text. For example, when comparing Figures 5.8 and 5.9, we observe that the last episode obtained with a threshold equal to 70 includes the 15th episode in addition to the 16th, 17th, and 18th. It represents the following set of modifications.

> A community of modifications is a series of successive insertions and/or deletions **at a specific point in the text**. For example, if you write "am" between "x" and "p" in the word "Exple", you get "Example". So "am" represents the community of modifications of the word "Exple". In graph terms, the community is the set of nodes **with successive numbers (chronological links)** and arcs (spatial links). However, due to the high number of nodes **in very large graphs**, it is sometimes **not easy** to observe communities.

The change in the text made in the 15th episode of Figure 5.5 is an insertion of 32 characters at the beginning of the text while the 3 episodes that follow concern modifications made at the end of the text.

5.5 Discussion and Conclusion

In this chapter, we defined the notion of "episode of modifications" which allows to divide the writing process into writing episodes, and we also showed how to represent these episodes to visually understand what the writer achieved at each step of the process. The chosen representation makes it possible to see the extent of the changes made in each episode, the position of these modifications in the text and their composition (insertions or deletions). One can also see the move of the cursor during the writing process.

Additional diagrams allow information to be synthesized in order to evaluate the quantitative contribution of each episode to the final text. We also categorized character insertions to determine how many of them are then removed and therefore do not appear in the final text. This makes it possible to determine whether the writer tends to rewrite his text several times before obtaining a result that suits him, or if, on the contrary, what he writes has a good chance of remaining in the text until the end.

We also showed how the fusion of episodes allows to have a more global view of the writing process. These fusions can be done when successive episodes have a small size (which may indicate that writers make a few adjustments to their text here and there), or when the cursor is only moved a few characters (which indicates that the modifications made remain in the same part of the text).

Our visualisation diagrams can be used in addition to other tools for analysing the writing process. Indeed, as our diagrams do not use any particular linguistic structure, they allow to have a general overview of the different aspects of the writing process. One possible application is in teaching. By adopting our visualisation model, the teacher can get an idea of the nature and impact of each text modification made by the student. To increase knowledge of the modifications made, all this can be coupled with other elements of text analysis in natural language processing such as the number of words, the number of sentences, the meaning of the words or even syntax. Text evaluation indices such as readability and amount of information can also be used to evaluate the impact of each episode of modifications on the quality of the final text.

Of course, these illustrations are far from exhaustive, and the model itself is not static, but could easily be improved or adapted. For instance, instead of considering the written text as a sequence of characters, it is possible to use another level of analysis such as words, sentences, paragraphs or even chapters. In that way, the model would better fit some applications, particularly in linguistic or literature where the basic text unit is the word, the sentence, or the paragraph. We note for instance that the current model, based upon isolated characters cannot handle the cut and paste function while it is an important tool for the writer. Still regarding possible improvements, episodes may be defined in a more sophisticated way that would include revision campaigns. Indeed, when a series of small modifications is achieved across a possibly large portion of text, always moving forward, it is possible that a revision campaign occurs, and this process should be considered as a single revision episode.

The models proposed in this chapter present a proof of concept, as previously indicated, but they deserve to be used as a new tool to study writing from keystroke logging. They may easily be implemented in dedicated software (such as GenoGraphiX-Log) or be used in a standalone manner from already collected logs.

Even if it is not directly visible, one of the main contributions of this model is certainly to provide statistics that are difficult to obtain otherwise, and which can prove useful. Namely, the classical units of analysis for text production are the character, word, paragraph, etc. However, these units refer to the final product and are linear in nature in the sense that they correspond to a sequence of consecutive characters in the text. In this chapter, we propose to split these sequences according to episodes, which is closer to the redaction dynamic. We believe that this approach will better fit the needs of researchers, and we expect that the statistics obtained in this way, instead of the classical word or character counts, will provide a new angle that is well suited to the study of the process. The visualisations associated to the model show some dimensions that are not easy to catch with other techniques, mainly because they are based upon episodes.

References

Abdel Latif, M.M. (2008). A state-of-the-art review of the real-time computer-aided study of the writing process. *International Journal of English Studies* 8(1), 29–50.

Allal, L., Chanquoy, L., Largy, P. (2004). *Revision Cognitive and Instructional Processes.* Kluwer Academic Publishers.

Baaijen, V.M., Galbraith, D., de Glopper, K. (2012). Keystroke Analysis: Reflections on Procedures and Measures. *Written Communication* 29(3), 246–277.

Bécotte-Boutin, H.-S. (2019). [Analysis and visualization of the writing process using graphs.] PhD Thesis, Polytechnique Montréal.

Caporossi, G., Leblay, C. (2011). Online Writing Data Representation: A Graph Theory Approach. *Lecture Notes in Computer Science* 7014. Springer, Berlin, Heidelberg.

Conijn, R., Dux Speltz, E., Chukharev-Hudilainen, E. (2024). Automated extraction of revision events from keystroke data. *Reading and Writing* 37, 483–508.

Emig, J. (1967). On Teaching Composition: Some Hypotheses as Definitions. *Research in the Teaching of English*, 1(2), 127–135.

Emig, J. (1971). The Composing Processes of Twelfth Graders. *National Council of Teachers of English.*

Fitzgerald, J. (1987). Research on Revision in Writing. *Review of Educational Research* 57(4), 481–506.

Flower, L., Hayes J.R. (1980). The Cognition of Discovery: Defining a Rhetorical Problem. *College Composition and Communication* 31(1), 21–32.

Flower, L., Hayes, J.R. (1981). A Cognitive Process Theory of Writing. *College Composition and Communication* 32(4), 365–387.

Hayes, J.R. (1996). A new framework for understanding cognition and affect in writing. *The Science of Writing: Theories, Methods, Individual Differences, and Applications.* Routledge.

Hayes, J.R. (2012). My past and present as writing researcher and thoughts about the future of writing research. In *Past, present, and future contributions of cognitive writing research to cognitive psychology* (pp. 3–26). Psychology Press.

Horning, A., Becker, A. (2006) *Revision: History, Theory, and Practice*, Parlor Press LLC.

Leijten, M., Van Waes, L. (2013). Keystroke Logging in Writing Research: Using Inputlog to Analyze and Visualize Writing Process.es. *Written Communication* 30(3), 358–392.

Lindgren, E., Knospe, Y., Sullivan, K.P. (2019). Researching Writing with Observational Logging Tools from 2006 to the Present. *Observing Writing*. Brill.

Mahlow, C., Ulasik, M.A., Tuggener, D. (2024) Extraction of transforming sequences and sentence histories from writing process data: a first step towards linguistic modeling of writing. *Reading and Writing* 37, 443–482.

Murray, D.M. (1978). Internal revision: A process of discovery. *Research on composing: Points of departure*, 85–103.

Rohman, D.G., Wlecke, A.O. (1964). *Pre-writing, the construction and application of models for concept formation in writing.*

Sharp, L. (2016). Acts of Writing: A Compilation of Six Models that Define the Processes of Writing. *International Journal of Instruction* 9, 77–90.

Witte, S.P. (1985) Revising, Composition Theory, and Research Design. *The Acquisition of Written Language: Response and Revision*. Bloomsbury Publishing, 250–284.

CHAPTER 6

Towards a 3-Sided Behavioural/Linguistic/ Machine Learning Analysis and Visualisation of Key-Log Data

Georgeta Cislaru, Nistor Grozavu and Maxime Olivié

6.1 Introduction

In high dimensional data analysis one of the main tasks is producing a simplified, usually visual, overview of data sets. This belongs to the field of information visualisation, defined as "the communication of abstract data relevant in terms of action through the use of interactive visual interfaces" (Keim et al., 2006: 10). The use of computer graphics and tools to produce visual interfaces, where data sets can be observed, raises several technical, ergonomic, and scientific challenges. These issues become even more challenging when it comes to representing writing data. In the context of writing, visualisation can be defined as a type of conceptualization which amounts to knowledge construction and representation. First of all, writing is in itself a visualisation technology, inscribing information contents on visual interfaces by means of graphic linguistic forms. Secondly, the usual result of writing is the most complex and complete linguistic unit, the text (see Halliday, 1977). Thirdly, writing is a multi-dimensional process, comprising at least two dynamic dimensions prior to the final text. The first is incremental, cumulative and spatially oriented (e.g., from left to right and top to bottom). It leads to a constant progression of the number of characters and words in the text. The second is non-linear, cumulative (insertion) or non-cumulative (deletion), and spatially non-oriented. In handwriting it leads to a multi-layered texture, accumulating the different fragments produced at different times, as well as the various rewriting marks such as insertions or deletions. In type writing, it leads to a variation in the number of characters and positions and to a redistribution of the association of a character with a position following insertions or displacements. Recording the writing process using keyloggers also makes it possible to integrate information on the temporal course of writing: chronology of the production and assembly of language units, chronology of revisions, pauses, etc. (see also Basnayake & Usoof, this volume, p. 48) All of this temporal and spatial information on the process constitutes multi-dimensional data articulating

 | HTTPS://DOI.ORG/10.1163/9789004760264-007

behavioural and linguistic data. These data call for multi-dimensional visual representations, in order to integrate the temporality of the process with the spatiality of the text.

How these representations are deployed depends on the objectives served by the visualisation. Do we need to represent the writing process, or some specific operations such as reformulating, deleting, etc.? Within the complexity of the writing process, do we need to focus on behavioral aspects, temporal dynamics, or language units? What is the final end of the visual conceptualization: to help writers to structure their process, to better understand writers' strategies or to analyse the writing process, its mechanisms and dynamics? The answers to these questions can be diverse, and they govern the nature of the visualisations to be crafted. Thus one can identify several features to be visualised: temporal dynamics, language data, relationships between language data and temporal dynamics. Furthermore, each of these features has more than one facet. Writing and rewriting processes are characterized by temporal dynamics, sequentiality, chronological series, and time duration. The process structure can also be represented as a writing model (Flower & Hayes 1980, Hayes & Flower 1980). The diversity of viewpoints and research issues underlines the need for a modular visualisation approach, giving the researcher-user autonomy of choice.

Unlike the product, which constitutes a visual trace, the process is only visually accessible—and partially so—in the form of direct observation, a trace of rewriting, or recording (video, keylogging) (see Cislaru, 2015). The visual representation of the writing process requires a distinct level of conceptualization, where temporal dynamics can be given a static representation based on sequentiality and duration measures. One of the difficulties lies in the fact that writing manipulates language, and language production is the primary objective of the process. But not only is the production of language structures part of the temporal dynamic, it can also be assumed to influence the course of the process. Upstream, the challenge is to analyse and model the links between language actualization and behavioural dynamics. In this way, we assume that visualisation is an integral part of an analytical approach to data. In order to capture and visually represent this multi-dimensionality of the writing process, our research articulates behavioural and linguistic points of view and relies on machine learning developments.

This article gives an overview of several possibilities for visual representation of the dynamics of the writing process, depending on analytical needs and techno-graphic possibilities, before presenting the keylog data visualisation platform developed within the Pro-TEXT project. In the following section, we discuss writing as a temporally constrained visualisation technology and its representations. We then present a few approaches to rewriting data based on draft analysis. In section 4, we discuss linear and multi-layer representations of keylogging data. Section 5 focuses on hierarchical representations of language data and their explicative potential. Section 6 is dedicated to the presentation of clustering results for writing bursts and their visualisation in several forms. Finally, section 7 presents the visualisation platform developed within the Pro-TEXT project, based on the various analysis and visualisation strategies presented in the previous sections. Based on various analyses and visualisation experiments in writing, we thus aim to develop a dynamic interface, allowing data exploitation in various domains—education, speech-language pathology and therapy, etc.

6.2 Writing as a Temporally Constrained Visualisation Technology

The written word, unlike speech, is the product of graphic semiotisation, i.e., the production and alignment of graphemes, which are visual traces of sounds, groups of sounds, words and so on. As well as being a linguistic practice, writing is also a visuo-spatial activity (Olive et al., 2010; Olive & Passerault, 2012), because of the need to structure the graphical traces in a spatially oriented way, which will enable text construction. Writing is a visual activity in that it is guided by the gaze; it is a spatial activity because of the layout of the graphic line in a space that is also the space for organizing the text. This visuo-spatial dimension attracted the attention of Hayes (1996), who incorporated it into his revisited model of writing.

Although it goes way back into the past, with clay tablets and papyri, the link between text and space was first observed in handwriting, on the page, which is spatially limited and visually constrained. Research in critical genetics showed how authors align the visual-spatial unit of a page with a unit of content by adjusting the size of margins and line spacing (Lebrave, 1999).

Given its spatial footprint, the text in turn exerts visuo-spatial constraints. For instance, the text already produced enacts in turn visuo-spatial constraints on the text to be produced or the revisions to be implemented, according to Olive et al. (2010: 43). But while the authors consider this impact particularly at the cognitive level, the already written text being assimilated to an external auxiliary memory that dispenses the writer from keeping a certain amount of information in memory; we would also include a dimension linked to the management of writing production and writing operations: adding to the right, inserting into what has already been written, substituting what has already been written, etc. On the other hand, Plane et al. (2010) see this interaction through the prism of temporal strata. Thus, temporal constraints intersect with spatial constraints, as we shall also see in the following sections.

As stated by Plane et al. (2010: 10), as a "physical act, the graphic gesture necessarily follows a linear sequence over time". But while the temporality of the writing process is linear and irreversible, the material trace that is writing can depart from this linearity and immutability. The graphic trace can be modified, restructured, and even erased—all these movements affect the spatiality of the written word. Space combined with the medium modify the course of the writing process itself. For instance, when a text is produced on a computer, a higher number of revisions are made than when the text is handwritten (Kellogg & Mueller 1993). Moreover, unlike handwriting, the spatiality offered by word-processing tools is more flexible, and the material trace is negotiable: deletions, for example, leave no visible trace. In order to keep track of changes to the text, one needs to either compare versions (section 3), use the track changes mode or keystroke recording tools (section 4).

6.3 Drafts, Versions, and Revisions

Drafting is part of the writing process: Ferrer (2011: 182) insists on the role and cognitive interest of drafts for textual configuration, considering variants as "protocols for making of a text". Rewriting, which is part of the drafting process, concerns the modification of a static preexisting version of a visual text—be it handwritten or typed. The critical genetics approach (Hay, 2002; Grésillon & Lebrave, 2008; Grésillon, 2016) takes into account this graphic dynamic of writing, and emphasizes the multi-layered nature of rewriting while pointing out the difficulty of accurately relating it to a chronology. In contrast, texts produced by means of digital tools are the result of multiple versions that were abandoned or modified during the process. While producing texts, writers may save different drafts in different files or produce in the same file. For one of our corpora, writers were asked to automatically record the status of their production every quarter of an hour, as a process of macro-segmentation, i.e., the creation of versions as working units on the writer's side and units of analysis on the researcher's side (Cislaru & Olive, 2018). The versions were then compared in order to identify changes to the text. Identifying and visualising text changes between two versions required the alignment of the versions and automatic comparison of version $n + 1$ with version n. Several software have been developed to compare two versions (EDITE MEDITE, Fenoglio & Ganascia, 2007) or each new text version with the previous one (ALLONGOS,

Lardilleux et al. 2013). Using the Allongos tool, we compared versions and identified which revision operations had been carried out from one version to another. First and foremost, this allowed a longitudinal approach in short diachrony, by comparing the versions of texts from each writing session and identifying variants that interfered with the linearity of the texts. In this way, text genetics can calculate insertions (characters or sequences added to the text), replacements (the substitution of one sequence by another), displacements (a text fragment moved up or down) and deletions (removed text sequences) to obtain an overall view of the modifications a text has undergone (Figure 6.1).

This representation of writing operations through the different versions gives a visual overview of the stages involved in producing a written text and the writing strategies involved. In the example shown, we can see that the process is very rich in the first seven versions and in the version that will become the final version. We can also see that the number of deletions and displacements is significantly lower than that of insertions and substitutions. Similarly, the production of writing—in the form of insertions—is particularly marked in the first seven versions.

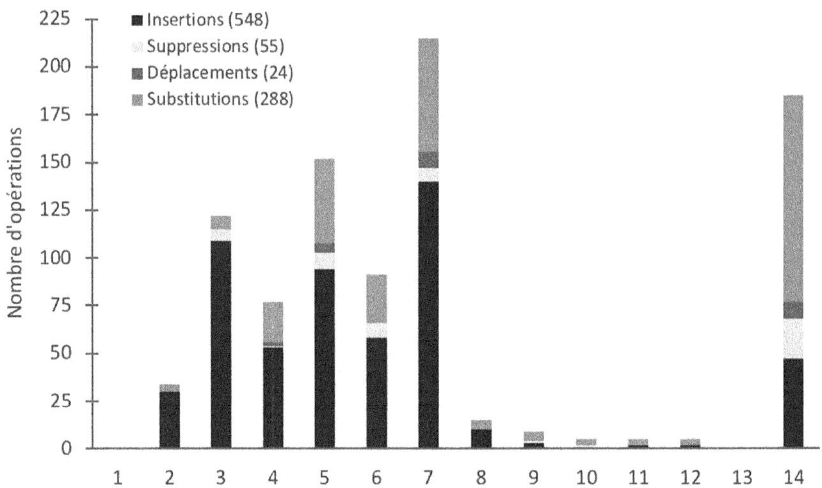

FIGURE 6.1 Number of rewriting operations for a 14-session writing process. The tool's interface is in French only.

The X-axis represents the compared versions. The Y-axis represents the number of writing operations. The listed operations are insertions, suppressions, displacements and replacements; figures in brackets represent the total number for each operation.

The visualisation of writing operations by comparing writing versions can also be exploited for application purposes, to support learning to write texts, where revision is a pillar, in line with the conception of writing as rewriting. As a cognitive aid aiming to encourage global revision, Xu and Shibata (2007) proposed an interface for relating revisions to sections and subsections of a text, in the form of writing blocks, along the lines of a textometry display, with text units represented as boxes.

Both analytical and pedagogical objectives are exploited by graphically representing the time course of writing and writing operations, notably insertions and deletions. The graph representation of the writing process through its operations (Leblay & Caporossi, 2015; Bécotte-Boutin et al., 2019) is an innovative strategy to visualise real-time recorded data. Developed through the synergy of critical genetics (see above) and graph theory, it visualises nodes representing production or deletion operations. Taken as a whole, the graph illustrates the writing process, which can take a linear or a circular form, depending on the writing strategies and degrees of expertise of the writers. An example of the use of graphs for research purposes is Zhong's thesis (2020) which analysed writing strategies deployed by Chinese French second language learners. In a didactic application of revision visualisation, writers were invited to take a reflexive look at their practices (Olmanson et al., 2015).

The word is the basic unit of the above-described tools, even though information beyond the word remains accessible. The observation of detailed revisions, however, requires a focus on character-level shapes—which becomes available through keystroke recordings, albeit more complex in their visual representation. The great contribution of these different visualisation methods is twofold: on the one hand, they have enabled us to advance our understanding and representation of the writing process, and on the other, they provide a tried-and-tested basis for visualising keylog data that are both similar but characterized by a dynamic dimension and multidimensionality.

6.4 Keylogging and Online Process Dynamics: from Linear to Multi-layered Representation

Key-stroke logging software provides a chronologically structured record of all the operations involved in writing on a keyboard: typing characters and spaces, revisions (deletions, insertions, displacements, etc.), pauses sequencing the process, or consultation of sources outside the document (Leijten & Van Waes, 2013; Lindgren & Sullivan, 2019; Wengelin et al., 2009). All these data can be updated in their longitudinal dynamics thanks to the rereading function of keyloggers, extracted by type (pause, typing, revision), classified by series, etc. Keylog outputs correspond to a large number of events and of evolving language data which follow one another in time (linearity) but sometimes overlap in space as is the case with revisions (non-linearity). Their visualisation involves three different approaches, which may follow one another or alternate: linearization to represent the time course, delinearisation to represent spatiality, and multi-layered representation to combine both.

6.4.1 *Linear and 2-Dimensional Representations*

By offering longitudinal access to the chronological unfolding of the writing process, keystroke recording tools stage a representational paradox. While the studies based on material archives and drafts demonstrate the non-linearity of the writing process (see above), the temporality of recorded writing is always linear. Only by relating this chronological linearity to the topology of the text is it possible to articulate temporality to the non-linearity of the process. For example, graphic representations of the writing process proposed by Leblay and Caporossi (2015) clearly illustrate the recursivity of revision operations, and Inputlog graphically represents the progress of writing in terms of characters typed or deleted, pause time, and sources consulted (Figure 6.2, Cislaru & Olive, 2018), in the same way as the LS-graph (Lindgren & Sullivan, 2002).

A similar linear cumulative principle is applied to keylogging data in the sentence-based model developed by Mahlow et al. (2022), in a tabular view where versions of sentences are schematized and aligned vertically on the horizontal axis representing the temporal dimension.

The behavioural dimension pertaining to writing events and revision practices is the one that contributes the most to non-linearity in the spatial framework. In Inputlog files, the identification of textual operations performed by writers when composing their text is based on S-notation, a language developed specifically to support the analysis of revision episodes (Severinson Eklundh & Kollberg 1996) and which describes writing as a decomposed linear process (Overview—Inputlog). As far as revisions are concerned, the output of keystroke recording software marks character deletions with backspaces in order to represent effects in a non-linear space frame; it can be considered as an example of linearization, or linear representation:

⌫⌫⌫⌫⌫⌫sjjss␣⌫⌫⌫⌫⌫⌫⌫

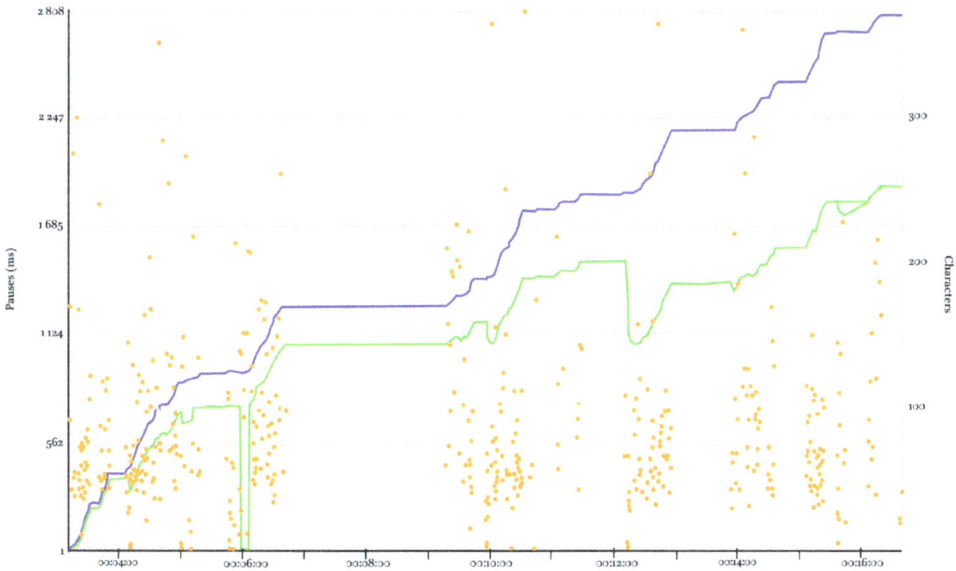

FIGURE 6.2 Inputlog representation of a writer's productivity during a social report writing session

The yellow dots indicate pauses, each of whose duration (in ms) is shown on the left vertical axis, with the moment of occurrence indicated on the horizontal axis. The green curve represents the sum of characters present in the text. The blue curve indicates the cumulative sum of characters typed since the start of the writing session. A descending green curve indicates the deletion of characters. The dotted green curve indicates the cursor position (Cislaru & Olive, 2018).

6.4.2 *Delinearization and Multi-layered Representations*

An alternative for the visualisation of deletions is proposed in the frame of the Pro-TEXT project by Serge Fleury (PROTEXT WIP (univ-paris3.fr)). Backspaces leave room for the reconstitution of deleted sequences with strikethrough markings, corresponding to a layered visualisation, while displayed in a bi-dimensional view:

0:<C'etait en décembre je connaisser ce garcçon depuis la marenelle il e~~tea~~>:69
68:<tait très gentil m~~a~~>:87

FIGURE 6.3 Reconstruction of deletions from Inputlog .idfx files and visualisation based on handwriting strategies

One may also want to have access to both text modifications and the final text—which is what the Pro-TEXT interface offers, with multiple windows displayed on the same page. This can be termed a flat multi-level representation.

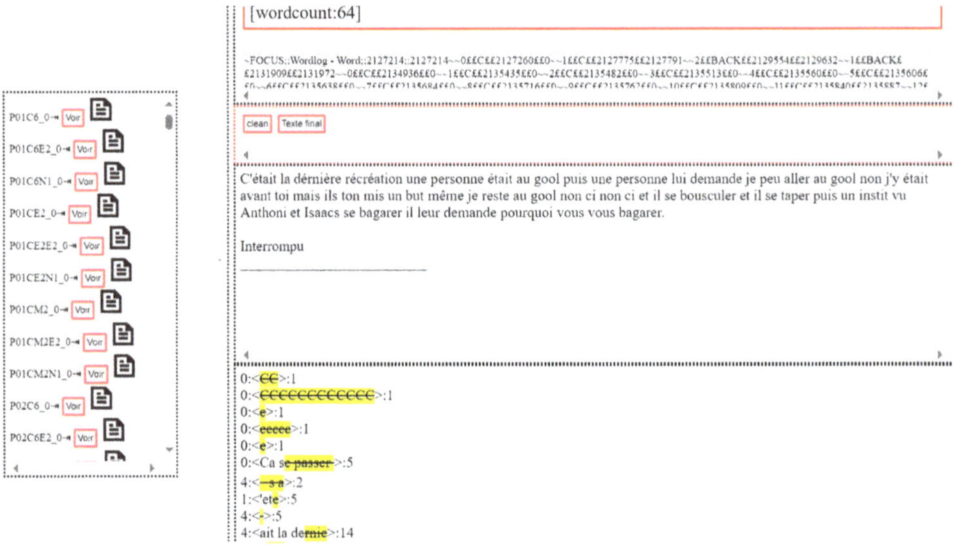

FIGURE 6.4 A flat multi-level representation: different text representations displayed in several windows

The naturally visible traces of writing are graphic characters which combine to form words, phrases, clauses, etc. Yet the writing flow is not continuous, but interspersed with pauses. Thus, another behavioral dimension of the writing process remains invisible: it relates to the temporal dynamics of the process, and therefore to the occurrence of pauses, or periods of language non-productivity. Pausology—which is the study of pauses in language production—is an essential part of any approach to the processual dimension of language production. Pauses provide a first level of segmentation of the language flow and make it possible to associate the production of textual units with the dynamics of the writer's or speaker's mental functioning (cf. Fayol, 1997). By setting the desired pause threshold, one can segment the language sequences produced between pauses, called bursts of writing (Chenoweth and Hayes, 2001). Like the visible part of the text that remains largely present (with the exception of deletions/modifications) throughout the writing process, bursts of writing can be a prime object of study (see Cislaru & Olive, 2018). The sets of writing bursts obtained are thus the result of the delinearisation of the writing flow.

In such a tabular view (Figure 6.5), pause visualisation is implicit, through the identification of language sequences produced in-between pauses of a fixed threshold, or: each burst frontier corresponds to a pause. An approach to writing that focuses both on language production and its temporal management—and therefore takes into account the behavior of writers—needs representations

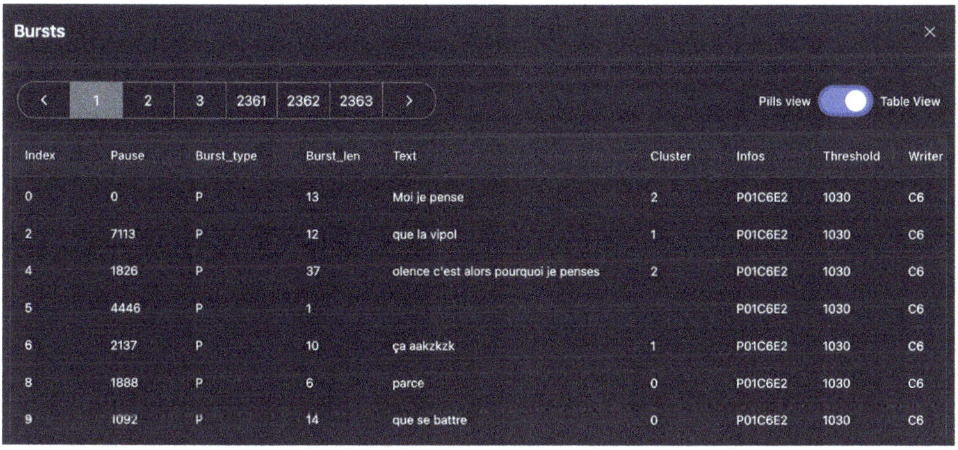

Index	Pause	Burst_type	Burst_len	Text	Cluster	Infos	Threshold	Writer
0	0	P	13	Moi je pense	2	P01C6E2	1030	C6
2	7113	P	12	que la vipol	1	P01C6E2	1030	C6
4	1826	P	37	olence c'est alors pourquoi je penses	2	P01C6E2	1030	C6
5	4446	P	1			P01C6E2	1030	C6
6	2137	P	10	ça aakzkzk	1	P01C6E2	1030	C6
8	1888	P	6	parce	0	P01C6E2	1030	C6
9	1092	P	14	que se battre	0	P01C6E2	1030	C6

FIGURE 6.5 Tabular view of the bursts (excerpt from the Pro-TEXT platform, see section 7). Some burst columns can be visualised via a horizontal scroll.

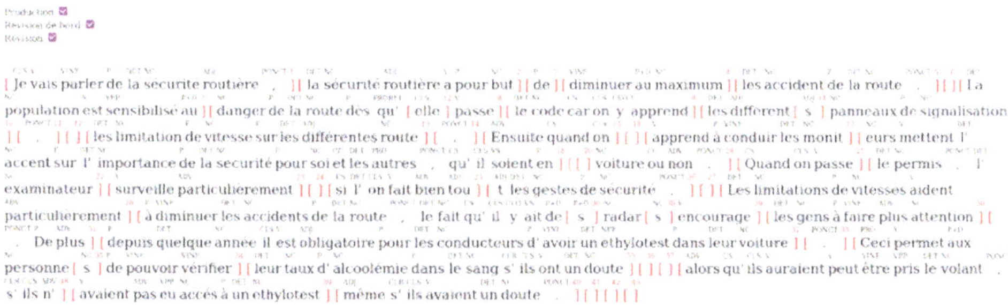

FIGURE 6.6 Text display with pause (or burst border) marking and POS (part-of-speech) marking option

that show both bursts and pauses in an orderly fashion. This can be achieved by integrating symbols, such as square brackets in the figure above (Figure 6.6), between burst concatenations. A supplementary layer concerns part-of-speech annotations that make it possible to calculate the correlation between pause segmentation and the linguistic nature of the sequences produced.

This kind of analytical and visualisation approach favours the linguistic analysis of bursts in particular, and of the writing process in general, by seeking to articulate behavioural dynamics to language structures and constraints. It is this dimension that is the focus of the Pro-TEXT project. However, linguistic analysis in turn benefits from a whole tradition of schematization and visualisation, which we address in what follows and explain how we draw on it for the project.

C'était [pause 2.371]

en décem [pause 3.183]

bre [pause 6.099]

je connaisser ce garçon depuis la marenelle il e [pause 3.729]

tait tr [pause 2.044]

FIGURE 6.7 Cascading representation compiling bursts and pauses (in seconds)

6.5 Hierarchical Representations for Targeted Linguistic Analysis

Aside from the multi-faceted nature of recorded writing data, which reinforces the importance of visualisation, language analysis has often resorted to schematization. Using maps, schemas or diagrams to represent language data is common in linguistics (Legallois, 2021; Mazziotta et al., 2023; Koponen this volume, p. 19); these schematics may concern language families or dialects, semantic layers and relations, syntactic structure and relations, or discourse structure. From the standpoint of linguistics, visualising writing and the writing process involves identifying the relevant linguistic forms and relationships to be highlighted. From the perspective of the study of writing, the identification of these linguistic objects is intimately linked to the dynamics of the process. The challenge is therefore to find visual means such as maps, schemas, diagrams, graphs, etc., preferably automatic or automatable, to construct a representation of the process, taking into account the sequence and the language.

While representational choices are often based on specific theoretical frameworks, we find that exploiting several schematizations enriches the points of view on the object. As already shown in some previous studies, the writing flow shares some features such as pauses, hesitations, and disfluencies, with the speech flow (Cislaru & Olive, 2018). For example, in order to understand the entailment of bursts, while at the same time highlighting the advancement of the flow of information, and thus, the accumulation of sequences into sentences and texts, we used a manual cascade representation, inspired by the syntax of spoken language (Blanche-Benveniste 1997, Figure 6.7).

A different layer is needed to mark revisions, as shown in Figure 6.3 reproduced below:

0:<C'etait en décembre je connaisser ce garcçon depuis la marenelle il e~~tea~~>:69
68:<tait très gentil m~~a~~>:87

These visualisations provide added value for analysis, as they show that some pauses are related to revision operations, as in the case of *~~etea~~* → *etait*.

However, not all pauses are related to revisions, and, from a linguistic viewpoint, the challenge is to determine whether pausal segmentation is underpinned by specific language principles. At sentence level, we sought to align the relationship between sentence structure and pause segmentation. Trees and tree-like schematizations are usually exploited to represent hierarchical relationships (Bosveld-de Smet & Verheggen, 2016). Using dependency annotations, we obtained representations of the relationships within sentences (Miletic et al., 2022; Figure 6.8A). The projection of the pauses on the schematization makes it possible to evaluate the degree of correspondence between sequences characterized by a dependency relationship and bursts (Figure 6.8B).

The analysis of bursts and their nature and length, as well as pauses and their length, reveals their significant heterogeneity. If, in addition, we wish to integrate the parameter of revision operations, it is clear that data processing would benefit from cross-sectional classification possibilities. To do this, we used machine learning methods and, more specifically, clustering algorithms based on a series of linguistic and behavioural parameters.

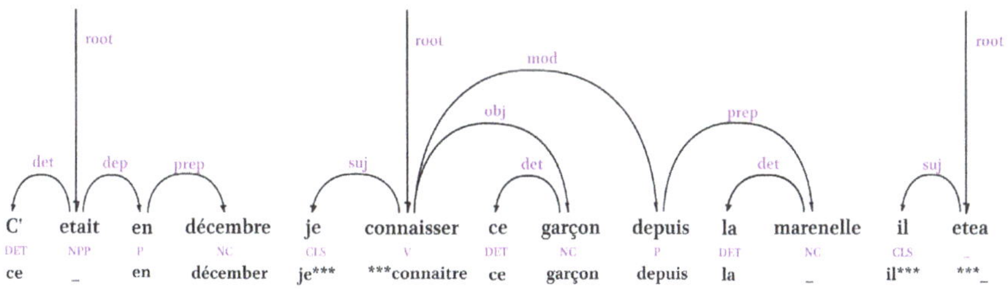

FIGURE 6.8A Dependency trees including part-of-speech annotations and lemmatization (bottom line)

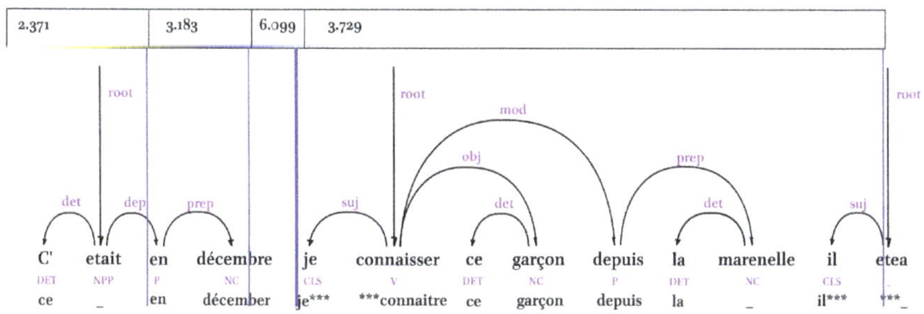

FIGURE 6.8B Dependency trees including pause visualisation. Pause length was measured in seconds.

6.6 Clustering and Cluster Visualisation

Topological learning is a field at the interface of topological data analysis (TDA) and machine learning. Neural network-based techniques are the most appropriate for topological learning as these approaches already represent a network. Topology captures multi-scale, global, and intrinsic properties of data sets based on homology (see Hensel et al., 2021 for a synthesis). Machine learning enables machines to learn from data, based on mathematical models. One possible outcome is clustering, which is a kind of categorization: data sharing the same parameters of similarity are grouped in clusters, which correspond to the sets of similar observations. Topological learning allows clustering and visualisation simultaneously. Clusters can be represented by more concise information than the rough listing of their patterns, such as their gravity center or different statistical moments.

6.6.1 *Clustering Parameters and Methodology*

As mentioned above, one of the characteristics of recorded writing data is its multi-dimensional nature. In order to subject these data to clustering methods, we had to identify similarity parameters that were both i) interesting for our research and ii) exploitable, i.e., available in the form of information and categorization of the data. Here again, analysis is a prerequisite for visualisation. We identified two groups of similarity parameters which are operational to date, but which can still be enriched: behavioral parameters (duration of pauses, production cycle, etc.) and linguistic parameters (length, content, POS-annotation).

Before clustering and visualising data, we need to apply an embedding approach in order to vectorize the semantic knowledge from the text. There are several methods to convert text data to numerical vectors, and among these methods two types of approaches can be found: Classic models such as TF-IDF and transformer-based models such as word2vec, Doc2Vec, fastText, Bert, etc. TF-IDF is a traditional NLP (Natural Language Processing) approach for text representation that shows the importance of a word in a document or in a collection of documents D, but it cannot capture the context and the semantic meaning of words, making it inadequate to represent textual documents for clustering. Thus, we need an advanced technique that can convert text to numerical vectors while capturing the important semantic information. We thus applied Doc2Vec and BERT embedding methods. Doc2Vec is a model that represents each document as a vector. BERT is a transformer-based language model developed by Google (Reimers & Gurevych, 2019) that learns contextual embeddings of words in sentences using the attention mechanism.

A word can have several representations depending on its context in the sentence. The model was pre-trained on a huge amount of textual data and it uses two training strategies: Masked Language Modelling (MLM) and Next Sentence Prediction (NSP). MLM consists in predicting the identity of a random masked input token using its context only while NSP predicts if two sentences are adjacent or not. Doc2Vec constructs representations of input sequences of variable length. It is applicable to texts of any length: sentences, paragraphs, and documents. The tool does not require task-specific tuning of the word weighting function nor does it rely on parse trees.

To cluster the data, we chose to use the HDBSCAN (Hierarchical Density-Based Spatial Clustering of Applications with Noise, Campello et al., 2013) algorithm which can automatically detect the number of clusters based on the density of points. DBSCAN is an unsupervised algorithm for clustering proposed by Ester et al. (1996). Given a number of points and an integer *k*, the algorithm organizes the points into k groups, called clusters, which are homogeneous and compact. Density estimation follows 4 stages:

– ε-neighbourhood of the observation, i.e., the number of points at most a distance ε from it.
– A core or high-density observation is an observation that has at least a certain number of neighbours including itself.
– All observations in the neighbourhood of a core observation belong to the same cluster.
– Any observation which is not a core observation, and which does not comprise a core observation in its vicinity, is considered an anomaly.

Based on DBSCAN adaptation, HDBSCAN constructs a cluster hierarchy tree and then uses a specific stability measure to extract flat clusters from the tree.

6.6.2 *Bursts Clustering Visualisation*

The data set can then be represented as a graph with data objects as vertices (a circle with a label), connected by weighted edges with the mutual reachability distances as weights. Using this graph to construct a minimum spanning tree and sorting its edges by mutual reachability distance results in a hierarchical tree structure (dendrogram). By choosing an epsilon as a global horizontal cut value and selecting all clusters with at least minPts points at this density level, we were able to retrieve the DBSCAN* clusters for this epsilon from the hierarchy.

Figures 6.9–6.12 below detail the graphical representations using each of the clustering methods.

The clusters identified in this way must also be “read” and analysed, giving access to the content of the bursts and to temporal information such as pauses.

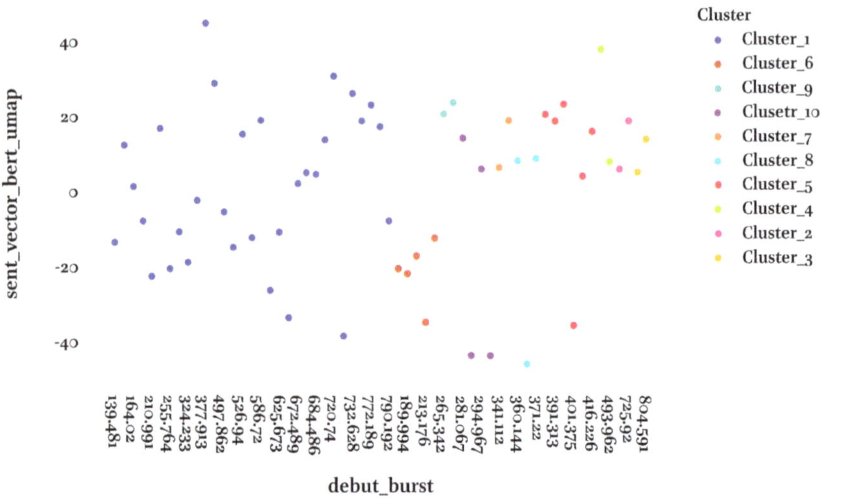

FIGURE 6.9 Bursts clustering visualisation based on the Bert-Sentence Transformer model

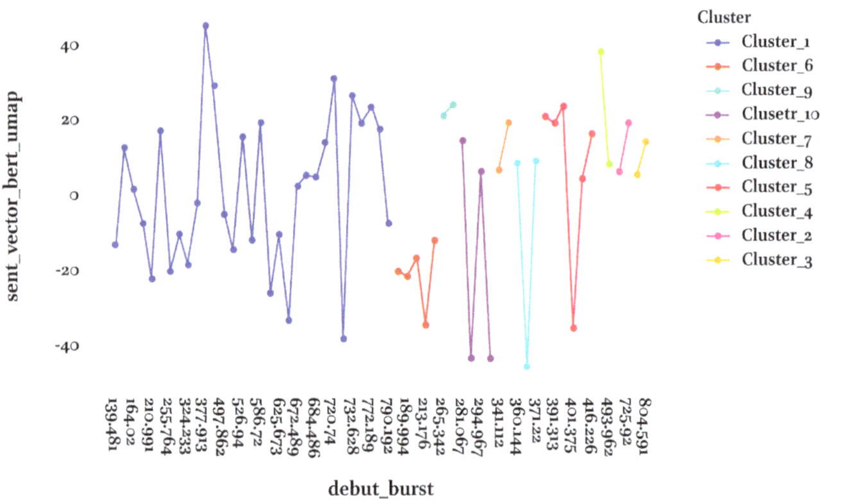

FIGURE 6.10 Dynamic behaviour of clusters based on the Bert-Sentence Transformer model

Below we illustrate the visualisation of burst content, with a colour associated with each identified cluster and the possibility of filtering.

Several clustering algorithms were integrated in the platform, in order to give access to different methodologies and various visualisation options. After the various treatments—we recall that, for us, visualisation is already the result of an analytical approach—the challenge is to articulate the different visualisation possibilities in a modular and flexible way.

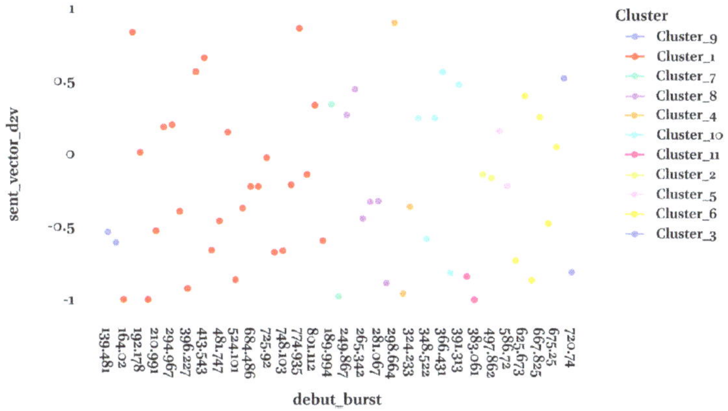

FIGURE 6.11 Clustering visualisation based on the Doc2Vec Method

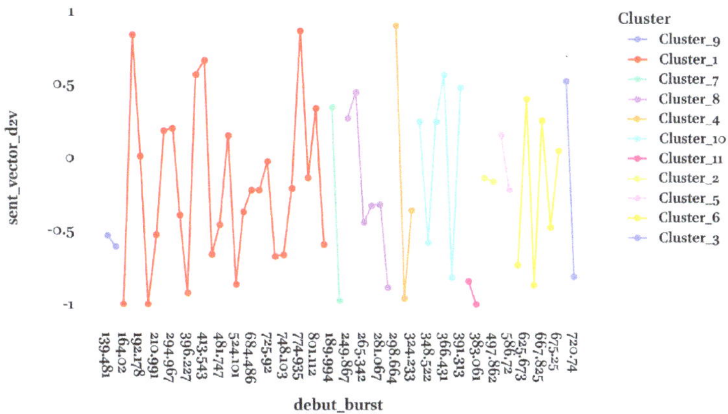

FIGURE 6.12 Dynamic behaviour of clusters based on the Doc2Vec method

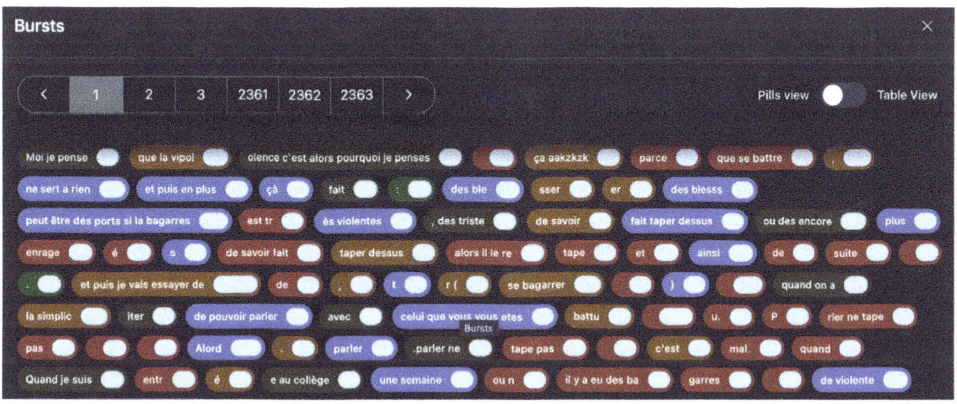

FIGURE 6.13 Burst content visualisation with color-coded information on cluster affiliation

6.7 The Pro-TEXT Bursts of Writing Visualisation Platform

Drawing visualisations for keylog behavioural and linguistic data and clustered burst data is quite challenging: visualisations have different shapes depending on the clustering algorithm chosen and its hyperparameters, or the pause threshold. Also, the cardinality of a burst set is large (> 15k bursts), and the number of attributes can exceed 15. Last but not least, additional attributes are often added when a raw Inputlog .idfx file is converted to a list of bursts (writer information, start time, end time, burst text, burst position ...). One of the prerequisites is to decide which visualisations are the most relevant, and the other one is the ability to generate different burst visualisations easily in order to compare them. These needs led us to create our own visualisation platform. This platform, related to the Pro-TEXT project, is user-friendly and enables researchers to build plots from burst data quickly, with no programming skills required, while allowing sufficient freedom over the choice of certain hyperparameters or visualisation types.

Given a list of bursts, usually presented as a .csv or .xlsx file, the platform lets the user choose the clustering algorithm and some related hyperparameters (number of clusters, max iterations ...) that will be applied to the burst dataset.

The visualisation platform offers the ability to:
- filter the data with conditions on the burst attributes, in order to reduce the amount of data, focusing on a burst subset, or by removing outliers that affect visualisation quality;
- obtain 1D, 2D and 3D visualisations with burst attributes chosen by the user as axes, and the possibility to switch axes/attributes instantly;
- view all bursts globally, while retaining chronological information;
- visualise and export subsets of the burst dataset.

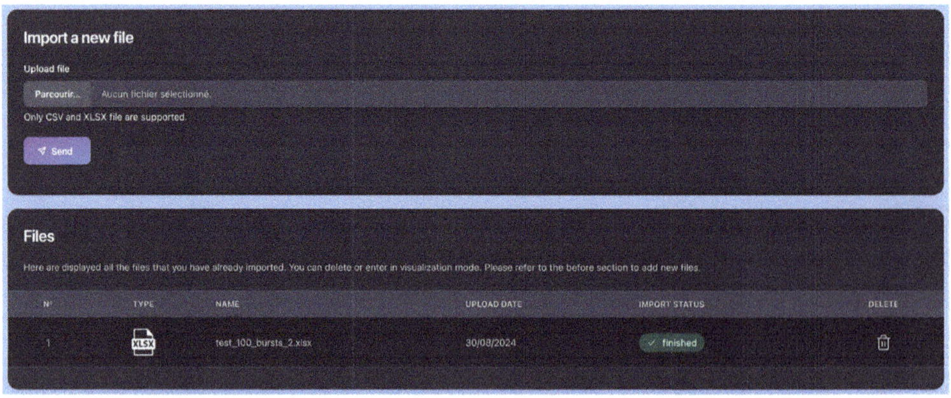

FIGURE 6.14 File import panel of the visualisation platform

Figure 6.15 below offers an example of a 1D visualisation (bar chart) on the *burst_len* (burst length) attribute. The data are filtered in order to retain only the bursts which satisfy the following parameters:
- burst_type: production
- burst_len: > −20 characters
- burst_len: < 50 characters

The same data can be exploited to draw a 2D chart by adding another attribute, as shown by Figure 6.16: by applying the same filters as in Figure 6.15, we draw a 2D scatter plot with *burst_len* on the X-axis, and *pause* on the Y-axis.

A 3D scatter plot can be created by adding another attribute. To obtain the graph in Figure 6.17, we draw a 3D scatter plot with *burst_len* on the X-axis, *pause* on the Y-axis, and the *cluster ID* on the Z-axis. To obtain this figure, the clustering algorithm chosen was K-Means, and the filters were the same as above (Figures 6.15 and 6.16).

During their research, users can visualise all the bursts or a selected subset of bursts as coloured pills (Figure 6.13), or preserve the classic table visualisation, which consists in displaying each burst, with all its attributes, in a row (see Figure 6.5 above).

In addition to the classic 1D, 2D and 3D plots, new types of charts can be added, depending on the research needs, thanks to the modularity of our platform. The overall goal of our project is to build an end-to-end solution for burst data visualisation, from the .idfx file to the construction of a variety of customized visualisations. A range of clustering algorithms can be integrated in the platform, making it possible to compare clusters and the different plots.

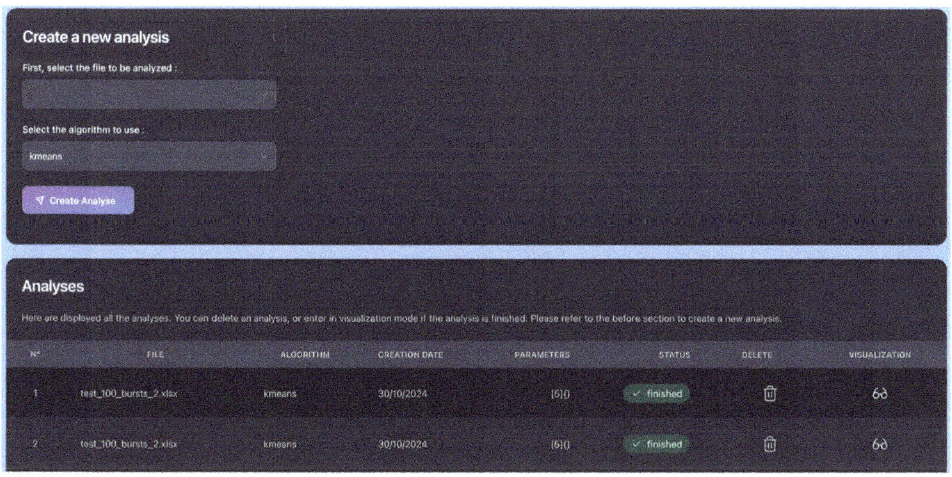

FIGURE 6.15 Analysis creation panel (i.e., choice of clustering algorithm) of the visualisation platform

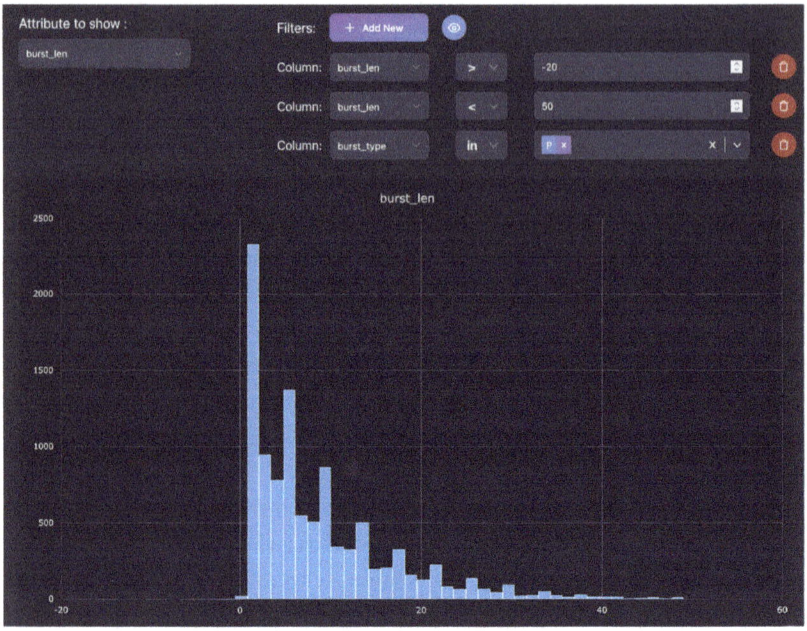

FIGURE 6.16 1D bar chart created with the visualisation platform

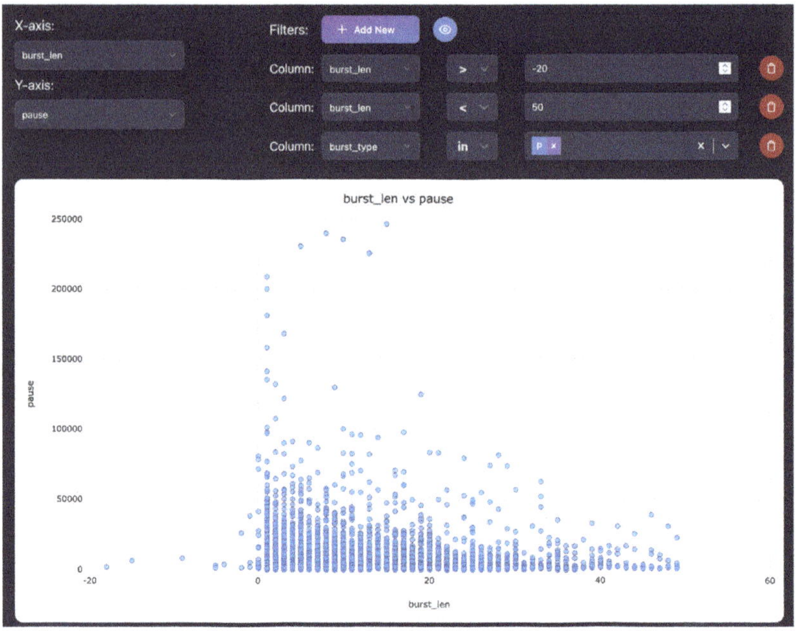

FIGURE 6.17 2D scatter plot created with the visualisation platform

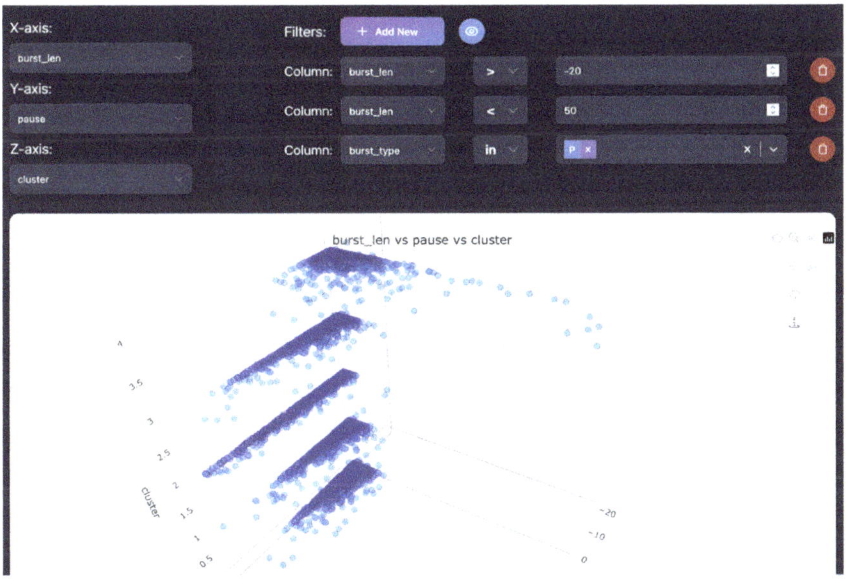

FIGURE 6.18 3D scatter plot created with the visualisation platform

6.8 Conclusions and Perspectives

This work is based on the observation that writing is defined by its visuo-spatial character, to which the temporal dimension is added as soon as the writing process is taken into account. It looks at the possibilities of visualisation that articulate both the behavioural and linguistic parameters of the writing process and questions the articulation between the temporal dimension (usually related to the behavioural dimension) and the spatial dimension, specific to text. This implies representing, at the same time or in parallel, the linear temporality of the process and the spatial non-linearity, which is particularly evident in revision operations. The review of several linear representations, delinearisation and layered representations illustrates a range of technical possibilities, but also the fact that the choice of visualisation strategy can depend on analysis needs and focus (on behaviour or on the language dimension, for example). Our starting point is the analysis of bursts of writing, defined as language sequences produced between two pauses with a predefined threshold of observation. The aim of the analysis is to understand whether and how the occurrence of a pause is determined by the nature of the linguistic units produced, and vice versa. The heterogeneity of the data then becomes apparent, with, on the one hand, the diversity of parts-of-speech or rewriting events and, on the other, the variability of pause duration and burst length. To cope with the heterogeneity of the data to be analysed, we used topological learning methods, which combine a topological approach with a machine learning approach. The need for prior analysis is in line with the statement made by Basso Fossali et al. (2022: 8–9), according to whom "visualisation should be precisely a perspective that modulates its [the mass of information] internal possibilities and then stabilizes itself where it encounters an interpretive question that can be associated with a body of objects emerging from the bottom of the information archive. And it is left to artificial intelligence and its deep learning to offer *salient* visualisations."

As part of the Pro-TEXT project, we have developed a platform for visualising keylog data. This platform integrates an analytical part, the different approaches to which have been developed in the article. Due to the analytical dimension, it is also designed to be user-friendly, modular and scalable, so as to provide users with a wide range of options. Users also have options for colour selection and data filtering. To sum up, the set of visualisations we have produced as part of our research into writing and their interpretation respond to two specific constraints:

- one concerns the perception of the writing process as dynamic, (non)linear and resistant to a monochrome two-dimensional visual representation, i.e., we need to exploit multi-layered or 3-dimensional visual representations, and enrich them with color-codes for distinct shapes and classes/clusters;
- the other concerns the identification of the research questions that determine the identity of the objects and features to be observed, as well as the links between them.

With a view to the operationalization of visualisations, a more in-depth digital exploitation of some of the graphic features identified by Bertin (1967) such as colour, pattern, shape, position, orientation—and also value—is an avenue to be explored and developed. As primary means to encode data graphically, these variables make information salient and relationships distinct. From this point of view, it is also important to distinguish between contrastive (unordered) and numerical or progressive (ordered) data.

References

Basso Fossali, P., Dondero, M.G., & Yoka, L. 2022. Semiotic approaches to big data visualization. *Punctum* 8(1): 5–12.

Bécotte-Boutin, H., Caporossi, G., Hertz, A., & Leblay, C. 2019. Chapter 4 Writing and Rewriting: the Coloured Numerical Visualization of Keystroke Logging. In Lindgren, E., & Sullivan, K. (eds) *Observing Writing*. Leiden, The Netherlands: Brill. https://doi.org/10.1163/9789004392526_006.

Bertin, J. 1967. *La Sémiologie Graphique.* Paris, La Haye, Mouton; Paris, Gauthier-Villars.

Blanche-Benveniste, C. (1997). *Approches de la langue parlée en français* [*Approaches to speech in French*]. Paris, Ophrys.

Bosveld-de Smet, L., & Verheggen, R.-J. 2016. Comparison of diagrams in producing and understanding hierarchies in three different application domains. In Jamnik, M., Usaka, Y. et Elzer Schwartz, S. (eds) *Diagrams 2016. Diagrammatic representation and inference*, Vol. 9781, Berlin, Springer, https://doi.org/10.1007/978-3-319-42333-3_23, pp. 272-279.

Campello, R.J.G.B., Moulavi, D., & Sander, J. 2013. Density-Based Clustering Based on Hierarchical Density Estimates. In: Pei, J., Tseng, V.S., Cao, L., Motoda, H., Xu, G. (eds) *Advances in Knowledge Discovery and Data Mining. PAKDD 2013. Lecture Notes in Computer Science*, vol 7819. Springer, Berlin, Heidelberg, pp. 160 172. https://doi.org/10.1007/978-3-642-37456-2_14.

Chenoweth, N.A., & Hayes, J.R. (2001). Fluency in Writing: Generating Text in L1 and L2. *Written Communication, 18*(1): 80–98.

Cislaru, G. 2015. Introduction: the process/product interface. In Georgeta Cislaru (ed.), *Writing(s) at the Crossroads: the process/product interface*, Amsterdam – Philadelphia: John Benjamins, pp. 1–17.

Cislaru, G., Olive, Th. 2018. *Le processus de textualisation* [*The process of textualisation*]. Bruxelles: De Boeck.

Ester, M., Kriegel, H.-P., Sander, J., & Xu, X. 1996. A density-based algorithm for discovering clusters in large spatial databases with noise. *Proc. 2nd Int. Conf. on Knowledge Discovery and Data Mining.* Portland, OR, pp. 226–231.

Fayol, M. 1997. *Des idées au texte Psychologie cognitive de la production verbale, orale et écrite.* Presses Universitaires de France.

Fenoglio, I., & Ganascia, J.-G. 2007. MEDITE: un logiciel pour l'approche comparative de documents de genèse. *Genesis* 27: 166–168.

Ferrer, D. 2011. *Logiques du brouillon. Modèles pour une critique génétique.* Paris: Éditions du Seuil.

Flower, L.S., & Hayes, J.R. 1980. The dynamics of composing: Making plans and juggling constraints. In Lee W. Gregg, Erwin R. Steinberg (Eds.). *Cognitive Processes in Writing.* Hillsdale, NJ: Lawrence Erlbaum, pp. 31–50.

Grésillon, A. 2016 [1994]. *Eléments de critique génétique.* Paris: CNRS Editions.

Grésillon, A., & Lebrave, J.-L. 2008. Linguistique et génétique des textes: un décalogue. *Le français moderne, numéro spécial « Tendances actuelles de la linguistique française »*: 37–49.

Hay, L. 2002. *La littérature des écrivains. Questions de critique génétique.* Paris: Corti.

Hayes, J.R. (1996). A new framework for understanding cognition and affect in writing. In C.M. Levy & S.E. Ransdell (eds), *The Science of Writing: Theories, Methods, Individual differences, and applications*, Mahwah (NJ): Lawrence Erlbaum Associates, 1–27.

Hayes, J.R., & Flower, L.S. 1980. Identifying the organization of writing processes. In L.W. Gregg, E.R. Steinberg (eds). *Cognitive processes in writing.* Hillsdale, NJ: Lawrence Erlbaum, pp. 3–30.

Halliday, M.A.K. 1977. Text as a semantic choice in a social context. In T. van Dijk, J.S. Petöfi (éds) *Grammar & Descriptions. Studies in Text Theory and Text Analysis,* Berlin: De Gruyter, pp. 175–225.

Hensel, F., Moor, M., & Rieck, B. 2021. A Survey of Topological Machine Learning Methods. *Frontiers in Artificial Intelligence* 4. URL = https://www.frontiersin.org/journals/artificial-intelligence/articles/10.3389/frai.2021.681108. DOI = 10.3389/frai.2021.681108.

Keim, D.A., Mansmann, F., Schneidewind, J., & Ziegler, H. 2006. "Challenges in Visual Data Analysis", *Proceedings of Information Visualization (IV 2006), IEEE*, pp. 9–16.

Kellogg, R.T., & Mueller, S. (1993). Performance amplification and process restructuring in computer-based writing. *Journal of Man-Machine Studies* 39, 33–49.

Lardilleux, A., Fleury, S., & Cislaru, G. 2013. Allongos: Longitudinal Alignment for the Genetic Study of Writers' Drafts. *Lecture Notes in Computer Sciences* 7817: 537–548.

Leblay, C., & Caporossi, G. 2015. A graph theory approach to online writing data visualization. In Georgeta Cislaru (ed.) *Writing at the Crossroads: The Process-Product Interface.* Amsterdam – Philadelphia: John Benjamins, pp. 171–182.

Lebrave, J.-L. (1999). Les manuscrits entre la substance de l'expression et la substance du contenu. In C. Cortès & A. Rousseau (eds). *Catégories et connexions. En hommage à Jean Fourquet pour son centième anniversaire.* Villeneuve d'Ascq: Presses Universitaires du Septentrion, 371–378.

Legallois, D. 2021. Illustrations et réflexions sur une opération cognitive fondamentale: la schématisation en linguistique—du lexique aux constructions grammaticales. In François, J. (dir.) *L'expansion pluridisciplinaire des grammaires de constructions,* Bibliothèque de Syntaxe & Sémantique, 21–46. Presses universitaires de Caen.

Leijten, M., & Van Waes, L. (2013). Keystroke logging in writing research: Using Inputlog to analyze and visualize writing processes. *Written Communication, 30*(3), 358–392.

Lindgren, E., Sullivan, K.P.H. 2002. The LS Graph: A Methodology for Visualizing Writing Revision. *Language Learning* 52(3): 565–595.

Lindgren, E., & Sullivan, K.P.H. (2019). *Observing writing: Insights from keystroke logging and handwriting.* In R. Fidalgo & T. Olive (Series Eds.), *Studies in Writing, Vol. 38.* Brill.

Mahlow, C., Ulasik, M.A., & Tuggener, D. 2022. Extraction of transforming sequences and sentence histories from writing process data: a first step towards linguistic modeling of writing. *Reading & Writing.* https://doi.org/10.1007/s11145-021-10234-6.

Mazziotta, N., François, J., & Kahane, S. 2023. Des outils graphiques pour étudier le langage et les langues. Les diagrammes en linguistique. *Travaux de linguistique* 87(2): 7–28.

Miletic Haddad, A., Benzitoun, C., Cislaru, G., & Herrera-Yanez, S. 2022. Pro-TEXT: An annotated corpus of key-stroke logs, *LREC 2022*.

Olive, T., Lebrave, J.-L., Passerault, J.-M., & Le Bigot, N. 2010. La dimension visuo-spatiale de la production de textes: approches de psychologie cognitive et de critique génétique. *Langages*, 177, p. 29–55.

Olive, T., & Passerault, J.-M. 2012. The visuospatial dimension of writing. *Written Communication*, 29(3), 326–344.

Olmanson, J., Kennett, K., Magnifico, A., McCarthey, S., Searsmith, D., Cope, B., & Kalantzis, M. 2015. Visualizing Revision: Leveraging Student-Generated Between-Draft Diagramming Data in Support of Academic Writing Development. *Technology, Knowledge and Learning*, *21*(1), 99–123. https://doi.org/10.1007/s10758-015-9265-5.

Plane, S., Alamargot, D., & Lebrave, J. 2010. Temporalité de l'écriture et rôle du texte produit dans l'activité rédactionnelle. *Langages*, n° 177(1), 7–28.

Reimers, N., Gurevych, I. 2019. Sentence-BERT: Sentence Embeddings using Siamese BERT-Networks. *arXiv preprint arXiv*:1908.10084.

Severinson Eklundh, K.S., & Kollberg, P. 1996. Computer tools for tracing the writing process: From keystroke records to S-notation. In Rijlaarsdam, G., Van den Bergh, H., Couzijn, M. (Eds.), *Theories, models and methodology in writing research* (pp. 526–541). Amsterdam, Netherlands: Amsterdam University Press.

Wengelin, A., Torrance, M., Holmqvist, K., Simpson, S., Galbraith, D., Johansson, V., & Johansson, R. (2009). Combined eye tracking and keystroke-logging methods for studying cognitive processes in text production. *Behavior Research Methods, 41*, 337–351. http://dx.doi.org/10.3758/BRM.41.2.337.

Xu, S., & Hirohito, S. 2007. Writing blocks: a visualization to support global revising. *Australasian Computer-Human Interaction Conference.*

Zhong, M. 2020. *Produire un texte cohérent dans une langue étrangère: l'exemple d'étudiants chinois de niveau intermédiaire et avancé de FLE en France.* PhD Dissertation, Université Sorbonne nouvelle.

CHAPTER 7

Visualising the Genesis of a Text: a Workflow for Analysing Keystroke Logging Data with a Text Genetic Approach

Lamyk Bekius and Floor Buschenhenke

What changes have been made to the text? There is much more to this seemingly simple question than meets the eye and depending on the field of study or research perspective, its meaning might vary. The effect of the changes on the quality of the text (Tanoï Namio et. al., this volume, p. 106), may be of interest for writing pedagogy, while a focus on professional writing may emphasise the cognitive and social dynamics of the writing process (Perrin, this volume, p. 176). In this chapter, we approach this question from the perspective of genetic criticism. Genetic criticism is a field within literary studies and textual scholarship which examines creative invention through the drafts, manuscripts, notes, and other textual evidence that have been preserved from a writing process (Grésillon, 1997; Deppman, Ferrer & Groden, 2004; Van Hulle, 2022). Contrary to other fields within textual scholarship, its main interest lies with the pre-publication stage of a work's trajectory. It studies literary works, but also scientifical and historically significant sources. This genetic perspective foregrounds a range of other questions, including, but not limited to: How do these changes affect our understanding of the text? How did an idea develop from a preliminary note to an integral part of the text? And how do the writing operations provide insights into the writer's poetics, or their creative process? To be able to approach such questions, genetic criticism aims to reconstruct the story behind how the text was written by looking at the traces of writing. On a single documentary source, such as for example a page from a handwritten manuscript (see Figure 7.1), one can find evidence of different periods of writing, such as a base text, with immediate revisions in the form of strikethrough words followed by new materials within the lines, and then there can be text added or removed at a later stage, with additions for example occurring in the margins or in between the already written lines, and deletions through crossing out or striking through. By examining the marginal and

HTTPS://DOI.ORG/10.1163/9789004760264-008

interlinear additions, the strikethrough words, different pen and pencil colours, and other scribbled corrections, an analysis of the process can be made.

However, now that present-day writers foremost write their (literary) texts on a computer, these 'analogue' traces of the writing process are replaced by digital traces. This poses challenges for genetic criticism—how to investigate the additions and deletions while word processors are initially programmed to visualise a clean text, without visible revisions (Mathijsen, 2009). One solution to this challenge is to collaborate with (literary) writers to log their writing process with a keystroke logger (Bekius 2021; 2023, Buschenhenke 2025). For the text genetic researcher, this brings along opportunities to study the creative writing process at an unprecedented level of detail, but it also requires them to adopt a new workflow that adapts the text genetic methodology to the keystroke logging data.

Long-term (literary) writing processes take place over many writing sessions, resulting in many session-versions and many hours of keystroke logging data. The material is fine-grained but can be overwhelming. Therefore, in this chapter, we will propose a workflow for analysing keystroke logging data from long-term writing processes using a text-genetic approach. Although we work with literary texts by professional writers, the method we propose is very well suited for other forms of long-term writing, such as academic writing by students and faculty, or business writing. In our exemplary workflow, we will draw specifically on our experience of working with literary writers to study the genesis of (literary) fiction and emphasise the role of text-based visualisations. For us, in this particular use case, a visualisation is the output of a scholarly act of making a visual display of information that emphasises a specific property of that information. It is not per se an 'image' or chart representing the writing process, but can use a range of visual aspects, such as colour or interactivity to draw attention to specific properties of the writing process. Bleeker, Buitendijk, and Haentjens Dekker (2019) emphasise that "the process of visualising data is a scholarly activity in line with the process of modelling, hence the resulting visualisation influences the ways in which a text can be studied" (158). The visualisations discussed in this chapter, therefore, are specifically meant to stimulate reading the text production along with the textual changes in their temporal and spatial context. This implies being able to follow the movements of the author or at least their cursor, through the working document (spatial) in chronological order (temporal) (Conijn, Dux Speltz, Van Zaanen, Van Waes & Chukharev-Hudilainen, 2022).

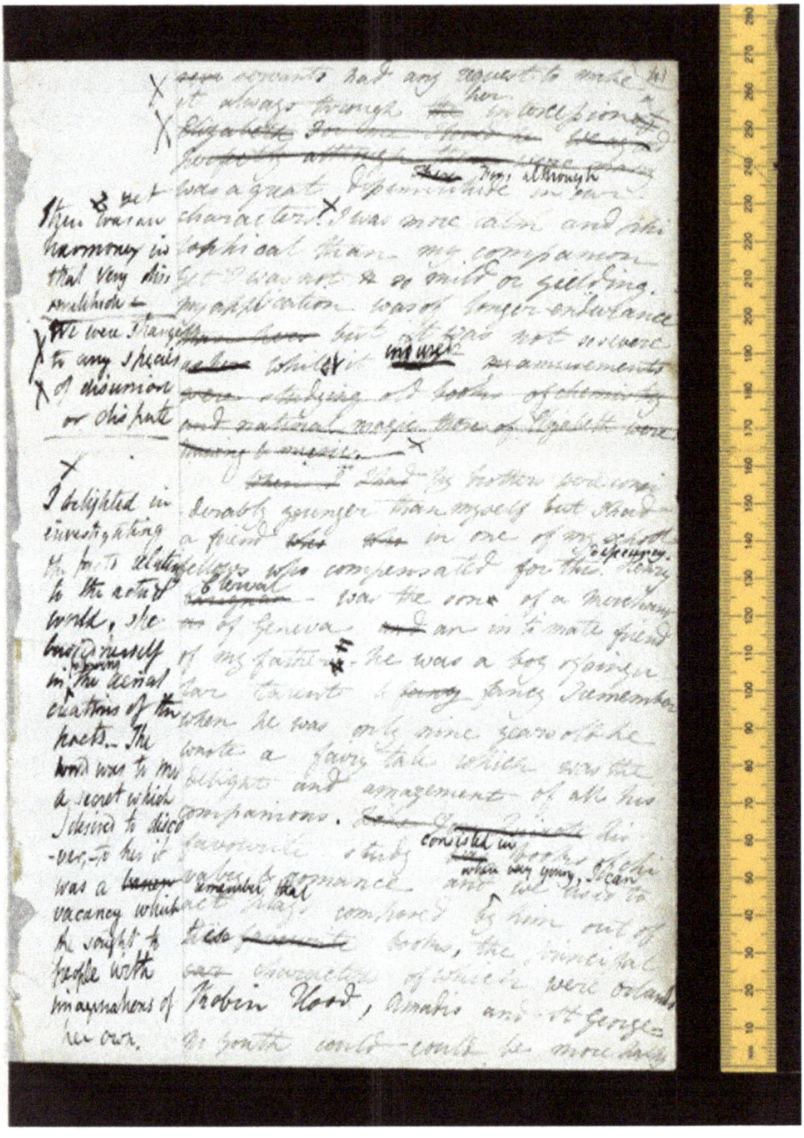

FIGURE 7.1 Page from Mary W. Shelley's draft of *Frankenstein*, MS. Abinger c. 56, r4, 1816 (Shelley)

7.1 Collaboration with Authors

The NWO-funded project Track Changes (2018–2024) was set up to study the born-digital writing processes of contemporary authors. We reached out to authors with the help of the Dutch and Flemish Literature foundations, the authors' unions in both regions, and various publishers. We also contacted several authors directly. Before announcing our call, we had obtained the green light from the university's ethics board, which is mandatory in most places when your research involves participants. We had prepared an author's agreement form as well as an information brochure, and had set a modest financial compensation for the authors' time. We met with interested writers, demonstrated the keystroke logging tool and further discussed our plans. Eleven writers decided to participate in our study.

As we wished to observe their writing in the most natural conditions possible, yet we also wanted to compare the processes and ensure that their work would be complete in time for our project, we asked them to write short stories of a minimum of 3000 words. For each individual writer, an agreement was made about the time period they would be working—though extensions were given as well. The topic of the story was free. Several writers indicated they already had a story commission, and would be working on that, and other writers created something specifically prompted by this experiment.

As Inputlog works with Windows, those participants who did not own a Windows machine were supplied with a rented laptop, on which we pre-installed Inputlog. The writers themselves were in charge of their project management; this included when and where to work on their stories and practically; when to switch the logger on and off again and when to share their logging data with the researchers. Apart from the occasional technical hiccup, the writers registered their processes quite faithfully. The keystroke data is stored in the form of working periods, so each episode where the writer switches the logger off again, a 'writing session' is stored with all files for this episode.

Together, our eleven participants created 175 hours of keystroke sessions. In this chapter, we will showcase our approach to visualisation of keystroke data with the help of one of these processes, namely the data from Roos van Rijswijk.[1] Van Rijswijk (1985) is a Dutch writer, moderator and book reviewer whose debut novel *Onheilig* (2016) was received very favourably. She also writes short stories and poetry. In 2020, when she joined the experiment, she

1 The visualisations of Van Rijswijk's writing process can be found on Nanogenesis Digital: https://nanogenesis-digital.github.io.

was finishing up the short story collection *De dwaler* (2021). She wrote the story *Zorgvlied* as one of the final stories for this manuscript, in seven keystroke logged sessions, spanning a little over 8 hours, in December 2020. In *Zorgvlied*, a mother and adult child take a lockdown stroll over the Zorgvlied cemetery. While they are affectionately bantering with each other, they are visited by their foremothers, who only the child can see. Mother and child reminisce about their close encounters with death, the state of the world during the pandemic, and the enduring crisis in the Dutch housing market. The child has gone through a rough time, and has been seeing their foremothers regularly—but kept this to themself.

7.2 Visualisations for a Text Genetic Analysis

Once the author has finished writing, it is the researcher's task to analyse the keystroke logging data, in this case with a text genetic perspective. The aim of genetic criticism is to investigate the genesis of texts in order "to construct a series of hypotheses on the operation of writing" (Grésillon, 1997, 106). This relates to the second of the two objectives of genetic criticism later outlined by Pierre-Marc De Biasi (2004). The first objective consists of the constitution of readable and analysable manuscripts, and the second entails the critical dimension: the reconstruction of the logic of the genesis. This entails that the manuscripts have to be presented in some particular way *before* the writing process can be analysed. According to De Biasi, therefore, "the essential objective of text genetics is to produce genetic editions" (De Biasi 2004, 61). In Elli Bleeker's definition, a digital genetic edition is a digital publication that presents the genetic dossier of a creative work and "contains one or several tools that enable further exploration of the content and thus further study of the genesis of the work" (2017, 59). Genetic editions, in this sense, offer 'visualisations' of the writing process that function as a research instrument. For our goal of analysing the keystroke logged writing process from a text genetic perspective we therefore need a visualisation resembling a genetic edition but constructed with keystroke logging material instead of paper manuscripts.

Genetic digital editions, such as the Samuel Beckett Digital Manuscript Project (Dillen, 2015), the Shelley Godwin archive and the Melville electronic library (which houses several fluid text editions of Melville's works) provide access to the transcribed texts ("You look at the manuscript and record what you see." Robinson, 2016, p. 184) with their changes, and a presentation of the facsimiles (scans of the original documents), often presented side-by-side.[2] Some form of interactivity, such as text searches and filters, is often possible. The digital edition of the novel *Frankenstein* within the Shelley Godwin archive, for example, offers a functionality to switch between the highlights of the hand in the manuscript. As Mary and Percy Shelley collaborated on the novel *Frankenstein*, the edition allows the reader/user to view only Mary's writings or, conversely, only Percy's revisions.[3] An example of an online archive of born-digital materials[4] (but not keystroke logged) is the Digital Variants project—now sadly defunct.[5] It offered various tools to explore the collection of differing drafts of digitally written poetry and prose by a number of Italian authors, including a 'genetic machine' that visualised textual differences in an interactive way (Fiormonte & Pusceddu, 2006). Worth a mention, although it is not a genetic edition per se, is the literary journal *Midst*, created by Annelyse Gelman.[6] Poets use a specifically designed word processor, which stores all of their textual development. The poems are then published as an 'interactive timelapse', allowing the readers to follow along the creation process.

For keystroke data, both text-based and movement-based visualisations are used. Movement-based visualisations show the writer's tracks through the working document, by visualising the cursor position over time, often along with document length and number of characters typed. Some examples of this kind of visualisation are the LS-graph (Lindgren & Sullivan, 2002; Leblay et al., this volume, p. 73), the progression diagram (Perrin, 2019; Fürer, 2017), and Inputlog's process graph (Leijten & Van Waes, 2013). Movement-based graphs can indicate when and to what extent the writer has revised their text-so-far, and when they were concentrating on expanding their working documents with new material.

An example of a text-based visualisation is the S-notation (Kollberg & Severinson Ekhlund, 2002, 91; Leblay et al., p. 73). The S-notation represents the changes in the text where they occur, and provides information about the extent, order and structure of the revisions (Kollberg & Severinson Ekhlund, 2002, 91). Due to inaccuracies in the recording itself and limitations of the software, these are not applicable to long-term writing processes in

2 http://www.beckettarchive.org; http://shelleygodwinarchive.org/; https://melville.electroniclibrary.org/editions (accessed on 2 February 2024).

3 In this case, revisions means visible changes to the text (Fitzgerald, 1987).

4 'Literature that is written within a digital environment' Bekius, 2023, p. 62.

5 https://web.archive.org/web/20230610235043/http://digitalvariants.org/ (accessed on 2 February 2024).

6 https://www.midst.press/read (accessed on 2 February 2024).

which the writers move through their documents not just from top to bottom, but non-linearly (Buschenhenke, Conijn & Van Waes, 2023). Moreover, various edits in a single text fragment impacts the legibility of the S-notation.

Combining the two, textual changes and chronological movement, is quite rare. The progressive graph visualisation (Bécotte-Boutin et al., 2015; 2017) is an example of the latter, which shows the text that is being changed along with the order in which the writer has made textual changes at various locations in the text. The text history visualisation by Mahlow et al. (2021) takes sentences as the unit of analysis, and although the content of the sentences is not shown, does provide a quantitative overview of how the text was changed. It achieves this by showing which sentences have been altered, in the context of an abstract representation of the whole text-so-far.

While these visualisations of keystroke data all offer valuable representations of the writing process, none of them offer a proper way of visualising the text suitable for a text genetic analysis. We have therefore applied the methodologies from digital scholarly editing projects to the keystroke logging data. In that way we have come to a workflow that leads to the creation of dynamic text-based visualisations that allow the reader to interact with it and promote reading the text with inclusion of the sequentiality of the writing actions.

7.3 Keystroke Logging and the Genetic Workflow

Since textual scholarship has a long tradition of studying analogue textual witnesses, we will look at methods and tools used in textual scholarship to see how they can be applied to working with keystroke logging data. In the workflow discussed below, we will focus on the steps of collation, text encoding, and eventually, visualisation. For illustrative purposes, we will focus primarily on Van Rijswijk's fifth writing session—and incidentally on the sixth writing session. The fifth session took place on 9th of December 2020, and had a duration of 2 hours, 55 minutes, and 42 seconds.

7.3.1 *Collation*

The first step in the workflow is to use collation tools to get a first impression of where changes were made during each writing session, which can help formulate more specific research questions. In essence, collation is the operation of comparing two or more texts to identify differences between them. Collation is used for various reasons, including examining textual variation, tracing the historical transmission of a text, producing a critical text, or—most relevant in this case—to study the creative writing process (Bleeker et al., 2019, 142). In textual scholarship, then, collation is used as a means in itself, and its output is the direct source of analysis. However, we use it as an intermediate step to support the next step in the workflow.

The keystroke logging data contains the version of the text at the beginning of the writing session as well as the version of the text at the end of the writing session. By making a collation of these two versions, the overall changes that have been made to the text can be visualised. While there are many collation tools and text comparison software's available, such as CollateX and its successor HyperCollate (for an overview, see Nury, 2018), we will discuss only two of them: MEDITE and Diff Annotator. We opted for these two since they offer, in a relatively simple way, an overview of the changes that have been made in the text.

MEDITE is developed in France as a collaboration between genetic critics at ITEM (Institut des Textes et Manuscrits Modernes) and Artificial Intelligence specialists from LIP6 (Laboratoire d'Informatique de Paris 6). It identifies deleted, inserted, replaced, moved and unaltered blocks of characters, and aligns these last three types. To visualise the results, the two texts are displayed side by side. Deletions, additions, and substitutions are highlighted in a specific colour (see Figure 7.1). Diff Annotator is developed by Vincent Neyt (University of Antwerp) for the eXtant Toolkit for Digital Scholarly Editing for the CLARIAH-VL Open Humanities Service Infrastructure (Shahidzadeh Asadi, Neyt and Bekius, 2024). It is a lightweight environment for annotating text-comparisons of two plain text files that produces a visualisation of the variation, based on Git Diff. Diff originated in computer science, where diff algorithms were designed to compare two different versions of the same code file, and to indicate the lines where the two versions differ. The text files are usually divided into segments (tokenized) based on carriage returns, which makes it less accurate when comparing prose with many changes (Nury 2018, 59). In Diff Annotator, the differences between the two texts are visualised in-line (see Figure 7.2). If needed, the text comparison can be corrected. Variants can then be annotated, and notes can be added in the right margin. While MEDITE, as specifically developed for text genetic research, is better at handling complex variations between the versions, Diff Annotator allows for manual correction and annotation of the variants.

Despite these differences, they both visualise the changes Van Rijswijk made to the text in session 5 quite accurately. The version comparison shows a revision that seems to be worthy of further analysis. In the preceding session, Van Rijswijk had written that the narrator does not ask her grandmother the reasons behind her 'visits', because such questions are dismissed with exasperated waving gestures as if she is asking about something boring like VAT

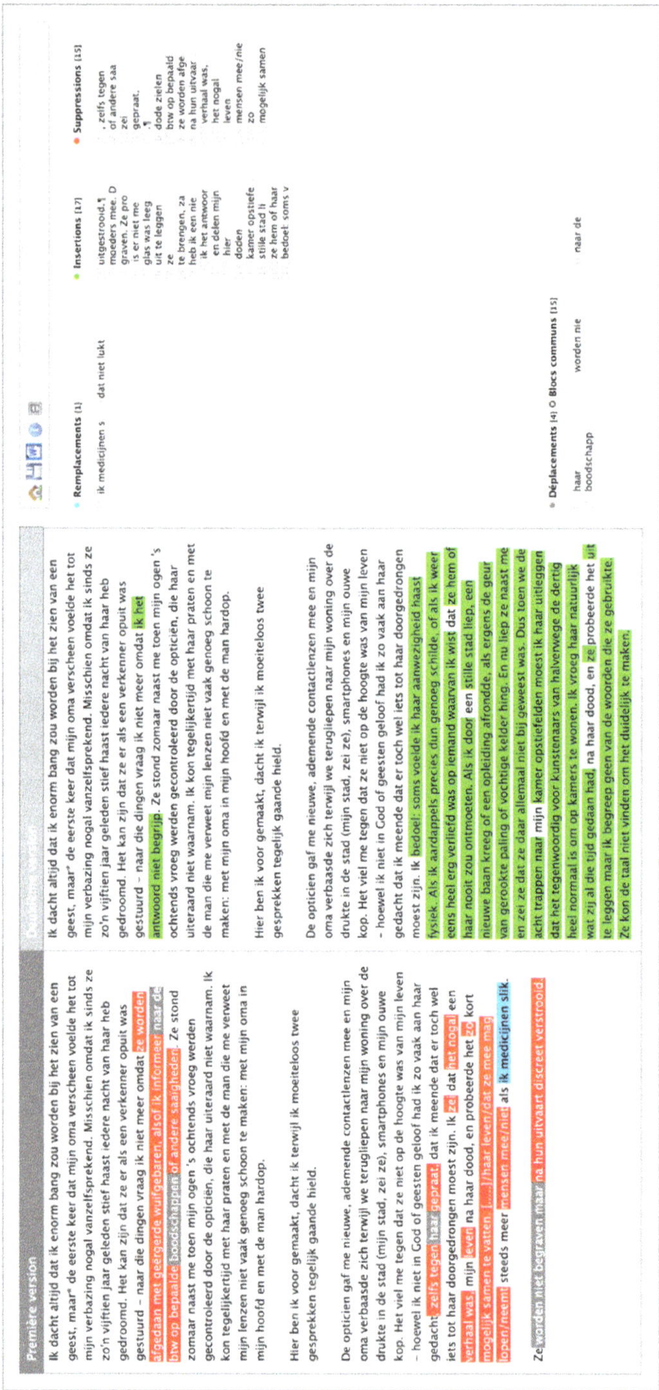

FIGURE 7.2 Visualisation of the collation output by MEDITE, comparing the end product of session 5 with the end product of the preceding session

DIFF ANNOTATOR

22 Ik dacht altijd dat ik enorm bang zou worden bij het zien van een geest, maar* de eerste keer dat mijn oma verscheen voelde het tot mijn verbazing nogal vanzelfsprekend. Misschien omdat ik sinds ze zo'n vijftien jaar geleden stief haast iedere nacht van haar heb gedroomd. Het kan zijn dat ze er als een verkenner opuit was gestuurd - naar die dingen vraag ik niet meer omdat ze worden afgedaan met geërgerde wuifgebaren, alsof ik informeer naar de btw op bepaalde boodschappen of andere saaïgheden. Ze stond zomaar naast me toen mijn ogen
het antwoord niet begrijp.
's ochtends vroeg werden gecontroleerd door de opticiën, die haar uiteraard niet waarnam. Ik kon tegelijkertijd met haar praten en met de man die me verweet mijn lenzen niet vaak genoeg schoon te maken: met mijn oma in mijn hoofd en met de man hardop.

23

24 Hier ben ik voor gemaakt, dacht ik terwijl ik moeiteloos twee gesprekken tegelijk gaande hield.

25

26 De opticien gaf me nieuwe, ademende contactlenzen mee en mijn oma verbaasde zich terwijl we terugliepen naar mijn woning over de drukte in de stad (mijn stad, zei ze), smartphones en mijn ouwe kop. Het viel me tegen dat ze niet op de hoogte was van mijn leven - hoewel ik niet in God of geesten geloof had ik zo vaak aan haar gedacht, zelfs tegen haar gepraat, dat ik meende dat er toch wel iets tot haar doorgedrongen moest zijn.
gedacht
Ik
zei
bedoel: soms voelde ik haar aanwezigheid haast fysiek. Als ik aardappels precies dun genoeg schilde, of als ik weer eens heel erg verliefd was op iemand waarvan ik wist
dat het nogal een
ze hem of haar nooit zou ontmoeten. Als ik door
verhaal was,
stille stad liep, een nieuwe baan kreeg of een opleiding afrondde, als ergens de geur van gerookte paling of vochtige kelder hing. En nu liep ze naast me en zei ze dat ze daar allemaal niet bij geweest was. Dus toen we de acht trappen naar
mijn
leven
kamer opstiefelden moest ik haar uitleggen dat het tegenwoordig voor kunstenaars van halverwege de dertig heel normaal is om op kamers te wonen. Ik vroeg haar natuurlijk wat zij al die tijd gedaan had,
na haar dood, en ze probeerde het uit te leggen maar ik begreep geen van de woorden die ze gebruikte. Ze kon de taal niet vinden om het duidelijk te maken.

27 Vreemd, zei ik.

FIGURE 7.3 Visualisation of the text comparison by Diff Annotator, comparing the end product of session 5 with the end product of the preceding session

on groceries. In session 5, Van Rijswijk modifies this sentence and changes the narrator's argument for not asking her grandmother questions like that anymore. Now it is just because she does not understand the answer.

Example 1

"Het kan zijn dat ze er als een verkenner opuit was gestuurd—naar die dingen vraag ik niet meer omdat *ze worden afgedaan met geërgerde wuifgebaren, alsof ik informeer naar de btw op bepaalde boodschappen of andere saaïgheden.*" ➔ "Het kan zijn dat ze er als een verkenner opuit was gestuurd—naar die dingen vraag ik niet meer omdat *ik het antwoord niet begrijp.*"

["It may be that she had been sent out as a scout—I don't ask about those things anymore because *they are dismissed with exasperated waving gestures, as if I were inquiring about* VAT *on certain groceries or other boring things.*" ➔ "It may be that she had been sent out as a scout—I don't ask about those things anymore because I don't understand the answer."]

The revision thus has the effect that the sentence changes from the narrator's detailed and slightly humorous interpretation of the grandmother's reaction to a somewhat dry statement that she does not understand the answer. This therefore seems to be a rather unusual revision, especially for Van Rijswijk, who usually makes revisions that make the text more detailed and specific. To better understand this revision, the keystroke logging data must be taken into account. We will further analyse the keystroke data underlying the textual changes found through collation, encoding and visualising the textual history in section 7.4.

7.3.2 *Text Encoding*

The second step in our workflow is therefore concerned with a method of capturing some of the characteristics of the writing process. To this end, we have chosen to encode all textual operations in TEI-compliant XML. The Text Encoding Initiative (TEI) is a consortium developing a standard for annotating texts in the humanities and social sciences in order to make them computer-readable for further processing. As a meta-markup language, XML, the extensible markup language, prescribes the 'syntactic' rules for annotating text in digital form (Burnard, 2014). According to these rules, text is annotated with tags, which are separated from the annotated text by angle brackets or chevrons (< and >) and should be properly nested. Tags can be further specified using attributes. The TEI Guidelines offer the vocabulary to fill this syntactical framework of XML and suggest using specific tags and attributes in a modular and adaptable way. The guidelines are intended to cover a wide range of texts, periods and purposes, including but not limited to literary texts, letters, linguistic corpora, dictionaries, written texts, spoken texts, blogposts and tweets. This flexibility has allowed us to adapt the tags and attributes currently available for encoding manuscripts so that they can also be applied to keystroke logging data.

Our encoding scheme captures all writing operations, such as additions, deletions, and the moving of text to a different location (translocations), in the context of the text, while also providing information about the process.[7] This allows us to analyse writing operations from both a product and a process perspective. The encoding itself is based solely on the overt writing operations

7 In this section, we will only briefly summarise the most important aspects of the encoding scheme for keystroke logging data. For more on encoding keystroke logging data in TEI, see Bekius 2021 & Bekius 2023. For the encoding manual, see: https://extant-cmg.github.io/eXtant-wiki/loxensis/encoding.

of the writer, and therefore leaves ample room for later analysis of the effects of the writing actions.

At its most basic level, digital writing involves only two writing operations: inserting and deleting. When text is typed in a word processor, it is inserted (added); when text is deleted, it is deleted by using the backspace or delete key to delete one character at a time, or by selecting the text to be deleted and deleting it, either through a delete or through over-writing. In essence, nearly every writing action is encoded using <add> (addition) and <del> (deletion) tags. These basic writing actions can then be specified using the attributes, indicating, for instance, the type of writing action and revision. In the encoding scheme, we distinguish between eleven *types* of writing actions: new text production, pre-contextual additions and deletions, contextual additions and deletions, typo related additions and deletions, returns to the leading edge, deletions, and additions for relocation of text fragments, and revised text production.

The first is, logically, the insertion of new text. For the encoding, we tagged the production of new text by encoding the addition of new sentences. For example, at a certain point in the sixth writing session, Van Rijswijk wrote ('added') a new sentence to the text produced so far: "De Aziatische man van eerder loopt langs met een kruiwagen vol macaroni" ["The Asian man from earlier walks by with a wheelbarrow full of macaroni."]. Table 7.1 offers an overview of the tags and attributes used to encode new text production and the other writing actions.

For the other types of writing actions, the encoding scheme builds on the taxonomy of Lindgren and Sullivan (2006), which distinguishes between 'pre-contextual' revisions ("revisions made before an externalised context is completed") and 'contextual' revisions ("revisions made within a completed externalised context"; see Lindgren, 2006, 159), and applies these types of revisions to the writing of a sentence. Thus, contextual revisions indicate revisions made in a previously written sentence. Van Rijswijk, for example, revised the newly added sentence described above somewhat later in session 6:[8]

8 For the sake of these examples, we are already jumping ahead to the final visualisations of the text encoding.

Example 2

[273]De Aziatische man van eerder loopt ~~nu [309]~~langs met een kruiwagen vol ongekookte [289]macaroni. (session 6)

[[273]The Asian man from earlier ~~now [309]~~walks past with a wheelbarrow full of uncooked [289]macaroni. (session 6)]

The first time Van Rijswijk returned to this sentence to revise it, she added the word “ongekookte” [“uncooked”] as an adjective to “macaroni”. The second time she returned to this sentence, she deleted the word “nu” [“now”]. These revisions are therefore contextual revisions since they were made *after* the initial production of the new sentence.

Taken together, a contextual deletion and a contextual addition sometimes form a substitution, but since this adds another level of interpretation, we did not encode this information. This stems from our choice to create a visualisation that is relatively free of interpretation.

In the encoding, the following contextual revisions—in which the word “raar” [“weird”] is replaced by the synonym “vreemd” [“strange”]—are just two separate revisions (one deletion and one addition), although after critical reading, you can conclude they form a single substitution:

Example 3

[67]~~Raar[424]~~Vreemd[425], zei ik. (session 6)

[[67]~~Weird[424]~~Strange[425], I said. (session 6)]

Contrary to contextual revisions, pre-contextual revisions take place more immediately, and at least before a sentence is completed. In example 4, Van Rijswijk started producing a sentence with “Wel ja,” [“Well yeah,”], but she immediately deleted this and started the sentence again by writing “Ze komen” [“They come”], which she then deleted again before settling on the formulation “Weer een nieuwe” [“Another new one”]. The deletion of “Wel ja,” and “Ze komen” are therefore pre-contextual deletions:

Example 4

~~[85]Wel ja, [186]~~~~[187]Ze komen[188]~~[189]Weer een n~~eu[190]~~[191]ieuwe. (session 5)

[~~[85]Well yeah, [186]~~~~[187]They come[188]~~[189]Another n~~eu[190]~~[191]w one. (session 5)]

Example 4 also illustrates another type of writing action, namely the correction of a typing error, or 'typo'. When Van Rijswijk was typing the word "nieuwe" ["new"], she missed the 'i'. She noticed this after writing 'eu', which she deleted to then continue typing 'ieuwe.' This fixed the typo. For genetic criticism, typos are not the most meaningful writing actions, but they can influence the writing process. For this reason, we have chosen to encode them as a separate type of writing action—which of course adds an interpretive layer to the encoding.

The pre-contextual deletions above were performed at the 'leading edge'. This is the location in a new, incomplete sentence where no more text follows. Often but not always this (moving) point is situated at the end of the working document, but it can occur anywhere "where new meaning is produced". (Lindgren et al., 2019). Pre-contextual revisions can also be made at another place within the sentence that is still in production, where some text does follow the revised segment. Example 5 illustrates such an instance. Van Rijswijk wrote the start of the sentence "Zonder iets te zeggen slaat ze het in, we moeten bukken om onder een overhangende hulst" ["Without saying anything, she enters it; we have to duck to get under an overhanging holly bush"]. Then she replaced the cursor to delete "onder" ["under"] and to type "langs" ["past"]. Since this revision is made before the sentence was finished, the separate addition and deletion are encoded as belonging to the type of pre-contextual revisions.

Example 5

[207]Zonder iets te zeggen slaat ze het in, we moeten bukken om ~~onder~~ ~~[208]~~<u>langs [209]</u>een overhangende hulst[210]struik te komen. (session 6)

[[207]Without saying anything, she enters it; we have to duck to get ~~under~~ ~~[208]~~<u>past [209]</u>an overhanging holly[210]bush. (session 6)]

After Van Rijswijk made the pre-contextual revision, she relocated the cursor back to the location at the end of the unfinished sentence where she wrote the end of the sentence: "struik te komen". This can be described as a 'return to the leading edge'. In the definition formulated by Lindgren et al. (2019), the leading edge is located "typically at the end of the text produced so far, but can also occur at the end of additions within previously written text where a writer inserts new ideas (not only revises form)" (347). When the author returns to the sentence to finish it and starts to create new meaning there after a modification elsewhere in the text, this finishing of the sentence would not be an addition. Therefore, to distinguish these returns to the leading edge from

TABLE 7.1 Overview of the different writing actions that can be encoded in the TEI-XML

Writing action	Description	XML tag with attribute
New text production	New sentences are added to the text produced so far	<add type="nt">*new text* </add>
Contextual additions	Text is added to a sentence that has already been written	<add type="context"> *addition*</add>
Contextual deletions	Text is deleted from a sentence that has already been written	<del type="pre-context"> *deletion*</del>
Pre-contextual additions	Text is added to a sentence that is in the process of being written	<add type="pre-context"> *new text*</add>
Pre-contextual deletions	Text is deleted from a sentence that is in the process of being written	<del type="pre-context"> *deletion*</del>
Typo related additions and deletions	Text is added to a sentence to correct a typo	<add type="typo"> *typo correction*</add>
Typo related deletions	Text is deleted from a sentence to correct a typo	<del type="typo"> *typo*</del>
Returns to leading edge	Text is added to finish a sentence after being away from the sentence	<mod type="pre-context"> *text*</mod>
Translocation deletion	A (part of) a sentence is deleted from the text to be relocated to another position in the text	<del type="translocation"> *deletion*</del>
Translocation addition	A (part of) a sentence is added as it comes from another position in the text	<add type="translocation"> *addition*</add>
Revised text	A sentence is retyped into the text in revised from	<add type="rt">*revised text* </add>

All tags listed above also require the attribute @seq and @id, respectively containing the date and timestamp of the writing action in the keystroke logging data and the id-number in the data of the first character of the encoded writing action, e.g., <add seq="20240524104459" type="nt" id="30" >*new text*</add>

'regular' additions, these actions are encoded differently in a <mod> tag and specified with the type 'continue'.

Some text may also be deleted and added again in a revised form; the inscription of this revised text is not necessarily 'new' text and is therefore classified as 'revised text'. The copy-pasting of text elements from one point in the document to another is accounted for in the encoding by giving it the type 'translocation'.

To be able to study the temporal aspect of the writing actions—specifically the sequentiality—we encoded the start time given in the keystroke logging data for each of the writing actions discussed above (in the @seq attribute). Based on this timestamp, we were able to chronologically order all the writing actions automatically and without much interpretation of the editor.

The resultant transcriptions of each writing session provide detailed information about the writing process and the location of the modifications in the text, but a visualisation of the transcription is essential to facilitate the analysis.

7.3.3 *Visualisation*

The third step in the workflow is therefore the visualisation of the writing process encoded in TEI-XML in the previous step. This can be done using the Keystroke Loxensis tool (Bekius, 2024). This tool provides an environment for further examination of the temporal and spatial dimension of textual changes and is made available by Lamyk Bekius as part of the eXtant Toolkit (Shahidzadeh Asadi, Neyt and Bekius, 2024). Once the writing process has been annotated, the document can easily be uploaded to Keystroke Loxensis, which will then give an overview of all the uploaded files, already providing an overview of some of the metadata, such as the title of the text, the author, the date of the session and its duration. It will also show the number of all the encoded modifications. Then, there are currently two visualisation-options available: the 'standard visualisation' and the 'annotation visualisation'. The standard visualisation is most suitable for the first exploration of the writing process. It can be used to make the annotations that can be visualised with the second visualisation option. This is especially useful for giving students feedback on their writing process, or giving additional information about how the writing process proceeded and how this can be interpreted. The visualisations discussed below, however, are part of both visualisation-options.

The default view in the given visualisation of the writing process is the state of the text at the beginning of the writing session—mostly, either a blank document or the text as it was at the end of the preceding writing session. By means of toggles, it is then possible to visualise the writing actions. The 'all modifications'-toggle activates the visualisation that offers a reconstruction of all the encoded types of writing actions in their textual context and encourages reading the text with all the changes made during this session (see Figure 7.3). The different types of writing actions are visualised in different colours: purple for new text production; orange for returns to the leading edge (returns to unfinished sentences); pink for pre-contextual deletions; light green for pre-contextual additions; dark red for contextual deletions; dark green for

Ik dacht altijd dat ik enorm bang zou worden bij het zien van een geest, maar* de eerste keer dat mijn oma verscheen voelde het tot mijn verbazing nogal vanzelfsprekend. Misschien omdat ik sinds ze zo'n vijftien jaar geleden stief haast iedere nacht van haar heb gedroomd. Het kan zijn dat ze er als een verkenner opuit was gestuurd - naar die dingen vraag ik niet meer omdat ~~ze worden afgedaan met geërgerde wuifgebaren, alsof ik informeer naar de btw op bepaalde boodschappen of andere saaïgheden~~ik het antwoord niet begrijp. Ze stond zomaar naast me toen mijn ogen 's ochtends vroeg werden gecontroleerd door de opticiën, die haar uiteraard niet waarnam. Ik kon tegelijkertijd met haar praten en met de man die me verweet mijn lenzen niet vaak genoeg schoon te maken: met mijn oma in mijn hoofd en met de man hardop.

Hier ben ik voor gemaakt, dacht ik terwijl ik moeiteloos twee gesprekken tegelijk gaande hield. ~~Later mertke kkte ik dat ik als ik mijn medicatie nam minder vaak bezoke ek kreeg van de overledenen, en omdat~~

De opticien gaf me nieuwe, ademende contactlenzen mee en mijn oma verbaasde zich terwijl we terugliepen naar mijn woning over de drukte in de stad (mijn stad, zei ze), smartphones en mijn ouwe kop. Het viel me tegen dat ze niet op de hoogte was van mijn leven - hoewel ik niet in God of geesten geloof had ik zo vaak aan haar gedacht~~, zelfs tegen haar gepraat,~~ dat ik meende dat er toch wel iets tot haar doorgedrongen moest zijn. Ik bedoel: soms voelde ik haar aanwezigheid haast fysiek. Als ik aardappels precies dun genoeg schilde, of als ik weer eens heel erg verliefd was ~~p~~op iemand waarvan ik wist dat ze hem of haar nooit zou ontmoeten. Als ~~k~~ ik door een stille stad liep, een nieuwe baan kreeg of een opleddiding aftrondde, als ~~ik~~ ergens de geur van gerookte paling of ~~eoh~~vochtige kelder hing. En nu liep ze naast me en zei ze dat ze daar allebmaal niet bij geweest was. Dus toen we ~~in mijn~~ de acht trappen naar mijn kamer opstiefelden moest ik haar uitleggn en dat ~~ik in een arme schrijver ben,~~ het tegenwoordig voor kunstenaars van halverwege de dertig heel normaal is om op kamers te wonen. Ik vroeg haar natuurlijk wat ze ij al die tijd gedaan had, na haar dood, en ze prbobeerde het uit te leggen maar ik begrep ep geen van de woorden die ze gebruikte ~~en~~, ~~z~~Ze kon ~~ze~~ de taal niet vindn en om het duidelijk te maken.

~~Raar~~Vreemd, zei ik.

Ja, zei zij.

Ik schonk ~~haar~~ons, ook al was het nog geen ~~elf uur 's~~tien uur 's ochtends, een glas wijn in ~~en nam er zelf ook een~~. ~~Ze vroeg of ze vaker langs zou komen, . Dat is goed, zei ik.~~

FIGURE 7.4 Visualisation that visualises all the writing actions in Roos van Rijswijk's sixth writing session

contextual additions; dark brown for typo related deletions; light brown for typo related additions; and lavender for revised text.

At a glance, this visualisation offers a first view into the dynamics underlying text production. This visualisation therefore also highlights the amount of information that was captured in the keystroke logging data and could not be reconstructed with collation of the Word documents. This visualisation, for example, immediately points at a sentence Van Rijswijk started writing in session 5, but decided to delete even before the sentence was finished:

Example 6

~~Later mertke kkte ik dat ik als ik mijn medicatie nam minder vaak bezokeek kreeg van de overledenen, en omdat~~

[~~Later I notidce ccced that when I took my medication I was not visietkdted as often by the deceased, and because~~]

This sentence production and its subsequent deletion are related to Van Rijswijk's decisions about whether or not to give a specific reason for the narrator's ability to perceive ghosts. In this sentence, she introduces the suggestion that this ability might be related to the narrator's mental state, since the narrator remarks that they have noticed that when they take their mediation, they are not visited as often by the deceased. While formulating this sentence, however, Van Rijswijk seems to change her mind about this explicit reference to the effect of the medication on the perception of ghosts and deletes the idea mid-sentence. In this way, the keystroke logging data provides valuable information about Van Rijswijk's decision-making process.

The visualisation tool further allows for respectively removing all the additions, deletions, and typos made during the writing session, which therefore allows for different reading modes. Obscuring the additions enables for the study of which text from the 'base layer'—the text at the start of the writing session has been deleted (Figure 7.5), whilst obscuring the deletions enables for studying how the text that made it to the end of the writing session was written (Figure 7.6). While these visualisation views already allow for the analysis of the types of writing actions, it does not provide any insights into the sequence of these writing actions. We have therefore implemented three visualisation features to enable the analysis of the sequentiality of the writing actions: a numerical representation of the chronology, a replay function and the writing path.

Ik dacht altijd dat ik enorm bang zou worden bij het zien van een geest, maar* de eerste keer dat mijn oma verscheen voelde het tot mijn verbazing nogal vanzelfsprekend. Misschien omdat ik sinds ze zo'n vijftien jaar geleden stief haast iedere nacht van haar heb gedroomd. Het kan zijn dat ze er als een verkenner opuit was gestuurd - naar die dingen vraag ik niet meer omdat ~~ze worden afgedaan met geërgerde wuifgebaren, alsof ik informeer naar de btw op bepaalde boodschappen of andere saaïgheden~~. Ze stond zomaar naast me toen mijn ogen 's ochtends vroeg werden gecontroleerd door de opticiën, die haar uiteraard niet waarnam. Ik kon tegelijkertijd met haar praten en met de man die me verweet mijn lenzen niet vaak genoeg schoon te maken: met mijn oma in mijn hoofd en met de man hardop.

Hier ben ik voor gemaakt, dacht ik terwijl ik moeiteloos twee gesprekken tegelijk gaande hield.

De opticien gaf me nieuwe, ademende contactlenzen mee en mijn oma verbaasde zich terwijl we terugliepen naar mijn woning over de drukte in de stad (mijn stad, zei ze), smartphones en mijn ouwe kop. Het viel me tegen dat ze niet op de hoogte was van mijn leven - hoewel ik niet in God of geesten geloof had ik zo vaak aan haar gedacht~~, zelfs tegen haar gepraat,~~ dat ik meende dat er toch wel iets tot haar doorgedrongen moest zijn. ~~Ik zei dat het nogal een verhaal was, mijn leven na haar dood, en probeerde het zo kort mogelijk samen te vatten. [.....]/haar leven/dat ze mee mag lopen/neemt steeds meer mensen mee/niet als ik medicijnen slik.~~

~~Ze worden niet begraven maar na hun uitvaart discreet verstrooid.~~

FIGURE 7.5
Visualisation that hides all the additions, from Van Rijswijk's 6th session

Ik dacht altijd dat ik enorm bang zou worden bij het zien van een geest, maar* de eerste keer dat mijn oma verscheen voelde het tot mijn verbazing nogal vanzelfsprekend. Misschien omdat ik sinds ze zo'n vijftien jaar geleden stief haast iedere nacht van haar heb gedroomd. Het kan zijn dat ze er als een verkenner opuit was gestuurd - naar die dingen vraag ik niet meer omdat ik het antwoord niet begrijp. Ze stond zomaar naast me toen mijn ogen 's ochtends vroeg werden gecontroleerd door de opticiën, die haar uiteraard niet waarnam. Ik kon tegelijkertijd met haar praten en met de man die me verweet mijn lenzen niet vaak genoeg schoon te maken: met mijn oma in mijn hoofd en met de man hardop.

Hier ben ik voor gemaakt, dacht ik terwijl ik moeiteloos twee gesprekken tegelijk gaande hield.

De opticien gaf me nieuwe, ademende contactlenzen mee en mijn oma verbaasde zich terwijl we terugliepen naar mijn woning over de drukte in de stad (mijn stad, zei ze), smartphones en mijn ouwe kop. Het viel me tegen dat ze niet op de hoogte was van mijn leven - hoewel ik niet in God of geesten geloof had ik zo vaak aan haar gedacht dat ik meende dat er toch wel iets tot haar doorgedrongen moest zijn. Ik bedoel: soms voelde ik haar aanwezigheid haast fysiek. Als ik aardappels precies dun genoeg schilde, of als ik weer eens heel erg verliefd was op iemand waarvan ik wist dat ze hem of haar nooit zou ontmoeten. Als ik door een stille stad liep, een nieuwe baan kreeg of een opleiding afrondde, als ergens de geur van gerookte paling of vochtige kelder hing. En nu liep ze naast me en zei ze dat ze daar allemaal niet bij geweest was. Dus toen we de acht trappen naar mijn kamer opstiefelden moest ik haar uitleggen dat het tegenwoordig voor kunstenaars van halverwege de dertig heel normaal is om op kamers te wonen. Ik vroeg haar natuurlijk wat zij al die tijd gedaan had, na haar dood, en ze probeerde het uit te leggen maar ik begreep geen van de woorden die ze gebruikte. Ze kon de taal niet vinden om het duidelijk te maken.

Vreemd, zei ik.

Ja, zei zij.

Ik schonk ons, ook al was het nog geen tien uur 's ochtends, een glas wijn in. Na haar vertrek ruimde ik de wijn en de glazen op. Uit de fles was maar een glas geschonken en haar glas was leeg en schoon.

FIGURE 7.6
Visualisation that obscures all the deletions, Van Rijswijk's sixth session

One way to gain insight into the sequentiality of the writing actions is to visualise the numbers of the writing actions, which represent the chronological order of the encoded writing actions (Figure 7.7). These numbers indicate that Van Rijswijk produced the new text (in Figure 7.7) in a fairly linear way, but that the splitting of the sentence "Ik vroeg haar natuurlijk wat zij al die tijd gedaan had, na haar dood, en ze probeerde het uit te leggen maar ik begreep geen van de woorden die ze gebruikte en ze kon de taal niet vinden om het duidelijk te maken" ["I asked her, of course, what she had been doing all this time, after her death, and she tried to explain but I didn't understand any of the words she was using and she couldn't find the language to make it clear"] took place much later in the writing process than the initial writing of the sentence. The sentence production itself took place from writing action 53–63, while writing actions 426–429 were performed to split the sentence:

Example 7

[53]Ik vroeg haar natuurlijk wat z~~e~~ [54][55]ij al die tijd gedaan had, na haar dood, en ze pr~~b~~[56][57]obeerde het uit te leggen maar ik begre~~p~~ [58][59]ep geen van de woorden die ze gebruikte ~~en~~[426]. [427] ~~z~~[428]Z[429]e kon ~~ze~~ [60][61]de taal niet vind~~n~~ [62][63]en om het duidelijk te maken.

[[53]I asked her, of course, what sh~~e~~ [54][55]e had been doing all this time, after her death, and she tr~~e~~[56][57]ied to explain but I didn't understa~~d~~ [58][59]nd any of the words she was using ~~and~~[426]. [427] ~~s~~[428]S[429]he couldn't find ~~she~~ [60][61]the language to ma~~e~~ [62][63]ke it clear.]

The transcriptions of the keystroke data and their visualisation represent a text that never actually appeared on the writer's screen as such, and with which they therefore never interacted. Of course, when writing in a word processor, deletions disappear from the screen and additions do not all occur at the same time. Therefore, the second visualisation feature to gain insight into the sequentiality offers a way to replay the encoded writing operations step by step: the additions are visualised in their order and the deletions are removed from the visualisation at the moment they are deleted. Before deletions are removed from the visualisation, the deleted text is briefly formatted in bold to help the reader/user detect the deleted text.[9] The reader/user can also 'walk' through the session at their own pace. In this way it is possible to reconstruct

9 Please consult https://nanogenesis-digital.github.io to see how the dynamic visualisation works.

Ik dacht altijd dat ik enorm bang zou worden bij het zien van een geest, maar* de eerste keer dat mijn oma verscheen voelde het tot mijn verbazing nogal vanzelfsprekend. Misschien omdat ik sinds ze zo'n vijftien jaar geleden stief haast iedere nacht van haar heb gedroomd. Het kan zijn dat ze er als een verkenner opuit was gestuurd - naar die dingen vraag ik niet meer omdat ~~ze worden afgedaan met geërgerde wuifgebaren, alsof ik informeer naar de btw op bepaalde boodschappen of andere saaïgheden~~[64]ik het antwoord niet begrijp[65]. Ze stond zomaar naast me toen mijn ogen 's ochtends vroeg werden gecontroleerd door de opticiën, die haar uiteraard niet waarnam. Ik kon tegelijkertijd met haar praten en met de man die me verweet mijn lenzen niet vaak genoeg schoon te maken: met mijn oma in mijn hoofd en met de man hardop.

Hier ben ik voor gemaakt, dacht ik terwijl ik moeiteloos twee gesprekken tegelijk gaande hield. [79]~~Later mertke k~~[80][81]~~kte ik dat ik als ik mijn medicatie nam minder vaak bezoke~~[82][83]~~ek kreeg van de overledenen, en omdat~~[84]

De opticien gaf me nieuwe, ademende contactlenzen mee en mijn oma verbaasde zich terwijl we terugliepen naar mijn woning over de drukte in de stad (mijn stad, zei ze), smartphones en mijn ouwe kop. Het viel me tegen dat ze niet op de hoogte was van mijn leven - hoewel ik niet in God of geesten geloof had ik zo vaak aan haar gedacht~~, zelfs tegen haar gepraat,~~[24] dat ik meende dat er toch wel iets tot haar doorgedrongen moest zijn. [25]Ik bedoel: soms voelde ik haar aanwezigheid haast fysiek. [26]Als ik aardappels precies dun genoeg schilde, of als ik weer eens heel erg verliefd was ~~p~~[27][28]op iemand waarvan ik wist dat ze hem of haar nooit zou ontmoeten. [29]Als ~~k~~[30][31]ik door een stille stad liep, een nieuwe baan kreeg of een ople~~di~~[32][33]iding af~~t~~[34][35]rondde, als ~~ik~~[36][37]ergens de geur van gerookte paling of ~~eoh~~[38][39]vochtige kelder hing. [40]En nu liep ze naast me en zei ze dat ze daar alle~~b~~[41][42]maal niet bij geweest was. [43]Dus t[44]oen we ~~in mijn~~[45][46]de acht trappen naar mijn kamer opstiefelden moest ik haar uitlegg~~n~~[47][48]en dat~~ik in~~[49][50]~~een arme schrijver ben,~~[51] het tegenwoordig voor kunstenaars van halverwege de dertig heel normaal is om op kamers te wonen.[52] [53]Ik vroeg haar natuurlijk wat z~~e~~[54][55]ij al die tijd gedaan had, na haar dood, en ze pr~~b~~[56][57]obeerde het uit te leggen maar ik begre~~p~~ [58][59]ep geen van de woorden die ze gebruikte~~en~~[426], [427]~~z~~[428]Z[429]e kon ~~ze~~[60][61]de taal niet vind~~n~~[62][63]en om het duidelijk te maken.

[67]~~Raar~~[424]Vreemd[425], zei ik.

[69]Ja, zei zij.

[71]Ik schonk ~~haar~~[93]ons[94], ook al was het nog geen ~~elf uur 's~~[72][73]tien uur 's ochtends, een glas wijn in~~en nam er zelf ook een~~[95]. [74]~~Ze vroeg of ze vaker langs zou komen,~~[75][76]~~.~~[77]~~Dat is goed, zei ik.~~[85]

FIGURE 7.7 Visualisation with the numbers indicating the order of the writing actions, representing a fragment of Van Rijswijk's sixth writing session

what the text looked like after any number of changes and to see the writers' movements through the text during text production.

The last way to get an overview of the route the writer followed through the document in a particular writing session, is to visualise this writing path (Figure 7.8) (see Bekius, 2023, p. 139). The visualised writing path enables a quick assessment of whether or not the writing was characterised by linearity (for other ways of measuring non-linearity, see Buschenhenke, Conijn & Van Waes, 2023; Section 7.4). The orange shaded lines indicate that the next change took place in the same line or below the previous change. Conversely, the blue shaded lines indicate that the next modification took place above the previous modification. In this way, the writing path can be used as a first examination of revision episodes, or to investigate what may have triggered certain revisions. With these visualisations we have created analysable keystroke logging data suitable for genetic criticism—equivalent to De Biasi's first objective. These visualisations of the text production alongside a selection of the temporal and spatial dimensions of the writing actions can now be used as a research instrument for the critical interpretation of the writing process.

7.4 Analysis

How do these visualisations help us in understanding the revision that caught our attention in the collation results? Does it offer a hypothesis as to why Van Rijswijk changed the sentence from the narrator's interpretation of the grandmother's reaction to the bland statement that she does not understand the answer? The visualisations of the way the writing session proceeded seems to indicate that this particular revision was triggered by new text production.

First of all, the writing path shows that Van Rijswijk moved the cursor upwards to the location of this specific sentence after producing a new sentence (the outer right blue line in Figure 7.8). A closer examination of this movement through the numbers that indicate the sequence of the revisions, as well as the replay function, show that this newly produced sentence also seems related to the revised sentence.

Example 8

^{53}Ik vroeg haar natuurlijk wat z~~e~~^{54}^{55}ij al die tijd gedaan had, na haar dood, en ze pr~~b~~^{56}^{57}obeerde het uit te leggen maar ik begre~~p~~^{58}^{59}ep geen van de woorden die ze gebruikte~~en~~^{426}. ^{427}~~z~~^{428}Z^{429}e kon ~~ze~~^{60}^{61}de taal niet vind~~n~~^{62}^{63}en om het duidelijk te maken.

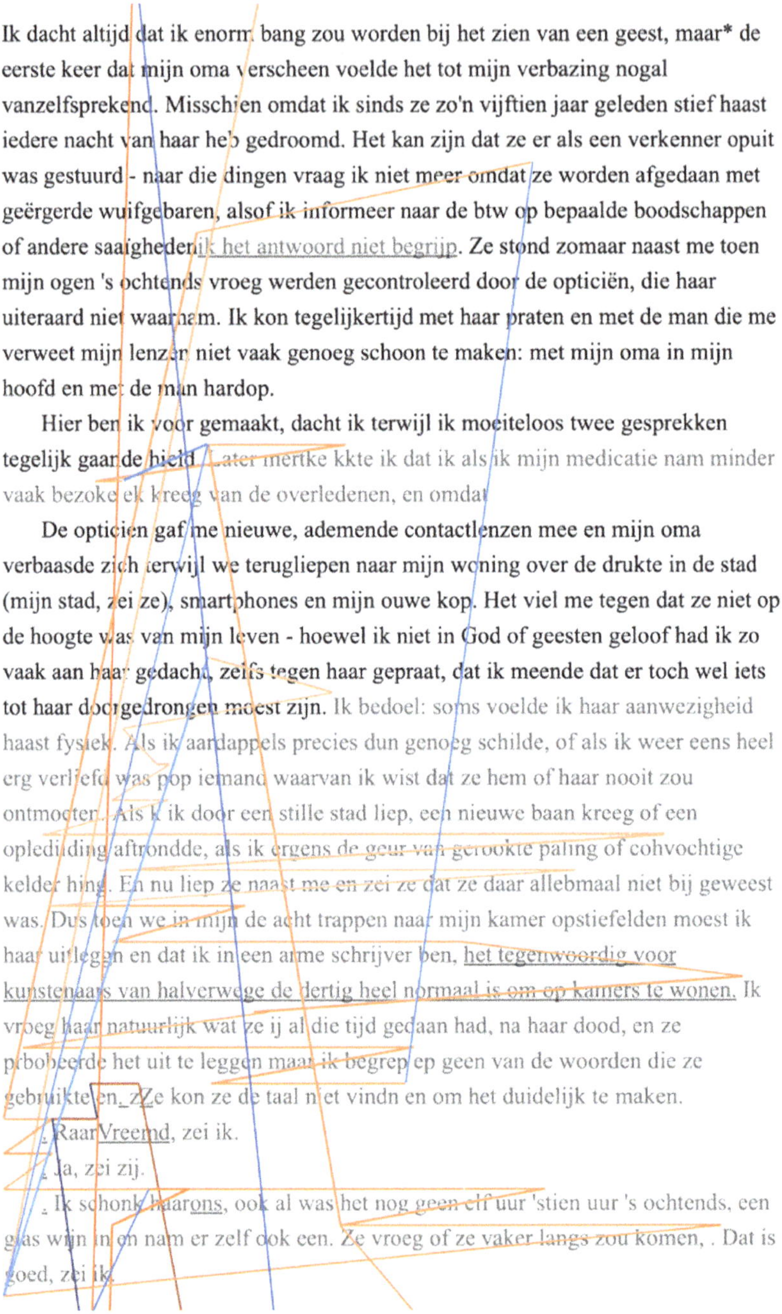
Ik dacht altijd dat ik enorm bang zou worden bij het zien van een geest, maar* de eerste keer dat mijn oma verscheen voelde het tot mijn verbazing nogal vanzelfsprekend. Misschien omdat ik sinds ze zo'n vijftien jaar geleden stief haast iedere nacht van haar heb gedroomd. Het kan zijn dat ze er als een verkenner opuit was gestuurd - maar die dingen vraag ik niet meer omdat ze worden afgedaan met geërgerde wuifgebaren, alsof ik informeer naar de btw op bepaalde boodschappen of andere saaigheden ik het antwoord niet begrijp. Ze stond zomaar naast me toen mijn ogen 's ochtends vroeg werden gecontroleerd door de opticiën, die haar uiteraard niet waarnam. Ik kon tegelijkertijd met haar praten en met de man die me verweet mijn lenzen niet vaak genoeg schoon te maken: met mijn oma in mijn hoofd en met de man hardop.

Hier ben ik voor gemaakt, dacht ik terwijl ik moeiteloos twee gesprekken tegelijk gaande hield. Later mertke kkte ik dat ik als ik mijn medicatie nam minder vaak bezoekek kreeg van de overledenen, en omdat

De opticien gaf me nieuwe, ademende contactlenzen mee en mijn oma verbaasde zich terwijl we terugliepen naar mijn woning over de drukte in de stad (mijn stad, zei ze), smartphones en mijn ouwe kop. Het viel me tegen dat ze niet op de hoogte was van mijn leven - hoewel ik niet in God of geesten geloof had ik zo vaak aan haar gedacht, zelfs tegen haar gepraat, dat ik meende dat er toch wel iets tot haar doorgedrongen moest zijn. Ik bedoel: soms voelde ik haar aanwezigheid haast fysiek. Als ik aardappels precies dun genoeg schilde, of als ik weer eens heel erg verliefd was pop iemand waarvan ik wist dat ze hem of haar nooit zou ontmoeten. Als ik ik door een stille stad liep, een nieuwe baan kreeg of een opleididing aftrondde, als ik ergens de geur van gerookte paling of cohvochtige kelder hing. En nu liep ze naast me en zei ze dat ze daar allebmaal niet bij geweest was. Dus toen we in mijn de acht trappen naar mijn kamer opstiefelden moest ik haar uitleggen en dat ik in een arme schrijver ben, het tegenwoordig voor kunstenaars van halverwege de dertig heel normaal is om op kamers te wonen. Ik vroeg haar natuurlijk wat ze ij al die tijd gedaan had, na haar dood, en ze prbobeerde het uit te leggen maar ik begrep ep geen van de woorden die ze gebruikte en. zZe kon ze de taal niet vindn en om het duidelijk te maken.

. RaarVreemd, zei ik.

. Ja, zei zij.

. Ik schonk haarons, ook al was het nog geen elf uur 'stien uur 's ochtends, een glas wijn in en nam er zelf ook een. Ze vroeg of ze vaker langs zou komen, . Dat is goed, zei ik.

FIGURE 7.8 Visualisation of the writing path, sample taken from Van Rijswijk's 5th writing session. Blue lines represent movement towards the top of the document, orange lines movements towards the bottom.

> [[53]I asked her, of course, what sh~~e~~[54][55]e had been doing all this time, after her death, and she tr~~e~~[56][57]ied to explain but I didn't understa~~d~~[58][59]nd any of the words she was using ~~and~~[426]. [427]~~s~~[428]S[429]he couldn't find ~~she~~[60][61]the language to ma~~e~~[62][63]ke it clear.]

> Het kan zijn dat ze er als een verkenner opuit was gestuurd—naar die dingen vraag ik niet meer omdat ~~ze worden afgedaan met geërgerde wuifgebaren, alsof ik informeer naar de btw op bepaalde boodschappen of andere saaïgheden~~[64]ik het antwoord niet begrijp[65].

> [It may be that she had been sent out as a scout—I don't ask about those things anymore because ~~they are dismissed with exasperated waving gestures, as if I am inquiring about VAT on certain groceries or other boring things~~[64]I don't understand the answer[65].]

The new sentence is part of a conversation the narrator has with the ghost of her grandmother. The narrator asks what her grandmother has been doing after she died, but she does not understand the words her grandmother uses, and the grandmother cannot find the language to make herself clear. The production of this new sentence ended with writing action 63, and the following writing action (number 64) is the deletion of the narrator's humorous interpretation of the grandmother's reaction which is replaced by the statement that the narrator does not understand her answer. This newly produced sentence thus inspired a change in the text-produced-so-far. After she had written that the narrator sometimes cannot understand what her grandmother says, she decides that this is also an appropriate reason for the narrator not asking the reasons behind her grandmother's 'visits'.

7.5 Discussion

Using a fragment from the process of Dutch writer Roos van Rijswijk as a case study, we have demonstrated the workflow of the genetic critic working with keystroke logged materials. Seeing the revisions Van Rijswijk made in their chronological and textual context allowed us to discover the internal logic of her work, specifically the way in which she increased the coherence of her story by adapting pre-existing text to accommodate a recent plot development. Thus, the two objectives of genetic criticism have come together; first, a relatively 'neutral' visualisation has been created, and then a critical interpretation of the textual development can be created.

Palermo (2017) made a bold suggestion to writing studies: what if we think about our data as an archive? He draws on digital humanities, and in particular on computational textual scholarship, for examples of how organised, annotated and visualised data collections can be shared within the research community to foster a practice of open science. Our text-based visualisation can be seen as such a bridge between writing studies and textual scholarship, as it is a sustainable, curated modelling of the process, at the midpoint between 'raw' materials and the scholars' analyses.

A concrete application of our visualisation would be in the field of writing pedagogy. The recent development in automated process feedback (Dux Speltz et al., 2022; Conijn, 2020) is currently focussed on process characteristics (such as moving the cursor to a previous sentence, or pausing before typing a new sentence), not on textual content. Complementing this approach with individualised process feedback based on textual development, may help students improve their writing. A visualisation that offers both a chronological overview of the textual development, as well as a hermeneutical classification of textual changes can therefore be helpful in the field of writing pedagogy (Leijten, Vandermeulen & Vangehuchten, 2022). The 'annotation visualisation' in Keystroke Loxensis can be used to provide feedback on the writing actions and to indicate parts of the writing process that need to be addressed by the student. As writers can also learn from (proficient) others' processes (Rijlaarsdam et al., 2008), discussing a visualisation of a sample process may help learning writers to reflect on their own strategies and develop the meta-cognitive skills needed to improve their texts.

More in general, as multi-session writing is understudied (see Sala-Bubaré et al., 2021), visualisations of multi-session keystroke logging data are few and far between. Our own proposal takes the writing session as a unit, but by visualising all sessions belonging to a process, we can nevertheless create a holistic overview. However, it would be informative to also find visual approaches that capture a multi-session process in its entirety. One can think of approaches that reach back from the final text version to indicate for each sentence how heavily it was revised. Or, in more of a genetic approach, a visualisation which shows the gaps; the locations where deletions have taken place. One could also think of the document space as a map, and the text as land on the map, and then visualise the growth of the text by layering collation outputs, much like a geographical map can show altitudes.

References

Bécotte-Boutin, H., Caporossi, G., & Hertz, A. (2015). The progressive visualization, a new tool for analyzing the writing process. Cahiers Du GERAD, 141, 1–12.

Bécotte-Boutin, H.-S., Caporossi, G., Hertz, A., & Leblay, C. (2019). Writing and rewriting: The coloured numerical visualization of keystroke logging. In E. Lindgren & Sullivan, K.P.H. (Eds.), Observing Writing (pp. 96–124). BRILL. https://doi.org/10.1163/9789004392526_006.

Bekius, L. (2024). Keystroke Loxensis (v0.1-beta). Zenodo. https://doi.org/10.5281/zenodo.13918953.

Bekius, L. (2023). Behind the computer screens. the use of keystroke logging for genetic criticism applied to born-digital works of literature. [Doctor of Philosophy in Literature]. University of Antwerp & University of Amsterdam.

Bekius, L. (2021). The Reconstruction of the Author's Movement Through the Text, or How to Encode Keystroke Logged Writing Processes in TEI-XML. Variants, 15–16, 3–43. https://doi.org/10.4000/variants.1245.

Bleeker, E., Buitendijk, B., & Haentjens Dekker, R. (2019). From graveyard to graph: Visualisation of textual collation in a digital paradigm. International Journal of Digital Humanities, 1(2), 141–163. https://doi.org/10.1007/s42803-019-00012-w.

Bleeker, E. (2017). Mapping Invention in Writing: Digital Infrastructure and the Role of the Genetic Editor [Doctor of Philosophy in Literature]. University of Antwerp.

Burnard, L. (2014). What is the Text Encoding Initiative?: How to add intelligent markup to digital resources. OpenEdition Press. https://doi.org/10.4000/books.oep.426.

Buschenhenke, F., Conijn, R., & Van Waes, L. (2023). Measuring non-linearity of multi-session writing processes. Reading and Writing. https://doi.org/10.1007/s11145-023-10449-9.

Conijn, R. (2020). The keys to writing. [Doctoral dissertation]. University of Tilburg & University of Antwerp.

Conijn, R., Speltz, E.D., van Zaanen, M., Van Waes, L. and Chukharev-Hudilainen, E. 2022. 'A Product- and Process-Oriented Tagset for Revisions in Writing'. Written Communication 39 (1): 97–128. https://doi.org/10.1177/07410883211052104.

De Biasi, P.-M. (2004). Toward a Science of Literature: Manuscript Analysis and the Genesis of the Work. In Jed Deppman, Daniel Ferrer, & Michael Groden (Eds.), Genetic criticism: Texts and avant-textes (pp. 36–68). University of Pennsylvania Press.

Deppman, J., Ferrer, D., & Groden, M. (2004). Genetic criticism: Texts and avant-textes. University of Pennsylvania Press.

Dillen, W. (2015). Digital Scholarly Editing for the Genetic Orientation: The Making of a Genetic Edition of Samuel Beckett's Works [Doctor of Philosophy in Literature]. University of Antwerp.

Dux Speltz, E., et al. (2022). 'Automating Individualized, Process-Focused Writing Instruction: A Design-Based Research Study'. Frontiers in Communication, 7. https://www.frontiersin.org/articles/10.3389/fcomm.2022.933878.

Fenoglio I., Ganascia, J.-G. (2007). MEDITE: un logiciel pour l'approche comparative de documents de genèse, Revue Genesis, 166–16.

Fiormonte, D., & Pusceddu, C. (2006). The text as product and process. History, genesis, experiments. Manuscript, Variant, Genese/Genesis, 109–128.

Fürer, M. (2017). Modeling, scaling and sequencing writing phases of Swiss television journalists. [Doctoral dissertation] University of Bern.

Grésillon, A. (1997). Slow: Work in progress. Word & Image, 13(2), 106–123. https://doi.org/10.1080/02666286.1997.10434276.

Kollberg, P., & Severinson Eklundh, K. (2002). Studying Writers' Revising Patterns with S-Notation Analysis. In Contemporary Tools and Techniques for Studying Writing (pp. 89–104). Springer Netherlands: Dordrecht.

Leijten, M., Vandermeulen, N., & Vangehuchten, L. (2022). Source-based writing in professional Spanish as a foreign language: Some pedagogical insights based on a quali-quantitative approach. RLA. Revista de Lingüística Teórica y Aplicada, 60(1), 127–151. https://doi.org/10.29393/RLA60-5SBML30005.

Lindgren, E. & Kirk P.H.S. (2002). The LS graph: A methodology for visualizing writing revision. Language Learning, 52(3), 565–595.

Mathijsen, M. (2009). Genetic textual editing: The end of an era. In G. Mitterauer, W.M. Bauer, & S. Hofer (Eds.), Was ist Textkritik? Zur Geschichte und Relevanz eines Zentralbegriffs der Editionswissenschaft. Niemeyer.

Nury, E. (2018). Automated Collation and Digital Editions: from Theory to Practice. [Doctor of Philosophy]. King's College London.

Palermo, G.J. (2017). Transforming Text: Four Valences of a Digital Humanities Informed Writing Analytics. Journal of Writing Analytics, 1, 33.

Perrin, D. (2019). Progression Analysis: Working with Large Data Corpora in Field Research on Writing. In Observing writing. (pp. 143–162). Brill. https://doi.org/10.1163/9789004392526_008.

Rijlaarsdam, G., et al. 'Observation of Peers in Learning to Write. Practise and Research.' Journal of Writing Research, 1, no. 1, June 2008, 53–83. https://doi.org/10.17239/jowr-2008.01.01.3.

Sala-Bubaré, A., Montserrat C., & Gert R. (2021). 'Writing Processes as Situated Regulation Processes. A Context-Based Approach to Doctoral Writing'. Journal of Writing Research, 30.

Shahidzadeh A., Nooshin, V.N. & Lamyk B. (2024, June 4). eXtant: a toolkit for digital scholarly editing and beyond. DH Benelux, Leuven, Belgium. Zenodo. https://doi.org/10.5281/zenodo.14011883.

Shelley, M.W. "Frankenstein, Volume I", in The Shelley-Godwin Archive, MS. Abinger c. 56, 4r. Retrieved from http://shelleygodwinarchive.org/sc/oxford/frankenstein/volume/i/#/p1.

Van Hulle, D. (2022). Genetic criticism: Tracing creativity in literature. Oxford University Press.

CHAPTER 8

Visualising Real-World Writing Processes with Progression Analysis

Daniel Perrin

Progression Analysis (PA) was developed to understand the material, cognitive, and social dynamics of text production processes in real-life contexts. By doing so, it has contributed to shifting the focus of writing research from the lab to classrooms and workplaces. In transdisciplinary projects, this in-depth understanding enables researchers to develop both empirically based theories and practical measures. Such measures can help writers realize and overcome the limitations of their repertoires of text production strategies, practices, and routines. However, sharing knowledge between research and professional practice requires effective ways to visualise the dynamics of an emerging text in context. These visualisations must allow for scaling up and down between details, from adding a character to shaping the big picture of value creation in collaborative text production.

8.1 Visualising Analyses of Real-Life Writing with Progression Analysis

Real-life writing in the professions combines patterns and routines with unpredictability (Haapanen & Perrin, 2024), which results in pattern variation and change. Artificial intelligence (AI) mimics this process by re-assembling linguistic units based on probabilities derived from large language datasets. Results include coherent text surfaces with certain flaws (e.g., Berber Sardinha, 2024). By contrast, meaningful writing requires critical thinking (Essien, Bukoye, O'Dea, & Kremantzis, 2024) in terms of making purposeful decisions and taking responsibility (e.g., de Villiers, Dimes, & Molinari, 2024).

This dichotomy between form and meaning requires analysis of human writing to capture both the assemblage of linguistic units at the surface of text production and the deeper processes of meaning-making in real-life contexts. Progression_Analysis (PA) has been developed to capture real-life writing from three complementary perspectives: the material view on composing signs, the cognitive view on making decisions about the emerging text product, and the

 | HTTPS://DOI.ORG/10.1163/9789004760264-009

social view on interacting with others by proceeding language, from defining the task to implementing the product (Perrin, 2003).

Ideally, PA visualisations help researchers understand the data generated in their analyses of real-life writing from these three perspectives. Moreover, they should facilitate academic discourse within and across the domains involved in writing research. Finally, they are meant to foster knowledge transformation across the boundaries of academic research, the practical fields under investigation, and society at large (e.g., Gravengaard, 2018). By doing so, the visualisations support the generation of shared knowledge in transdisciplinary research projects (Perrin & Kramsch, 2018).

Throughout this chapter, I draw on data from the YOGY case. In times of austerity measures, an ethically conscious journalist and a video editor collaborated to produce a piece for the evening news. The YOGY case study was part of a large research project, Idée suisse, investigating the interplay of three drivers: the Swiss national broadcaster's public mandate; the demands of competitive media markets; and the journalists' practices of overcoming what the management conceived as discrepancies between the public mandate and the media markets (Perrin, 2013, 71–79).

Zooming into the YOGY case, I focus on problems of multilingual communication in public discourse—a driver of "glocalization", the interplay of localization and globalization (Khondker, 2004). Translating news content and its source materials can overcome linguistic and cultural divides in the global competition for attention (e.g., Gomaa, 2024). In this process, visually accessible data on multilingual news production help to understand language-related inequalities, as addressed in both political movements and sociolinguistic study programs (e.g., Perrin, 2025, in prep.).

8.2 The Micro Level of Formulating Written Language

On a micro level, *text production* consists of composing patterns that are supposed to be seen and heard as complexes of signs. In the case of writing in the Western world, these patterns are linguistic units such as characters, syllables, words, phrases, sentences, or paragraphs. *Composing* consists of inserting and deleting such units until the writer considers the result appropriate to fulfil the intended function among the target readership or audience. Progression Analysis visualises this process using a standard called S-notation (Severinson-Eklundh & Kollberg, 1996).

S-notation shows in ^{n}[square brackets]^{n} what was deleted in an emerging text, while insertions are put in ^{n}{curly braces}^{n}. The superscript numbers ^{n} indicate the order of these so-called revisions in the writing process. Vertical bars | indicate where a writer jumped off in the writing flow to move the point of insertion to another place in the emerging text. In the following simplified example, the writer deletes a period right after writing it (Revision 59 in Figure 8.1), then continues with "tiré" and finishes the entire sentence. Only then does he jump back, inserts "j'ai" (63) and deletes the typo "t" (64):

J'ai entendu deux explsions et ^{59}[.|$_{59}$]^{59,63}{j'ai }^{63}|$_{64}$tiré quatre personnes hor^{64}[t]^{64}s de l'avion|$_{63}$.

FIGURE 8.1 S-notation basics shown in a simplified example

The following real example from the YOGY case illustrates the complex back-and-forth movements that can occur in writing processes when authors are chiseling their sentences. The revisions (i.e., insertions and deletions) can be interpreted, for example, as mere corrections of typos (Revision 64 in Figure 8.2), as traces of syntactic fine-tuning (Revisions 65–68), or as the results of a decision to alter the order of building blocks in the piece. In any case, S-notation shows what was done to the text in terms of material activity, step by step, as a sequence of revisions.

J'ai enténdu deux explsions et ^{59}[.|$_{59}$]^{59,63}{j'ai }^{63}|$_{64}$tiré ^{60}[.|$_{60}$]^{60,61}[.|$_{61}$]^{61,62}[.|$_{62}$]^{62}quatre personnes hor^{64}[t]^{64}s de l'avion|$_{63}$^{65}[.|$_{65}$]^{65,66}[.|$_{66}$]^{66,67}[.|$_{67}$]^{67,68}[.|$_{68}$]^{68}....saine^{76}[ ]^{76}|$_{77}$s^{77}[te]^{77}|$_{78}$^{78}{ et ^{79}[.|$_{79}$]^{79}|$_{80}$}^{78} sauves.

FIGURE 8.2 S-notation of screen activity in the text production window (extract)

Why does PA build on such ordinal writing process data, the sequence of revisions—instead of, for example, counting the milliseconds between key strokes (Conijn, Roeser, & van Zaanen, 2019)? Throughout our 30 years of research, we have focused on analyzing meaning-making in transdisciplinary projects. Considering the chunks of characters inserted or deleted in one go as the smallest units of analysis enables researchers to reconstruct linguistic composing at a level that is still accessible to the writers under investigation. In their self-perception, writers assemble texts, much more so than punching keys.

Moreover, foregrounding the process of linguistic assemblage in the micro-analysis of writers' situated activity allows for the annotation of these smallest units of analysis, i.e., the chunks of language inserted (or deleted) in one go. To give an example, since writing in the professions is often based on sources, the insertions can be color-coded to reflect the source texts that the chunks of language were copied from (e.g., Perrin, 1999). In any case, the analysis of such observational data on the formulation of written language benefits from complementary data on why the writers did what they did.

Analyzing writing from a cognitive perspective can only draw on indirect data, such as transcriptions of writers' cue-based retrospective verbal protocols (RVP). In Progression Analysis, these RVPs result from showing the writers video recordings of their text production processes right after writing. Aside from keystroke logging (Basnayake & Usoof, this volume, p. 48) and screen recording, generating this verbal data is obtrusive. While it opens a window into writers' repertoires of writing practices and strategies, it risks influencing their language awareness for any follow-up writing processes (e.g., Kuusela & Paul, 2000).

This is where recording negotiations in collaborative text production comes in. In our large, transdisciplinary research projects, we use the first of five years to prepare the field: We start by developing the goals and discussing the methods together with the practitioners under investigation. Second, we get everybody's consent for collecting data by keystroke logging, video recording, and the like at all the workplaces for at least a year. In parallel, we develop measures that allow everyone to withdraw collected data securely. Only then do we install the technical tools.

Once the writers have got used to the cameras and microphones at their workplaces, which tends to be after four to six weeks, we start to record collaborative text production as natural data. Visualising these data follows standards of transcription, according to the aim of the analyses. In the following example (Figure 8.3), a journalist (J) is negotiating with a video editor (V) about the correct translation of the English phrase I *pull* from the source material into French, the language of the emerging news item. The highlighted parts show a negotiation on whether to *pull* means *pousser* (to push) or *tirer* (pull).

This extract highlights a rich point from the data analysis in our projects on newswriting: Whereas most journalists are prepared to handle the interplay of verbal language and images with professional finesse and rigor, they hardly dispose of any elaborate practices to deal with the transition from one natural language to another. Put simply: They are amateurs when it comes to translating, as they depend on friends who happen to speak a source language

0713	J:	i pull four victims out of the plane
0714		j'ai poussé quatre victimes hors de l'avion
0715		on peut pas dire victimes puisque-
0716		j'ai poussé quatre survivants
0717	V:	j'ai tiré
0718	J:	j'ai tiré pull push ah
0719		j'ai tiré j'ai tiré
0720	V:	sorti oui
0721	J:	pull out j'ai poussé hors pull to pull
0722	V:	push
0723	J:	push ah c'est push pull
0724		non c'est pull
0725	V:	ah tu tires
0726	J:	j'ai tiré ouais heu- personnes hors de l'avion
0727	V:	moi j'le prends un peu quelque part avec-
0728		j'comprends plus ou moins
0729	J:	j'ai tiré quatre-
0730		elles étaient-
0731		they were safe
0732		and they were safe
0733		ça veut dire
0734		elles ont été sauvées à cause du fait-
0735		oui
0736	V:	oui

FIGURE 8.3 Transcription of collaborative text production (extract)

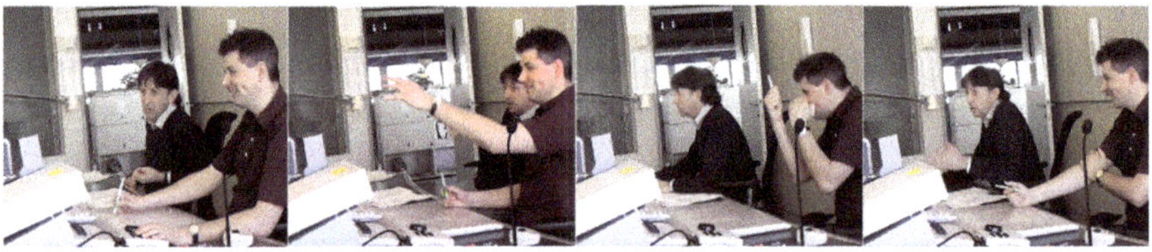

FIGURE 8.4 Key stills of video-recorded collaborative text production

they don't understand. This even applies to the staff of well-established media companies (e.g., Ehrensberger-Dow, Perrin, & Zampa, 2018).

Besides the translation problem, another culturally interesting phenomenon is mirrored in the data from the YOGY case: the influence of individual psychobiographies (Layder, 2005; Layder, 2021) on organizational text production in the newsroom. In the following example, four stills from the video recording show the body language of the journalist in the background and the video editor in the foreground while dealing with footage (Figure 8.4). The images on their screen show a passenger aircraft that overshoots the end of the runway, catches fire, and goes up in flames.

The visualisation with stills feeds the assumption that the journalist (J) is shocked by the images while the video editor (V) shows some excitement. This assumption is supported by the transcript of the workplace dialogue. J foregrounds the risk of showing brutal images during prime time when children may be watching the news, whereas V says "wow, that's awesome." Biographical data reveal that J was a teacher for two decades before journalism school, whereas V normally works on action movies and has been supporting the newsroom team in the context of austerity measures.

8.3 The Meso Level of Writing a Text

On a meso level, Progression Analysis visualisations quite literally show, the big picture of an entire text production process—or of one session in a multi-session process, which is defined as being followed by closing the file and doing something other than writing. These visualisations, instead of depicting the details of individual revisions, show the shift of the writer's focus of attention while composing a piece or its large parts. Like the micro level, the meso level of Progression Analysis is covered by visualisations that show either observable or interpreted aspects of writing processes.

Progression graphs are automatically generated based on the data from keystroke logging. They show the composing process in writing sessions from a material perspective, as a trace of activities in time and space (for "material traces" cf. Leblay et al., this volume, p. 73). Technically speaking, progression graphs are two-dimensional ordinal-numeric visualisations. On the x-axis, they display the order of all the revisions made during a writing process or session in chronological order from left to right. On the y-axis, the revisions are arranged from top to bottom in the order they appear in the final product.

With this in mind, phases (Mutta et al., this volume, p. 214) of linear writing, from top to bottom, with some immediate corrections of typos only, but without jumping back and forth in the emerging text, result in a straight line from the upper left to the lower right of a progression graph. Such a phase can be observed in the following progression graph between revisions 50 and 70 (Figure 8.5). In other phases, the graph shows larger jumps back and forth while writing. In the YOGY case, the writer added stage directions for the recording team at the end of the process—but they appear at the very beginning of the final product.

While progression graphs display the movement of the insertion point in an emerging text, they tell us little about why the writers moved the way they did. These cognitive aspects are at the core of the complementary visualisation on the meso level: the progression score. Again, time runs from left to right, as displayed at the bottom of the score in terms of revisions and characters produced. The first 16 lines, the main parts of the score, represent the 16 fields of activity identified in newsroom writing research following the principles of Grounded Theory (Perrin, 2013, 181–188).

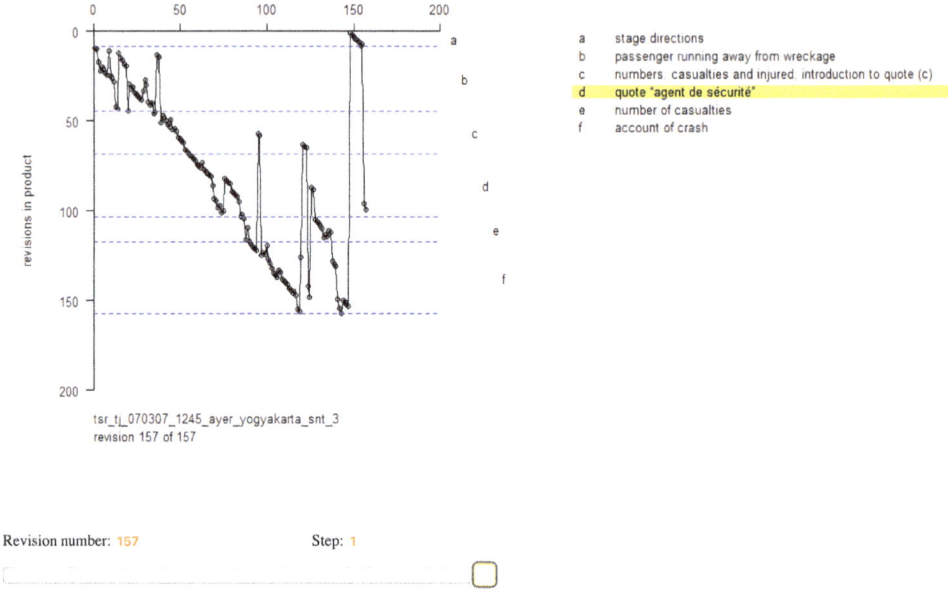

FIGURE 8.5 Dynamic progression graph. On screen, moving the slider plots the graph dot by dot, revision by revision, in the order of their appearance in the writing process

Technically speaking, progression scores relate the coded meaning from writers' talk *about* writing to the sequence of observable, material activities. In other words, what writers said in their workplace negotiations or RVPs (see above, Part 7.2) is allocated, through manual coding, both to specific revisions (insertions, deletions) in the text production process and to one or several of the 16 activity fields. This results in an Excel-generated visualisation that resembles a musical MIDI score, showing the activities over time depicted as red bars bundled onto 16 activity channels.

The progression score below (Figure 8.6) reveals that the writer started and ended his process by *handling task environment* (such as writing stage directions at the very end), but also engaged in *goal setting* early in his process. While activities of *controlling* increase throughout the process, *finding the sources* decreases. The fact that the line of *planning* remains empty throughout the score hints at issues with collecting and coding verbal data. Interview data show that this experienced journalist did engage in planning—but took it for granted, not worth mentioning in the RVP.

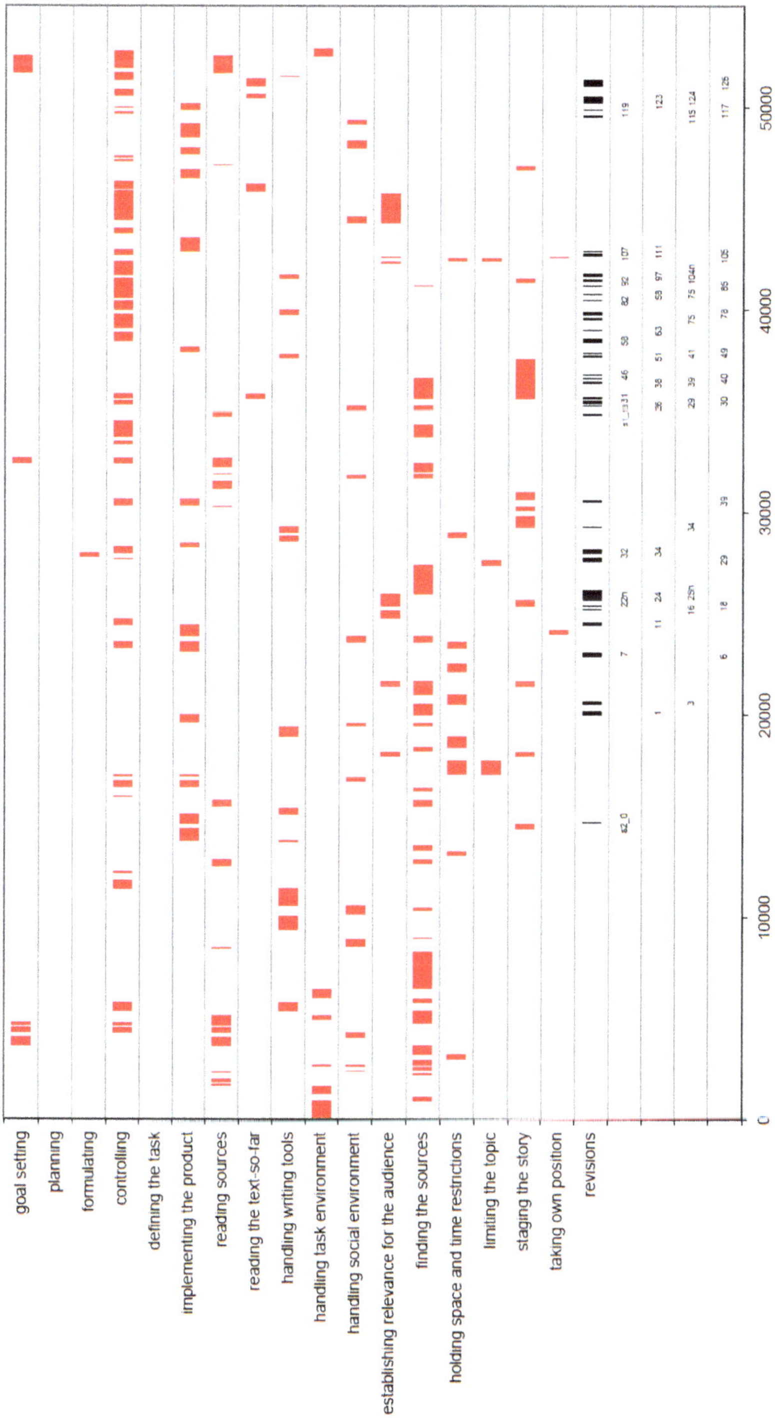

FIGURE 8.6 Progression score based on writer's cue-based retrospective verbal protocol

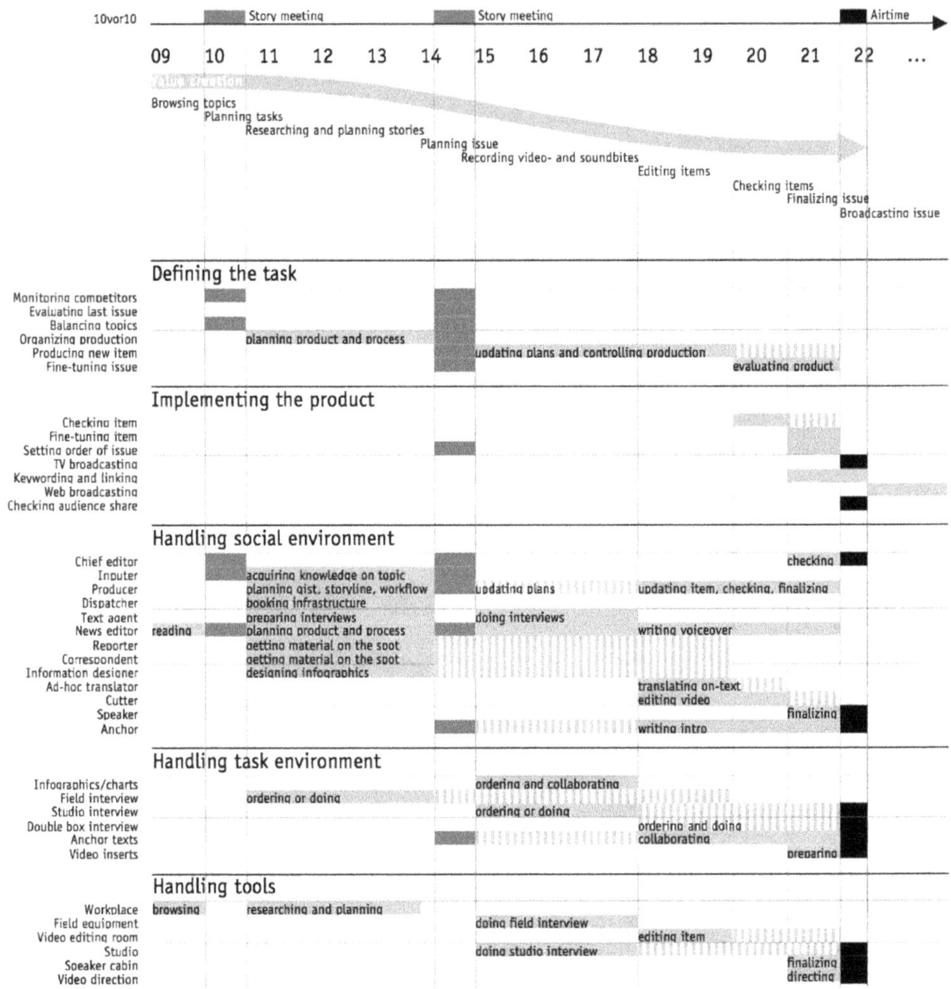

FIGURE 8.7 Daily newsroom workflow and predominant activity fields

8.4 The Macro Level of Controlling Organizational Workflows

On a macro level, writing research can look at individuals' and organizations' text production processes and products across long time frames. This includes lifespans of individual writers (e.g., Tusting, Barton, McCulloch, Papen, & Potts, 2019) or complex collaborative text production patterns in organizations (e.g., Schindler & Wolfe, 2014). An example from the TV newsroom investigated in cases such as YOGY is the daily workflow. Progression Analysis visualises such collaboration patterns in workflow charts. Just as with the progression score, time is displayed on the x-axis while activity fields are listed on the y-axis.

In the workflow chart below (Figure 8.7), time on the x-axis is counted in office hours, whereas the activity fields on the y-axis—a subset of the same fields as in the progression score—are specified along the distinctions that matter most in the newsroom under investigation. The bars indicate the occurrence of these activities over time. Dominant occurrence is indicated by a solid bar, occasional occurrence by a hatched one. The chart visualises averaged data collected over a year. The pattern repeats on a daily basis during the week and differs slightly on weekends.

A closer look at the details of *handling social environment* shows that one of the related key agents is the "ad hoc translator." Indeed, in many newsrooms, collaboration with professional translators is close to absent. If, in cases such as YOGY, translators are included in the process of newswriting, they tend to be laypeople who are familiar with the source language to a certain extent and happen to be available for short-term advice towards the end of the text production process. So, in this respect, the YOGY case is typical of the workflow in the field under investigation.

Of course, macro-level charts visualising complex collaboration patterns in writing research are not limited to the object of research, which is text production processes. Instead, they can also visualise the modular interplay of the research processes and products themselves. In this manner, they help contextualize the research questions and angles, the methods applied and combined, as well as the type of data gathered. In long-term multi-method projects resulting in large data corpora, this facilitates communication within the project group and beyond (Perrin, 2019).

The research chart for the Idée suisse project, during which the YOGY case emerged, shows the main characteristics and interconnections of four research modules (Figure 8.8). Each of these modules, as listed in the first column, focuses on specific stakeholders in newswriting: (a) on media policymakers, (b) on media management, (c) on newsroom practitioners, and (d) on addressees' follow-up discourses as reflected in newsroom conferences. The second column shows the data types gathered per module and their connection to the methods combined in the project, as explained in the third column.

The background knowledge for the YOGY case (see above, section 7.1) was generated in research modules A and B. Analyzing the interviews from module A resulted in knowledge about media policymakers' expectation that the public service broadcasting company had to reach wide audiences and foster their political awareness. In module B, it became clear that the media management felt overburdened with the mandate. Module C, however, provided evidence that some experienced journalists found ways to cope with contradictory expectations, for example, regarding multilingualism.

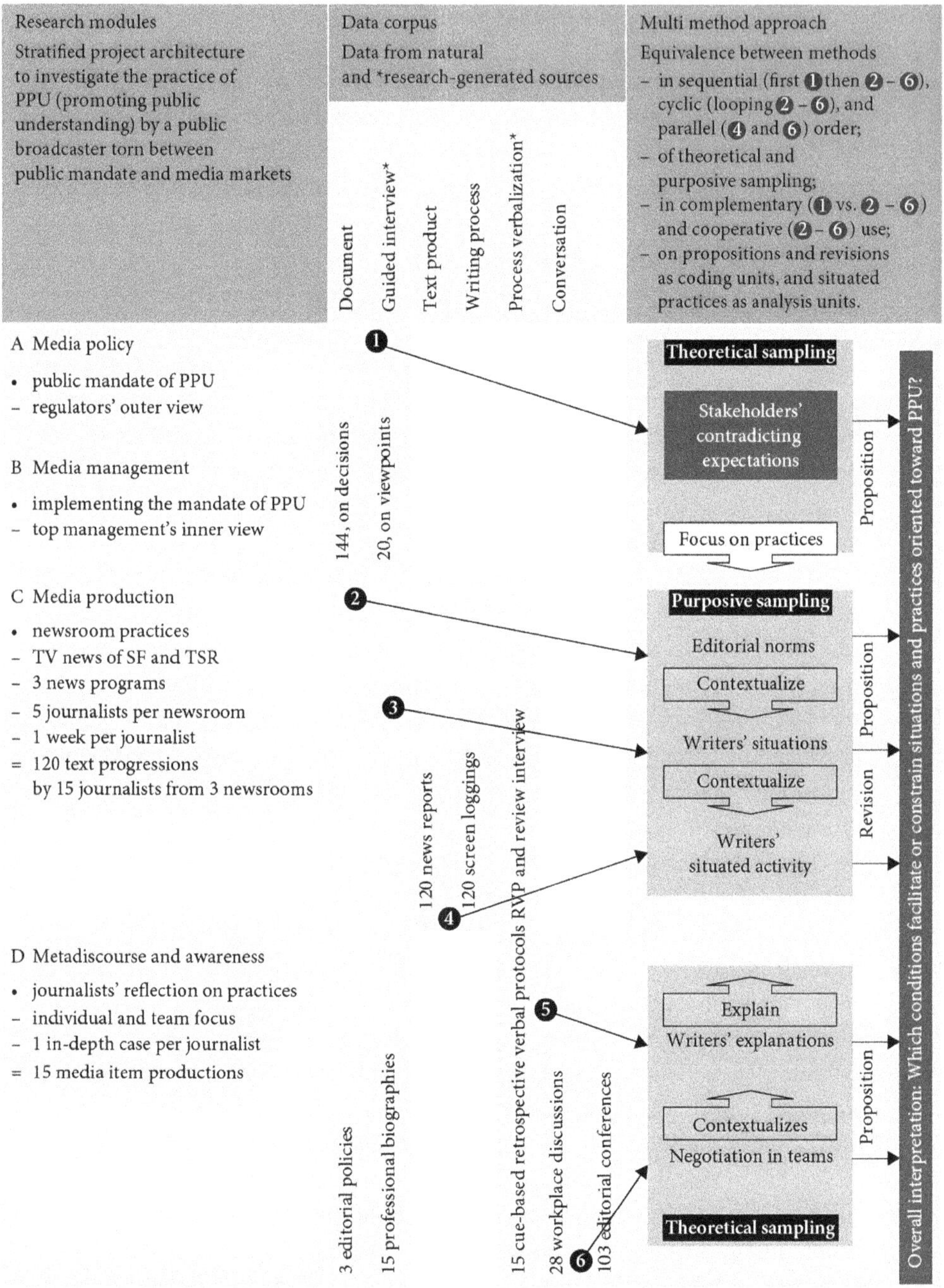

FIGURE 8.8 Synopsis of research activities in the Idée suisse project

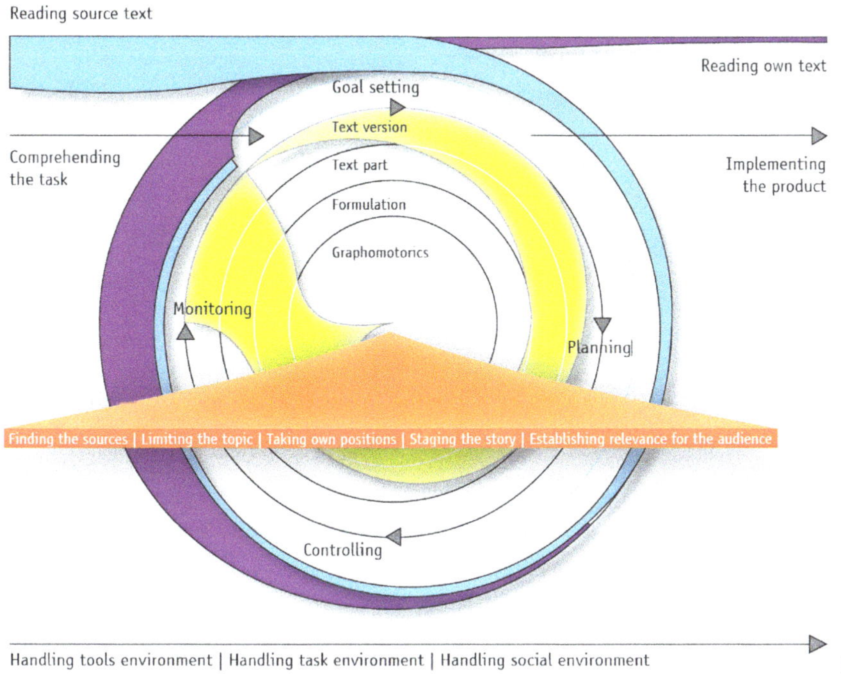

FIGURE 8.9 Interplay of activity fields in professional real-life writing

In the YOGY case, the journalist and the video editor found a third way out of the conflict between explaining politically relevant aspects of a plane crash in Yogyakarta and including pictures that sell but cause distress. The austerity measures that had created the unusual collaboration of a very concerned, pedagogically driven journalist with a stand-in video editor from the action movie business resulted in a prudently construed, yet visually attractive educational piece for the evening news—even if the (partly very basic) translation issues happened to be solved only by chance.

8.5 Visuals beyond Case Studies and Big Data

Visualisation does not stop at the end of the knowledge generation process with Progression Analysis. Quite the opposite, knowledge transformation can benefit from visuals, too. In training, coaching, and organizational development based on research with Progression Analysis, the interplay of the 16 activity fields identified with Grounded Theory is illustrated using a figure called the writing helix (Figure 8.9). The helix metaphor highlights that the four basic

FIGURE 8.10 Visualisation of empirically based good practices
HTTPS://TINYURL.COM/WRITERS-TOOLBOX

activities of *goal setting, planning, controlling,* and *monitoring* reoccur incrementally and in loops while a text is being produced.

They do so on levels ranging from punching keys up to connecting and altering formulations and entire sections of text or even text versions. *Goal setting* activities tend to be pursued consciously on the levels of entire texts and larger text sections. *Controlling* activities consist of inserting and deleting micro elements of texts. MONITORING the result can apply to activities that range from local to global scopes. These activities are documented in RVPs and recordings of the text producers' workplace negotiation.

The four core activities of writing interact with *reading source text* and *reading one's own text* as it emerges. Value creation is addressed directly in the activity fields of *comprehending the task* and *implementing the product*. Throughout a writing process, authors deal with the situational context by handling *tools, tasks,* and *social environments*. Finally, the orange triangle visualises the activity fields of *finding the sources, limiting the topic, taking own positions, staging the story,* and *establishing relevance for the audience,* the results of which are directly observable in the text products.

An example of using the writing helix to visualise the interplay of writing activities: With AI, translation shifts towards *handling tools environment*. However, making sure that the result suggested by the AI tool is culturally appropriate and thus fit for purpose calls for double-checking with, if possible, professional translators—which shifts parts of the issue back to *handling social environment*. The absence of options to translate from languages a newsroom team is not familiar with can result in neglecting or even excluding sources instead of FINDING THE SOURCES from this linguistic region.

Finally, knowledge transformation based on Progression Analysis also draws on visuals in narrative videos on good practice techniques in the newsroom. These practices were identified in cases such as YOGY and on projects such as Idée suisse. An example is the "re-explaining test" (Perrin, 2013, 271), in which representatives of the target audience are asked to explain what they understood when reading, for instance, the news item in the making. Here, narrative visualisation helps understand and memorize at a glance the core ideas of a good practice technique.

In a nutshell: Progression Analysis was developed to connect writing research with text production in the real world. This is why visualisations are oriented towards supporting both theory building in the academic world and knowledge transformation between academia and the practical fields under investigation. This makes the task of developing suitable visualisations both challenging and rewarding. In the three decades of developing, applying and refining Progression Analysis, close collaboration with visualisation experts and artists has proven to be a productive move.

References

Berber Sardinha, T. (2024). AI-generated vs human-authored texts: A multidimensional comparison. Applied Corpus Linguistics, 4(1), 100083. doi: https://doi.org/10.1016/j.acorp.2023.100083.

Conijn, R., Roeser, J., & van Zaanen, M. (2019). Understanding the keystroke log: the effect of writing task on keystroke features. Reading and Writing, 32(9), 2353–2374. doi: 10.1007/s11145-019-09953-8.

de Villiers, C., Dimes, R., & Molinari, M. (2024). How will AI text generation and processing impact sustainability reporting? Critical analysis, a conceptual framework and avenues for future research. Sustainability Accounting, Management and Policy Journal, 15(1), 96–118. doi: 10.1108/SAMPJ-02-2023-0097.

Ehrensberger-Dow, M., Perrin, D., & Zampa, M. (2018). Multilingualism and media. Reconsidering practices and ideologies of media-linguistic research. In C. Cotter & D. Perrin (Eds.), Handbook of language and media (pp. 373–387). London: Routledge.

Essien, A., Bukoye, O.T., O'Dea, X., & Kremantzis, M. (2024). The influence of AI text generators on critical thinking skills in UK business schools. Studies in Higher Education, 49(5), 865–882. doi: 10.1080/03075079.2024.2316881.

Gomaa, Y.A. (2024). Deciphering linguistic and cultural hurdles in English-Arabic media translation. Insights from the BBC online news articles. Cadernos de Tradução, 44(1), 1–21. doi: https://doi.org/10.5007/2175-7968.2024.e94510.

Gravengaard, G. (2018). Transforming knowledge. Cooperation with journalism's stakeholders. In C. Cotter & D. Perrin (Eds.), Handbook of language and media (pp. 489–504). London: Routledge.

Haapanen, L., & Perrin, D. (2024). Embracing the unexpected. Exploring the role of serendipity in newswriting. Discourse & Communication, 19(1), 25–45. doi: https://doi.org/10.1177/17504813241281709.

Khondker, H.H. (2004). Glocalization as Globalization. Evolution of a sociological concept. Bangladesh e-Journal of Sociology, 1(2), 12–20.

Kuusela, H., & Paul, P. (2000). A Comparison of Concurrent and Retrospective Verbal Protocol Analysis. The American Journal of Psychology, 113(3), 387–404. doi: 10.2307/1423365.

Layder, D. (2005). Understanding social theory. London: Sage.

Layder, D. (2021). Social sciences, social reality and the false division between theory and method. Some implications for social research. Springer Nature Social Sciences. Springer Nature Social Sciences, 1(2), 47.

Perrin, D. (1999). Woher die Textbrüche kommen. Der Einfluß des Schreibprozesses auf die Sprache im Gebrauchstext. Zeitschrift für Deutsche Sprache, 2, 134–155.

Perrin, D. (2003). Progression analysis (PA). Investigating writing strategies at the workplace. Journal of Pragmatics, 35(6), 907–921.

Perrin, D. (2013). The linguistics of newswriting. Amsterdam et al.: John Benjamins.

Perrin, D. (2019). Working with large data corpora in real-life writing research. In K. Sullivan & E. Lindgren (Eds.), Observing writing: insights from keystroke logging (pp. 143–162). Leiden: Brill.

Perrin, D. (2025, in prep.). On, for, and with practitioners. Fostering transdisciplinary dissertations in times of science criticism. Swiss Academies Communications, 20(1), 1–36.

Perrin, D., & Kramsch, C. (2018). Transdisciplinarity in applied linguistics. Introduction to the special issue. AILA Review, 31, 1–13.

Schindler, K., & Wolfe, J. (2014). Beyond single authors. Organizational text production as collaborative writing. In D. Perrin & E.-M. Jakobs (Eds.), Handbook of writing and text production (Vol. 10, pp. 159–173). Boston: De Gruyter.

Severinson-Eklundh, K., & Kollberg, P. (1996). Computer tools for tracing the writing process. From keystroke records to S-notation. In G. Rijlaarsdam, H. Van den Bergh & M. Couzijn (Eds.), Current research in writing. Theories, models and methodology (pp. 526–541). Amsterdam: Amsterdam University Press.

Tusting, K., Barton, D., McCulloch, S., Papen, U., & Potts, D. (2019). Researching writing across the lifespan. The value of literacy studies for highlighting social and contextual aspects of change. Writing and Pedagogy, 10(3), 401–422. doi: 10.1558/wap.34589.

CHAPTER 9

Visualising the Process of Answering Clinical and Diagnostic Linguistic Tests

Andreas Sellstone, Linda Sandström and Kirk P.H. Sullivan

The development of keystroke logging tools has offered new opportunities to study the writing process. Thus far, it has primarily been used as a research tool (see Lindgren et al., 2019 for an overview); however, keystroke logging technology has the potential to be useful in non-research environments, such as clinics and schools. Digitized tests in a keystroke logging environment provide in-depth accounts of the writing processes. These accounts could aid the diagnosis of language impairments and neuropsychiatric disorders. Moreover, they can give detailed information about learning progress and be used longitudinally to monitor the effects of, and continually individualise treatment, as suggested by Johansson-Malmeling et al. (2020) for individuals diagnosed with aphasia. Yet, despite several researchers calling for the use of keystroke logging in clinical and educational settings (e.g., Holm et al., 2022; Johansson-Malmeling et al., 2020), take-up has been slow in the real-world. One of the challenges facing non-writing researchers is the less-than-intuitive data representation of many keystroke logging programs. This chapter suggests how the visualisation of keystroke logging data can be tailored to the requirements of the clinic and school.

9.1 The Problem of Visual Representation for Clinicians and Teachers

Keystroke logging programs produce enormous amounts of data that at times can feel overwhelming. Visual representations are an attempt to make the data less obscure and more readily interpretable (Brath, 2021; Koponen, this volume, p. 19). For example, if we look at the linear representation of a keystroke log[1] that displays the sequence of keystrokes and mouse (see Sullivan and Lindgren, 2006) actions for one participant diagnosed with aphasia in

1 Johansson-Malmeling et al. (2020) used New Scriptlog (Wengelin et al., 2019) in their research study.

 | HTTPS://DOI.ORG/10.1163/9789004760264-010

Johansson-Malmeling et al. (2020, p. 155), we can see that the data would be strenuous and too time consuming to decipher for a therapist or teacher:

- *<5.810>c<2.331>y<2.065>ke<6.938>r<BACKSPACE1>l<4.336>käe<BACKSPACE2><6.525>ej<BACKSPACE1>l<4.591>j<BACKSPACE1><2.905><MOUSECLICK><8.925><MOUSECLICK>an<2.078><MOUSECLICK>r<BACKSPACE1><3.655><MOUSECLICK>j<2.071><MOUSECLICK><BACKSPACE1>ä<BACKSPACE1><2.201>e<BACKSPACE1><6.598>e<4.774>d<7.161><BACKSPACE1><2.426>d<10.708><MOUSECLICK><10.271><MOUSECLICK><BACKSPACE1><2.271><BACKSPACE1>d<6.448>j<3.089><MOUSECLICK><MOUSECLICK><BACKSPACE1><17.505><MOUSECLICK><5.093>k<2.015><BACKSPACE1><11.186><MOUSECLICK><BACKSPACE1><3.119><MOUSECLICK><.*

This example linear representation is only a small part of this participant's keystroke log and one of several example keystroke logs which Johansson-Malmeling et al. use to illustrate their participants approach revising their writing, that is there editing strategies (see Sullivan and Lindgren, 2006; Lindgren and Sullivan, 2019). It is not intuitive to the inexperienced reader of such logs where the writing was edited, nor which type of editing strategy was used.

The need for the development of visual representations has inspired various ways of visualising the writing process; some incorporate as many writing dimensions as possible, for example, progression visualisation (Bécotte-Boutin et al., 2019), and others focus on a single dimension, for example, S-notation (Kollberg, 1998) while others have focussed on visualising real-world writing processes (Perrin, 2013). Even if these visualisations assist in the interpretation of a keystroke log, the process of analysing the results is still time-consuming. The time an analysis takes is of importance in clinical and diagnostic settings. For example, clinical consultations are limited in time, and the therapist sees many clients during the day. Similarly, in school-settings, for keystroke logging to be accepted as a diagnostic tool, it is necessary that it saves the teacher time rather than create additional work. Hence, if keystroke logging programs are to be used outside the research environments, the keystroke logged data need to be sifted to present relevant information tailored to the test administrator's needs. That is, the development of bespoke visual representations for these settings ought to be of interest to the keystroke logging programmers and developers.

Keystroke logging's potential comes from the ability to provide information about writing and cognitive processes that cannot be captured by traditional diagnostic tests taken with pen and paper—since with pen and paper, the test administrator is limited to the test results, the session's duration, and any notes made by the administrator during testing. However, without easily accessible visualisations and analytic tools, keystroke logging will not find its way into clinics and classrooms; this is despite promising research into the use of keystroke logging as a diagnostic and pedagogic tool. Thus, for therapists and teachers to be able to use keystroke logging technology, they must be able to access the data of interest rapidly. To date, the available visualisation tools (see Bécotte-Boutin et al., 2019 for an overview of keystroke log visualisations) are unsuitable for classrooms or clinics. Yet, as Basnayake & Usoof (this volume, p. 48) point out, there are possibilities for new visualisations of the writing process. Hence, the objective of this chapter is to consider and suggest useful visualisations of keystroke logging data for clinicians and teachers from their clinical and diagnostic linguistic tests.

9.2 Keystroke Logging and Diagnostic Tests

Multiple studies have shown that keystroke loggers can be used to elucidate and provide useful data about the writing process of people with writing difficulties, for example, aphasia (e.g., Behrns et al., 2008; Johansson-Malmeling et al., 2020) and dyslexia (e.g., Torrance et al., 2016; Wengelin, 2007) in the clinic and the classroom. Moreover, keystroke logging can also be informative for the clinician when diagnosing and monitoring degenerative dementia (Alfalahi et al., 2022; Van Waes et al., 2017).

9.2.1 *Keystroke Logging for Language Assessment*

In the area of aphasia, Johansson-Malmeling et al. (2020) found that the most common editing strategy used by individuals diagnosed with aphasia was repeatedly revising the same letter. This aligns with Behrns et al. (2008) who found that an individual diagnosed with aphasia tended to edit most at the word and letter level. Johansson-Malmeling et al. (2020) suggest that "both correctness of spelling as well as the presence and nature of any editing difficulties should be taken into account and treatment for writing difficulties should include training in successful editing strategies" (p. 146) and that "[t]he fitting of digital writing aids for persons with aphasia should be individual, since many of the editing strategies used were individual" (p. 146). The development and integration of new data visualisation into keystroke logging programs would facilitate these suggestions and make keystroke logging a viable tool in the clinical setting.

In the area of dyslexia, there is an abundance of published keystroke logging research. Among other things this has shown that people diagnosed with dyslexia display a word-level focus when writing (e.g., Torrance et al., 2016;

Wengelin, 2007). In comparison with other writers who tend to pause the longest at sentence and paragraph levels, writers with dyslexia tend to pause longer and more frequently before writing words and within words.

In the area of degenerative dementia, Van Waes et al. (2017) found that when participants performed a simple task that consisted of copying a set of words, bigrams and sentences, elderly people with Alzheimer's disease had longer average pause lengths compared to both healthy elderly people and young adults. Van Waes et al. suggest that a writing test taken with a keystroke logger can provide beneficial information for diagnostic assessment of patients with disorders such as Alzheimer's disease. More recently, based on their meta-analysis of published literature, Alfalahi et al., (2022) argued that keystroke logging could be a useful tool for the early diagnosis of neurological and/or psychiatric disorders that affect fine motor skills.

In sum, this research suggests that it may be fruitful to apply keystroke logging in assessment situations since pausing, revision, and editing are aspects that are not visible when taking tests with pen and paper. Tests that can be easily moved to keystroke logging environments are currently used clinically, and in the classroom to detect students with writing difficulties. Although, without bespoke visualisations, clinicians and teachers will find it challenging to access the relevant information.

9.2.2 *Areas with Potential for Keystroke Logging beyond Free Writing*

As keystroke logging captures interaction with a computer keyboard and mouse, it can be used for digitized tests, including multiple-choice tests as well as those requiring free-text answers. In the case of multiple-choice tests, a keystroke logger could highlight points of increased cognitive effort that are evidenced with pauses and answer revisions. These measures can hint at planning and evaluation challenges. Hence, the type of diagnostic test that offers possibilities for the use of keystroke logging is not limited to free-text written tasks (Usoof et al., 2020), that has been the traditional focus of keystroke logging research, including visualisation. Both in the clinic and school many tests include non-free text writing elements. In the following sub-sections, we present some examples of such elements that we consider to be suited for moving to a keystroke logging environment. Such a move would however place new demands on the visualisation of the data recorded by the keystroke logging program.

9.2.2.1 Keystroke Logging in the Clinic

Johansson-Malmeling et al. (2020) argue that key writing difficulties faced by persons with aphasia can be captured by keystroke loggers. Although diagnostic tests for aphasia differ, that is they target different language-related processes, the majority assess writing in one way or another (Castro et al., 2023). These writing tasks generally consist of copying words, and sentences, and writing words, nonwords, and sentences from spoken prompts. Although keystroke logging might not inform the diagnosis of aphasia, there is evidence that suggests that it is useful as a tool to tailor treatment for writing difficulties as a result of aphasia (Johansson-Malmeling et al., 2020).

To diagnose dyslexia many language-related aspects are evaluated. These include reading accuracy and speed, reading comprehension, word comprehension, listening comprehension, spelling, writing ability, and working memory. The Swedish Agency for Health Technology Assessment and Assessment of Social Service (SBU, 2014) found that more than 50 diagnostic tests for dyslexia were used in Sweden in 2014 for the assessment of dyslexia. One of the most widely used tests is Logos (Logometrica, 2024), a computer-based test battery that covers a wide range of the skills listed in the SBU report (SBU, 2014). By incorporating keystroke logging into computerized tests such as Logos, it is possible to collect detailed information about the areas where test-takers may face difficulties. Although this information might not be crucial for diagnosis, it would still provide valuable insights to clinicians when making recommendations and when planning targeted interventions.

For neuropsychiatric disorders such as Alzheimer's, screening tests for dementia such as the Mini Mental State Examination (MMSE) (Folstein et al., 1975) include a task that requires participants to spontaneously write a sentence that should "contain a subject and verb and be sensible" (p. 198), but correct grammar and punctuation is inconsequential for the judgement of the writing. In line with Van Waes et al. (2017), one might perform this and similar writing tasks in a keystroke logging environment. While the use of writing tasks in screening tests for dementia is rare, there is evidence that supports its efficacy for early diagnosis of Mild Cognitive Impairment (MCI), the stage that precedes disorders such as Alzheimer's disease. Early signs of MCI are motor skill decline, thus detecting early signs of motor decline is important. However, it is a major challenge to distinguish early motor skill decline from the effects of typical aging (Alfalahi et al., 2022). Yet, on the basis of a meta-analysis of 41 studies, Alfalahi et al., (2022) concluded that keystroke dynamics can provide valuable additional information to the clinician. Hence, keystroke logging, with its sensitivity to temporal aspects of typing as biomarkers for fine motor decline, could provide valuable diagnostic data for the clinician in ways that current MCI tests do not—these tests focus on other motor skills, such as drawing a clock, drawing a copy of a cube, remembering and repeat a string of numbers.

Some of the diagnostic tests in these three example areas could fruitfully be transferred to a computer keystroke logging environment. In this way, keystroke logging technology could be tailored for non-research purposes, with visualisations of the collected data directed towards the clinician.

9.2.2.2 Keystroke Logging in the Classroom

Many researchers have suggested that keystroke logging has potential in the language classroom for supporting argumentative and descriptive writing (e.g., Bušić & Sullivan, 2022; Holm et al., 2023; Lindgren & Sullivan, 2003; Lindgren et al., 2008; Skein et al., 2020; Sullivan et al., 1998; Sullivan & Lindgren, 2002; Thomas et al., 2022, Thomas & Sullivan, 2022). They argue that capturing challenges during writing with keystroke logging software can give the teacher access to students' writing challenges. In the special education setting, such information, when appropriately visualised, can tailor the support required to help students in need. However, to date, computer keystroke logging is rarely, if at all, used in the classroom. This is not least due to the enormous amount of data collected and the time required to analyse it for educational purposes.

Diagnostic tests in the classroom, on the other hand, do not demand long free-text answers in the way argumentative and descriptive tasks, or long-term writing (Bekius & Buschenhenke, this volume, p. 148) do. Indeed, many diagnostic tests consist of multiple-choice or short answer questions. For example, the test battery Diagnostic Reading and Writing Test (DLS, Järpsten & Taube, 2018; a frequently used screening tool in schools for identifying reading and writing difficulties), assesses word and reading comprehension with 64 multiple-choice questions. If taken with a keystroke logger, pauses and revisions during the answering process would be captured; data which would provide teachers with insights into how students' approach the answering of such tasks. DLS also includes a dictation task in which 36 words are to be written down by the participants. It is easy to imagine this dictation task being taken with a keystroke logger to provide further information about the writing of the participants. DLS for Swedish school years 7–9 (age 13–15) and upper secondary school year 1 (age 16–17), are already digitized and can be taken on a computer. Creating customised visualisations based on keystroke logging data for the needs of classroom teachers has the potential of individualising the educational context for individual students.

9.3 Piloting a Morphological Diagnostic Test in a Keystroke Logging Environment

Before piloting a test in a keystroke logging program, it is pertinent to consider what the diagnosis test aims to reveal. This is particularly necessary when planning how the data may be visualised. Equally, it is important to bear in mind that not all tests are immediately suitable for moving from pen-and-paper to the computer. Sellstone (2023) investigated whether a morphological test undertaken in the keystroke logging program GenGraphiX-LOG (GGXLog) (Caporossi et al., 2023) could provide data that afford tailored data visualisation. His pilot study also aimed to find out if it was possible to generate useful information about the test-taking process beyond the information provided by the test results alone. The morphological test that Sellstone adapted and placed in a keystroke logging environment was based on the gamified diagnostic test *Monster, P.I.* (Goodwin, Petscher, Tock, et al., 2022). This gamified test assesses written language skills, such as morphology, vocabulary, and syntax—language skills of importance for reading comprehension, and writing (e.g., Goodwin, Petscher, & Reynolds, 2022). Monster, P.I. includes multiple-choice questions and word dictation tasks, that can readily be transferred to a computer keystroke logging environment. Sellstone's pilot study used tasks and questions from the morphological part of Monster, P.I.—four linguistic morphological abilities were included (see Table 9.1 for examples of items from each subtest).

The pilot test was in English and was taken by 21 first language Swedish speakers in upper secondary school. The subtest was carried out over the duration of an English class (85 min) and the students proceeded at their own pace within the time limit, except for the first subtest which was dictated by the test administrator simultaneously the whole class. Each of the six subtests required the student to upload the corresponding subtest document and an answer sheet with numbered rows on which to write the answers. Before writing, the students clicked the record button which made it possible to write the answers. When the participants were finished, they raised their hand, upon which the keystroke logging files were collected.

Sellstone's (2023) pilot study reported no relationship between the test score and the number of cognitive pauses or revisions as evidenced by the log-file at group level. This was surprising since previous studies have shown that an increase in cognitive demand results in increased pauses and errors (e.g., Conijn et al., 2019; Wengelin, 2006). A more detailed analysis of Sellstone's data, however, revealed that the morphological spelling subtest score was indeed related to pauses ($R^2 = .33$, $F(1, 19) = 9.49$, $p = 0.006$). This supports the value of collecting keystroke logging data when individual's undertake tests. Moreover, when Sellstrone's data was investigated at the individual level, variation between students' score, cognitive pauses, and revisions were noted. For example, some students had high test scores, yet their keystroke logs contained a high number of pauses and revisions that suggests that they might have challenges deciding on the correct answers. Such information about these students' processes when taking the test would have been lost if their keystrokes had not been

TABLE 9.1 Morphological skill and subtest with an example (Sellstone, 2023)

Skill and subtest	**Example question**
Morphological-Orthographic Knowledge	
Morphological Spelling	We must endeavour to make the justice system *nondiscriminatory.*[a] [nondiscriminatory*]
Morphological-Syntactic Knowledge	
Real Word Suffix	John wants to make a good _____ on his date. [impressive, impression*, impressionable, impressively]
Making it Fit	The cook wanted them to share the last piece of pie, but it was too small to be ____ (divide) into two pieces. [divided*]
Morphological Awareness	
– *Meaning Puzzles*	Write the word that could help you figure out the meaning of MOVEMENT. – [*men, mover**, *over, meant*]
– *Odd Man Out*	Which word shares the same part but has a different meaning? [mushroom*, bedroom, classroom]
Morphological-Semantic Knowledge	
– *Word Detectives*	People were FEARLESS even as the big storm approached. The people could be described as – [*A. brave**, *B. tired, C. sad, D. scared*]

a Words and sentences were not seen, only read aloud.
Note: The linguistic skill that was measured is written in the left column in italics, whereas the subtest/subtests designed to measure the skill is/are written beneath the skill in bold text. The alternatives and answers are bracketed beneath the example item and the correct answer is marked with an *.

logged. The question though is how best to visualise this information at group and individual level (Cohen et al., 2008) for non-writing researchers who are unfamiliar with keystroke log-files and who expect data to be presented familiar ways.

9.4 Visualising the Test-Taking Process: an Ideal Future

The objective for clinicians and teachers is rarely to answer research questions. It is rather to understand the data in relation to their client or student. Hence, the data need to be visualised in a consistent and intuitive way that makes it possible to reliably detect deviations from the norm that might indicate difficulties. Our starting point for the development of the visualisations we present in this chapter, was thus, to create visualisation with which clinicians and teachers are familiar. We, therefore, read a range of books and articles aimed at clinicians and teachers to acquaint ourselves with the types of data visualisation with which they are familiar. This revealed that it would be wise to delimit data visualisation, as much as possible, to bar charts, scatter plots, along with basic descriptive statistical information such as mean and standard deviation. This is not to say that other more complex visualisations, as proposed in many of this volume's chapters (e.g., Tanoï Namio et al., this volume, p. 106) might not be useful in clinics and schools. However, in our visualisation proposals we avoid such complex visualisations, not least as these research-driven visualisations may have contributed to the slow uptake of keystroke logging technology by non-writing researchers.

In the following sections, we present examples of how keystroke logged data can be visualised at group and individual levels to encourage the implementation of keystroke logging as a tool for diagnostic tests in non-research settings.

9.4.1 *Group Level Visualisations*

To be able to present group level visualisations, it is necessary for keystroke logging analysis and visualisation software to merge individual logfiles into a single database. Ideally, individuals would be able to upload their own logfiles to this database. Scripts can easily be created to grade multiple choice-based tests, spelling tests and word/morphological segmentation tests. However, free-text written answers need human judgement. Such judgements need to be manually entered into the keystroke log database as a separate data point.

After scores are available in the database, it would be possible to create group level visualisations. For example, the score data from Sellstone's (2023) 21 participants can be presented as shown in Figure 9.1(a). Here the various subtests (see Table 9.1) are reported.[2] As clinicians and teachers consider results in relation to a larger population, they expect such figures to also include mean and standard deviation. Figure 9.1(a) can readily be overlayed with such information (see Figure 9.1(b)); the calculation of this information can be either internal to the group, or based on normative data, either from a published standardised test, or from a dynamic database that continuously recalculates these values as more files are added to the database. Thus, in Figure 9.1(a) and 9.1(b) the distribution of scores between subtests can be seen, as well as specific individual scores that lie outside of two standard deviations. The dual representation (the unstandardised and standardised) allows clinicians and teachers to evaluate both absolute and relative performance.

Moving beyond the test score, the test-taking process can also be visualised at the group level to provide an in depth understanding of the test-taking process. Figure 9.2 shows how this data can be visualised. Pauses[3] (Figure 9.2(a)), and deletions (Figure 9.2(b)) are plotted for each test (see Table 9.1). The visualisation shown in Figure 9.2(a) and 9.2(b) is interpreted in the same way as Figure 9.1(b), but with pauses or deletions represented in the y-axis instead of subtest scores, and a categorical distribution of subtests in the x-axis. This gives access to each measure allows a more nuanced view of the test taking process, as deletions and pauses can be indicative of increased cognitive effort and difficulties with certain subtests.

To assist the relationship between test scores and the process (pauses and revisions), we envisage these graphs as interactive. For example, clicking on a subtest label (e.g., morphological spelling) on the x-axis would result in Figure 9.3 that shows details about this subtest's number of pauses in relation to final scores. All variables can be plotted against each other, depending on the information in which the reader is interested, including mean and standard

2 The x-axis in figure 9.1 and 9.2 are categorical and jittering has been applied to distinguish overlapping data points in figures 9.1–9.4.

3 The represented pauses are equal to or longer than 2 seconds.

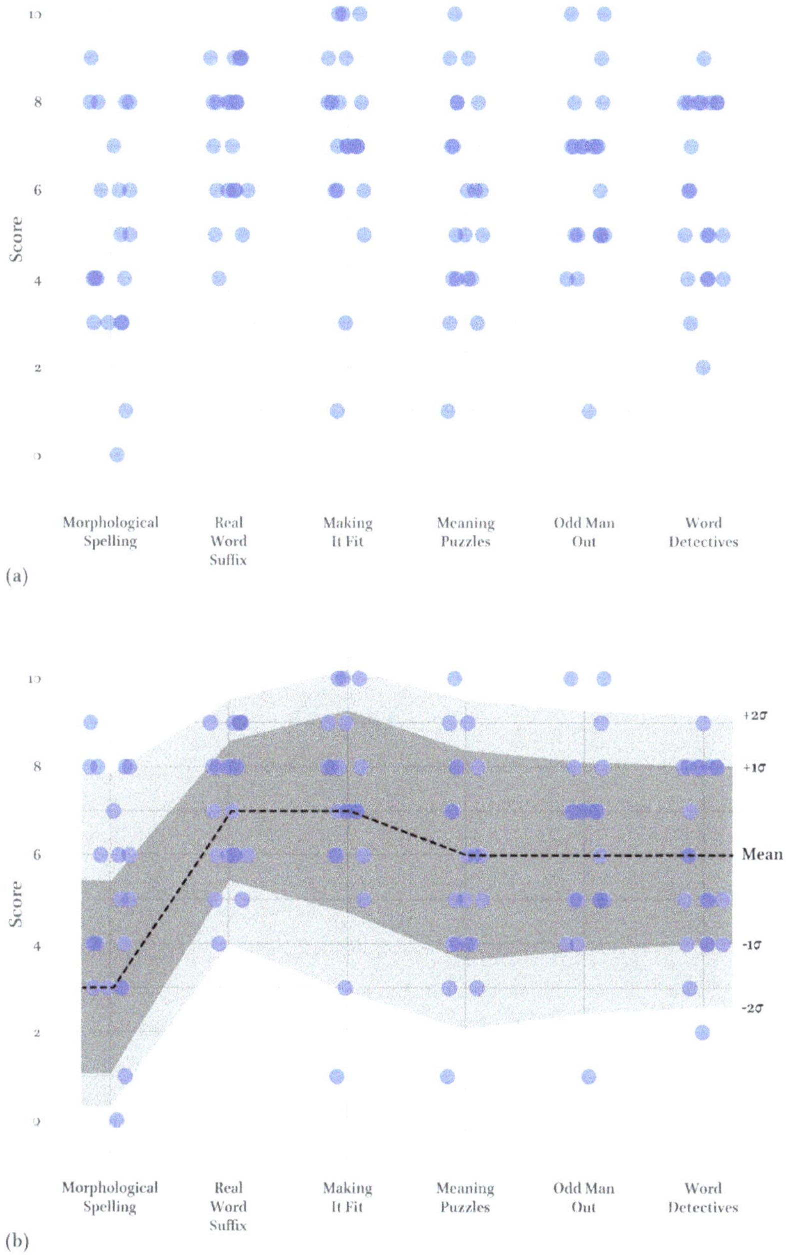

FIGURE 9.1 Overview of the total score for each participant over each subtest—(a) displaying unstandardised test scores and (b) displaying standardised test scores
The test scores are visualised in the y-axis, while each subtest is categorically divided and visualised in the x-axis.

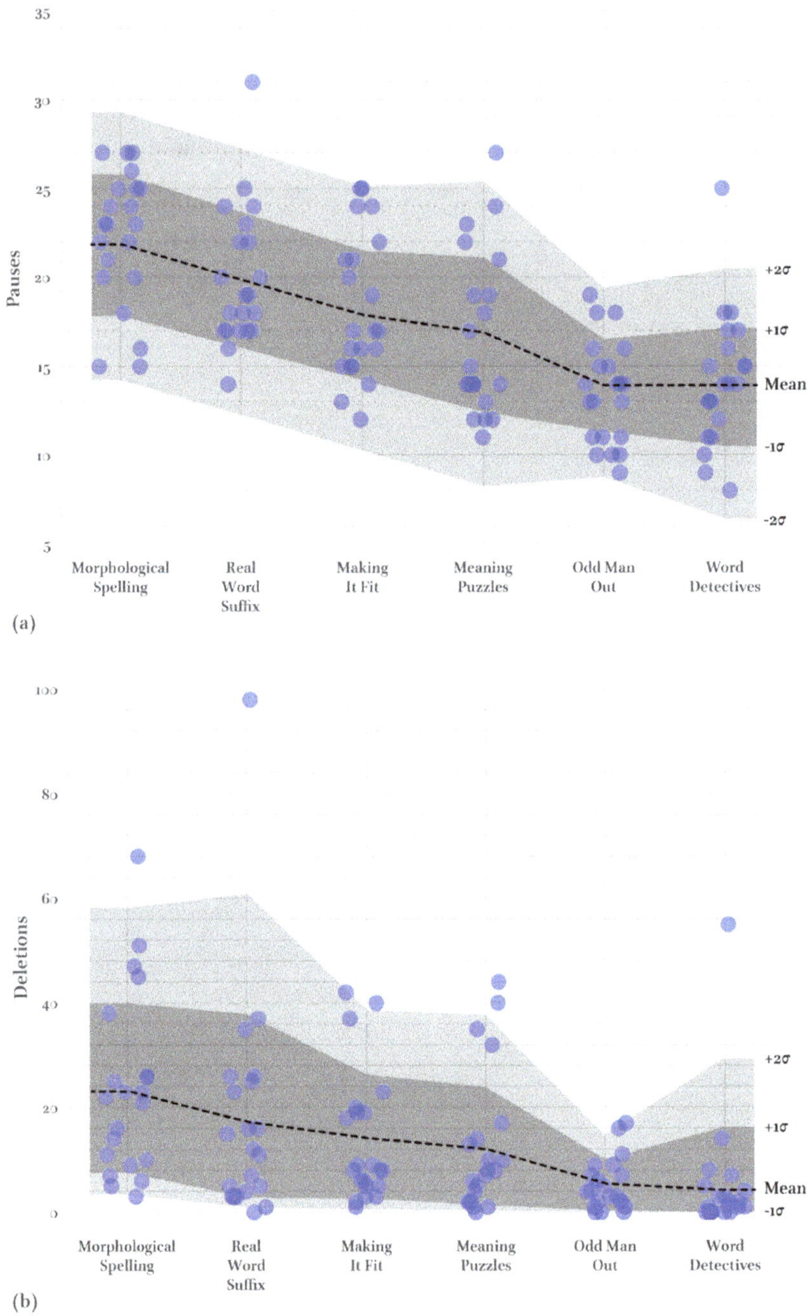

FIGURE 9.2 Overview of the number of pauses (a) and deletions (b) for each subtest

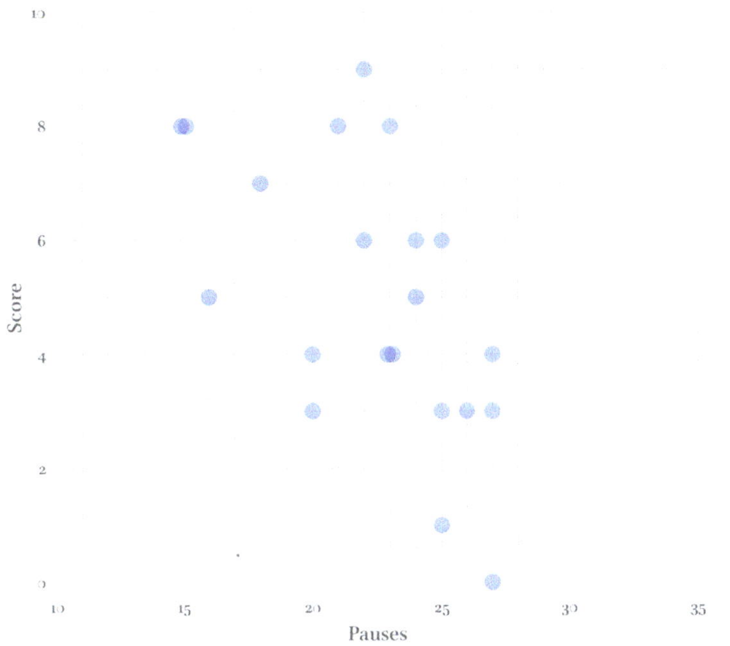

FIGURE 9.3 Each participant's number of pauses in the x-axis and score in the y-axis for the Morphological Spelling subtest

information data (see Figure 9.4(a) and 9.4(b)). As well as placing an individual in relation to other people's performance, in the clinic and the school, it is also useful to understand the individual's test-taking process in detail. In his way, clinicians and teachers can more easily identify certain patterns, such as correlations between scores and pauses or deletions.

9.4.2 *Individual Level Visualisations*

Individual level visualisations, we propose, can be accessed via the group visualisations; by clicking on an individual's datapoint in a group level visualisation, more detailed information can be visualised. Figure 9.5(a)–(c) presents individual test scores, along with number of pauses and deletions in relation to normative data. Thus, how a single participant performed in relation to the standardised test scores in each subtest is visualised.

Further, clicking on a subtest label on the x-axis would result in Figure 9.6 that shows detailed information about each item in the subtest, for example, the number of pauses (9.6(a)), mean pause length (9.6(b)) and deletions (8.6(c)) for each word in the Morphological Spelling subtest. These measures reflect different aspects of writing the answers. This allows a closer look at

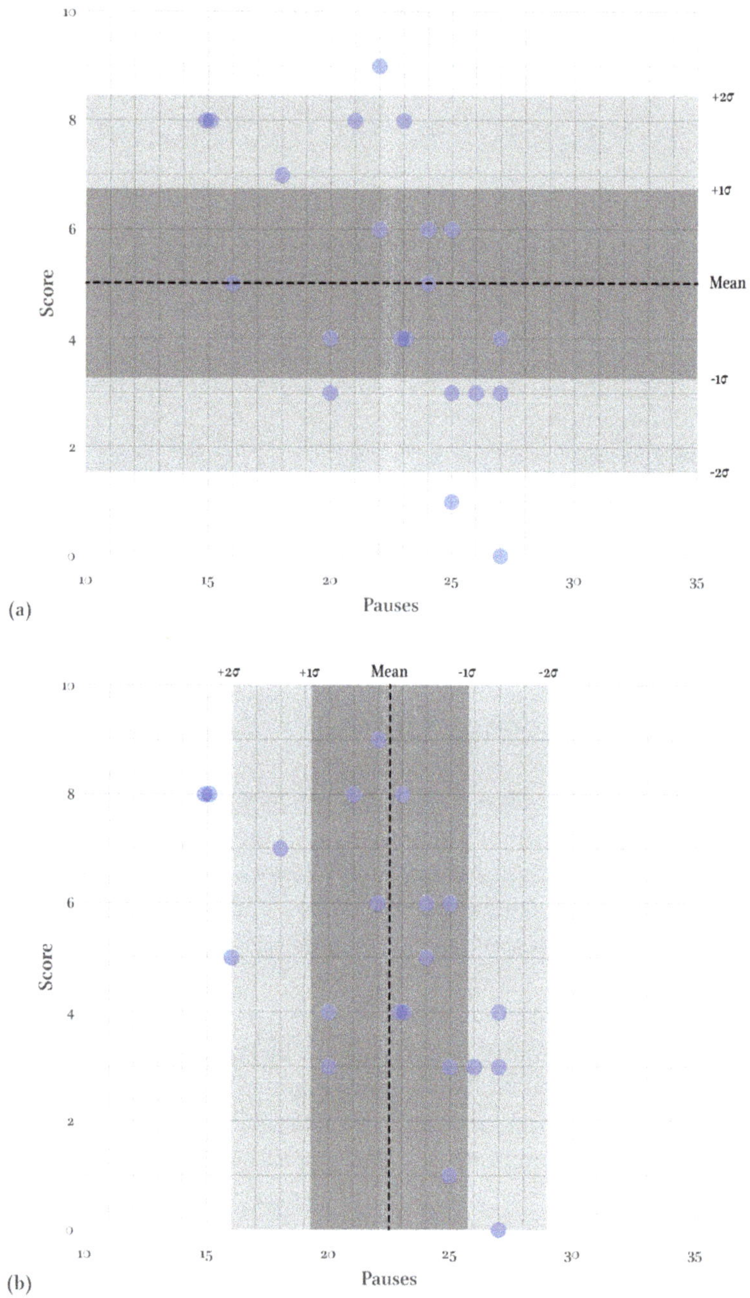

FIGURE 9.4 Each participant's number of pauses in the x-axes and score in the y-axes (a) displaying standard deviations and mean for score and (b) displaying standard deviations and mean for number of pauses

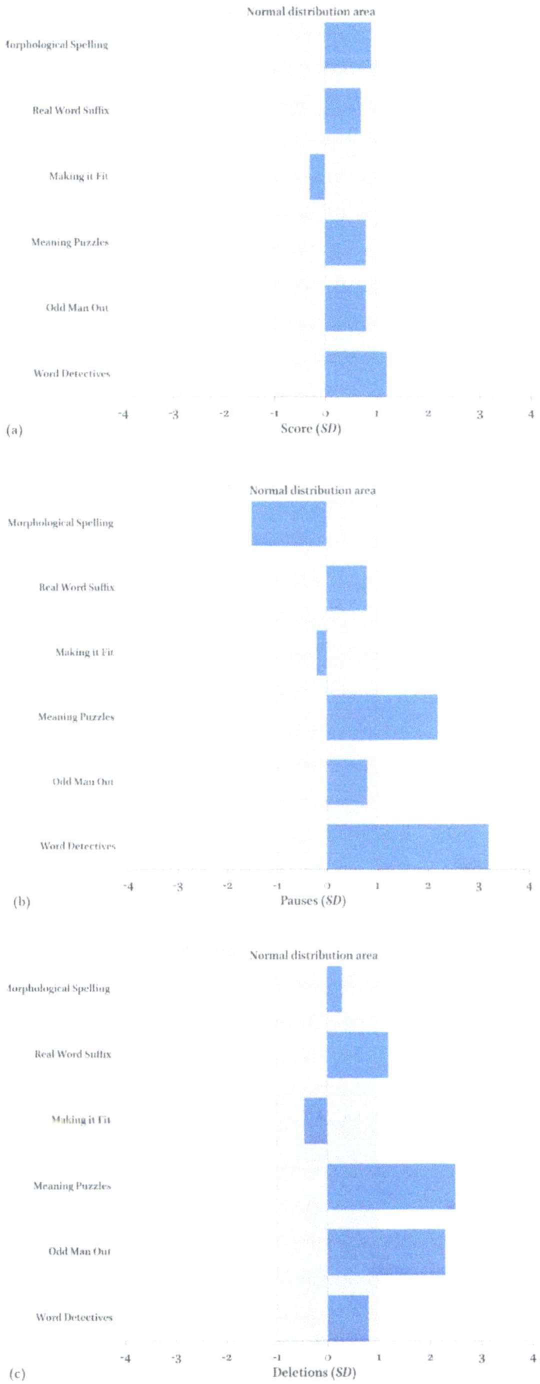

FIGURE 9.5
Individual and standardised overview of one participant's number of scores (a), pauses (b), and deletions (c) for each subtest
Each subtest is categorically represented in the y-axis, while the participants' standard deviations of each measurement (score, pauses, or deletions) are represented in the x-axis.

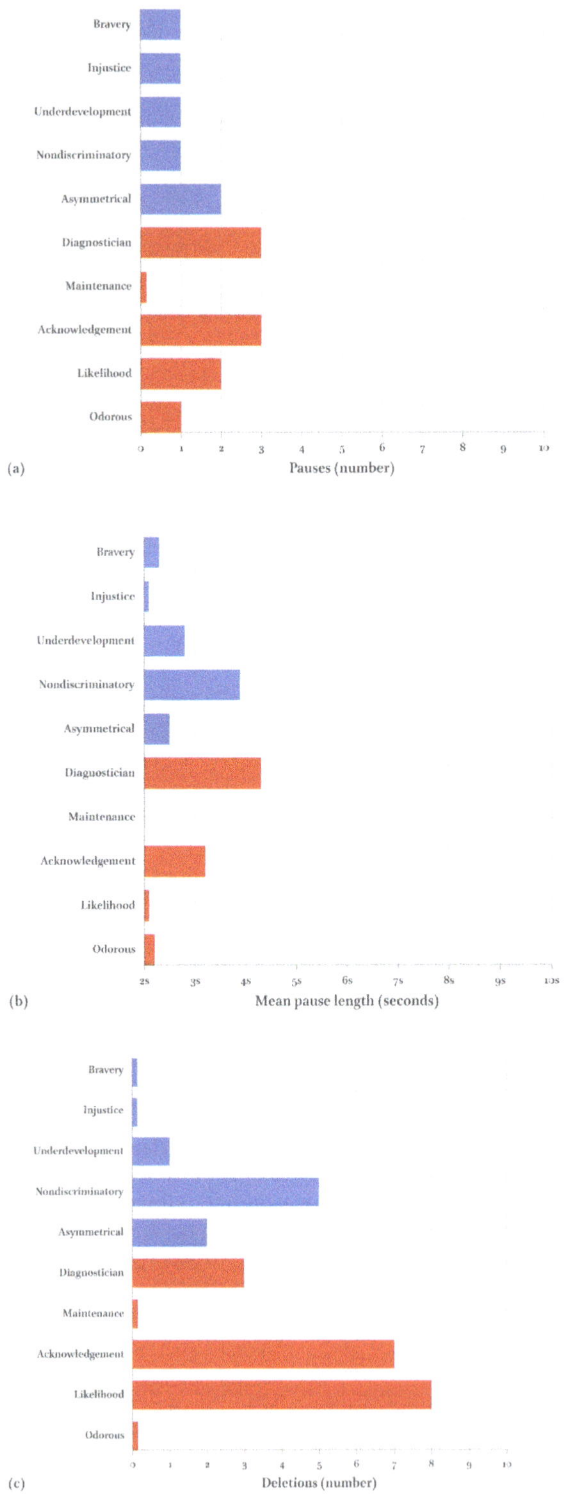

FIGURE 9.6
Individual overview of the number of pauses (a), mean pause length (b), and number of deletions (c) for each item in the Morphological Spelling subtest
Correct answers are represented by blue bars and incorrect answers by red bars. Each target word is categorically represented in the y-axis, while the measures (pauses, mean pause length, or deletions) are represented in the x-axis.

the participant's performance on a specific subtest through the visualisation of where the participant spent more time pausing, presumably thinking, and revising their answer.

For multiple choice subtests, an additional visualisation is necessary as these tests only allow the test-taker to select and revise their choice(s). Hence for these tests, the revision sequence becomes pertinent. It is necessary to know between which choices a test-taker moves, how many times they revise their selection, and how long the test-taker takes between answer selections.

Figure 9.7 presents one of Sellstone's (2023) participants' multiple-choice subtest process (Word Detectives). The figure visualises the answer the participant first provided, if and to what the participant changed the answer, which answer was correct or incorrect, and how long it took for the participant to change their answer—indicating the degree of cognitive effort and the participants certainty in their given answers. The test-taker visualised in Figure 9.7 did not make more than one revision per question. However, it is not difficult to imagine how this visualisation could include multiple revisions for a single answer.

The clinician and teacher might also want to gain an impression about how the test-taker divided their time when answering a subtest's items. For example, Figure 9.8 visualises how one of Sellstone's (2023) participants undertook the subtest morphological spelling using the GGXLog Pause Analysis Graph, together with vertical lines indicating the start of each question item.

FIGURE 9.7 Answer revisions for one participant in the multiple-choice task Word Detectives and the duration between answers, with the question-number in the y-axis, time in the x-axis
Correct answers are represented by blue data points and incorrect answers by red data points.

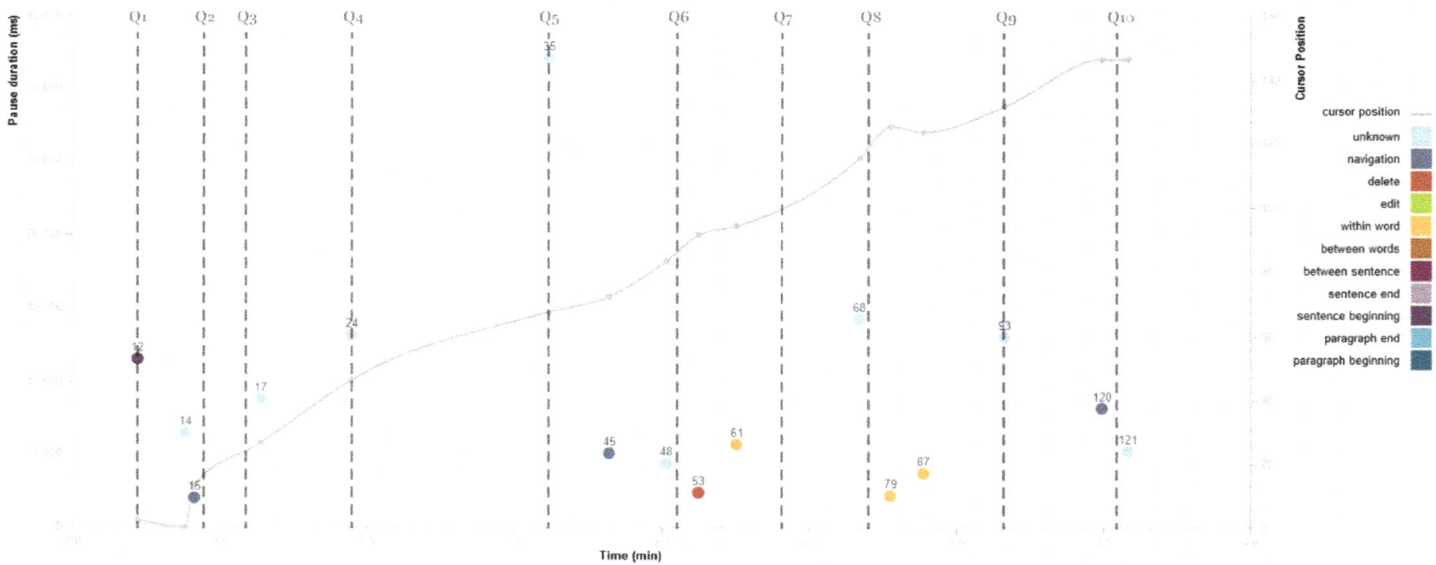

FIGURE 9.8 Pause graph analysis with the start of each item by the participant visualised by a dotted line (Q1–Q10)
The left y-axis represents the pause duration in milliseconds, the right y-axis represents the cursor position in characters, and the x-axis represents the time in minutes of the whole subtest session. Each dotted line (Q1–Q10) represents the time at which the participant started writing a word. Each dot is a type of pause, and its colour indicates what type of pause it was (as seen in the right-hand graph legend). The grey line represents cursor position.

This is a useful way to visualise and easily identify different types of pauses, some of which are known to be associated with various types of learning disabilities—for example, increased within-word pause rate is associated with dyslexia (Torrance et al., 2016; Wengelin, 2007). This item demarcation could be applied to multiple graph visualisations such as Burst and Fluency Analysis.

In sum, keystroke logging data affords a way to visualise group and individual diagnostic test processes in ways that are familiar to non-writing researchers working in clinics and schools. Not all the visualisations discussed are currently available in keystroke logging programs. In the following section we discuss the program specifications necessary to generate the proposed visualisations.

9.4.3 *Keystroke Logging Development for the Future*

Keystroke logging software is currently not optimised for clinical and diagnostic testing in the way that was explored in Sellstone (2023). A keystroke logging program optimized for diagnostics tests requires several features, over and above the fundamentals of temporal logging of keystrokes. One, some diagnostic tests require editing of existing texts. This requires the presentation of the question, and the logging of the editing of questions. Two, in order to record logging data that accurately captures the starting point of a subtest or item, a way to step through the test is required. In this way the time from seeing the test to completing the test is possible to log accurately. Three, an interface for presenting, answering, and recording multiple-choice questions is needed. Four, diagnostic tests frequently include oral instructions in addition to the written instructions. Hence, the keystroke logging program needs a text-to-speech module, or be able to play pre-recorded audio instructions as and when required by the diagnostic test. Five, in order to present group-level data, it is imperative that individual logfiles be entered into a single database; and six, a visualisation module that is able to calculate and visualise the data in the ways expected by clinicians and teachers as outlined in this chapter. One way forward would be to have a new project type (see Usoof et al., 2020), that could be called *Diagnostic Testing*. For example, in GGXLog this would be a project type alongside *Free-writing, Translating, Post editing*, and so on. This new project type would be specifically designed for diagnostic tests, and examinations with multiple subtests and questions, in which each question is isolated, and one can traverse the test by clicking through each question. Of importance is that this project type would allow the sub-tests of a diagnostic test to be linked.

9.5 Concluding Remarks

The current visualisation repertoire of keystroke logging programs has been driven by the research interests of the program development teams. Not surprising this has focussed on providing writing researchers with novel forms of data visualisation that interrogate keystroke logging data so that it supports research questions relating to the writing process of various groups of writers composing various types of texts. However, as we have highlighted in this chapter, the goal for clinicians and teachers is different. These professionals primarily use diagnostic test results to provide their clients and students appropriate interventions and support. Using keystroke logging during diagnostic testing affords new opportunities for these professionals to access nuanced temporal data relating to the writing of test answers. These data need to be visualised in a consistent and intuitive way that makes it possible to reliably detect performance variation of importance. This is not to say that current keystroke logging visualisations might not be useful in clinics and schools, but it is possible that the focus on research-driven visualisations makes keystroke logging programme unattractive to clinicians and teachers. This chapter has presented a range of visualisations of keystroke logging data that has been collected during the taking of a diagnostic test and these visualisations aim to make keystroke logging more attractive in these settings. The automation of this visualisation within a keystroke logging environment would extend the use of computer keystroke logging to new domains that translate computer keystroke logging research experience in novel ways.

References

Alfalahi, H., Khandoker, A.H., Chowdhury, N., Iakovakis, D., Dias, S.B., Chaudhuri, K.R., & Hadjileontiadis, L.J. (2022). Diagnostic accuracy of keystroke dynamics as digital biomarkers for fine motor decline in neuropsychiatric disorders: a systematic review and meta-analysis. *Scientific Reports*, *12*(1). https://doi.org/10.1038/s41598-022-11865-7.

Brath, R. (2021). *Visualizing with Text*. CRC Press.

Bécotte-Boutin, H.-S., Caporossi, G., Hertz, A., & Leblay, C. (2019). Writing and rewriting: The coloured numerical visualization of keystroke logging. In E. Lindgren, & K.P.H. Sullivan (Eds.), Observing writing: Insights from keystroke logging and handwriting (pp. 96–124). Brill. https://doi.org/10.1163/9789004392526_006.

Behrns, I., Ahlsén, E., & Wengelin, Å. (2008). Aphasia and the process of revision in writing a text. *Clinical Linguistics & Phonetics*, *22*(2), 95–110. https://doi.org/10.1080/02699200701699603.

Bušić, V., & Sullivan, K.P.H. (2022). Skrivande och metaspråkande i modersmålsundervisningen [Writing and metatalk in mother tongue education]. In A. Norlund Shaswar, E. Lindgren, C. Hermansson, & S. Areljung (Eds.), *Skrivdidatik* [*The teaching and learning of writing*]. Studentlitteratur.

Caporossi, G., Leblay, C., & Usoof, H. (2023) *GenoGraphiX-LOG* (Version 2.1.0) [Computer software]. HEC Montréal & University of Turku. https://ggxlog.net.

Castro, N., Hula, W.D., & Ashaie, S. (2023). Defining aphasia: Content analysis of six aphasia diagnostic batteries. *Cortex*, *166*, 19–32. https://doi.org/10.1016/j.cortex.2023.05.005.

Cohen, A.L., Sanborn, A.N., & Shiffrin, R.M. (2008). Model evaluation using grouped or individual data. *Psychonomic Bulletin & Review*, *15*(4), 692–712. https://doi.org/10.3758/PBR.15.4.692.

Conijn, R., Roeser, J., & Van Zaanen, M. (2019). Understanding the keystroke log: the effect of writing task on keystroke features. *Reading and Writing 32*, 2353–2374. https://doi.org/10.1007/s11145-019-09953-8.

Folstein, M.F., Folstein, S.E., & McHugh, P.R. (1975). Mini-mental state. *Journal of Psychiatric Research*, *12*(3), 189–198. https://doi.org/10.1016/0022-3956(75)90026-6.

Goodwin, A.P., Petscher, Y., & Reynolds, D., (2022) Unraveling Adolescent Language & Reading Comprehension: The Monster's Data, *Scientific Studies of Reading, 26*(4), 305–326. https://doi.org/10.1080/10888438.2021.1989437.

Goodwin, A.P., Petscher, Y., Tock, J., McFadden, S., Reynolds, D., Lantos, T., & Jones, S. (2022). Monster, PI: Validation evidence for an assessment of adolescent language that assesses vocabulary knowledge, morphological knowledge, and syntactical awareness. *Assessment for Effective Intervention*, *47*(2), 89–100. https://doi.org/10.1177/1534508420966383.

Habib, M., & Giraud, K. (2013). Dyslexia. *Handbook of clinical neurology*, *111*, 229–235. https://doi.org/10.1016/B978-0-444-52891-9.00023-3.

Holm, H., Skein, E., & Sullivan, K.P.H. (2022). Using computer keystroke logging in the second language composition classroom. In J. Qin & P. Stapleton (Eds.), *Technology in second language writing: advances in composing, translation, writing pedagogy and data-driven learning* (pp. 167–181). Routledge. https://doiorg/10.4324/9781003279358-11.

Johansson-Malmeling, C., Wengelin, Å., & Henriksson, I. (2020). Aphasia and spelling to dictation: Analysis of spelling errors and editing. *International Journal of Language & Communication Disorders*, *56*(1), 145–160. https://doi.org/10.1111/1460-6984.12591.

Järpsten, B., & Taube, K. (2018). DLS. För skolår 7–9 och år 1 i gymnasiet. Rättstavning, ordförståelse, läshastighet och läsförståelse. [Assessment of reading and writing. For school years 7–9 and year 1 in upper secondary school. Orthography, word comprehension, reading fluency, and reading comprehension]. Elanders.

Kollberg, P. (1998). S-notation—a computer based method for studying and representing text composition (Licentiate Thesis. Royal Institute of Technology). https://urn.kb.se/resolve?urn=urn:nbn:se:kth:diva-808.

Lindgren, E., Knospe, Y., & Sullivan, K.P.H. (2019). Researching Writing with Observational Logging Tools from 2006 to the Present. In E. Lindgren, & K.P.H. Sullivan (Eds.), *Observing Writing: Insights from Keystroke Logging and Handwriting* (pp. 306–325). Brill. https://doi.org/10.1163/9789004392526_002.

Lindgren, E., Stevenson, M., & Sullivan, K.P.H. (2008). Supporting the reflective language learner with computer keystroke logging. In B. Barber and F. Zhang (Eds.), *Handbook of Research on Computer Enhanced Language Acquisition and Learning.* (pp. 189–204) IGI Global Inc. https://doi.org/10.4018/978-1-59904-895-6.ch011.

Lindgren, E., & Sullivan, K.P.H. (2003). Stimulated recall as a trigger of increasing noticing and language awareness in the L2 writing classroom: A case study of two young female writers. *Language Awareness, 12*(3–4), 172–186. https://doi.org/10.1080/09658410308667075.

Lindgren, E. & Sullivan, K.P.H. (Eds.), Observing Writing: Insights from Keystroke Logging and Handwriting. Brill.

Logometrica. (2024, January). *Logos*. https://logometrica.se/logos.

Perrin, D. (2013). *The linguistics of newswriting*. John Benjamins Publishing Company.

Rastle, K., Davis, M.H., Marslen-Wilson, W.D., & Tyler, L.K. (2000). Morphological and semantic effects in visual word recognition: A time-course study. *Language and Cognitive Processes, 15*(4–5), 507–537. https://doi.org/10.1080/01690960050119689.

SBU (2014). Dyslexi hos barn och ungdomar—Tester och insatser. En systematisk litteraturöversikt [Children and teenagers with dyslexia—tests and interventions. A systematic literature review] (SBU-rapport nr 225). Statens beredning för medicinsk utvärdering.

Sellstone, A. (2023). *From Keystrokes to Cognitive Processes: Analyzing Morphological Knowledge Using Keystroke Logging* [Master's (one year) thesis, Umeå University]. DiVA. Retrieved from https://urn.kb.se/resolve?urn=urn:nbn:se:umu:diva-210609.

Skein, E., Knospe, Y., & Sullivan, K.P.H. (2020). Supporting advanced multilingual speakers as individuals: Translanguaging in writing. In G. Neokleous, A. Krulatz, & R. Farrelly (Eds.), Handbook of research on cultivating literacy in diverse and multilingual classrooms (pp. 577–595). IGI Global. https://doi.org/10.4018/978-1-7998-2722-1.ch027.

Sullivan, K.P.H., Kollberg, P., & Pålson, E. (1998). Trace-it—a computer tool with application to the second language classroom. *BABEL: Journal of the Australian Federation of Modern Language Teachers Associations Inc*, *33*(1), 22–28.

Sullivan, K.P.H., & Lindgren, E. (2002). Self-assessment in autonomous computer aided L2 writing. *ELT journal*, *56*(3), 258–266. https://doi.org/10.1093/elt/56.3.258.

Sullivan, K.P.H., & Lindgren, E. (2006) (Eds.). *Computer keystroke loggins and writing*. Elsevier.

Thomas, E., Owen, C.M., Hunt, F., Young, N., Dafydd, M., Fontaine, L., Aldridge-Waddon, M., Sullivan, K., Lloyd-Williams, S.W., ap Gruffudd, G.S., & Caulfield, G. (2022). Gweithio tuag at ddiagnosis o alluoedd llythrennedd plant dwyieithog: Rhai ystyriaethau allweddol i athrawon yng Nghymru [Working towards diagnosing bilingual children's language abilities: issues for teachers in Wales], *Cylchgrawn Addysg Cymru/Wales Journal of Education*, *24*(2). https://doi.org/10.16922/wje.24.2.4.

Thomas, E., & Sullivan, K.P.H. (2022). Pausing and revision around mutations: the case of L1 and L2 speakers of Welsh. In E. Lindgren, K.P.H. Sullivan, C. Hermansson, M. Levlin, E. Norlin Rehnmark, N. Vandermeulen, & E. Sturk (Eds.), *Sig Writing Conference 2022* (pp. 81–82). http://umu.diva-portal.org/smash/get/diva2:1694524/FULLTEXT01.pdf.

Torrance, M., Rønneberg, V., Johansson, C., & Uppstad, P.H. (2016). Adolescent Weak Decoders Writing in a Shallow Orthography: Process and product. *Scientific Studies of Reading*, *20*(5), 375–388. https://doi.org/10.1080/10888438.2016.1205071.

Usoof, H., Leblay, C., & Caporossi, G. (2020). GenoGraphiX-Log version 2.0 user guide. *Les Cahiers Du GERAD G-2020-68*, 1–63.

Van Waes, L., Leijten, M., Marin, P., & Engelborghs, S. (2017). Typing competencies in Alzheimer's disease: An exploration of copy tasks. *Computers in Human Behavior*, *73*, 311–319. https://doi.org/10.1016/j.chb.2017.03.050.

Wengelin, Å. (2006). Examining Pauses in Writing: Theory, Methods and Empirical Data. In K. Sullivan, & E. Lindgren (Eds.), *Computer Keystroke Logging and Writing: Methods and Applications* (pp. 107–130). Brill. https://doi.org/10.1163/9780080460932_008.

Wengelin, Å. (2007). The word-level focus in text production by adults with reading and writing difficulties. In M. Torrance, L. van Waes, & D. Galbraith (Eds.), *Writing and Cognition: Research and Applications* (pp. 67–82). Brill. https://doi.org/10.1163/9781849508223_006.

Wengelin, Å., Frid, J., Johansson, R., & Johansson, V. (2019). Combining keystroke logging with other methods: Towards an experimental environment for writing process research. In E. Lindgren, & K.P.H. Sullivan (Eds.), *Observing Writing: Insights from Keystroke Logging and Handwriting* (pp. 30–49). Brill. https://doi.org/10.1163/9789004392526_003.

CHAPTER 10

Visualising Multilingual Writers' Bursts and Profiles in the Initial Writing Phase

Maarit Mutta, Mari Mäkilä, Päivi Laine and Anne-Maj Åberg

10.1 Introduction

The aims of this chapter are to show how different types of bursts can be used to study the writing process, to offer a new type of burst based on visualisations, and to provide examples of how bursts and visualisations can help identify writers' profiles in the initial phase of writing. This chapter combines theory with term definition to present an empirical study that uses a visualisation tool in a data-driven way.

Writing process research seeks to understand the cognitive processes that underlie final output by examining the actions that take place during the writing process. Such studies may focus on different elements and have specific purposes. For instance, fluency features, including automatically processed linguistic elements (e.g., multiword sequences; Perez-Bettan, 2015; Wray, 2002), and disfluency features, such as pauses and revisions (Baaijen & Galbraith, 2018; Cislaru & Olive, 2018; Ellis & Yuan, 2004), may be investigated. Fluency in writing is a cognitive process that can be studied through the relationships between uninterrupted text production—also known as bursts (i.e., an index of fluent writing)—pauses, and revisions (Cislaru & Olive, 2018). Pauses tend to be more frequent, and bursts tend to be shorter in second language (L2) compared to first language (L1) writing (Chenoweth & Hayes, 2001). Following conventions in writing research, we adopted a pause threshold of ≥ 2 seconds for cognitive pauses when studying bursts, as this pause length is considered a mental preparation of the text from a psycholinguistic point of view (Cislaru & Olive, 2018). This was the threshold set in the visualisation tool used in the current study.[1]

Using keystroke logging (KSL) programmes such as ScriptLog and InputLog offers possibilities to study linear text production, but it can be difficult for someone unacquainted with the method to decipher the depicted linearity of

1 The GenoGraphix-Log programme uses this default threshold, but it can be modified according to study purposes.

HTTPS://DOI.ORG/10.1163/9789004760264-011

the writing process. Therefore, it can be useful to illustrate various aspects of the writing process to examine how it progresses, how writers construct texts, and what strategies are used to transform ideas and thoughts into coherent linear texts (cf. Cislaru & Olive, 2018). To respond to the need to illustrate writing processes more clearly, the keystroke logging software GenoGraphiX-Log (GGXLog) was created using a graph theory-based visualisation tool (i.e., a progressive graph tool), allowing for visualisation of the writing process at various stages of the writing session (Caporossi & Leblay, 2015; Usoof et al., 2020). In this chapter, we theoretically discuss how bursts can be identified using GGXLog (Caporossi & Leblay, 2015). This tool allows for more detailed and illustrative analyses of writing processes that are accessible to different audiences, including learners, teachers, and researchers (see, e.g., Mutta & Laine, 2022). Visualisations and learning analytics are often used in education to help learners understand complex themes or phenomenon (Vieira et al., 2018), for instance, visual models representing contexts of practices and attitudes (Storto et al., 2023) or process graphs illustrating the dynamics of the writing process (Leblay et al., 2015, 2022) or displaying different sources used during the process (Kruse, 2024).

This chapter concentrates on the initial phase of writing, meaning the title and the first sentence ending with a punctuation mark. This choice was made for two reasons. First, we wanted to discuss the definition of "bursts" according to different criteria and to provide our own definition. Bursts can include the linguistic material produced between pauses (P-bursts) or between pauses and revisions (R-bursts), as well as other actions (e.g., a mouse or arrow-key movement) away from the leading edge (I-bursts; Baaijen & Galbraith, 2018; Cislaru & Olive, 2018; Conijn et al., 2021). Our definition is based on the visualisations made by GGXLog. Due to the nature of the GGXLog visualisation tool, it was reasonable to illustrate only the beginning of the writing process (see the next section; Basnayake & Usoof, this volume, p. 48 and Leblay et al., this volume, p. 73), as visualisations based on longer productions were too complex for our analysis purposes. Second, we wanted to study how fluently writers begin a text during spontaneous sentence production with no materials (i.e., dictionaries) other than the task assignment and their mental lexicon, which reflects their implicit understanding of the topic (Baaijen & Galbraith, 2018).

The empirical case study focuses on writers' profiles in the initial writing phase and the production of bursts, which indicate fluent text production. In spontaneous text production, writers seem to make relatively short pauses and bursts (Baaijen & Galbraith, 2018). Writer profiles have been studied in relation to writing processes and certain features. For instance, some researchers have distinguished between writing profiles that describe structural variability and the organisation of processes and writer profiles that are specific to individual writers (Van Waes, 1992; see also Mutta, 2020; Mutta & Laine, 2022; Van Waes & Schellens, 2003).[2] These two profiles seem to intertwine on several points; therefore, in the present chapter, the term writer profile is used to describe writers' behaviours, including bursts and pauses as well as text production when writing on a computer. The empirical aspect of this chapter examines fluency in university-level, first language (L1) Finnish writers' (n = 30) writing processes in three second languages (L2s): English, French, and Swedish. All the examples were taken from this data and therefore may contain erroneous forms.

10.2 Defining Bursts: Comparing Linear Text and Visualisations

In this section, we compare different ways of identifying various types of bursts (i.e., P-bursts, R-bursts, I-bursts; Baaijen & Galbraith, 2018; Cislaru & Olive, 2018; Conijn et al., 2021) and examine how a visualisation tool can help define them and reveal differences in L1 and L2 writing fluency. As explained in Cislaru et al. (this volume, p. 124), studies using log files record various process-related data, such as the time and occurrence of each keystroke, enabling an examination of different phases of the writing process (Spelman Miller et al., 2008). Compared to other KSL programmes, GGXLog enables a more detailed analysis of writing processes at various stages, as it combines log files and linear text analysis with a progressive graph tool. The tool represents a writing session as nodes (vertices) and edges (links); each node is a cluster of continuous events (e.g., inserted, appended, or deleted text, or a pause), and each edge represents relationships between nodes, such as chronological order, flow in the final text, or deletions (Caporossi & Leblay, 2015; Usoof et al., 2020, p. 27, 38). Comparing linear texts and visualisations provides a more comprehensive understanding of how the writing process starts and what strategies are used to construct a text.

In earlier studies in which writers created texts using pen and paper, average burst length was calculated in words—more experienced writers averaged 10–12 words, while less experienced writers averaged 5–6 words (Kaufer et al., 1986)—and the delimiting criterion was a pause of two or more seconds (Chenoweth & Hayes, 2001, p. 83). In studies examining typing on a computer,

2 Van Waes and Schellens (2003, pp. 836–837; see also Van Waes, 1992) proposed a typology of five writer profiles: initial planners, fragmentary first-phase writers, second-phase writers, non-stop writers, and average writers. This last category is omitted in some studies (see, e.g., Mutta, 2020).

burst type is defined based on the nature of the interruption of the writing process at either end of the burst (Conijn et al., 2021). According to Baaijen and Galbraith (2018), P-bursts (*pause bursts*) begin and end with a cognitive pause (≥ 2 secs) and represent a text production without modifications (e.g., revisions or deletions; see also Hayes, 2009). The GGXLog programme illustrates a P-burst only when no revisions were made by the writer and when the burst starts and ends with a pause. Table 10.1 shows a case in which the linear text and the visualisation align, as the writer's actions included only bursts (nodes 1 and 3) and pauses (node 2). It is notable that a mouse event started the process, which is illustrated with a green node (= event 0). In the GGXLog programme, when the cursor is placed on the progressive graph, it is marked with node 0 [START], indicating the starting position of the graph. In the linear text, the numbers in angle brackets indicate the length of pauses in milliseconds. In the visualisation, the green nodes represent pauses, and the red nodes represent text insertion. The final pause is not included in either the linear text or the illustration, as a punctuation mark came before the pause.

Table 10.1 illustrates a student's (ID 2019) entire initial phase (i.e., the first sentence in its final form) alongside the linear text and its visualisation; the student did not write a title at the beginning of the session. In this study, the analysis focuses on the visualisation and the linear text; thus, the final text has been excluded from all other examples provided to highlight the production of bursts during the writing process.

The orthographic correction of a few letters is considered a revision.[3] It is rare that a writing process is entirely free of orthographic or content-related corrections and there are no revisions or deletions. Some learners primarily

TABLE 10.1 Example of GGXLog's different presentation tools (ID 2019, L2 Swedish, C1 level)

Final text	Linear text	Visualisation
Jag tycker att det är inte lika viktigt längre att ha körkort. I think it is not as important anymore to have a driving licence.	<MOUSE EVENT>Jag tycker att det är <2135>inte lika viktigt längre att ha körkort.	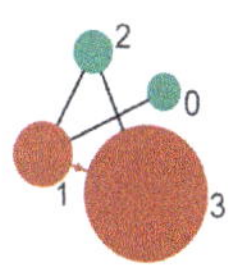

3 When writing by hand, P-bursts are likelier to contain more complete words due to the use of a pen or pencil (i.e., there are usually fewer mistakes; Kaufer et al., 1986).

TABLE 10.2 Example of P-bursts alternating with pauses (ID 2013, L2 English, B2 level, time 01:32)

Visualisation	Linear text
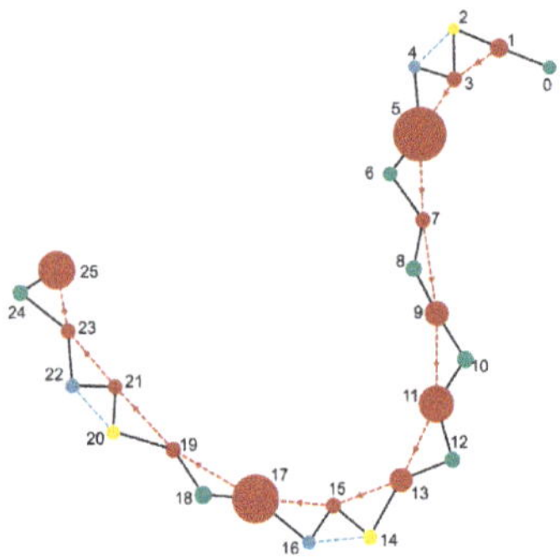	<MOUSE EVENT>Student exchanf <BACKSPACE>ge and its advantages and disadvantages<2672> <RETURN><RETURN><7153>**Student exchange** <2017>**was brought to my attention** <2545>in highschool and i<BACKSPACE>I had a few friends who would go and <14545>study for a <BACKSPACE3> <5666>about a year and come back.

use the strategy of pausing and then producing text, meaning they mentally plan the text before writing it down all at once. This occurs especially when a learner is reliant on the use of multiword sequences comprising words or other units stored in memory as single units and retrieved automatically (e.g., "bring to one's attention"), which can enhance the flow of writing (Tavakoli & Uchihara, 2020; see also Mutta et al., to appear). Table 10.2 illustrates a case in which P-bursts consist of a compound word and a multiword sequence ("Student exchange" and "was brought to my attention", respectively), which alternate with pauses from nodes 6–12. These words are bolded. The blue and yellow nodes represent deletion by backspace or other methods (see Usoof et al., 2020, p. 25). It is important to note that revisions by backspace occurred in other places in the linear text.

R-bursts (*revision bursts*) are more typical than P-bursts during the writing process. They end with a revision at the leading edge (Baaijen & Galbraith, 2018; Conijn et al., 2021; Hayes, 2009), but existing definitions do not specify how the bursts begin. GGXLog delimits an R-burst as an activity starting with a pause and ending with a revision, starting with a revision and ending with a pause, or terminated by revisions on both sides. Table 10.3 illustrates an example that includes several R-bursts.

In this example, the first cognitive pause <3153> occurs just before the final word (*cultures*) of the first sentence. The learner wrote quickly, completing the sentence in only 40 seconds. The only pause was short, and the deletions

TABLE 10.3 Example of R-bursts in text production (ID 2017, L2 English, B1 level, time 00:40)

Visualisation	Linear text
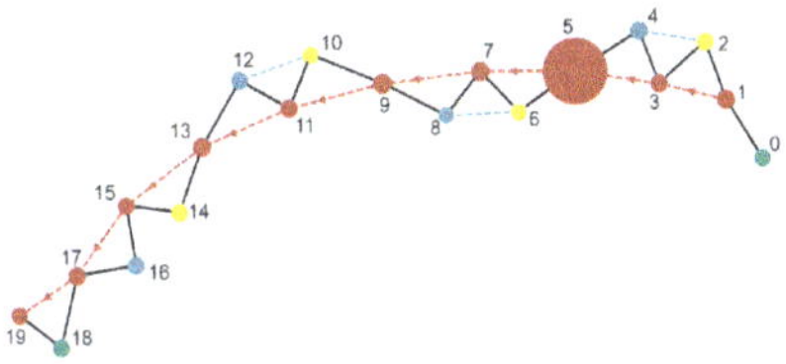	<MOUSE EVENT>Student exchange <RETURN><RETURN><BACKSPACE2>—is it worth it?<RETURN><RETURN> I have always been interested in global issues, multiculturalism <BACKSPACE>, <BACKSPACE2> and exchanginf <BACK-SPACE2>g <3153>cultures. I

were typing corrections. This writer was thus considered to have a fluent writing process (see also Table 10.10). The illustration of the R-bursts details what occurred between cognitive pauses and how the writer started the text; however, analysing only P-bursts without modifications can lead to a great deal of information about the writing process being lost. Whether it is meaningful to study only P-bursts or to include revisions and modifications is dependent on a study's objectives (see, e.g., Cislaru & Olive, 2018).

According to Baaijen and Galbraith (2018), I-bursts (*insertion bursts*) start with a mouse or arrow-key movement followed by text production, all of which move away from the leading edge of the current writing point. It is rare to find I-bursts in the initial writing phase; the exception is writers who make an explicit plan and then insert text into this plan (for an example, see Table 10.6 in Section 10.4).

In earlier studies relying on linear text, researchers (see, e.g., Mäntylä et al., 2020) examined P-bursts and accepted some typing corrections (e.g., one to two backspaces) when defining burst length. The challenges of such delimiting criteria include how many backspace deletions are accepted without impacting the flow of writing and at what point a text is no longer produced automatically and efficiently—that is, fluently (cf. Mutta, 2020). Table 10.4 exemplifies such a case.

This writer started slowly, writing a title surrounded by pauses and followed by small typing corrections. After the title (*Student exchange*), there occurred a sequence of several backspace deletions (11 and 3). Revisions are often accompanied by pauses of different lengths (see, e.g., Cislaru & Olive, 2018; Mutta, 2020); however, in this example, the pauses were not closely related

TABLE 10.4 Example of pauses and revisions in text production (ID 2011, B2 level, time 01:11)

Visualisation	**Linear text**
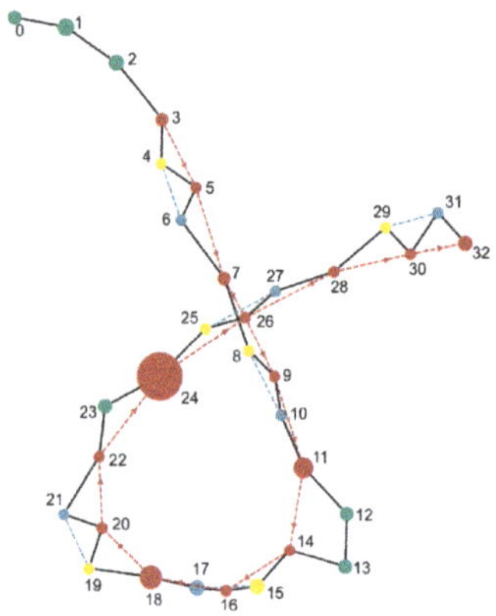	<12594><MOUSE EVENT><6952> T<BACKSPACE>Studeny<BACKSPACE> t Exchange<RETURN><RETURN> <4704><3329>Start<RETURN> <RETURN>I thi<BACKSPACE11>tudent exhange can be <BACKSPACE3>be a <3473>fun and insighful period in a studne'<BACKSPACE3>entä <BACKSPACE>'s life.

to revisions. This leads to the question of whether such corrections should be interpreted as not interrupting the flow of writing or if ending with a change of structure impacts the cognitive process. An advantage of using GGXLog is that all revision events are analysed in the same way, and visualised bursts are easy to recognise. Thus, the analysis is systematic, and the difference between automatic typing corrections (i.e., one or two letters) and longer strategic revisions is ignored. Furthermore, the GGXLog visualisation tool does not define I-bursts (i.e., contextual insertions) separately, as all revisions and pauses are addressed in the same way.

The examples in Tables 10.2–10.4 indicate that analysing R-bursts and visualising revisions provide valuable information about how the processes reinforce each other. P-bursts reveal what learners process as an entire unit between cognitive pauses, whereas R-bursts show the problematic places where learners correct and revise a text sporadically, often, or systematically, which may also reveal a lack of keyboarding skills.

The earlier definitions of the different types of bursts are partly in line with our definition. However, the criteria of the earlier definitions, including where and how bursts start and end, are not always clear. GGXLog enables bursts to be defined precisely by consistently using the same criteria. In the present study, a new type of burst based on the GGXLog analysis is introduced: *visualisation bursts* (V-bursts). These are defined according to the visualisations produced by the GGXLog tool, and the graphical representation includes seven possible

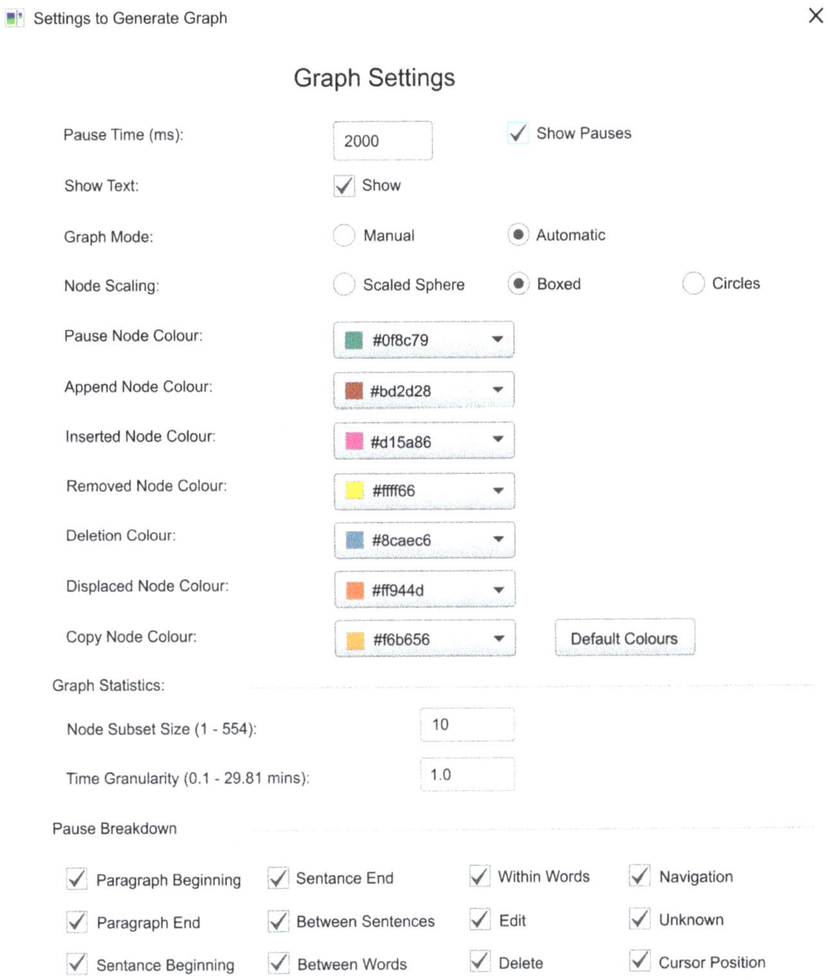

FIGURE 10.1 Criteria for V-bursts in GGXLog

types of nodes: append, insert, removed, deletion, displaced, copy and pause. Figure 10.1 shows the criteria settings; for instance, uncategorizable pauses are listed as "unknown" (see Usoof et al., 2020, pp. 27, 32).

As mentioned, studying bursts according to previous definitions is appropriate in different contexts. The following demonstrates how V-bursts can be used to study writer profiles. With the help of V-bursts and visualisations (see Section 10.4), we were able to identify various writer profiles in the initial phase—in other words, how the writers started a text during spontaneous text production. Before presenting these profiles, we present the empirical data.

10.3 University Students' L1 and L2 Writing Processes—a Case Study in Finland

The empirical data were collected at a university in Southern Finland in 2021 and 2022 following the EU's General Data Protection Regulation (GDPR) and with consideration for the anonymity of the students, all of whom participated voluntarily. The data are a part of the KISUVI project,[4] a larger body of research on writing fluency and the use of multiword sequences. For the current study, 30 students were recruited from various degree-programme courses in English, French, and the Scandinavian languages. Prior to data collection, the students completed a questionnaire addressing background information and language repertoire, and they gave their informed consent to participate in the study. The students were considered multilingual, as their language repertoires included one to three L2s in addition to their L1 (Finnish). They all studied L2s as their major or minor at the university level.

The students wrote two argumentative texts on a QWERTY keyboard with Finnish layout. There were three possible language combinations: Finnish–English, Finnish–French, and Finnish–Swedish. Thus, the students wrote one text in Finnish (n = 30) and the other in English (n = 10), French (n = 10), or Swedish (n = 10). Each writing task consisted of a 30-minute spontaneously written text with no extra tools (e.g., dictionaries). The students were asked to provide a title for their text; however, it is important to note that some of the students may have added their title later and not during the initial phase of the writing process. The students first wrote a text in one language; after a short pause, they wrote a text in their other language. The order of the languages of writing was counterbalanced, that is, some students wrote first in L1, some others in L2. Topics were chosen based on the writers' familiarity with the topic in their everyday lives in the Finnish context (cf. Baaijen & Galbraith, 2018). The task assignments were short and always the same: "Write a short argumentative text in your L1/L2. Title your topic." However, due to the study design of the KISUVI project,[5] the topics varied as follows:

4 The KISUVI project is funded by the Kone Foundation (2022–2026) and focuses on multilingual writers' writing processes, especially formulaic sequences and fluency patterns in writing (https://sites.utu.fi/kisuvi/en/).

5 In the KISUVI project, the L1 topic was always the same, and the L2 topic was the same if two languages were used; however, for three languages, the third language had a different topic. For instance, the Finnish–Swedish group wrote texts in three languages (Finnish, English, Swedish); thus, the topic in Swedish differed from that of English and French. In the current

- L1 Finnish: Mitä mieltä olet töiden tekemisestä opiskelun ohessa? Mitä hyviä ja huonoja puolia siinä on? (What do you think about working while studying? What are the advantages and disadvantages?)
- L2 English and L2 French (same topic): Qu'est-ce que vous pensez des études en échange? Quels sont les avantages? Quels sont les inconvénients? (What is your opinion on student exchange? What are the advantages? What are the disadvantages?)
- L2 Swedish: Tycker du att det är viktigt att ha körkort? Vilka för- och nackdelar finns det med att ha bil? (Do you think it is important to have a driver's licence? What are the advantages and disadvantages of having a car?)

The L2 texts were evaluated by two project researchers; a third evaluator was invited in case of disagreement. For comparability, we excluded the lowest (A1–A2 in L2 French) and highest (C2 in L2 English) levels (for a comparison of the role of proficiency level in the initial phase, see Mutta et al., to appear). Only productions written by students at the intermediate or advanced levels (B1–B2–C1) according to the Common European Framework of Reference for Languages (CEFR; Council of Europe, 2001) were included to ensure adequate proficiency levels for our purposes (see Table 10.5).

The proficiency levels of the L2 French students were generally lower than those of the other language groups. In Finland, English is studied by over 90% of learners as their first L2, while Swedish is the country's second official language and thus obligatory for Finnish-speaking students at school; however, the number of pupils studying additional languages, such as French, is low (Finnish National Agency for Education, 2019).

The following section examines how the students began to write their texts, the writer profiles that were identified based on their burst behaviour, and how visualisations can help identify writers' profiles in the initial phase of writing.

TABLE 10.5 Number of writers at each CEFR level in English, French, and Swedish

Language	B1	B2	C1
English	1	5	4
French	6	3	1
Swedish	1	5	4
Total	8	13	9

study, the English texts written by the Finnish–Swedish group were excluded from the analysis, as only two-language combinations were examined.

10.4 Writer Profiles and Visualisations of Bursts in the Initial Phase of Writing

Often, researchers examine limited criteria for creating writer profiles as part of a larger analysis. For example, one case study relied on time spent writing, number of words, and percentage of cognitive pauses (≥ 2 seconds) throughout the entire writing process to study writers' fluency (Mutta & Laine, 2022). Based on these criteria, three participants' L1 (Finnish) and L2 (French) writings were compared. The analysis showed that two of the writers had the same profiles in their L1 and L2: one was a fragmentary and one was a non-stop writer (cf. Van Waes, 1992; Van Waes & Schellens, 2003). The latter was due to the writer using the 10-finger typing method and being highly proficient in their L2 (French). The third writer was a non-stop writer in their L1 and a fragmentary writer in their L2. This was related to the fact that the writer was accustomed to writing texts in their L1, but their L2 proficiency level was relatively low.

As language learners use various strategies to achieve diverse communication goals, there is a need for more thorough analyses of learner profiles, for instance, comparing language learners' own profiles in their L1 and L2 instead of comparing L2 production with production by native users (see, e.g., Lintunen et al., 2020). Furthermore, mixed-methods studies should be conducted to increase teachers' and researchers' understanding of L2 writing processes (cf. Révész et al., 2022). In a fluency study (Mutta et al., 2025), the spoken and written L1 and L2 productions of 11 university-level students were compared to create a more comprehensive picture of L2 English students' fluency profiles. The written products and processes were objectively measured based on time spent on the writing process, word count, words per minute, mean length of bursts, pause time (% of cognitive pause ≥ 2 seconds), deletions (percentage of characters), and product-to-process ratio. The data collection and analysis of written productions were conducted using the GGXLog programme. As there are no earlier studies that compare different modes of fluency, the researchers used a data-driven method to identify different categories. With regard to writing, four different fluency profiles (Mutta et al., 2025) were derived: fast and productive, fast, slow but productive, and slow and reflective.[6] The study found that seven out of 11 writers had the same profile in their L1 and L2.

Similarly, the research of the current chapter also used a data-driven method. New criteria for analysing writer profiles were created, as the focus was on the initial writing phase instead of the entire process. Our measures, which were

6 The study examined fluency across modes by the same participants. For the spoken results, see Mutta et al. (2005).

based on V-bursts and visualisations, included number and content of events (e.g., bursts, deletions, pauses), number of nodes, and time spent until the end of the first sentence ending with a punctuation mark. Each researcher categorised the productions separately, after which we created the final categorisations in discussion together. Using this data-driven method, six writer profiles were identified: explicit planner, implicit planner, slow starter, tentative starter, quick starter, and quick and productive starter. Tables 10.6–10.11 exemplify the different profiles, including illustrations and the linear texts of the data. The GGXLog analysis tool explicitly shows the number and content of bursts (see the Session Bursts and Parameters file; Usoof et al., 2020), and a progressive graph illustrates the writing process node by node (see the Representation of Progressive Graph; Usoof et al., 2020). The progressive graph cannot present the content of all the nodes at the same time, as the content only becomes visible in the programme when you place the cursor on the node. For this reason, the linear text has also been included.

Explicit planners started with (a title and) a plan. It usually took them time to complete the first sentence, and sometimes text was inserted into the middle of their plan. In Table 10.6, inserted node colour alternates with pauses, between nodes 17–26 (according to earlier studies, this would be defined as an I-burst; see Section 10.2). There were often many writing process events (e.g., a sequence of inserted, appended, or deleted characters, or a pause in the writing; Usoof et al., 2020, p. 27); however, some writers planned quickly and briefly.

Implicit planners started slowly (with long pauses), which suggests that they created a mental plan. Their first sentence was completed quickly, and there were few corrections in the output after the start. Long bursts distinguished these writers from slow starters. In Table 10.7, R- and P-bursts are differentiated in the linear text, while all V-bursts are illustrated as red nodes.

Slow starters began slowly and took a long time (more than five minutes) to complete the first sentence. There were a considerable number of pauses and few long bursts in these writers' process. Lengthy revisions were common; therefore, output was scarce, although a lot of time was spent on the initial writing phase. The visualisation in Table 10.8 highlights the role of pauses (green nodes) during the initial phase compared to the linear text presentation.

Tentative starters typed and revised the beginning of the text multiple times; therefore, there were many events involved in writing the first sentence. The writers started fairly quickly and planned during text production rather than prior to beginning. These writers did not spend much time writing the first sentence. The visualisation in Table 10.9 illustrates the fragmentary nature of text production. It is worth noting that if only P- or R-bursts were studied, a lot of process-related information would be overlooked.

TABLE 10.6 Explicit planner

Example: ID 2031 (L2 Swedish, B2, time 02:35)	
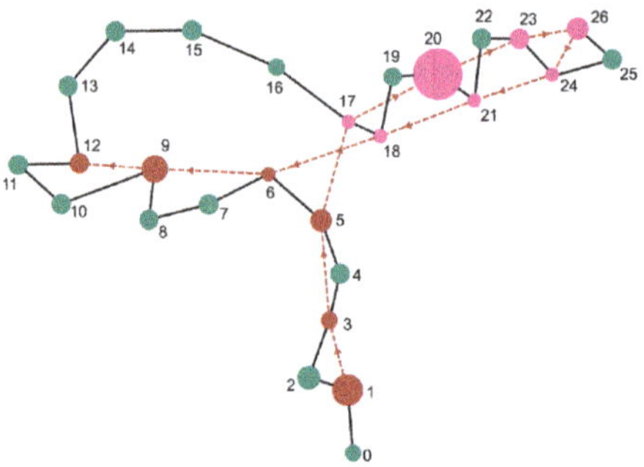	<MOUSE EVENT><RETURN>Är det viktigt <2267>att <23466><MOUSE EVENT>ha körkort? <RETURN> <RETURN><2342><6144><MOUSE EVENT>Förnackdelar <2988><2089><MOUSE EVENT>att ha bil?<5032><4877><MOUSE EVENT><12055><MOUSE EVENT><MOUSE EVENT><2335><MOUSE EVENT><RETURN><RETURN><51183>Jag tycker att trafik är nä<3520>stan som <4075>grupparbet. <11190>

Translation

<MOUSE EVENT><RETURN>Is it important <2267>to <23466><MOUSE EVENT>have a driver's licence?<RETURN> <RETURN><2342><6144><MOUSE EVENT>Benefits <2988> <2089><MOUSE EVENT>of having a car? <5032> <4877><MOUSE EVENT><12055><MOUSE EVENT><MOUSE EVENT> <2335> <MOUSE EVENT> <RETURN><RETURN><51183>I think traffic is the cl<3520>osest thing to <4075>group work. <11190>

TABLE 10.7 Implicit planner

Example: ID 2012 (L2 English, B2, time 00:48)	
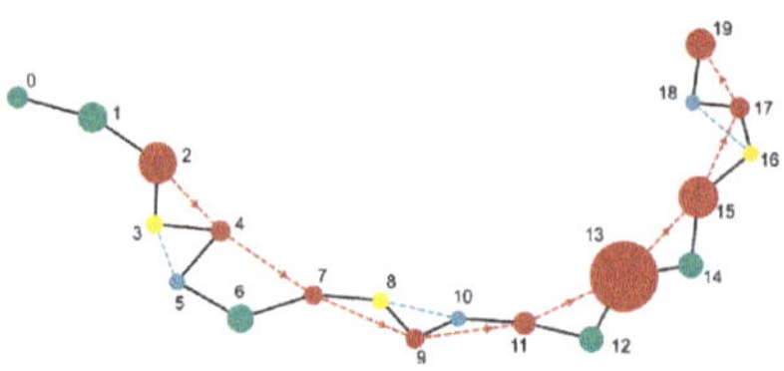	<MOUSE EVENT><11961>Student exchange gi<BACKSPACE2><3553>is <BACKSPACE3>can be <3361>viewed as a richness in the <4657>highger education v<BACKSPACE>community.

TABLE 10.8 Slow production starter

Example: ID **2005 (L1 Finnish, time 05:07)**

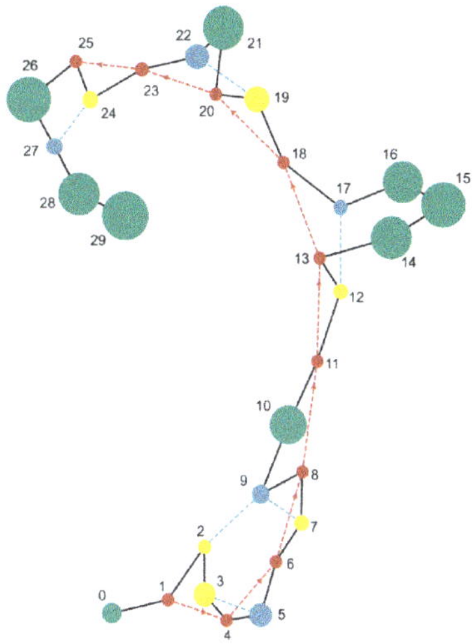

<MOUSE EVENT>jbhhhhhh
<BACKSPACE6> r
<BACKSPACE4><2675>
h<3534><15642><MOUSE EVENT>
<2024><BACKSPACE5>
mmmmmm
<33707><BACKSPACE13>
mmn<27233> <BACKSPACE3><13221>

<MOUSE EVENT><148334><MOUSE EVENT><BACKSPACE3>
y<DOWN><5632><MOUSE EVENT>
<BACKSPACE><DOWN><8174>

<RETURN> m<BACKSPACE>
<22457>Ennen opintojen alkamista mietin, että muutama vuoro vaikkapa lähiaku<BACKSPACE3>kaupassa

<MOUSE EVENT>viikossa, <MOUSE EVENT>, onnistuisi mainiosti<2060> ja <2946><BACKSPACE4>. Sen myötä olisi myös

Translation

<MOUSE EVENT>jbhhhhh<BACKSPACE6> r<BACKSPACE4><2675> h<3534><15642> <MOUSE EVENT><2024><BACKSPACE5>mmmmmm<33707><BACKSPACE13> mmn<27233><BACKSPACE3>

<13221><MOUSE EVENT><148334><MOUSE EVENT><BACKSPACE3>y<DOWN> <5632><MOUSE EVENT><BACKSPACE><DOWN><8174><RETURN> m<BACKSPACE> <22457>Before starting my studies I was wondering, that a few shifts in, say, a convenience store<BACKSPACE3>in <MOUSE EVENT>week, <MOUSE EVENT>, would be fine<2060> and <2946><BACKSPACE4>. It would also

TABLE 10.9 Tentative starter

Example: ID 1003 (L2 French, B1, time 03:05)

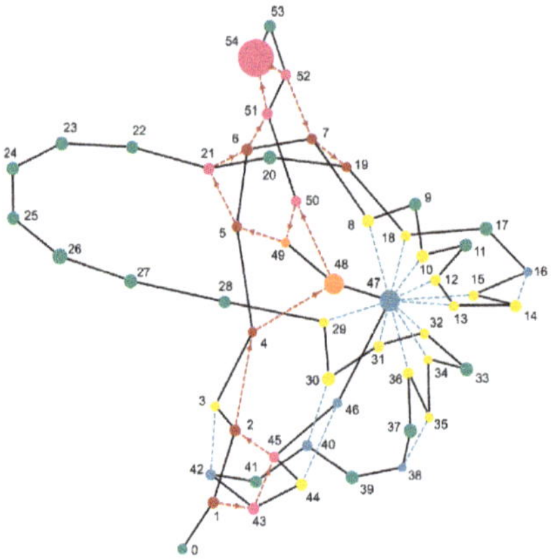

<MOUSE EVENT>Porraient les études <2289>en échange <2769>—P<BACKSPACE3>

<7488><RETURN><RETURN> <18457><MOUSE EVENT>u<3379> <14865><15003><11060><15001> <15000><7966><MOUSE EVENT> aggraver <4354>les <3554><3217> <BACKSPACE13><4377>

<MOUSE EVENT><BACKSPACE> Comment le<BACKSPACE2> <RIGHT10><MOUSE EVENT><CUT><MOUSE EVENT><PASTE>p<MOUSE EVENT> être <2705>une mauvaise chose. <RETURN><RETURN>C'est commun que les é

Translation

<MOUSE EVENT>Would studies <2289>in exchange<2769>—. P<BACKSPACE3> <7488>

<RETURN><RETURN><18457><MOUSE EVENT>u<3379><14865><15003><11060> <15001><15000>

<7966><MOUSE EVENT>aggraver <4354>les <3554><3217><BACKSPACE13><4377> <MOUSE EVENT><BACKSPACE>How the<BACKSPACE2><RIGHT10><MOUSE EVENT><CUT><MOUSE EVENT><PASTE>p<MOUSE EVENT>be <2705>a bad thing. <RETURN><RETURN>It's common for e

TABLE 10.10 Quick starter

Example: ID 2017 (L2 English, B1, time 00:40)

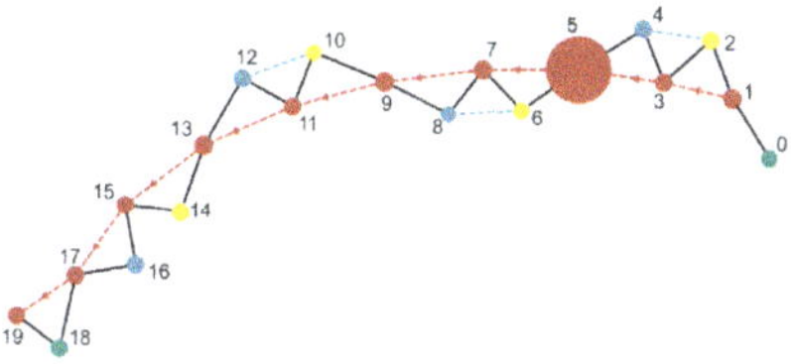

<MOUSE EVENT>Student exchange

<RETURN><RETURN><BACKSPACE2>—is it worth it?<RETURN><RETURN>I have always been interested in global issues, multiculturalism <BACKSPACE>, <BACKSPACE2> and exchanginf <BACKSPACE2>g <3153>culturcs. I

Quick starters began quickly (a pause of under two seconds or no pause at all), and the first sentence was short. Writing time was less than a minute, and there were few events and corrections. The visualisation in Table 10.10 shows a number of short V-bursts, one larger V-burst, and no pauses. All corrections made were backspaces and are clearly visible in the illustration. In earlier studies, this kind of production would have been considered a single P-burst with some typos (Mäntylä et al., 2020).

Quick and productive starters began quickly and produced a lot of text with few corrections or pauses. With regard to the number of characters, these writers were productive in a fairly short time. The visualisation in Table 10.11 shows V-bursts starting and ending with pauses or revisions.

After categorisation, the writers' L1 and L2 profiles were compared. The majority (21 participants) had different profiles in their L1 and L2, while nine had the same profile in both languages. The number of each type of L1 and L2 starter profile is shown in Table 10.12.

Table 10.12 reveals some language-related tendencies. For example, there were more tentative starters in L2 than L1 and more quick starters in L1 than L2. Furthermore, all quick and productive starters were L1 writers, but all slow starters were also L1 writers. The visualisation tool contributes to profiling writing processes, as it makes the different profile types easy to recognise (e.g., tentative and slow starters).

TABLE 10.11 Quick and productive starter

Example: ID 2019 (L1 Finnish, 00:54)

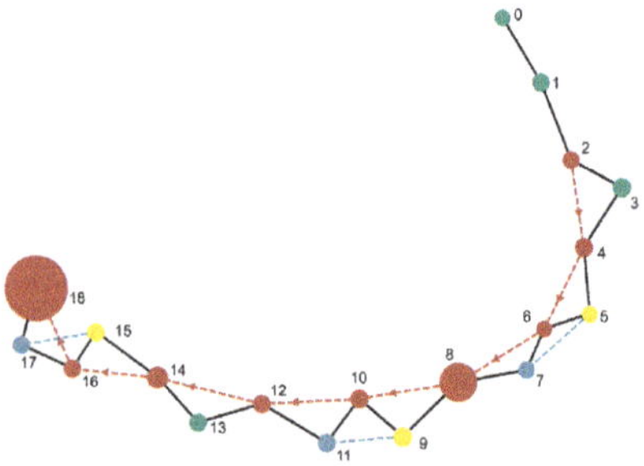

<MOUSE EVENT><3609>Töiden<3114> tekeminne<BACKSPACE2>en opintojen ohella<RETURN><RETURN><RE-TURN>Töiden tekeminen opintojen ohella on aihe, jotai<BACKSPACE> olen <2405>pohtinut viime aikoina todl <BACKSPACE>ella paljon. Aluksi tein töitä, sillä olin ollut kaupassa jo aiemminkin, ja minun oli loogista tienata hima

Translation

<MOUSE EVENT><3609>Working<3114> alongside your<BACKSPACE2> studies <RETURN><RETURN><RETURN>Working alongside your studies is a topic that<BACKSPACE> I've been <2405>thinking about a lot lat<BACKSPACE>ely. At first I worked because I had been in the shop before, and it was logical for me to earn some money.

TABLE 10.12 Number of starter writer profiles in L1 and L2

Profiles	L1 n = 30	L2 n = 30
Explicit planner	3	4
Implicit planner	2	3
Slow starter	3	0
Tentative starter	8	16
Quick starter	11	7
Quick and productive starter	3	0

10.5 Discussion and Conclusions

This chapter defined and discussed different types of bursts, with visualisations of the data provided by the GGXLog programme. Bursts, which represent fluency in the writing process, can be defined in various ways depending on the purpose of a study. Previous studies have included three main types of bursts: P-bursts, R-bursts, and I-bursts (e.g., Baaijen & Galbraith, 2018; Cislaru & Olive, 2018; Conijn et al., 2021; Hayes, 2009). Studying P-bursts allows researchers to examine what writers are able to process with regard to whole units, specifically between cognitive pauses (≥ 2 seconds). P-bursts are unmodified, as corrections and revisions are ignored; however, they may contain a number of single characters (e.g., punctuation marks) when the writing is being done on a computer (see, e.g., Cislaru & Olive, 2018). Thus, depending on a writer's typing skills, there may be few multiple-word bursts (e.g., Van Waes et al., 2021).

In studying writing processes, P-bursts may be analysed alongside R-bursts. R-bursts allow researchers to study problem areas in the writing process, as they highlight corrections and revisions and reveal elements that writers miss or correct. Analysing I-bursts, which are bursts starting with a mouse event or arrow key that is not situated at the leading edge of the current writing point, helps researchers evaluate sentence linearity and distinguish between bursts that are inserted into a text and bursts that occur during forward text production (Baaijen & Galbraith, 2018, p. 208). Unless a writer makes an explicit plan and continues producing text within that plan, there are generally fewer I-bursts in the initial phase of writing.

With the GGXLog programme, these three types of bursts can be studied using the visualisation and linear text tools. However, it can be difficult to decide which elements should be included in the bursts and how many corrections might be due to typos, which do not necessarily influence the flow of writing (cf. Mäntylä et al., 2020). Indeed, a writer can be efficient and productive, even without 10-finger-typing capability and when constantly correcting typos. Thus, earlier definitions of bursts are useful but sometimes lack systematicity with regard to distinguishing criteria. This led us to create a new type of burst, V-bursts, based on visualisations provided by the GGXLog tool, in which bursts are limited by several different events (e.g., append, insert, removed, deletion, displaced, copy, and pause). The definition of these bursts always follows the same criteria, thereby enabling more precision (see Figure 10.1). However, this definition is limited, as research categories are dependent on the tools utilised and their exploitation. Every research design is limited by different measures and assumptions, and our definition of a V-burst proves that it is important to pedagogically and methodologically study all kinds of bursts. The use of other visualisation tools provided by GGXLog, such as pause graph analysis, linear text, and statistics, would be required to conduct a detailed and complex analysis of the entire writing process (cf. Usoof et al., 2020).

This chapter also analysed how Finnish writers began the writing process in their L1 and in three different L2s (English, French, and Swedish) during spontaneous sentence production without extra materials (i.e., dictionaries); thus, they could only rely on their existing understanding of the topic (Baaijen & Galbraith, 2018) and the task assignment. Writer profiles for L1 and L2 writers during the initial writing phase were created based on how fluently text production began under these conditions. With the help of V-bursts and the visualisation tool and based on several measures (i.e., number and content of events, number of nodes, and time spent until the end of the first sentence ending with a punctuation), six writer profiles were identified: explicit planner, implicit planner, slow starter, tentative starter, quick starter, and quick and productive starter. The visualisations allowed for trends and strategies related to the ways the writers began their texts to be recognised. While many writers had different profiles in their L1 and L2, nine writers had the same profile in both of their languages (for the role of proficiency level, see, e.g., Mutta et al., to appear).

Pedagogically, it is useful to examine different kinds of bursts and various complex elements of the writing process together with learners (see, e.g., Kruse, 2024; Storto et al., 2023; Vieira et al., 2018). A visualisation of the interplay between V-bursts, pauses, and revisions can clearly demonstrate how a text is created. Examining writers' strategies and profiles in the initial phase of writing increases knowledge of writing behaviours, which may help prevent fear of a blank page. Moreover, the 10-finger typing method might help to make the writing process more fluent and include fewer typos; however, the impact of using an unfamiliar or different keyboard (e.g., QWERTY vs. AZERTY) should be highlighted. The usefulness of this method could be discussed with students to enhance their understanding of their writing processes in different languages. This chapter encapsulates the complexity of the writing process in the initial phase of text production. The knowledge provided by this study could be used in various ways, for instance, to discuss different writer profiles and help writers recognise their bursts and profiles in spontaneous writing tasks in the classroom.

References

Baaijen, V.M., & Galbraith, D. (2018). Discovery through writing: Relationships with writing processes and text quality. *Cognition and Instruction, 36*(3), 199–223. https://doi.org/10.1080/07370008.2018.1456431.

Caporossi, G., & Leblay, C. (2015). A graph theory approach to online writing data visualization. In Georgeta Cislaru (Ed.), *Writing(s) at the crossroads: The process–product interface* (pp. 171–181). Amsterdam: John Benjamin.

Chenoweth, A.N., & Hayes, J.R. (2001). Fluency in writing: Generating text in L1 and L2. *Written Communication, 18*(1), 80–98. https://doi.org/10.1177/0741088301018001004.

Cislaru, G., & Olive, T. (2018). Le processus de textualisation. Analyse des unités linguistiques de performance écrite [The textualisation process. Analysis of linguistic units of written performance]. Bruxelles: De Boeck.

Conijn, R., Dux Speltz, E., & Chukharev-Hudilainen, E. (2021). Automated extraction of revision events from keystroke data. *Reading and Writing*. https://doi.org/10.1007/s11145-021-10222-w.

Council of Europe. (2001). *Common European Framework of Reference for Languages: Learning, teaching, assessment*. New York, NY: Cambridge University Press. Retrieved 19 December 2023 from https://www.coe.int/en/web/common-european-framework-reference-languages.

Ellis, R., & Yuan, F. (2004.) The effects of planning on fluency, complexity, and accuracy in second language narrative writing. *Studies in Second Language Acquisition, 26*(1), 59–84. https://doi.org/10.1017/S0272263104026130.

Finnish National Agency for Education. (2019). *Facts express 1C/2019: What languages do pupils study in basic education?* Retrieved 23 November 2023 from https://www.oph.fi/sites/default/files/documents/factsexpress1c_2019.pdf.

Galbraith, D., & Baaijen, V.M. (2019). Aligning keystrokes with cognitive processes in writing. In Eva Lindgren & Kirk P.H. Sullivan (Eds.), *Observing writing: Insights from keystroke logging and handwriting* (pp. 306–325, Vol. 38). Brill. Advance online publication. https://doi.org/10.1163/9789004392526_015.

Hayes, J.R. (2009). From idea to text. In Roger Beard, Debra Myhill, Martin Nystrand & Jeni Riley (Eds.), *The SAGE handbook of writing development* (pp. 65–79). London, England: SAGE. https://doi.org/10.4135/9780857021069.

Hayes, J.R., & Flower, L.S. (1980). Identifying the organization of writing processes. In Lee W. Gregg & Erwin R. Steinberg (Eds.), *Cognitive processes in writing* (pp. 3–30). Hillsdale, New Jersey: Lawrence Erlbaum Associates.

Kaufer, D.S., Hayes, J.R., & Flower, L.S. (1986). Composing written sentences. *Research in the Teaching of English, 20*(2), 121–140. Retrieved 18 December 2023 from https://www.jstor.org/stable/40171073.

Kruse, M. (2024). Problem-solving activity during the foreign language writing process: A proposal for categorisation and visualisation of source use and a new take on fluency in multilingual writing. *Journal of Writing Research, 16*(1), 129–161. https://doi.org/10.17239/jowr-2024.16.01.05.

Leblay, C., & Caporossi, G. (2015). A graph theory approach to online writing data visualization. In Georgeta Cislaru (Ed.), *Writing(s) at the Crossroads: The Process-Product Interface* (pp. 171–181). Amsterdam: John Benjamins.

Leblay, C., Usoof, H., & Caporossi, G. (2022). Kirjoittamisprosessin dynaaminen visualisointi [Dynamic visualisation of the writing process]. *Kieli, koulutus ja yhteiskunta, 13*(3). https://www.kieliverkosto.fi/fi/journals/kieli-koulutus-ja-yhteiskunta-toukokuu-2022/kirjoittamisprosessin-dynaaminen-visualisointi.

Lintunen, P., Mutta, M., & Peltonen, P. (2020). Synthesising approaches to second language fluency: Implications and future directions. In Pekka Lintunen, Maarit Mutta & Pauliina Peltonen (Eds.), *Fluency in L2 learning and use* (pp. 186–201). Bristol: Multilingual Matters.

Mutta, M. (2020). L2 fluency and writer profiles. In Pekka Lintunen, Maarit Mutta & Pauliina Peltonen (Eds.), *Fluency in L2 learning and use* (pp. 63–80). Bristol: Multilingual Matters.

Mutta, M., & Laine, P. (2022). Tapaustutkimus monikielisten kirjoittajien kirjoitusprosesseista: Näppäilyntallennus apuna sanastokeskittymien tunnistamisessa [A case study of multilingual writers' writing processes: Using keystroke logging to identify formulaic sequences]. *Lähivõrdlusi. Lähivertailuja, 32*, 120–149. doi:10.5128/LV32.04. https://doi.org/10.5128/LV32.04.

Mutta, M., Laine, P., Lahtinen, S., Mäkilä, M., Åberg, A.-M., & Lintunen, P. (to appear). Writers' L1 and L2 Fluency: The impact of proficiency level on the use of multiword sequences in the initial writing phase. In Gustaf Bernhard Uno Skar, Paul Rogers & Jonathan Marine (Eds.), *Writing research across borders: From early literacy learning to writing in professional life* (working title). The WAC Clearinghouse.

Mutta, M., Peltonen, P., Laine, P., & Lintunen, P. (2025). Fluency across modes: An exploratory study of L1 and L2 spoken and written fluency. *International Review of Applied Linguistics in Language Teaching*, 1–30. https://doi.org/10.1515/iral-2024-0187.

Mäntylä, K., Lahtinen, S., & Toropainen, O. (2020). Processing L2 vocabulary in writing. In P. Booth & J. Clenton (Eds.), *First language influences on multilingual lexicons* (pp. 107–126). New York, NY: Routledge.

Perez-Bettan, A. (2015). Apprentissage et utilisation du langage préfabriqué chez des apprenants de français langue étrangère [Learning and use of prefabricated language among learners of French as a foreign language] [Doctoral dissertation, Paris 8 Université Vincennes Saint-Denis]. Sciences Cognitives. Retrieved 5 October 2023 from https://tel.archives-ouvertes.fr/tel-01714531/document.

Révész, A., Michel, M., Lu, X., Kourtali, N., Lee, M., & Borges, L. (2022). The relationship of proficiency to speed fluency, pausing, and eye-gaze behaviours in L2 writing. *Journal of Second Language Writing, 58*(December 2022), 100927. https://doi.org/10.1016/j.jslw.2022.100927.

Spelman Miller, K., Lindgren, E., & Sullivan, K.P.H. (2008). The psycholinguistic dimension in second language writing: Opportunities for research and pedagogy using computer keystroke logging. *TESOL Quarterly, 42*(3), 433–454. Retrieved 5 October 2023 from https://www.jstor.org/stable/40264477.

Storto, A., Haukås, Å., & Tiurikova, I. (2023). Visualising the language practices of lower secondary students: outlines for practice-based models of multilingualism. *Applied Linguistics Review, 15*(5), 2035–2059. https://doi.org/10.1515/applirev-2022-0.

Tavakoli, P., & Uchihara, T. (2020). To what extent are multiword sequences associated with oral fluency? *Language Learning, 70*(2), 506–547. https://doi.org/10.1111/lang.12384.

Usoof, H., Leblay, C., & Caporossi, G. (2020). *GenoGraphiX-Log version 2.0 user guide.* Les Cahiers Du GERAD G-2020-68.

Van Waes, L., & Schellens, P.J. (2003). Writing profiles: The effect of the writing mode on pausing and revision patterns of experienced writers. *Journal of Pragmatics, 35*(6), 829–853. https://doi.org/10.1016/S0378-2166(02)00121-2.

Van Waes, L., Leijten, M., Roeser, J., Olive, T., & Grabowski, J. (2021). Measuring and assessing typing skills in writing research. *Journal of Writing Research, 13*(1), 107–153. https://doi.org/10.17239/jowr-2021.13.01.04.

Van Waes, L. (1992). The influence of the computer on writer profiles. In H. Pander Maat & M. Steehouder (Eds.), *Studies of functional text quality* (pp. 173–186). Amsterdam & Atlanta, GA: Editions Rodopi B.V.

Vieira, C., Parsons, P., & Byrd, V. (2018). Visual learning analytics of educational data: A systematic literature review and research agenda. *Computers and Education, 122,* 119–135. https://doi.org/10.1016/j.compedu.2018.03.018.

Wray, A. (2002). *Formulaic language and the lexicon.* Cambridge: Cambridge University Press.

CHAPTER 11

The Visualisation of Writing

Thierry Olive

This concluding chapter addresses two central themes explored throughout the volume. The first, which underpins all preceding chapters, concerns the dynamics of writing—a concept introduced by Leblay, Caporossi, and Usoof (this volume, p. 73). While each author approaches this dynamic from a different perspective, the temporality of writing remains a core focus across the contributions. The second theme pertains to the nature of the data being visualised. The recording of writing processes—whether handwritten or typed—generates extensive datasets from which a wide range of variables can be extracted. Although this heterogeneity presents certain challenges, it also offers a valuable opportunity for cross-perspective analysis and deeper insight.

Moreover, while data visualisation can enhance the description of data and reveal previously unobserved phenomena, its primary role as a medium for conveying information requires that it support effective information processing. It is therefore essential to select visualisation methods that are appropriately aligned with both the nature of the data and the specific communicative objectives. These methods must not only serve the representation of the phenomena under study but also facilitate reader comprehension. In this regard, Koponen's contribution (this volume, p. 19) offers a compelling example of how data gathered from writing recordings can be transformed into meaningful visual representations, tailored to both the characteristics of the data and the phenomena to be illuminated (see also Basnayake & Usoof, this volume, p. 48).

11.1 Visualising the Dynamics of Writing

If there is one aspect of writing that is indisputable, it is its inherently dynamic nature: writing unfolds over time. One might even argue that writing necessitates time. This dynamic dimension can be further divided into two key sub-dimensions. The first relates to the very act of writing itself. Composing a text involves multiple temporal stages—planning, formulating, and revising—all of which require time and cognitive effort. Second, writing requires long and formal instruction to learn the multiple skills that are necessary to produce texts. One can even ask if learning to write ever truly ends? As

 | HTTPS://DOI.ORG/10.1163/9789004760264-012

Kellogg (2008) suggests, every writer continues to learn with each new writing task encountered.

While the temporal dynamic of learning to write is essential, the present volume focuses more specifically on the temporality inherent in the act of writing—that is, the visualisation of the writing process as it unfolds. This process begins with an initial idea and culminates in a written text that adheres to both linguistic and communicative constraints. But what exactly do we mean by the term *writing process*?

The notion of *writing process* can vary significantly depending on disciplinary perspectives and theoretical orientations. For instance, within cognitive psychology, this process is conceptualized in terms of task temporality. It begins when the writer becomes aware of the writing prompt or instruction, continues through the phases of composition—including planning (with or without drafting), formulation, and revision—and concludes when the text is finalized and made public. From this perspective, the central objective is to understand the temporal organization of the cognitive processes involved in writing. In other words, cognitive psychology seeks to describe how the mental activities that enable text production are structured over time.

A substantial body of research has investigated how the major components of writing—planning, linguistic formulation, and revision—are temporally interconnected within a writing session, moving beyond a simplistic, linear view of the writing process. Findings indicate that these processes occur throughout the act of writing, with planning predominating in the early stages and revision becoming more prominent toward the end. Additional studies have examined the transitions between these phases, highlighting the recursive nature of the writing process, i.e., the fact that any process can interrupt or modify another at any moment (Levy & Ransdell, 1995; see also below). Research has further demonstrated that the timing of specific processes is critical. For example, in the context of argumentative writing, planning episodes occurring at the beginning of a session are more predictive of final text quality than those that occur later (Rijlaarsdam & van den Bergh, 1996). Other studies have focused on the concurrent coordination of writing processes. This line of work shows that the development of writing skills is associated not only with changes in the way processes are coordinated but also with increased flexibility in their regulation. Skilled writers can indeed adapt their process coordination strategies according to task demands, often employing overlapping cognitive processes to optimize performance (Olive, 2014).

From a psychological perspective, understanding the cognitive dynamics underlying writing involves designing experiments that manipulate factors likely to influence these dynamics, with the goal of identifying observable indicators that reflect cognitive processes. Typically, when psychology seeks to investigate temporal dynamics, it does so by measuring durations—or more broadly, temporal characteristics—associated with tasks, activities, or specific stages of activity. One prominent example is the study of pauses, initially developed in the context of spoken language production, which has since been adapted to the analysis of written language (Schilperoord, 2002).

Although pauses were originally interpreted primarily as indicators of planning and revision processes, subsequent research has demonstrated that they can reflect a much broader range of cognitive operations. These include sub-lexical, morphological, lexical, and morphosyntactic processes, among others. With advances in technology and increasingly precise experimental methods, psychologists have expanded their investigation of writing dynamics to include additional dimensions such as eye movements (Alamargot et al., 2007), neural activation patterns (Dufor & Rapp, 2013; Perret & Laganaro, 2013), and the evolution of cognitive load, as measured by reaction times (for a review, see Olive, 2022). Moreover, the temporal structure of writing processes—and transitions between them—has been explored through verbal protocol analysis (Levy & Ransdell, 1994).

These methodological developments have led to several tools and perspectives, generating a diverse array of data. Yet within this complexity, the phenomena of interest often remain embedded and must be carefully uncovered through rigorous analysis.

For text genetics, the dynamic nature of writing also pertains to the temporality of the task, but it is conceptualized differently from the psychological perspective. Rather than focusing on the writer's internal cognitive processes, the writing geneticist seeks to reconstruct and describe all the phases and stages that lead to the production of the final text (Grésillon, 1973). This may include documentary research, correspondence with editors or proofreaders, successive drafts, and other external elements that contribute to the evolution of the text. The primary object of study is not the writer's mental activity, but rather the progressive construction of the text as it unfolds over time. The aim of this approach is to understand how a text emerges and develops—from an initial instruction or idea to a fully formed piece of writing, whether a few paragraphs or a multi-chapter work (see, for example, Bekius & Buschenhenke, this volume, p. 148). Textual genetics thus foregrounds the relationship between *avant-textes* (pre-texts) and the final text, seeking to describe the various states of a text and the transformations that lead from one state to another. As such, the geneticist of writing places particular emphasis on revision processes, not only identifying key operations but also their temporal organization.

As noted in several chapters of this volume, text genetics laid important groundwork for what is now known as keystroke logging. With the increasing use of word processors, traditional traces of revision—previously visible in handwritten drafts—were at risk of being lost, since digital environments often erase intermediate stages of writing. To address this, researchers recognized the need to preserve the ephemeral traces of development of the text. This led to the creation of the first keystroke logging tools, designed specifically to capture the evolving nature of text production in digital contexts.

While the writing geneticist or the linguist typically directs their attention primarily toward the text itself, the study of writing dynamics requires analytical tools capable of revealing the underlying processes that drive development of the text. Writing recording technologies are increasingly employed to capture the temporal evolution of texts, not with the goal of analysing the writer's cognitive states—as is common in psychological approaches—but rather to trace the linguistic operations that give rise to the text (De Biasi, 2004). In this regard, the text-reconstruction functionalities offered by keystroke logging software have proven particularly valuable. These tools also facilitate the automatic identification of revision operations. By tracking the movement of the insertion point, it becomes possible to distinguish between operations aimed at continuing the text (typically occurring at the right edge) and those intended to modify previously written content. Studying the different versions of a text likewise necessitates aligning these states of the text. Several alignment tools now enable researchers to visualise a text's development across its various stages (Fénoglio & Ganascia, 2007; Laridilleux et al., 2013).

More recently, Cislaru and Olive (2018) proposed an interdisciplinary approach to studying writing temporality, drawing on insights from psychology, text genetics, linguistics, and natural language processing. Their work focuses on bursts of writing—the segments of text produced during uninterrupted transcription phases (see also Olive & Cislaru, 2015). This approach seeks to uncover the internal structure of these segments and the rules governing their sequential assembly, which ultimately result in a coherent final text.

In summary, describing the dynamics of writing relies on the evolving states of the text and the cognitive processes that drive these changes (Cislaru, Doquet & Olive, 2025). From this perspective, an ideal mode of visualising writing dynamics would be itself dynamic—capable of representing not only the successive states of the text but also the transitions and mechanisms underlying those transformations.

The chapters collected in this volume all engage with the dynamics of writing—often referred to as the *writing process*. Whether the focus is on various modes of visualisation (Koponen, this volume, p. 19; Basnayake & Usoof, this volume, p. 48) or on specific visual representations of particular datasets, the overarching scientific aim is to deepen our understanding of the writing process and the phenomena it encompasses. For instance, Leblay et al. (this volume, p. 73) apply graph-based visualisation theory to represent writing as a series of revision episodes. As the authors emphasize, their objective is to treat writing time as a central object of observation. Similarly, Tanoï Namio et al. (this volume, p. 106) examine the temporal flow of writing through the lens of revision episodes. Their work focuses on visualising these changes at the level of linguistic structures, particularly at the sentence level. They propose a multi-tiered approach to visualisation, ranging from minimally aggregated to highly aggregated levels, thereby offering readers varying depths of analysis concerning textual transformations. This chapter thus underscores the importance—and, indeed, the necessity—of employing multiple visualisation methods to illuminate the complexity of the phenomena under study. In this same perspective, Cislaru et al. (this volume, p. 124) introduce a platform that supports multiple types of data visualisations centred on bursts of writing in order to represent the dynamics of textualization. Notably, these authors incorporate artificial intelligence techniques to extract meaningful patterns from recorded data: clustering algorithms are used to categorize bursts of writing which are subsequently visualised or subjected to statistical analysis. Bekius and Buschenhenke (this volume, p. 148) approach the question of the temporality of writing from the standpoint of text genetics. Their work focuses on visualising text modifications by reintegrating them into the linear progression of the text. This visualisation approach enables not only the identification of revision operations during composition, but also the tracking of their temporal occurrence. As in several other chapters, here too revision operations serve as key segmentation markers of the writing process. Mutta et al. (this volume, p. 214) offer a comparative study of the sequences of bursts of writing of multilingual writers. In this case, the temporal segmentation markers extend beyond revision episodes to include uninterrupted transcription phases, categorized according to their functional role in either production or revision (Galbraith & Baaijen, 2019; Kaufer et al., 1986).

Perrin (this volume, p. 176) addresses a different aspect of temporality—more precisely, he seeks to capture the multiple temporalities that unfold as journalists compose short news stories. Adopting an applied and practice-oriented perspective, Perrin introduces a set of complementary models designed to account for both the cognitive and social dynamics involved in the writing process, particularly those arising in interactions between journalists and editors. His approach includes microstructural visualisations that represent the internal structure of the text and the writing process itself. In addition, he presents visualisations that aim to capture broader task-related dynamics by incorporating information related to source reading, task management, and the surrounding social environment. These multimodal representations offer a nuanced understanding of how writing is embedded in complex cognitive and collaborative contexts.

11.2 Visualising Heterogeneous Data

The visualisation of writing data relies on a heterogeneous set of information. These data can range from quantitative variables to character strings and categorical labels, all of which can reflect various aspects of writing dynamics. However, their diverse nature presents challenges for visualisation, particularly when attempting to represent multiple variables simultaneously within a single framework.

The writing process can be approached from the perspective of the evolving text, with the aim of illustrating its progressive construction over time. In this context, visualising the text in progress should reveal its genesis and support analytical interpretation by making visible the transformations of the written product. Writing bursts, for instance, may serve as foundational units of this construction (Cislaru & Olive, 2018). Alternatively, the writing process may be conceptualized through the lens of textual operations, focusing on the sequencing and classification of revision activities—such as insertions, deletions, movements, and substitutions—thereby providing insight into the writer's writing strategies.

Visualisation can also serve to account for the writer's cognitive activity. In such cases, variables related to the durations of mental processes are typically recorded, alongside performance indicators that reflect the writer's output. These varied dimensions of writing—textual and cognitive for example—can be studied independently or in combination.

Importantly, integrating these levels offers rich interpretive potential by linking observable text features with mental processes. This integrated perspective helps to identify key moments in the writing process when the linguistic or rhetorical demands of the task intersect with the writer's cognitive capacities. For example, a segment characterized by intensive rewriting might coincide with observable hesitation, such as prolonged pauses or production breaks.

Some recent research already employs multi-modal data collection systems that synchronize various types of input: keystroke logging, eye tracking, electroencephalographic (EEG) recordings, and source consultation. By cross-referencing these visualisations, researchers can identify recurring patterns, model cognitive profiles, and develop adaptive tools for writing support and instruction. Such dynamic representations of text production enable a reflective analysis of writing practices and provide educators and learners with tools to better understand the underlying mechanisms of text development (see Sellstone et al., this volume, p. 191).

To conclude this section, it is important to underscore that data visualisation is by no means limited to information derived from keystroke logging. While keystroke recording is central to the present volume, various other data sources also lend themselves to visualisation and offer valuable insights into the dynamics of writing. For instance, the Eye and Pen software (Chesnet et al., 2024) enables the recording of handwriting, generating a dataset comparable to that obtained through typing—even if the latter allows for more automated forms of processing.

More broadly, virtually any type of data can be visualised, including those that might initially appear to be less compatible with formal modelling. A notable example comes from the work of Levy and Ransdell (1995), who applied visualisation techniques to data collected through think-aloud protocols. Rather than limiting their investigation to the verbatim transcriptions of verbalizations, the authors systematically coded and segmented the data into distinct cognitive episodes—planning (P), translating/text production (T), evaluating (E), and revising (R). From this segmentation, they computed transition probabilities between these cognitive processes. For example, they were able to quantify the likelihood that a given writer would shift from planning to translating, or from translating to revising. These probabilities were calculated individually for each writer, segmented in 10-minute intervals across multiple 40-minute writing sessions. The resulting data were presented as transition matrices (see Figure 11.1), which revealed unique patterns for each writer—what the authors termed *writing signatures* (Levy & Ransdell, 1996). These writing signatures offered compelling evidence of individualized strategies in the use of writing processes. Remarkably, each writer tended to exhibit a consistent transition profile, both across different segments of the same session and across separate writing sessions. For example, Writer 1 in Figure 11.1 demonstrates frequent alternation among all four processes, while Writer 2 alternates primarily between planning and translating, returning frequently to planning. One of the most significant findings from this study is the relationship between these process profiles and the quality of the resulting texts. Writers who displayed highly recursive profiles—characterized by frequent alternation between all writing processes—tended to produce higher-quality

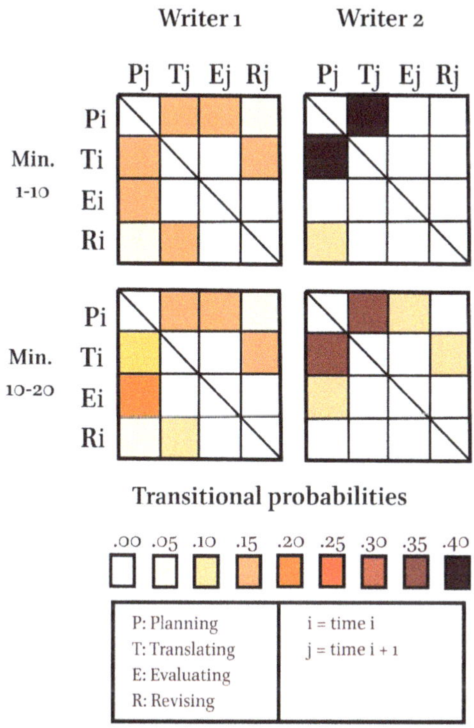

FIGURE 11.1
A figure depicting the transitional probabilities between the writing processes of Planning (P), Translating (T), evaluating (E), and revising (R) of two writers in different phases of a writing session

'i' indicates the first process of a couple of consecutive processes, and 'j' the second process. Darker cells indicate high transitional probabilities, i.e., low recursivity in the writing processes. By contrast, light yellow cells indicate low transitional probabilities, i.e., highly recursive writing strategies. Adapted from Levy & Ransdell (1995)

texts. Levy and Ransdell (1996) thus concluded that effective writing is supported by a strategic and dynamic coordination of cognitive processes, particularly through the recursive use of planning, translating and revision.

Visualising the text in production and cognitive processes of writing thus opens multiple windows, which offer varied but complementary points of view on a complex phenomenon. The intersection of these levels, by articulating visible and invisible data, product and process, constitutes a promising way to deepen our understanding of the act of writing. However, it calls for critical reflection on the tools chosen and the interpretations that these visualisations make possible.

11.3 Visualise but Not Too Much!

Visualisation plays an important role in the process of knowledge/information transmission by rendering complex information more accessible through graphic or schematic representations. In particular, it facilitates the structuring of abstract data and the identification of underlying patterns or trends. However, the effective interpretation of visualisations depends on specific literacies and interpretive skills, which can vary considerably across individuals. As such, a visualisation that is not appropriately designed for its intended audience may become a barrier to understanding—or even a source of confusion. Consequently, the design of visualisations must be approached with methodological rigor, ensuring alignment between the visual format, the intended message, and the cognitive capacities of the target users. A well-constructed visualisation is not merely an aesthetic enhancement but a communicative tool that supports comprehension and interpretation.

Although visualisations are typically intended to facilitate cognitive processing, they can paradoxically produce the opposite effect when they become overly complex. A dense diagram—characterized by multiple layers of interpretation, visual codes, and cross-references—may overload the user's working memory and impede comprehension. This is because interpreting a visualisation involves the simultaneous integration of diverse semiotic elements, including symbols, colors, spatial and graphical relationships. When these elements are too numerous, poorly organized, or insufficiently prioritized, users must expend significant attentional resources to understand it. This phenomenon is well-documented within cognitive psychology and aligns with an *intrinseque cognitive load* (Sweller et al., 2019). According to Sweller's Cognitive Load Theory (2010), all information processing draws from a limited pool of mental resources. When a visualisation is embedded within a written text, it not only needs to be understood in isolation but need also be integrated with the surrounding discourse. This entails interpreting the image, linking it to the accompanying verbal explanation, extracting its implications, and potentially comparing it with other representations within the same document. For the writer, this presents a particular challenge: integrating visual elements in a way that supports rather than disrupts the argumentative flow. Poorly integrated visualisations can become "floating objects"—detached from the main line of reasoning and burdensome to the reader. Furthermore, a sequence of complex visualisations may impose a high *extraneous cognitive load* (Sweller et al., 2019), resulting from the cognitive effort required to manage multiple formats of information simultaneously.

The overall readability of a text containing visualisations thus depends on the careful orchestration of attention. This involves avoiding redundancy, establishing clear informational hierarchies, and ensuring that each visualisation is meaningfully situated within the rhetorical progression of the text. A poorly calibrated visualisation—intended to clarify—may in fact obscure the very concept it is meant to illustrate, becoming not only ineffective but counterproductive by diverting attention away from the most relevant content. The challenge, then, is to design visualisations that are rich enough to convey meaningful insights, yet simple enough to be immediately intelligible.

Moreover, any visualisation is a constructed representation that involves deliberate choices, simplifications, and hierarchies. As such, it is never entirely neutral. The act of visualisation necessarily entails the selection of certain elements over others, a process guided by the researcher's objectives and interpretive framing. These decisions foreground particular aspects of a phenomenon while rendering others less visible or entirely absent, thereby shaping the viewer's interpretation. Visualisation is thus embedded within a prior research question or theoretical orientation that directs attention toward specific phenomena. This framing influences representational choices, including the selection of variables, spatial organization, and the type of graphical display employed. While these choices enable researchers to highlight salient patterns or dynamics, they also carry the inherent risk of obscuring other dimensions of the data. For example, a heat map illustrating the frequency of gaze fixations on a written text may effectively reveal areas of visual concentration but simultaneously obscure the sequence or trajectory of eye movements—details that may be crucial for understanding revision strategies or reading behaviour. In this sense, visualisation functions as both a lens and a filter: it facilitates perception while inevitably excluding certain information.

Thus, visualisation not only structures the perception of data but also conditions its interpretation. It frames what is made intelligible, what is emphasized, and what remains marginal. Recognizing these functions is essential for critically engaging with visual representations in research and for designing visualisations that remain meaningful, and therefore useful.

11.4 To Conclude

As these research examples demonstrate, the dynamics of writing can be approached from multiple perspectives by analysing a range of dimensions. Consequently, the study of the writing process relies on data of varying types: quantitative data such as durations, categorical data relating to the nature of textual operations, qualitative data derived from verbal protocols, and segments of text among others ... The analysis of this diverse data may open up avenues for exploring the cognitive mechanisms involved in writing and to help designing and evaluating pedagogical interventions.

In particular, the recording of handwriting represents a valuable source of information for researchers investigating the temporal and cognitive dynamics of writing. However, visualising the data generated by such recordings also requires the integration of multiple kinds of information—often from heterogeneous sources. Visualisation, in this context, becomes an essential analytical tool, enabling researchers to reveal patterns and phenomena that might otherwise remain obscured in raw or unstructured data. As illustrated by the various contributions discussed throughout this volume, visualisation is not merely a representational aid, but a methodological device that supports discovery and interpretation in writing research. To accommodate the complexity and heterogeneity of writing data, new forms of visualisation will likely need to be developed. These emerging tools have the potential to illuminate the diverse strategies employed by writers—whether cognitive, linguistic, or discursive—and their tangible effects on the texts they produce.

Crucially, the value of visualisation extends beyond academic research. It offers significant utility for clinicians, educators, and learners, providing a means for reflective engagement with writing practices (Sellstone et al., this volume, p. 191). For clinicians, such tools can support diagnostic insights into writing difficulties. In educational contexts, visualisation tools can enhance the teaching of writing by offering instructors a window into students' compositional behaviours and strategies, and by providing learners with meaningful feedback on their writing processes and outcomes.

Furthermore, data visualisation plays a particularly important role in digital technologies capable of processing large volumes of information in real time. These technologies can deliver immediate, individualized feedback to both students and teachers, thus contributing to more adaptive and responsive instructional practices (Bach et al., 2024; Dux-Speltz et al., 2022).

Visualising writing and its associated cognitive processes will represent a significant advance in the study of the psychological and linguistic mechanisms of writing. They not only facilitate a deeper understanding of writing dynamics and support the development of explicit models that are beneficial for research, clinical practice, teaching, and personalized interventions. Visualisation thus emerges as a bridge between empirical inquiry and practical application—offering new pathways for interpreting, modelling, and supporting dynamics of writing.

References

Alamargot, D., Dansac, C., Chesnet, D. & Fayol, M. (2007). Parallel processing before and after pauses: A combined analysis of graphomotor and eye movements during procedural text production. In M. Torrance, L. van Waes, & D. Galbraith (Eds.), *Writing and cognition: Research and applications* (pp. 13–29). Elsevier Science.

Bach, B., … & Capendale, S. (2024). Challenges and Opportunities in Data Visualization Education: A Call to Action. *IEEE Transactions on Visualization and Computer Graphics, 30*, 649–660. https://doi.ieeecomputersociety.org/10.1109/TVCG.2023.3327378.

Chesnet, D., Solier, C., Bordas, B., & Perret, C. (2024). A quick briefing on the new version of Eye and Pen (version 3.01): news and update. *Reading and Writing, 37*, 253–264. https://doi.org/10.1007/s11145-022-10267-5.

Cislaru, G., Doquet, C., & Olive, T. (2025). Operating units in written language performance: linguistics and behavioral perspectives. *Journal of Writing Research, 16*(3), 359–375. https://doi.org/10.17239/jowr-2025.16.03.01.

Cislaru, G. & Olive, T. (2018). *Le processus de textualisation. Analyse des unités linguistiques de performance écrite* [*The textualisation process. Analysis of linguistic units of written performance*]. Bruxelles: De Boeck.

De Biasi, Pierre-Marc. (2004). Toward a Science of Literature: Manuscript analysis and the Gcenesis of the work. In Jed Deppman, Daniel Ferrer, & Michael Groden (Eds.), *Genetic criticism: Texts and avant-textes* (pp. 36–68). University of Pennsylvania Press.

Dufor, O., & Rapp, B. (2013). Letter representations in writing: an fMRI adaptation approach. *Frontiers in psychology, 4*, 781. https://doi.org/10.3389/fpsyg.2013.00781.

Dux Speltz, E. et al. (2022). Automating Individualized, Process-Focused Writing Instruction: A Design-Based Research Study. *Frontiers in Communication, 7*. https://www.frontiersin.org/articles/10.3389/fcomm.2022.933878.

Fenoglio, I., & Ganascia, J.-G. (2007). [MEDITE: software for the comparative analysis of genesis documents], *Genesis, 166–16.*

Galbraith, D., & Baaijen, V.M. (2019). Aligning keystrokes with cognitive processes in writing. In Eva Lindgren & Kirk P.H. Sullivan (Eds.), *Observing writing: Insights from keystroke logging and handwriting* (pp. 306–325, Vol. 38). Brill. Advance online publication. https://doi.org/10.1163/9789004392526_015.

Kaufer, David. S., Hayes, John R., & Flower, Linda S. (1986). Composing written sentences. *Research in the Teaching of English, 20*(2), 121–140.

Kellogg, R.T. (2008). Training writing skills: A cognitive developmental perspective. *Journal of Writing Research, 1*(1), 1–26. https://doi.org/10.17239/jowr-2008.01.01.1.

Lardilleux, A., Fleury, S., & Cislaru, G. (2013). Allongos: Longitudinal alignment for the genetic study of writers' drafts. In *International Conference on Intelligent Text Processing and Computational Linguistics* (pp. 537–548). Springer. https://doi.org/10.1007/978-3-642-37256-8_44.

Levy, C.M., & Ransdell, S. (1995). Is writing as difficult as it seems? Memory & Cognition, 23(6), 767–779. https://doi.org/10.3758/bf03200928.

Levy, C.M., & Ransdell, S.E. (1996). Writing signatures. In C.M. Levy & S. Ransdell (Eds.), *The science of writing: Theories, methods, individual differences, and applications* (pp. 149–161). Lawrence Erlbaum Associates, Inc.

Olive, T. (2014). Toward an Incremental and Cascading Model of Writing: A review of research on writing processes coordination. *Journal of Writing Research, 6*, 173–194.

Olive, T. (2022). Working memory in beginning and skilled writing. In J.W. Schwieter & J. Cheng (Eds.), *Cambridge Handbook of Working Memory and Language (pp. 504–525)*. Cambridge University Press.

Olive, T. & Cislaru, G. (2015). Linguistic forms at the process-product interface: Analyzing the linguistic content of bursts of production. In G. Cislaru (Ed.), *Writing(s) at the crossroads: the process/product interface* (pp. 99–123). John Benjamins.

Perret, C., & Laganaro, M. (2012). Comparison of electrophysiological correlates of writing and speaking: a topographic ERP analysis. *Brain topography*, *25*(1), 64–72. https://doi.org/10.1007/s10548-011-0200-3.

Rijlaarsdam, G., & Van den Bergh, H. (1996). The dynamics of writing: An agenda for research into an interactive compensatory model of writing. Many questions, some answers. In C.M. Levy and S. Ransdell (Eds.), *The science of writing: Theories, methods, individual differences, and applications* (pp. 107–126). Lawrence Erlbaum Associates.

Sweller, J. (2010). Cognitive Load Theory: Recent theoretical advances. In *Cambridge University Press eBooks* (pp. 29–47). https://doi.org/10.1017/cbo9780511844744.004.

Sweller, J., Van Merriënboer, J.J.G., & Paas, F. (2019). Cognitive Architecture and Instructional Design: 20 years later. *Educational Psychology Review*, *31*(2), 261–292. https://doi.org/10.1007/s10648-019-09465-5.

Glossary

This glossary is not intended to be exhaustive. It is a preliminary compilation of fundamental terms that are representative of the field of data visualisation in relation to *Humanities* and especially to the writing process.

This glossary comprises terminology used in different chapters of this volume. It goes beyond the simple indexing of terms (lists and pagination) by pairing terms with definitions used by the authors, including reference and chapter distribution. It is founded upon two questions:

(1) Can the same term have divergent definitions?

(2) Can different terms converge on the same definition?

The responsibility to answer these questions lies with the reader.

A

B

Born digital material	**Definition**	**References**
VII-153	Literature that is written within a digital environment.	Bekius (2023)

Burst (of writing)	**Definitions**	**References**
VI-132	By setting the desired pause threshold, one can segment the language sequences produced between pauses, called bursts of writing. Like the visible part of the text that remains largely present (with the exception of deletions/modifications) throughout the writing process, bursts of writing can be a prime object of study (see. The sets of writing bursts obtained are thus the result of the delinearization of the writing flow.	Chenoweth and Hayes (2001); Cislaru & Olive (2018)

HTTPS://DOI.ORG/10.1163/9789004760264-013

(*cont.*)

Burst (*of writing*)	Definitions	References
X-214	Burst is an index of fluent writing.	Cislaru & Olive (2018)
X-231	Three main types of bursts: P-bursts, R-bursts, and I-bursts. Studying P-bursts allows researchers to examine what writers are able to process with regard to whole units, specifically between cognitive pauses (≥ 2 seconds).	Baaijen & Galbraith, (2018); Cislaru & Olive, (2018); Conijn et al., (2021); Hayes (2009)
X-215	Can include the linguistic material produced between pauses (P-bursts) or between pauses and revisions (R-bursts), as well as other actions (e.g., a mouse or arrow-key movement) away from the leading edge (I-bursts). I-bursts (insertion bursts) start with a mouse or arrow-key movement followed by text production, all of which move away from the leading edge of the current writing point.	Baaijen & Galbraith, (2018); Cislaru & Olive, (2018); Conijn et al., (2021)
X-220	*Visualisation burst* (*V-burst*) are defined according to the visualisations produced by the GGXLog tool, and the graphical representation includes seven possible types of nodes: append, insert, removed, deletion, displaced, copy and pause. Number and content of events (e.g., bursts, deletions, pauses), number of nodes, and time spent until the end.	This volume

C

Cartogram	Definitions	References
II-27	A graphic that combines statistical and geographical information, where areas of geographical regions are scaled in proportion to some statistic	Nusrat &Kobourov (2016)

(cont.)

Cartogram	**Definitions**	**References**
II-27	*Dorling cartogram* A cartogram where each region is drawn as a circle with its area in proportion to its population or other another statistic and is then treated as an object in a gravity model which is repelled by other circles with which it overlaps, but is attracted to circles which were neighbouring regions on the original map	Dorling (1996)

Chart	**Definitions**	**References**
II-29	A visual representation of quantitative data that employs graphic symbols with varying dimensions and positions within a Cartesian or polar coordinate system to express numerical relationships	This volume
II-21	*Statistical chart* A synonym of chart	This volume
II-19; III-57; VI-141; IX-199	*Bar chart* A stylized graph where data in the form of a bar or a line is plotted against x and y axes	Weaver (2014)
II-26	*Line chart* A chart consisting of data points that are connected to each other with a line representing an approximation of the values between the recorded observations	Koponen & Hildén (2019)
II-31	*Pie chart* A circular chart that encodes data using central angle, wedge area, and arc length	Kosara & Skau (2016)
II-30	*Area chart* A line chart in which the areas between the lines have been filled—the line chart	Koponen & Hildén (2019)

(*cont.*)

Chart	**Definitions**	**References**
VIII-184	*Workflow chart* Time is displayed on the x-axis while activity fields are listed on the y-axis	Koponen & Hildén (2019)

Collation	**Definition**	**References**
VII-154	Operation of comparing two or more texts to identify differences between them. Collation is used for various reasons, including examining textual variation, tracing the historical transmission of a text, producing a critical text, or—most relevant in this case—to study the creative writing process	Bleeker et al. (2019)

Computer-based text development	**Definitions**	**References**
III-49	Capturing data such as mouse movements, clicks, system tasks (cut-copy-paste), use of external applications, screenshots, audio recordings and even eye-tracking	Anderson et al. (2006); Stromqvist et al. (2006); Leijten & Van Waes (2013)
III-49	Insights into the writing process with the cognitive processes involved and the development of the text itself	Miller & Sullivan (2013)
VII-158	*TEI* (*Text Encoding Initiative*) Consortium developing a standard for annotating texts in the humanities and social sciences in order to make them computer-readable for further processing. As a meta-markup language, XML, the extensible markup language, prescribes the 'syntactic' rules for annotating text in digital form.	Burnard (2014)

D

Diagram	Definitions	References
	A hypernym for *charts* and other non-map graphical representations of data	
II-35	*Network diagram* Visualisation that displays the relationships between objects or concepts using connecting lines, typically in such a way that connected elements are fairly close to each other. See *mathematical graph.*	Koponen & Hilden (2019)
II-35	*Tree diagram* A network diagram with a hierarchical structure	Koponen & Hilden (2019)
II-37	*Flow diagram* Tree structure diagram where the connections have numeric values or weights attached to it, and which is visualised using line thickness.	This volume

Draft	Definition	References
VI-127	Part of the writing process: insists on the role and cognitive interest of drafts for textual configuration, considering variants as "protocols for making of a text".	Ferrer (2011)

E

Episode (of modifications)	Definitions	References
V-110	Refers to an event or a group of events occurring as part of a larger sequence. Synonym of a *writing phase* defined as a maximal set of consecutive actions made without using the mouse or keyboard arrows to move the cursor.	This volume

(*cont.*)

Episode (*of modifications*)	Definitions	References
V-117	*Episode merging* When revising a text, it sometimes happens that small changes are made in parts of text that are close to each other. The movement of the cursor, to move a little to the right or to the left, makes these modifications appear in different episodes while it could be interesting to group these changes so that they constitute only one episode.	This volume
V-117	*Proximity of the episode* The first type of fusion concerns successive episodes which only require a small movement of the cursor to move from one episode to the next. The principle is therefore to merge two successive episodes if the movement of the cursor between the two episodes is less than a given threshold. This reflects the fact that the author makes changes to various parts of the text that are close to each other.	This volume
V-117	*Size of the episode* The second type of fusion concerns the extent of the changes made in a episode. When two successive episodes have only few modifications, we can decide to group them. The number of modifications made in an episode is defined as the sum of the lengths of the red and blue parts and therefore corresponds to the number of newly inserted characters which are visible at the end of the episode at which we add the number of characters that were present at the start of the episode and that have been removed.	This volume

F

G

Genesis, Text Genetics	Definitions	References
IV-74	(1) Collect the material traces of the creative processes, (2) relate these traces to each other and to the works to which these processes have generally led, (3) arrange these traces in a chronological sequence that reflects the stages of the work's development and (4) analyse these traces and interpret them as clues to the temporal and spatial course of the genesis to identify recurring elements and regularities, or on the contrary, singularities, ruptures.	See https://www.item.ens.fr/thematique/
VI-127	The critical genetics approach takes into account this graphic dynamic of writing, and emphasizes the multi-layered nature of rewriting while pointing out the difficulty of accurately relating it to a chronology.	Hay (2002); Grésillon & Lebrave (2008); Grésillon (2016)
VII-148	*Genetic criticism* Field within literary studies and textual scholarship which examines creative invention through the drafts, manuscripts, notes, and other textual evidence that have been preserved from a writing process. Contrary to other fields within textual scholarship, its main interest lies with the pre-publication stage of a work's trajectory. It studies literary works, but also scientifically and historically significant sources. […]	Grésillon (1997); Deppman, Ferrer & Groden (2004); Van Hulle (2022)
IV-93	*Macrogenesis* (*macroscopic view*) An initial macroscopic examination of the graph, devoid of specific node analysis, and devoid of examination of node types distinguished by colour, and content, serves to differentiate whether the writing process is predominantly linear or exhibits a more dynamic and iterative processes. These observations provide insights into potential scenarios, including the writer's predisposition for preplanned compositional tasks, engagement in copying text, execution of a simplistic or rudimentary writing task, involvement in a complex cognitive process during writing, continuous revision, development of a sophisticated textual structure, or simply the manifestation of frequent errors.	This volume

(*cont.*)

Genesis, Text Genetics	Definitions	References
VI-127	The creation of versions as working units on the writer's side and units of analysis on the researcher's side	Cislaru & Olive (2018)
IV-93	*Microgenesis* (*microscopic view*) Investigating into a closer examination at the microscopic level allows for a thorough understanding of specific events through the utilization of graphs.	This volume
VII-152	*Digital genetic edition* As a digital publication that presents the genetic dossier of a creative work and "contains one or several tools that enable further exploration of the content and thus further study of the genesis of the work"	Elli Bleeker (2017)

(Mathematical) graph	Definitions	References
II-35	The network consists of data points called *nodes* that are connected to each other by *lines*, often called *edges*, which depict the relationships between the nodes. In the case of a *directed graph*, in which the edges have an associated direction, the nodes are connected by *arrows* (also called *directed edges*).	Koponen & Hildén (2019)
III-53	*Real-time graph* Real-time graph indicates the in-progress writing session related to short texts in the text editor.	Usoof et al. (2021); Zong (2020)
III-53	*Graph representation* Using graph theory to visualise the writing session	Caporossi et al. (2020)
VI-137	The data set can then be represented as a graph with data objects as vertices (a circle with a label), connected by weighted edges with the mutual reachability distances as weights.	This volume

(*cont.*)

(*Mathematical*) *graph*	**Definitions**	**References**
IV-74	Modelling pairwise relations between objects, intersects ideally with the linguistic theory of process.	Caporossi & Leblay (2011)
IV-77	In the mathematical sense, a graph is a set of points called nodes that are eventually linked by arcs. These hyperlinks, or arcs may be used to exhibit relations between portions of writing that remove constraints on the x-axis or the y-axis.	Caporossi & Leblay (2011)
V-107	Used to structure the information contained in the file contained the keystroke record	Caporossi and Leblay (2013); Bécotte-Boutin et al., (2019)
X-216	Writing session as nodes (vertices) and edges (links); each node is a cluster of continuous events (e.g., inserted, appended, or deleted text, or a pause), and each edge represents relationships between nodes, such as chronological order, flow in the final text, or deletions	Caporossi & Leblay (2015); Usoof et al. (2020)
III-53; IV-76; X-215	*Graph replay* (*progressive*) The Progressive Graph allows for the visualisation of the Graph at various stages of the writing session. The concurrent text is displayed in the text area below the graph.	Caporossi et al., (2020)
III-53	*Graph statistics* Graph statistics provide both numerical statistics and visual summaries of the session graph.	Caporossi et al., (2020)
VII-154	*Progressive graph* The x-axis is associated to topography and the chronology is represented by the y-axis (in that way, each keystroke is alone on one line). Combining [...] textual changes and chronological movement, progressive graph visualisation [...] shows the text that is being changed along with the order in which the writer has made textual changes at various locations in the text.	Bécotte-Boutin et al. (2015, 2017)

(*cont.*)

(*Mathematical*) *graph*	Definitions	References
IV-78	*Atomic DNA graph* When no editing is done, the graph simply represents the sequence of letters that appear in the text. The solid line indicates the chronological order of the keystrokes, and in this case, it is the same as the topographical order of the characters in the text.	This volume
IV-82	*Aggregated DNA graph* A sequence of nodes may be merged if the following conditions are met: (1) They are of the same nature, either addition/insertion or deletion. (2) They occur chronologically in consecutive order. (3) They are consecutive in space. (4) They are additions/insertions that happen to be deleted and their deletion is consecutive.	This volume
IV-85	*Enhanced DNA graph* Only the characters that appear in the final text may properly be analysed, and thus some information is lost with this model. It may, however, be enhanced by keeping a record of topographical arcs that used to exist	This volume
IV-85	*Atomic-lossless graph* Using only additions of nodes and arcs, and no removal. The rules to build such a graph are the following: (1) For any addition of character, identify the node corresponding to the last visible character before the insertion, say c. Then find the following node on the lower boundary of the graph, say s. Add then the new character, say k and connect it to c and to s. By adding arcs (arrows) from c to k and from k to s. (2) Suppose now the deletion of a character c. Consider the node corresponding to the character before c, say b and the node after, say s. The new deletion node k will be added as well as arcs from b to k and from k to s.	This volume

(*cont.*)

(*Mathematical*) *graph*	Definitions	References
IV-86	*Aggregated lossless graph* Using the following rules: (1) two addition/insertion nodes may be merged if they are consecutive (by their numbers), adjacent, have one same neighbour and either none of them was later deleted or they were deleted consecutively (by consecutive deletion keystrokes); and (2) two deletion nodes may be merged if they are adjacent, and their corresponding deleted nodes are adjacent and consecutive.	This volume

H

Histogram	Definition	References
II-34; III-57	A bar, line, or area chart that shows the distribution of a variable, where individual data points are classified into bins of equal intervals, and the chart shows the number of observations that fall into each	Koponen & Hilden (2019)

Human–computer interaction (*HCI*)	Definitions	References
III-51	Finding significant insights about user behaviour by facilitating the execution of advanced analysis and developing personalised services	Hinbarji et al., (2016)

I

Infographic	Definitions	References
II-20	Information graphics that have primarily an exploratory purpose, "graphics that tell a story"	Koponen & Hilden (2019)
II-37	*Qualitative infographic* A *diagram* that is not a *chart* or *map* and depicts information that is typically more conceptual than structured in nature	This volume
II-38	*Timeline* A historical diagram that depicts chronology using straight, curved, branching, or crossing line(s)	Rosenberg & Grafton (2010)
II-38	*Word cloud* or *Wordle* A diagram that visualises frequencies of words in text by varying font size, so that the most common words are shown in a larger size than less common ones.	Koponen & Hilden (2019)
II-39	*Word bubbles* A visualisation of word frequencies where words are located inside circles whose size is proportional to their frequency	Koponen & Hilden (2019)

Information graphic	Definitions	References
II-20	Hypernym of visualisation that covers both *infographics** and *visualisations* proper*	Koponen & Hilden (2019)
VI-124	Hypernym of *information visualisation* defined as the communication of abstract data relevant in terms of action through the use of interactive visual interfaces	Keim et al. (2006)

J

K

Keystroke log(ging) (*KSL*)	Definitions	References
III-49	Recording every event within the process of writing, allowing researchers to observe writing procedures and enhance their comprehension of the underlying dynamics during text production	Leijten and Waes (2015); Edwards et al. (2020)
III-49	Recording of key presses and releases on a computer keyboard	Sullivan & Lindgren (2008)
	Related to data visualisation	Andersson et al. (2006); Leijten & Van Waes (2013)
III-54	Typically consist of key characters, modifier keys (e.g., Shift, Ctrl), and navigation keys (e.g., arrows, Home, End) logged with timestamps for both keypress and key release events. Additionally, cursor position data, including caret and anchor positions, is often captured.	Andersson et al. (2006); Angelino et al. (2013); Caporossi et al. (2020); Hinbarji et al. (2016); Leijten & Van Waes (2013)
III-54	Keystroke logging may also encompass key depression duration, key hold duration, pauses between key releases and subsequent keypresses, and time elapsed since the writing session began.	Granville et al., (2009). Christopulos et al. (2004)
VI-129	KSL software provides a chronologically structured record of all the operations involved in writing on a keyboard: typing characters and spaces, revisions (deletions, insertions, displacements, etc.), pauses sequencing the process, or consultation of sources outside the document.	Leijten & Van Waes (2013); Lindgren & Sullivan (2019); Wengelin et al. (2009)

L

LS-graph	Definition	References
IV-75	*Lindgren-Sullivan graph* Statistics are computed all along the process and drawn as curves on a 2d-plot where the x-axis is associated to the sequence (either chronological or temporal) while the y-axis is associated to the statistics. Those statistics are typically the total number of keystrokes, the number of characters in the text, the position of the cursor, or other measure that may be of interest.	Lindgren & Sullivan (2002)

Linear text	Definitions	References
III-53	The linear text format illustrates the writing session employing two notational structures, summarising the progression of events throughout the session utilising textual descriptions and symbolic representation.	Caporossi et al. (2020)

M

Map	Definitions	References
II-23	A measurement-based miniature image of a geographical area	Koponen & Hildén (2019)
II-23	*Data map* or *thematic map* A map designed to illustrate some particular subject or to serve some special purpose, depicting spatial patterns in predominantly non-geographic phenomena	Thrower (1969); this volume

(*cont.*)

Map	Definitions	References
II-24	*Dot map* or *dot distribution map* A map which shows single recordings or observations of a phenomenon as dots of equal size	Koponen & Hilden (2019)
II-24	*Symbol map* or *graduated symbol map* A map similar to dot maps, where the dots are replaced by a symbol, usually a circle, the size of which is based on the value of a variable of interest	Koponen & Hilden (2019)
II-25; III-57	*Choropleth* or *heat map* A map where the region being depicted is divided into smaller areas which correspond to previously defined geographic regions and are assigned a color based on the value of a specific variable	Koponen & Hilden (2019)
III-57	Can represent the frequency or intensity of keystrokes across the keyboard. Each key is coloured based on the number of times it's pressed, with dark colours indicating higher activity.	This volume

Mouse movement tracking	Definition	References
III-55	Mouse movement tracking data typically includes the x and y coordinates of the cursor, along with event categorization such as left click, right click, double click, and move events.	Hinbarji et al. (2016); Vertega et al. (2001)

N

O

P

Pausology (pause)	Definition	References
VI-132	*Pausology* The study of pauses in language production is an essential part of any approach to the processual dimension of language production. Pauses provide a first level of segmentation of the language flow and make it possible to associate the production of textual units with the dynamics of the writer's or speaker's mental functioning.	Fayol (1997)
IV-91	*Psychomotor pause* Brief interruptions in the physical activity of writing caused by the need for motor adjustments, such as finger movements, key transitions, or hand repositioning.	Alves & Limpo (2015); Van Waes et al. (2010)
IV-91; IX-197; X-214	*Cognitive pause* These pauses occur when the writer stops to think, plan, or solve a problem during the writing process. Pause threshold of ≥ 2 seconds for cognitive pauses when studying bursts, as this pause length is considered a mental preparation of the text from a psycholinguistic point of view.	Cislaru & Olive (2018)
IV-91	*Strategic pause* These pauses taken by the writer to revise, re-read, or reflect on the written text.	Alves & Limpo (2015); Van Waes et al. (2010)
IV-91	*Technical pause* These pauses occur due to technical or external interruptions, such as dealing with software issues, system delays, or non-writing-related distractions.	Alves & Limpo (2015); Van Waes et al. (2010)

(*cont.*)

Process	Definition	References
VI-124	*Multi-dimensional process* Comprising at least two dynamic dimensions prior to the final text. The first is incremental, cumulative and spatially oriented (e.g., from left to right and top to bottom). It leads to a constant progression of the number of characters and words in the text. The second is non-linear, cumulative (insertion) or non-cumulative (deletion), and spatially non-oriented.	This volume

Plot	Definitions	References
II-29	A synonym of *chart*, used especially for more complex variants with a large number of data points; in contemporary usage, a plot often refers specifically to the *graphical* part of a chart, not the accompanying text labels.	This volume
II-32; III-36; VI-141; IX-199	*Scatter plot* A chart consisting of data points whose two characteristics are recorded as values on the horizontal and vertical axes, revealing the relationship between the variables and their distributions.	Koponen & Hilden (2019)
II-31	*Box plot* (*Tukey's box plot*) A chart that is made up of five components, chosen to give a robust summary of the distribution of a dataset: the median, two hinges showing the upper and lower quartiles, the data values adjacent to the upper and lower fences, two whiskers that connect the hinges to the fences, and outliers as individual points.	Wickham & Stryjewski (2011); Tukey (1977)
II-32	*Univariate scatter plot* *Scatter plots* where quantitative data is plotted only along one dimension (x or y), are instead used to visualise distributions.	This volume

(*cont.*)

Plot	**Definitions**	**References**
II-33	*Beeswarm plot* A *univariate scatter plot* where some of the dots are moved to the side to prevent overlap, so that the varying breadth of the "swarm" gives an indication of the shape of the distribution.	This volume

Progression analysis (PA)	**Definition**	**References**
VIII-176	*Progression Analysis* has been developed to capture real-life writing from three complementary perspectives: the material view on composing signs, the cognitive view on making decisions about the emerging text product, and the social view on interacting with others by proceeding language, from defining the task to implementing the product.	Perrin (2003)
VIII-181	*Progression graph* Progression graphs are automatically generated based on the data from keystroke logging. They show the composing process in writing sessions from a material perspective, as a trace of activities in time and space. Technically speaking, progression graphs are two-dimensional ordinal-numeric visualisations. On the x-axis, they display the order of all the revisions made during a writing process or session in chronological order from left to right. On the y-axis, the revisions are arranged from top to bottom in the order they appear in the final product.	This volume
VIII-181	*Progression score* Relate the coded meaning from writers' talk about writing to the sequence of observable, material activities. In other words, what writers said in their workplace negotiations or RVPs is allocated, through manual coding, both to specific revisions (insertions, deletions) in the text production process and to one or several of the 16 activity fields.	This volume

Q

R

Raw data (unprocessed data)	Definition	References
III-54	In computer-based writing research, can include logged keystrokes, stylus tracking, mouse movements, eye tracking and application tracking	Andersson et al. (2006); Caporossi et al. (2020); Graesser & McNamara (2017); Liu et al. (2020); Stromqvist et al. (2006)

Real-life writing in the profession	Definitions	References
VIII-176	Real-life writing in the profession combines patterns and routines with unpredictability which results in pattern variation and change.	Haapanen & Perrin (2024)
VIII-179	*Newswriting* Whereas most journalists are prepared to handle the interplay of verbal language and images with professional finesse and rigor, they hardly dispose of any elaborated practices to deal with the transition from one natural language to another.	Ehrensberger-Dow, Perrin & Zampa (2018)
VIII-180	*Still* From a video recording show the body language of the journalist in the background and the video editor in the foreground while dealing with footage	This volume

(*cont.*)

Representation	Definition	References
IX-191	*Visual representation* Attempt to make the data less obscure and more readily interpretable through a graphical representation that makes patterns perceptually visible.	Brath (2021)
IX-191	*Linear representation of log* Displays the sequence of keystrokes and mouse	Sullivan & Lindgren (2006)

Retrospective verbal protocol (RVP)	Definition	References
VIII-179	In Progression Analysis, these RVPs result from showing the writers video record-ings of their text production processes right after writing.	This volume

Revision	Definition	References
V-107	Making visible changes to the text	Fitzgerald (1987)
IV-88; V-121	*Revision campaigns* When a series of small modifications is achieved across a possibly large portion of text, always moving forward, it is possible that a revision campaign occurs, and this process should be considered as a single revision episode.	This volume
VII-159	*Contextual vs precontextual* 'Pre-contextual' revisions are made "before an externalised context is completed") and 'contextual' revisions are made "within a completed externalised context".	Lindgren & Sullivan (2006)

(*cont.*)

Rewriting	Definition	References
V-106; **VI-127**	Part of the drafting process: concerns the modification of a static pre-existing version of a visual text—be it handwritten or typed.	Hay (2002); Grésillon & Lebrave (2008); Grésillon (2016)

S

Sentence-based model	Definition	References
VI-130	A tabular view where versions of sentences are schematized and aligned vertically on the horizontal axis representing the temporal dimension.	Mahlow et al. (2022)

Simultaneous contrast	Definitions	References
II-26	Phenomenon of colour vision which causes adjoining areas of colour to influence the perception of each other	This volume
II-26	The apparent change in the hue, lightness, or saturation of a colour as a result of juxtaposition with other colours	Arnkil (2013)

S-notation	Definitions	References
III-52; **IV-76**; VI-130; VII-153; VIII-177; IX-192	The edition of the text is the main focus while temporality or chronology is difficult to follow. S-notation provides a visualisation that looks like a text where no character is removed (deletions are represented by crossed characters); it implicitly associates the x-axis to topography while chronology is represented by hyperlinks. Therefore, in essence, the S-notation is linear.	Kollberg (1998); Nilsson & Kollberg (1994)
VI-130	A language developed specifically to support the analysis of revision episodes and which describes writing as a decomposed linear process	Severinson, Eklundh & Kollberg (1996)

(*cont.*)

S-notation	**Definitions**	**References**
VIII-178	S-notation shows in ^{n}[square brackets]^{n} what was deleted in an emerging text, while insertions are put in ^{n}{curly braces}^{n}. The superscript numbers ^{n} indicate the order of these so-called revisions in the writing process. Vertical bars | indicate where a writer jumped off in the writing flow to move the point of insertion to another place in the emerging text.	This volume

Stylus tracking data	**Definition**	**References**
III-54	Stylus tracking data typically includes x and y coordinates at the beginning and end of an event, the pressure exerted by the stylus, timestamps for both the beginning and end of the event, and event categorization (e.g., pen up, pen down, move). Additional data points may include the time between the event's start and end and the distance travelled between the starting and ending points.	Gong et al. (2004)

Substitution	**Definition**	**References**
VI-128; VII-155	Replacing one segment of text with another	Bekius (2023)

T

Text production	**Definition**	**References**
VIII-177	On a *micro level*, text production consists of composing patterns that are supposed to be seen and heard as complexes of signs. In the case of writing in the Western world, these patterns are linguistic units such as characters, syllables, words, phrases, sentences, or paragraphs. Composing consists of inserting and deleting such units until the writer considers the result appropriate to fulfil the intended function among the intended readership or audience.	This volume

(cont.)

Topological learning	**Definition**	**References**
VI-136	*Topological learning* Field at the interface of topological data analysis (TDA) and machine learning. Neural network-based techniques are the most appropriate for topological learning as these approaches already represent a network. Topology captures multi-scale, global, and intrinsic properties of data sets based on homology. Machine learning enables machines to learn from data, based on mathematical models. Topological learning allows clustering and visualisation simultaneously. Clusters can be represented by more concise information than the rough listing of their patterns, such as their gravity center or different statistical moments.	Hensel et al. (2021)
II-39; III-62; **VI-136**; X-216	*Cluster* Kind of categorization: data sharing the same parameters of similarity are grouped in clusters, which correspond to the sets of similar observations.	Hensel et al. (2021)

U

V

(Visual) sign	**Definitions**	**References**
II-22; VII-176	*Sign* Division into *monosemic* (having a single meaning) vs *polysemic* (having multiple meaning)	Bertin (2011)
VI-126	*Graphic semiotisation* The production and alignment of graphemes, which are visual traces of sounds, groups of sounds, words and so on	This volume
VI-126	*Visuo-spatial activity* Need to structure the graphical traces in a spatially oriented way, which will enable text construction	This volume

(*cont.*)

(Data) visualisation	Definitions	References
II-19	Graphical representation of data to make patterns perceptually visible	Brath (2021)
II-19	Based on (non-visual) data, produces an image, and the result is readable and recognizable; based on an agreed-upon set of rules for converting the information into visual form	Kosara (2007); Koponen & Hildén (2019)
III-48	The creation, design and utilisation of graphical depictions to convey information effectively such that it supports enhancing comprehension and interpretation of data, facilitating informed decision-making processes	Amaar & Stasko (2013); Gandhi & Pruthi (2020); Munzner (2014)
II-19	*Visualisation as a process* Based on (non-visual) data, produces an image, and the result is readable and recognizable	Kosara (2007)
II-19	*Visualisation as a product* An information graphic that depicts at least some structured information, such as numbers	Koponen & Hilden (2019)
II-20	*Exploratory visualisation* (*thinking aid*) Visualisation meant to help the person creating the graphic to understand the data better themselves	Koponen & Hilden (2019)
II-20	*Explanatory visualisation* (*communication aid*) Visualisation that aims to disseminate some information that the person creating the graphic already has	Koponen & Hilden (2019)
VII-149	*Text-based visualisation* These visualisations indicate when and to what extent the writer has revised their text-so-far, and when they were concentrating on expanding their working documents with new material.	Buschenhenke, Conijn & Van Waes (2023)

(*cont.*)

(*Data*) *visualisation*	**Definitions**	**References**
VII-153	*Movement-based visualisation* These visualisations show the writer's tracks through the working document, by visualising the cursor position over time, often along with document length and number of characters typed.	Buschenhenke, Conijn & Van Waes (2023)
VII-154	*Text history visualisation* These visualisations take sentences as the unit of analysis, and although the content of the sentences is not shown, it does provide a quantitative overview of how the text was changed. It achieves this by showing which sentences have been altered, in the context of an abstract representation of the whole text-so-far.	Mahlow et al. (2021)
II-42; VIII-180	*Narrative visualisation* A technique borrowed from visual journalism where the visualisation is interspersed with text to contrast the data with more qualitative information. Helps understand and memorize at a glance the core ideas of a good practice technique	Segel & Heer (2010); this volume
IX-199	*Individual vs group level visualisation* An individual visualisation is based on data from one person. A group visualisation is based on data from more than one person.	Cohen et al. (2008)
X-215	*Visualisation as a pedagogical tool* Visualisations and learning analytics are often used in education to help learners understand complex themes or phenomenon, for instance, visual models representing contexts of practices and attitudes or process graphs illustrating the dynamics of the writing process or displaying different sources used during the process.	Vieira et al. (2018); Storto et al. (2023); Leblay et al. (2015, 2022); Kruse (2024)

W

Writing	**Definitions**	**References**
III-53; VII-165	*Writing (session) replay* Replaying the session allows for observation of the writing session as seen on Text Editor. Keystroke logging can facilitate this by means of its playback function, where a keystroke log can be replayed an infinite number of times.	Caporossi et al. (2020) Wengelin & Johansson (2023)
VI-128; VII-148	*Writing operation(s)* Textual genetics can calculate insertions (characters or sequences added to the text), replacements (the substitution of one sequence by another), displacements (a text fragment moved up or down) and deletions (removed text sequences).	Lardilleux et al. (2013)
VI-129	*Writing block* A textometry display, with text units represented as boxes	Xiu & Shibata (2007)
VI-134; VII-178	*Writing flow* Including features such as pauses, hesitations, and disfluencies, (the speech flow)	Cislaru & Olive (2018)
VIII-187	*Writing helix* The helix metaphor highlights that the four basic activities of goal setting, planning, controlling, and monitoring reoccur incrementally and in loops while a text is being produced.	This volume
IX-194	*Writing diagnostic test* The type of diagnostic test that offers possibilities for the use of keystroke logging is not limited to free-text written tasks, that has been the traditional focus of keystroke logging research, including visualisation.	Van Waes et al. (2007); Alfalahi et al. (2022)
IX-194	*Writing free-text task* Free-text tasks allow the writer to create original text. This is the most common option used for writing and common writing research scenarios.	Usoof et al. (2020)

(*cont.*)

Writing	Definitions	References
X-215	*Writing profile* Describe structural variability and the organisation of processes. Writer profiles that are specific to individual writers.	Van Waes (1992); Mutta (2020); Mutta & Laine (2022); Van Waes & Schellens (2003)
X-225	*Writer profile in the initial phase* Explicit planners started with (a title and) a plan. It usually took them time to complete the first sentence, and sometimes text was inserted into the middle of their plan. Implicit planners started slowly (with long pauses), which suggests that they created a mental plan. Slow starters began slowly and took a long time (more than five minutes) to complete the first sentence. There were a considerable number of pauses and few long bursts in these writers' process. Tentative starters typed and revised the beginning of the text multiple times; therefore, there were many events involved in writing the first sentence. The writers started fairly quickly and planned during text production rather than prior to beginning. Quick starters began quickly (a pause of under two seconds or no pause at all), and the first sentence was short. Quick and productive starters began quickly and produced a lot of text with few corrections or pauses.	This volume

Writing data	Definitions	References
III-55	*Application logging data* Include the application name, timestamps for when the application gains and loses focus, and the name of the opened file or UR. may also capture screenshots of the application window	Garnefski et al. (2010)
III-59	*Aggregated data* From the letter-to-word level considering the logging data with lexica and natural language processing (NLP) tools focusing on linguistics aspects in writing	Leijten & Van Waes (2013)

(*cont.*)

Writing process	**Definition**	**References**
V-106	A linear activity in which writers produce a draft that they then revise.	Rohman and Wlecke (1964)
VII-151	*Writing session* The keystroke data is stored in the form of working periods, so each episode where the writer switches the logger off again, a 'writing session' is stored with all files for this episode.	Bekius (2021, 2023); Buschenhenke (2025)
X-214	*Fluency vs. disfluency* Cognitive processes that underlie final output by examining the actions that take place during the writing process. Studies may focus on different elements and have specific purposes, for instance fluency features, including automatically processed linguistic elements and disfluency features, such as pauses and revisions. Fluency in writing is a cognitive process that can be studied through the relationships between uninterrupted text production—also known as bursts (i.e., an index of fluent writing)—pauses, and revisions.	Baaijen & Galbraith (2018); Cislaru & Olive (2018); Ellis & Yuan (2004)

X

Y

Z

www.ingramcontent.com/pod-product-compliance
Ingram Content Group UK Ltd.
Pitfield, Milton Keynes, MK11 3LW, UK
UKHW022227051026
15624UKWH00002B/395

9 789004 758193